CONDUCT and
COMMUNITY

A RESIDENCE LIFE PRACTITIONER'S GUIDE

CONDUCT and COMMUNITY

A RESIDENCE LIFE PRACTITIONER'S GUIDE

edited by

JoCynda Hudson
Alan Acosta
Ryan C. Holmes

Conduct and Community: A Residence Life Practitioner's Guide

Copyright © 2018 by the Association of College & University Housing Officers-International. All rights reserved. No part of this book may be reproduced or transmitted in any form or by any means, electronic or mechanical, including photocopying, recording, or by any storage and retrieval system, without written permission from the publisher.

Association of College & University Housing Officers-International (ACUHO-I)
1445 Summit Street
Columbus, Ohio 43201 USA

To order additional copies of this book, or other titles published by ACUHO-I, please visit our website at www.acuho-i.org.

Publishers Cataloging-in-Publication Data
Hudson, JoCynda 1976–
Acosta, Alan 1981–
Holmes, Ryan C. 1978–

Conduct and community: A residence life practitioner's guide
p. cm.

Includes bibliographical references

ISBN 978-0-9907763-3-8

1.Student housing—Handbooks, manuals, etc. 2. College discipline 3. Residence and education—Handbooks, manuals, etc.

1.Association of College and University Housing Officers, International 2. Title

Text design and typesetting by Jennifer Shoffey Forsythe
Cover design by James A. Baumann

Printed by Integrated Books International

The paper used in this publication meets the minimum requirements of the American National Standard for Information Sciences—Permanence of Paper for Printed Library Materials. ANSI Z39.48—1992.

9 8 7 6 5 4 3 2 1

Contents

Foreword

"Disciplined: A place where individuals accept their obligations to the group and where well-defined governance procedures guide behavior for the common good."

— Ernest Boyer's Six Principles of Community

I WAS FIRST attracted to a career in campus housing and residence life due to the sense of community it evoked in me. My need for this sense of community, I am sure, was grounded in my own adolescence. I grew up in a small town where everyone knew one another; activity revolved around a courthouse in the middle of town; and all people felt safe, engaged, and proud. When it came time for me to head off to college, I subconsciously wanted to recreate this same sense of community and, fortunately, I found a school where this occurred.

I lived in campus housing for seven years as an undergraduate, graduate student, and young professional. They were some of the best years of my life, not only because of the experiences I had in the community, but because of the overwhelming sense of community I felt. This book, *Conduct and Community,* is the first to examine the role student conduct plays in establishing such a campus community. Also, by using a social justice lens, the authors challenge readers to acknowledge that the strongest communities are diverse and inclusive. Building community where historically marginalized groups feel a sense of belonging, purpose, and engagement is at the core of the residential experience. These authors propose that, while much literature documents the impact of the conduct process on students' moral, ethical, and intellectual development, the conduct process is also a strategy for establishing, building, and maintaining community.

Anyone who works in residence life understands that establishing community is easier said than done. As both a goal (individuals contributing to the formation and maintenance of the community) and a process (a means to an end with an emphasis on individuals within a group), communities are a dynamic whole that emerges when a group participates in common experiences, depends upon one another, makes decisions together, commits to the group's long-term well-being, and is socially interdependent. In housing, we employ many strategies for building community (i.e., residential curricula, hiring residential staff, providing numerous community development activities and educational programs), but there is a point to be made: Student conduct is key to establishing community.

The student conduct process is designed to support the educational mission of the institution and provide members of the community with direction. Those who only view conduct as a punitive process are being shortsighted, for it is the conduct office that allows members to attain the most desirable characteristics of community. The student conduct process allows residents to hold individual members accountable, set direction and purpose for the community, and create a sense of belongingness. In short, the conduct process is essential to helping participants develop emotional connections and instill the belief that members' needs will be met by their commitment to live, work, and play together. It is the conduct process that allows members to view their community as a reference group — one where there are boundaries for what is appropriate behavior and what is not, as well as an understanding of the roles good members of the community engage in.

This latest contribution to the literature on student conduct provides a timely, practical, and comprehensive understanding of the conduct process and its role in creating community. It is an insightful publication that adds to the theoretical knowledge base and offers real-world strategies and practices for implementing best practices in student conduct. The book is organized into 10 chapters so each chapter builds upon the previous ones and readers can pick and choose what to read. This book will be a valuable professional development resource for higher education administrators in both conduct and residence life, as well as training for student staff, since it provides them with knowledge and skills to customize the conduct process in a way appropriate for their institutional context.

The authors begin by providing perspectives on community, specifically identifying factors affecting the residential community and offering readers an evolution of changes in conduct philosophies. These two chapters set the stage for the title and focus of the book. Subsequent chapters offer knowledge on topics such as understanding laws, the role and preparation of staff, conduct and issues of social justice, conduct and mental health, conflict resolution, and assessment. The overall premise is that by challenging themselves to reconsider conduct as a community-builder, housing professionals can use their knowledge of community and conduct to establish residential communities that are participatory, interdependent, and cohesive — communities where members are responsible and hold others accountable for actions. Especially helpful in illustrating the idea of conduct as a community-builder is the variety of case studies, training exercises, and best practices shared at the end of the book.

For many, this collection will challenge their perceptions of how they view the conduct process and engage in their work. Ideally, it will generate new discussions and dialogue while encouraging higher educational professionals to engage in open and candied discussions about the role of conduct in enhancing residential community. As student development educators, we must remember that we possess the power to design residential environments where residents feel a sense of belonging, purpose, and engagement; in other words, a sense of community. Creating such communities is necessary for students to reach their educational potential and experience success.

Tony W. Cawthon, PhD
Alumni Distinguished Professor
Clemson University Higher Education and Student Affairs

Foreword

A DECADE AGO, in our book *Reframing Campus Conflict: Student Conduct Practice Through a Social Justice Lens*, we introduced Schrage's concept of "magic real estate." We also advocated for reframing campus conflict and conduct management based on principles, values, and expanded process options aligned to social and restorative justice and exemplified in the Spectrum of Resolution Options (or Spectrum Model) developed by Schrage and Thompson.

As educators and practitioners in an increasingly legalistic context, seeking to sustain access to a full continuum of options to respond effectively to students in conflict and crisis who have diverse personal stories and needs, we recognize the value of magic real estate now more than ever. We see magic real estate not as a place but a space; between incident and process, in which a course of action has yet to be determined and a pipeline into a predetermined outcome is, as yet, unformed. This space makes room for the interpersonal messiness that is confrontation and dialogue, individual empowerment and civility, ownership and accountability, shared problem-solving and working a thing out, living and learning, resilience and growth, and growing up. It is in this space we find the truest expression of challenge and support.

There is no better embodiment of magic real estate than the common ground shared by students and staff who live together in campus residential housing. Here, we find complex social systems that connect diverse individuals. Students live among peers and peer leaders. Peer leaders find support in graduate and professional staff, and these staff members bridge their living, learning communities with the greater campus academic and social structure. What was once discounted as largely faculty- or staff-free dormitory dwellings and "extra" to the curricular classroom priority is now seen as the heart of a traditional-aged student's lived experience. Constructive communities formed in residence foster a sense of inclusion vital to a healthy campus climate. Without it, students often feel isolated and disconnected from their institutions of choice. In this way, residential communities staffed with competent and compassionate colleagues can be a campus's best defense against mental health challenges, poor academic performance, toxic expressions of culture, and, ultimately, high attrition rates.

With this highly anticipated publication, editors JoCynda Hudson, Alan Acosta, and Ryan Holmes, along with a diverse team of authors, remind us of the magic real estate created in residential living and the importance of investing in and supporting the team of colleagues serving in this educational and dynamic space. The safety officers, residential peer leaders and advisors, residence education colleagues, and other housing administration staff build relationships that allow them to meet students on common ground in the earliest moments of crisis and conflict. In turn, they are positioned to engage students effectively as frontline threat assessors, conflict resolvers, social justice advocates, and community builders working at all hours to secure a safe and just living and learning community for students.

This book is an important resource for properly equipping these valued colleagues and developing sound policies, protocols, and practices so no student falls through a gap or misses the opportunity for a more-accessible, inclusive, restorative, and educational experience, particularly in the moments that follow a conflict or crisis.

Relationships facilitated in residence are perhaps the single most underestimated ingredient in the success of a student searching for community in their home away from home, and we celebrate it here. We endorse this publication as a fresh take and timely reminder that rules, mandates, and guidance, however well intended, do not shape constructive campus climates or grow a culture of inclusion; people in community, building diverse and lasting relationships, do.

Nancy Geist Giacomini
Jennifer Meyer Schrage
Editors of Reframing Campus Conduct: Student Conduct Practice
Through a Social Justice Lens

Acknowledgments

"No one who achieves success does so without the help of others. The wise and confident acknowledge this help with gratitude."

— *Alfred North Whitehead*

FIRST AND FOREMOST, the editors would like to thank the authors for their time and contributions. This project is the result of collaboration between not just the two associations or three editors, but also between numerous authors who represent various institutions in many locations. Without your knowledge and experience, this project would not have been possible.

James Baumann, we thank you for all that you have contributed to drive this book to completion. You fought through all of our competing schedules, familial priorities, and various styles to lead us to a win. James' ability to maintain an umbrella of understanding while choosing when to have a laser focus was immeasurable. Working with you has been an invaluable masterclass and has helped us, as editors, in our further development.

We would like to thank the Association of College and University Housing Officers – International (ACUHO-I), under the leadership of Mary DeNiro, and the Association for Student Conduct Administration (ASCA), led by Dr. Jennifer Waller, for their efforts in supporting this book. We are grateful that ACUHO-I partnered with ASCA on this publication, having recognized the need to increase the literature and knowledge about student conduct in the residence halls. In addition, we'd like to recognize Martha

Compton and Von Stange for representing the boards of both associations and for their behind-the-scenes work.

The editors are grateful for this opportunity and acknowledge the honor it is to contribute to both the housing and conduct professions through this project. We appreciate the associations for giving us avenues to grow in the field, contribute through various leadership opportunities, and continue to be a resource in the changing world of conduct and housing from the institutional to the international levels. We believe both the student conduct and residence life fields will benefit from this book. May ACUHO-I and ASCA continue to advance student affairs practice, especially the student conduct profession, through continued collaboration.

Alan Acosta

My biggest thank you goes to my amazing partner in life, Danielle Morgan Acosta, who was a constant source of inspiration, humor, encouragement, and calming presence throughout this process. She gave me ideas when I felt like I had none. I am immensely grateful to her for all of the support throughout this fun experience. I'm very appreciative of Florida State University, particularly Dr. Amy Hecht, vice president for student affairs, and Dr. Vicki Dobiyanski, dean of students, who supported my participation in this groundbreaking project. To everyone at ACUHO-I and ASCA who entrusted this book to us as editors, thank you. And to Dr. JoCynda Hudson and Dr. Ryan Holmes, thank you so much for being an editing dream team. You helped make me a better writer, editor, and professional along the way. I could not have asked for better collaborators on this journey.

Ryan C. Holmes

I want to thank my family, who are always along for the ride when a new project is presented. My wife, Maria, and my children, Remaliah and Raziel, are constant supporters and cheerleaders even when time away from them is necessary. To my children — when you are older, I hope you understand why my work was necessary at this point in history, and may the landscape of society be changed by the time your years match mine.

I would also like to thank Martha Compton for believing I could contribute in this capacity. I would like to thank Dr. Alan Acosta and Dr. JoCynda Hudson for being the consummate teammates. Many hands make light work, and I feel we did a good job of showing how teammates can selflessly support each other for the benefit of the project. Also, while I have not been at the University of Miami long, the editorial process has taken place while I was a part of the UM community, so I would like to thank Dr. Patricia Whitely, Miami's vice president for Student Affairs, as well as my colleagues in the Dean of Students Office for their constant support as I continue to keep irons in the fire.

JoCynda Hudson

The first person I would like to thank for their patience and continued support is my partner, Marcus Moore. I would not be successful if it were not for Marcus reminding me to eat and sleep, and giving me space when I need to "think it out." My sisters have been an inspiration of strength who have kept me motivated to stretch myself and take on projects that intimidate me, such as this book.

At the University of Florida, I am grateful to Calvin Mosley for giving me the grace to work on this project and balance it with a full-time job while also defending a dissertation. Thank you to ACUHO-I and ASCA for allowing me this opportunity. The experience has been one of the most professionally fulfilling I have ever had. As for my co-editors, I have never worked with more professional individuals. I thank Dr. Alan Acosta and Dr. Ryan Holmes for their knowledge, insights, collaboration, and trust in me. Lastly, I would like to thank my staff and co-workers for their work and understanding. I could not take on projects such as this without a talented team in my corner.

Introduction

CONSIDERING THE CONDUCT MISSION

Alan Acosta, JoCynda Hudson, and Ryan C. Holmes

RESEARCH INDICATES living on campus has a positive correlation with college students' success on a variety of metrics, including enrollment, retention, and graduation rates (Blimling, 2014; Pascarella & Terenzini, 2005). Numerous aspects of the campus residential experience promote student learning and success, including academic collaborations, educational and social activities, involvement opportunities, and mentoring opportunities. While these facets of on-campus housing have been studied to some degree (Astin, 1993; Dunkel & Baumann, 2013; Dunkel, Schuh, & Chrystal-Green, 2014; Pascarella & Terenzini, 2005), one critical part of the college student residential experience that is underrepresented in the literature is an examination of the student conduct process.

The student conduct process has demonstrated a positive impact on the moral and ethical development of college students, while promoting a safe campus environment in which students can learn (Lancaster & Waryold, 2008; Schrage & Giacomini, 2009; Waryold & Lancaster, 2013). While practitioners can draw on numerous scholarship options about the broad topic of student conduct, little information exists specifically about the intersection between student conduct and college and university residence halls, and how those dynamics influence the work of residence life professionals and the experience of the students living in the residence halls. This book serves as a practical resource for higher education professionals while filling a significant gap in the literature about student conduct in the on-campus residential setting.

The editors of this text believe the most-effective tools are ones where the theoretical foundations in multiple bodies of scholarship are synthesized into a guide that practitioners can use to seamlessly and effectively incorporate theory into practice. This book takes that approach with student conduct in on-campus residence halls. It also solidifies the professional values that residence life and student conduct professionals espouse in the practical work they do every day, as outlined by the Association of College and University Housing Officers – International (ACUHO-I) and the Association for Student Conduct Administration (ASCA). Readers will not only learn the theoretical underpinnings necessary for effective student conduct processes, but will also get first-hand knowledge from the editors, chapter authors, and resource contributors. These individuals are scholars and practitioners in the fields of student conduct and residence life who understand how to integrate student conduct into on-campus residential communities effectively to maximize student learning, student development, and community accountability.

This book discusses many issues for higher education professionals to be aware of when considering the student conduct process within the residence halls. First and foremost, the student conduct process is meant to support the educational missions of higher education institutions and is designed to accomplish this goal (Waryold & Lancaster, 2013). While elements of the student conduct process are universal throughout higher education institutions, each campus's approach to implementing and executing student conduct processes in its residence halls can and should be customized to fit the institutional needs based on a variety of factors, such as state laws, institutional mission and culture, and desired learning outcomes.

Student conduct can often be framed merely as punishing students for misdeeds. In the on-campus residential setting, professionals are encouraged to rethink of conduct as an effective community builder. At almost no other time in higher education professionals' careers can they meet with a student at a potentially critical or life-altering moment and help students reshape their lives into productive and healthy collegiate experiences.

Part of facilitating an effective student conduct process is to consider dynamics related to social justice. Diversity, inclusion, and social justice are essential competencies for all higher education professionals to possess (Eanes & Perillo, 2015). Having these competencies is particularly important for residence life and student conduct professionals (Schrage & Giacomini, 2009), since engaging in work with an inclusion mindset can help all students, particularly historically marginalized or underrepresented student populations, feel that they have a sense of belonging or home in the residence hall (Harper & Quaye, 2009; Pascarella & Terenzini, 2005; Smith, 2009).

This makes it imperative for the student conduct process, both in and out of the residence halls, to have a social justice lens, because this allows for maximum learning opportunities and for students to believe the conduct process has been as fair as possible (Schrage & Giacomini, 2009). In addition, it helps students find their home in the residence halls and on campus. Approaching student conduct processes with this lens also provides another way to build social justice systematically in higher education institutions to achieve greater student equity, inclusion, and success (Adams & Bell, 2016; Harper & Quaye, 2009; Schrage & Giacomini, 2009; Smith, 2009).

While professionals whose work connects to residence life and on-campus housing may be more likely to take away information to use in their daily practice, any higher education professionals seeking to learn more about student conduct, on-campus housing, or the connection between the two will gain valuable insight from this book. Although many theories undergird the work of residence life professionals, and a few are referenced throughout this work, this book takes a practitioner's approach to the topic. Most chapters have some sort of supplemental materials, case studies, or other appendix items designed to increase professionals' practical use of the knowledge contained within the text.

Each chapter concludes with a series of discussion questions. These questions offer readers an opportunity to actively engage with the chapter and move their learnings from the pages to practical application. The questions are designed not only to encourage thoughts about what professionals and institutions believe is philosophically important about their conduct process, but also to identify concrete ways for them to update or improve their processes. The discussion questions can also serve as staff or professional development exercises, or be used during staff training to expand professionals' knowledge and skills.

Throughout this book, the authors use and incorporate examples of best practices from housing operations and institutions around the world. These examples exemplify numerous institutional types, institutional sizes, geographic locations, and student demographics, and are intended to give readers a chance to see how institutions — both alike and different from their own — approach and facilitate the conduct process. Ideally, readers will be inspired by both the discussion questions and the real-life examples to thoughtfully establish or critically re-examine student conduct in the residence halls on their campuses.

Although readers can go to any chapter of interest in any order they wish and have the flexibility to engage with the parts they deem most critical at any point in time, and still glean the knowledge in those pages, the book's chapters are intended to build upon each other. The layout of the chapters explains how residence life professionals successfully combine conduct and community to promote a vibrant, trusting, safe, productive, enriching, and engaging residence life experience for students where maintaining and holding community members accountable for community expectations are seen as an inseparable part of the residential experience.

The editors and authors believe this type of residential community is possible. The elements of an ideal student conduct process in an on-campus residential community, which are expounded upon in the following chapters, include: building community in the halls (Blimling, 2014); determining individual and campus philosophies regarding conduct (Lancaster & Waryold, 2008); understanding underlying rights, laws, and freedoms (Stoner & Lowery, 2004); preparing staff to work toward the goals of the community (Blimling, 2014); crafting student conduct processes that support student learning, growth, and professional development (Lancaster & Waryold, 2008; Waryold & Lancaster, 2013); the integration of social justice and inclusion (Schrage & Giacomini, 2009); understanding the role of student mental health on the student experience broadly and the student conduct process particularly (Kadison & DiGeronimo, 2004; Lancaster & Waryold, 2008); establishing and enforcing sanctions and outcomes that are both deterrents, but also educational (Waryold & Lancaster, 2013); achieving appropriate resolutions in both an active and reactive manner (Lancaster & Waryold, 2008); and assessing the student conduct process and associated outcomes (Schuh, Biddix, Dean, & Kinzie, 2016; Waryold & Lancaster, 2013).

Compiling the research and work of others, ordered in this way and combined with the insights of the professionals who wrote these chapters, provides readers with the foundational elements that optimize community development and student success. The book features new knowledge about the on-campus residential experience from scholars conducting research. The information is shown through the eyes of practitioners who are in the halls having these complex conversations and are hearing students' stories. Together, this book truly puts theory into practice. This new understanding of the function of student conduct as a community builder and student developer in a practical sense is further supplemented by the appendices containing case studies, training exercises, resources, and added insights.

Although this book has many unique elements and considerations for student conduct in the residence halls, it is by no means an exhaustive list. There are elements of crisis management often related to student conduct (such as behavioral intervention or threat assessment teams) that are touched on either briefly or not at all. The editors and authors, using their current understanding of the student experience, higher education trends, and professional best practices, determined the topics included are most appropriate at this time. Future editions may include or remove topics based on changes in the higher education landscape.

Student conduct is an essential part of community building and student accountability in the residence halls, but not much information regarding this topic is known or found in the literature. Many important elements are necessary to craft a student conduct process in the residence halls that increases student growth and community engagement. This book provides higher education professionals with a practical tool to use in their daily work to merge student conduct processes effectively into the on-campus residential experience. The authors have shared their expertise with readers in the hope of providing clarity to a process that can, at times, seem overwhelmingly complicated. By focusing on community building as the core component of residence life, the authors reinforce foundational expectations of basic human interaction.

REFERENCES

Adams, M., & Bell, L. A. (Eds.). (2016). *Teaching for diversity and social justice* (3rd ed.). New York, NY: Routledge.

Astin, A. W. (1993). *What matters in college? Four critical years revisited*. San Francisco, CA: Jossey-Bass.

Blimling, G. S. (2014). *Student learning in college residence halls: What works, what doesn't, and why*. San Francisco, CA: Jossey-Bass.

Dunkel, N. W., & Baumann, J. A. (Eds.). (2013). *Campus housing management (Volumes 1–6)*. Columbus, OH: Association of College and University Housing Officers – International.

Dunkel, N. W., Schuh, J. H., & Chrystal-Green, N. E. (2014). *Advising student groups and organizations* (2nd ed.). San Francisco, CA: Jossey-Bass.

Eanes, B. J., & Perillo, P. A. (Co-chairs). (2015). *Professional competency areas for student affairs educators*. Washington, DC: ACPA-College Student Educators International and NASPA-Student Affairs Administrators in Higher Education.

Harper, S. R., & Quaye, S. J. (Eds.). (2009). *Student engagement in higher education: Theoretical perspectives and practical approaches for diverse populations*. New York, NY: Routledge.

Kadison, R., & DiGeronimo, T. F. (2004). *College of the overwhelmed: The campus mental health crisis and what to do about it*. San Francisco, CA: Jossey-Bass.

Lancaster, J. M., & Waryold, D. M. (Eds.). (2008). *Student conduct practice: The complete guide for student affairs professionals*. Sterling, VA: Stylus Publishing.

Pascarella, E. T., & Terenzini, P. T. (2005). *How college affects students: A third decade of research (Volume 2)*. San Francisco, CA: Jossey-Bass.

Schrage, J. M., & Giacomini, N. G. (2009). *Reframing campus conflict: Student conduct practice through a social justice lens.* Sterling, VA: Stylus Publishing.

Schuh, J. H., Biddix, J. P., Dean, L. A., & Kinzie, J. (2016). *Assessment in student affairs* (2nd ed.). San Francisco: Jossey-Bass.

Smith, D. G. (2009). *Diversity's promise for higher education.* Baltimore, MD: Johns Hopkins University Press.

Stoner, E. N., & Lowery, J. W. (2004). Navigating past the "spirit of insubordination": A twenty-first century model student conduct code with model hearing script. *Journal of College and University Law, 31*(1), 1–77.

Waryold, D. M., & Lancaster, J. M. (Eds.). (2013). *The state of student conduct: Current forces and future challenges: Revisited.* College Station, TX: Association for Student Conduct Administration.

ESTABLISHING AND BUILDING COMMUNITY

Leah A. Barrett, Denise M. Baumann, Donna L. Hight, and Amanda J. Mesirow

ONE OF THE fundamental functions of campus housing is to facilitate a sense of community for its residents. A sense of community is " ...a feeling that members have of belonging, a feeling that members matter to one another and to the group, and a shared faith that members' needs will be met through their commitment to be together" (McMillan & Chavis, 1986, p. 9).

Since the 1990s, researchers and thought leaders in higher education have found a sense of community on the college campus is one of the most-important factors in student retention and persistence (Boyer, 1990; Gardner, 1996; Tinto, 1993). Practitioners suggest a sense of community supports healthy decision-making and fosters effective interpersonal communication, conflict resolution, and positive student conduct.

Creating a sense of community in campus housing is paramount, but it does not occur naturally. It takes intentionality in building and developing an inviting community environment from opening day. The students who arrive on campus are a diverse lot, representing a variety of ages, ethnicities, races, religious beliefs, sexual orientations, birth orders, birthplaces, transfer status, socio-economic statuses, academic majors, years in school, and many other aspects. In many cases, the only true commonality between these students is their current place of residency. What happens and how it happens in campus housing is a critical marker for student development and success.

Campus housing leaders are charged with creating a community from this diverse collection of backgrounds. Even before opening day, the physical design, reputation, and ingrained historical decisions about a wing or a floor of a residence hall already has influenced the community. Traditional corridor-style living is often allocated to first-year students to helped them build community. In this formation, students are, in essence, forced to interact with one or maybe two roommates in their room, as well as with other students in the hallways, shower facilities, and shared floor lounges. Suites and apartments influence the creation of smaller communities because lounges and bathroom facilities are exclusive to the unit and the space includes four or more students. Semi-suites are a current trend in combining more students in a single setting, sharing bathrooms but no lounge space.

The results of a qualitative study by Clemons, McKelfresh, and Banning (2005) suggest students need flexibility in their furnishings and the ability to personalize their space with surfaces that can be decorated. The students in their study suggested these little things matter for them to have a sense of belonging — the foundation for creating a sense of community.

The reputation of the residence hall, the wing, or the floor is another factor in understanding its sense of community. Sadly, this sense of community could be either positive or negative. When evaluating community, professionals will want to consider whether there is evidence the space has been successful. Do quantitative or qualitative data suggest vandalism or other violations are common? What do the custodial and maintenance staff have to say about the students living in the community? What are the retention and completion rates for students who have lived there? Such analysis will help to with understanding any factors that have created a negative reputation, and can help maintain a positive one.

Institutional decisions and priorities also influence the foundations of residence hall communities. The location of a residence hall may be ideal for specific students. For example, a hall near athletic facilities may draw more student-athletes, while a hall close to the performing arts facilities may attract theater and music majors. When a residence hall is open year-round, it may be more attractive to international students/students studying abroad, since they may not leave campus as often as other students. Special designations or requirements may also influence where students choose to live — a residence hall or wing may be designated for honors students, living-learning communities, or fraternities and sororities that have pre-determined requirements for its residents. Residential living philosophies and procedures that require first-year students to live on campus and provide preferential choice for returning students also influence the demographics of on-campus communities. Another critical factor that may influence student choice is the cost to live in the facility. A pricing structure that charges a premium for newer facilities may exclude students with lower expected family contributions or who pay for college themselves.

Physical space, reputation, and prior institutional decisions are environmental factors that influence the work of housing and conduct professionals. In some ways, the over-simplified premise of a residence life community — asking individuals to bond over the shared experience of simply living near each other — reads like a naïvely optimistic social experiment. Still, there are years of academic research on student development and engagement where the pros heavily outweigh the cons of students residing on campus (Chambliss & Takacs, 2014; Pascarella & Terenzini, 2005; Tinto, 1993).

In many ways, establishing and nurturing community in a residence hall — and, frankly, society as a whole — comes down to balancing the rights of individuals versus those of the whole. When students live with others in very close spaces, both unique opportunities and challenges often occur. Students gain the opportunity to get to know others both like and unlike themselves. Students may share bedrooms with others for the first time in their lives. They learn how their habits, good or bad, rub against the habits of those in their room, suite, or hallway. Often, today's college student has not learned how to communicate directly with others and relies on text or social media to convey acceptance of or displeasure with others. The opportunity and often-appropriate need for free expression or reflection can transform a roommate conflict into an incident that requires a college-wide response.

Residence life professionals have to respond at the student level and support institution-level responses. Some colleges, like Northern Wyoming Community College, use the foundational principles of the Federal Emergency Management Agency's Emergency Management Institute when a situation goes viral. This calls for establishing an incident command center and then the campus activities and residence life staff lead the restoration of the community. The public information office staff coordinate the communications to those affected, the college community, and then the public at large. Colleges can benefit from tabletop exercises on viral social media occurrences just as much as natural disasters.

FACTORS AFFECTING THE RESIDENTIAL COMMUNITY

Consider the following scenario. A resident assistant (RA) approaches a residence hall room and knocks on a door vibrating from the loud music playing inside. A student answers the knock and peers around the corner of the door. The RA says, "Hey there. I'm an RA and we have a quiet hours policy. Can you please turn down your music?" Without saying a word, the student slams the door shut. The RA, understandably, becomes irritated and knocks again. This time, when the door is answered, the RA barks, "I am going to have to document this incident."

Such a scene is not uncommon in campus residence halls. One still may wonder, what would lead the student to react in such a way? The fact is students do not arrive in residence life as blank slates. They bring personalities, identities, ideas, values, and notions of community formed throughout their earlier lives and everything they have experienced up to that point. Some of them come from large urban cities, while others are from rural areas. Some arrive on move-in day by themselves with only the bare necessities, while others show up with a moving truck, full wardrobe, and flat-screen television. Some students are eager to befriend their roommates, while others plan to get into a single room as soon as possible. New students face situations as simple as never having had to do their own laundry to the much-more-complex of never having lived where no one else speaks their native language. All of these qualities and circumstances are not, in and of themselves, positive or negative, but they certainly do play a role in a student's individual sense of identity and these differences will have an impact on the community's collective identity.

Visible and invisible diversity are part of campus communities. Professional and paraprofessional staff may have to address certain beliefs and values that may harm or enhance the student's progress on campus. Without looking to degrade students' former community identities, staff have to be aware of these beliefs and values as the new residential community develops. To assist with including underrepresented students in the residence halls, social justice and diversity training, along with several other concepts, should be incorporated into training and development for all staff. These include social and teambuilding activities with staff from areas on campus devoted to diversity initiatives, such as LGBTQ, multicultural, disability, and international student centers. Many campuses offer formal training focused on issues of diversity, and how a student's background will inform their current experiences. These may use large- and small-group discussions, case studies, and scenarios on common policy violations, including how to approach those violations when they involve underrepresented populations. These initiatives should incorporate student voices to ensure the training is based on feedback and real-life experiences of underrepresented students in residential communities, without putting the burden of the education on those students. The following sections explore qualities that may inhibit forming a cohesive campus community.

Distrust of Authority

Their very first day on campus, students are usually met by cheerful and welcoming staff members handing out keys, giving instructions, and directing move-in traffic to stairs and elevators. Signs advertise mandatory meetings for residents, invite them to social activities, and educate them about policies. All students are expected to respect the policies and expectations of their new home, regardless of whether these are or are not similar to expectations set before coming to college.

Some of the violations that occur in these early days can be explained reasonably. The students are experiencing their first days of freedom away from watchful parents, flexing their desire to have the "real college experience," or feeling the pressure of wanting to meet and fit in with others. A common example is accepting the invitation to drink in a residence hall room.

Some students, understandably, will ignore the mandatory student meeting requests, be barely polite when the student staff introduce themselves at check-in, and seem to want to have nothing to do with community building. Again, part of this is the desire to fit in — wanting to look as though they have adjusted to the college experience and do not need anyone looking after them.

There is a difference, though, between those students and students who come in with a distrust of authority for valid reasons. Distrustful students may have come from communities where authority is seen as unfair, unjust, or even violent. They may have come from communities where there were active uprisings against those in power. Some students come from homes where there was no authority, or the authority was negative — neglectful or abusive. They may also have come from homes where they were the authority because they had to take care of younger siblings or aging family members, and faced a great deal of responsibility as young adults. Finally, and perhaps most significantly, students of color, international students, or underrepresented students may have a distrust of authority based on their experiences with systemic racism and oppression.

For students who distrust authority, the act of an RA knocking on the door and asking for the music to be turned down can have a deeper meaning. It could escalate as an opportunity to assert their autonomy or protest a policy they find unfair, or simply be a typical response to being told what to do and when to do it, particularly by someone who is the same age. An RA untrained in considering identities may perceive this situation as a student who needs an even stronger authoritative response. The approach of the RA could potentially create an even more-hostile environment for the student.

As an example, a study of Black students' experience with racism in residence halls in recent literature "… describes hostile campus racial climates as encompassing the entire institutional environment that extends beyond college classrooms into communal spaces, including residential domiciles" (Hotchkins & Dancy, 2017, p. 43). When the authority figure is a White student, as is the case at many predominantly white institutions, these interactions can create a feeling described as perpetual homelessness for students of color. This manifests itself in micro-aggressions, physical and emotional separateness, and racially charged interactions with authority, particularly security. As Hotchkins and

Dancy (2017) state, "The process of being repeatedly racially confronted by White peers, staff[,] and police had a cumulative, deleterious effect on study participants who frequently expressed regret with living in the residential halls on their campuses" (p. 48).

When working with campus or local law enforcement, a community policing philosophy can be a helpful model for building trust between students, student staff, and law enforcement. A study for the United States Department of Justice by Reaves and Goldberg (1996) found high numbers of institutions of higher education engaging in community policing. Over half of respondents had a written policy for relations with residence life, conduct, and victim services staff. Evidence of community policing on a college campus includes police officers providing educational programming on sexual assault prevention, alcohol and other drugs, and crime prevention. The College at Brockport, State University of New York, invites university police to walk the halls, spend time in common areas, and talk to students on a regular basis, not just when an incident occurs. Each residence hall has an assigned officer who meets regularly with the staff and residents and is visible in the hall during their shifts. The officer and the hall director work together, both proactively and reactively, to prevent problems and address the culture of the community.

The community-policing model encourages a more-regular police presence in the residence hall community, not just when a student has presumably broken the law. Police become partners with residence life staff to provide educational programming on safety and prevention, discuss the impact of using alcohol or other drugs, and deter crime in the residence halls. Although a community-policing model may not be ideal for all campuses, it is an approach that has shown success in building relationships and reducing crime on campuses and in municipalities.

It is important for residence life and conduct professionals to gain a sense of students' feelings toward authority and how best to address these feelings. In each situation, professionals need to assess the situation to identify triggers in the environment that may have elicited a negative response, such as racial or gender dynamics, the language used by staff members, and the position of staff members. By ferreting out the reaction to authority, staff can better manage how to respect their experiences and background, while ensuring they are successful members of their community and campus.

Codes of Silence and Support

Some students come to campus with the ingrained belief one does not speak up against someone of the same identity or "snitch" on others from home. Others are on campus when there is a pronounced mistrust in society (or perhaps in the particular geographic area where the college is located) of individuals of their ethnicity (consider the Muslim student in post-9/11 America, as just one example). Is it possible a student feels targeted by authority and is responding to that? Absolutely.

Silence can be extremely detrimental to a community for many reasons. First, continued mistrust of authority means students are much less likely to seek help with other issues (academic, personal, etc.). Second, if violations occur repeatedly in a community, they do have to be addressed even though an even tougher response from staff may only reinforce these students' silence. Finally, and most alarmingly, students may not report serious, dangerous violations if they think doing so puts a member of their own community at risk.

When members of an underrepresented community perceive another member is at risk from an authority figure, this code of silence may serve to protect their identified community. Again, consider the RA and the noise violation — only this time, nobody answers the knock on the door. In this case, the RA turns to other students nearby and asks, "Does anyone know if they are home?" If those being asked are members of the same group as the confronted students, they may be reluctant to respond — they may not want to be seen as an ally of unfair authority figures, or they may hope to protect other students from consequences and a continued negative perspective of their group as a whole. This reaction may be especially true if staff in that community are perceived as biased against certain groups.

In fact, in their study, Hotchkins and Dancy (2017) found Black students also knew and shared with each other "when and where not to be on this campus" (p. 49) and practiced group self-care by "providing navigational information about how to literally avoid being traumatized" (p. 49). If a residential community, staff members, or both have a reputation for being places where students of color are not valued or where they experience racism, actions such as including membership and engagement opportunities outside the residence halls to protect members of a group from micro-aggressions and unfair treatment will increase as a measure of protection and resilience (Hotchkins & Dancy, 2017).

Hotchkins and Dancy also say White staff need to "educate themselves about practicing visual, cultural inclusiveness in geography and place" (p. 48), and call for "increased hiring of Black students in positions like residential assistants" (p. 48) to provide important perspectives and demonstrate inclusivity. Training initiatives should not be mere checklists of "we discussed diversity issues already." These students live with their experiences every day. Care should be taken to speak with RAs frequently about trends and issues they are seeing, the outreach they are doing to students from different backgrounds, and how their involvement in the community has developed. The difference between diversity and inclusion must also be highlighted as efforts are made to ensure every member of the community feels included at all times.

Inclusive Language and Consistent Confrontation

Returning to the earlier scenario, what could it mean if a Black student answered the door and shouted at the RA, "You're asking me to turn down my music, but you haven't asked the White students to turn theirs down!" Bias, or the perception of bias, absolutely has to be addressed in the community. In some cases, it can be as simple as considering the statistical facts. Are more students of color being referred to conduct than White students? Are more males being referred than females? When bias-related incidents do occur, is the response swift and severe, or do the victims feel unheard? Is the response genuine or a boilerplate platitude?

In addition to the confrontation process, consider the language used by staff. In America, there is an increase in more schools toward using phrases such as "written up," "referring the situation," or "documenting the situation" rather than "you are being documented." This nuance is beneficial, first of all, because it keeps the focus on the behavior, rather than the student. In addition, its relation to immigration status is less threatening to students who are undocumented or whose families are undocumented, and who understandably have a fear of any process using that terminology. Professionals can also make sure students know that to document something is part of the administrative process and not meant to intimidate students.

Students with Different Abilities

More and more residence life and conduct professionals are recognizing a need for better training and information about working with students who have different abilities, particularly students on the autism spectrum; students diagnosed with post-traumatic stress disorder, depression, and anxiety; and students needing physical accommodations. For example, think about the above scenario if it involved a student with autism; the importance of training becomes clear.

Professionals and paraprofessionals have to be trained to address different responses to authority, rules, and extreme stress effectively. Bringing staff from disability services, counseling services, or local community resources is strongly recommended. These professionals can help professional staff and RAs understand how to interact with various students during confrontations, resolve conflict, and build a universally accessible community for these students.

Privilege

Think about the loud-music interaction with a student who has always had strong parental support and has not been confronted for violations, or who had parents who were able to advocate on their behalf. A student from that background may also have a disrespect for authority and may be more likely to have a parent involved with disciplinary issues, to ask to consult an attorney, or even just make the pronouncement of "my parent is an attorney" and expect staff will not push the issue further. This student is also less likely to be deterred by sanctions of fines or restitution, since these consequences will not have the same impact as they would on a student who is struggling with finances.

Safety concerns can also stem from a privileged upbringing. A student who grew up in a community where they could leave their car or home unlocked, or they had easy access to safe parks and schools, is not going to have the same level of awareness in the community as students who grew up in less-safe areas. Disrespect for authority may manifest itself with a privileged student as well, but in more of a mocking sense of, "It's no big deal if I lend someone my keys." They may be less likely to take the conduct process seriously, since their privilege may have protected them from harm or consequences in the past. Discussing with staff how to approach students wielding privilege is just as important as discussing how to approach students whose backgrounds did not provide that privilege.

DEALING WITH CONFLICT

The idea of conflict typically scares most individuals. Human nature creates, for most people, the need to be liked, and conflict contradicts these natural impulses. For traditional-age college students living in residential communities, particularly first-year students, the collegiate experience necessitates being incorporated into the social fabric of the institution. For residence life professionals, recruitment and retention also require teaching social skills that allow people to live in community with many more people. At least some conflict will be a natural result of this closeness.

The Merriam-Webster Dictionary (2017a) cites, as the first definition of conflict, "fight, battle, war, an armed conflict." The definitions move to internal or mental conflict within an individual, and finally, to a dramatic opposition between individuals or groups. Conflict, as defined, appears as a scary high-stakes clash with losers and winners. As others in a community are drawn to take sides, these losers and winners often extend well beyond the people in conflict. The community suffers to the detriment of all.

More simply, conflict is a disagreement or a divergence of views, opinion, or facts. The drama often stems from an unwillingness as individuals, organizations, or communities to face a disagreement head on and work through it for the good of all. In these cases, the community proceeds with a scarcity mentality that believes, "If you have this, I will have less than you do." Such an approach creates and reinforces a notion of winners and losers.

Rather than winners and losers as individuals, campus housing organizations can strive to create a civic awareness that values the needs of the community over the needs of the individuals within the community. Western philosophy has reinforced the values of competitiveness and individualism, while Eastern philosophy has taught the values of cooperativeness and community. Much could be learned from Eastern philosophy about individual decision-making with community as a central value in conflict resolution.

Conflict Resolution

Conflict resolution includes the various processes that facilitate a peaceful end to disagreement. Individuals attempt to resolve conflict through active, direct communication about their conflicting ideologies (i.e., intent, reasons for holding certain beliefs, behavior) and by finding a collectively acceptable resolution. Often, the most challenging part of conflict resolution can be moving past individual ideology to honor community values.

Schrage and Giacomini (2009) identified what they called "conflict culture" (p. 15). Conflict culture addresses the unique lens or stories individuals bring to a conflict and the manner in which these worldviews influence how conflict unfolds. To resolve conflict effectively, residence life professionals have to help those involved understand the stories shaping the view of conflict, work through these worldviews, and create a resolution that honors the community and its members. Campus communities also can construct value sets for a civil community. For example, the University of South Carolina has "The Carolinian Creed," developed by a task force in the 1980s. The task force objective was to explore: (a) the characteristics that define relationships in the campus community, (b) the expectations of the university regarding student relationships, and (c) suggestions for the most-effective way to present these standards and civility aspirations to the student body (University of South Carolina, 2017). Many other institutions have adopted similar values statements to shape community dialogue and relationships.

Students may find themselves not only at odds with one another, but also with institutional community values with which they may or may not agree. In today's campus residential communities, students also tend to communicate through social media rather than directly to one another (or campus authorities, including RAs). Students often sit in the same room while fighting via text message or having social media wars on SnapChat, Twitter, or Instagram. As a result, residence life professionals can experience greater challenges in understanding what has unfolded between individuals because conversations disappear within seconds of being shared or can occur anonymously on certain social media sites.

Not only must professionals try to resolve conflict, but they also find themselves teaching communication skills, community values, and cultural inclusion. To understand how to mitigate conflict, professionals must also understand how issues escalate and how to respond when they do.

De-escalation

The Merriam-Webster Dictionary (2017b) defines de-escalation as "to decrease in extent, volume, or scope." Residence life professionals want to help the individual and the community address the impact of inappropriate behavior, especially if individual students fail to understand how their behavior hurts or affects anyone other than them because they are the ones facing the consequences of poor choices. Arguably, behavior always has an impact, whether one recognizes it or not. For example, if a resident breaks the glass and pulls the fire alarm on a nightly basis, the floor has to evacuate the building nightly, affecting fellow residents' ability to study, sleep, or visit with friends. If a resident punches a roommate, they create the belief they may be dangerous to others in the community. Every behavior creates a ripple in the pond of community, depending on how positive or negative and at what magnitude the behavior occurs.

Kriesberg (2003) provides a model for how conflict emerges and how it can be resolved. He believed conflict eventually resolves or de-escalates, although not necessarily with positive result. Without processes to resolve conflict appropriately, individuals and the community continue to feel pain. Additionally, due to this pain, other members of the community can cycle from hurting back

FIGURE 1.1 Kriesberg De-escalation Stages (2003)

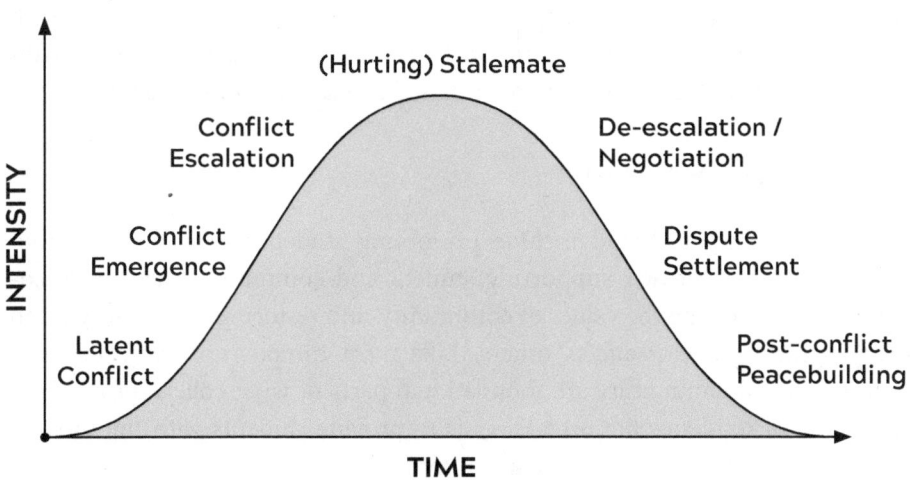

to the latent conflict, continually re-igniting the conflict until an appropriate method of dispute resolution or conflict resolution brings the issue to a conclusion. For example, roommates who cannot discuss deepening conflicts that are more personal wind up in fights over sweeping the floor. A deeper dialogue in these situations usually unveils longstanding interpersonal conflict that has not been addressed because someone does not want to make someone else angry or they are best friends.

In residence life, but also as the greater goal of the collegiate experience, residence life professionals build communities on residential floors, in buildings, throughout campus housing, and across campus. When approached with care and intentionality, these communities keep students in college, improve enrollment, promote student engagement, and increase retention. At the Ohio State University at Mansfield, students in on-campus housing have higher average grade point averages and a 10% higher retention rate from year one to year two, compared to non-residential students (Ohio State University Office of Enrollment Services-Analysis and Reporting). When intentionality goes into creating an inviting environment for students to live, students thrive.

Using techniques such as de-escalation has benefits to students that last far beyond an individual incident. When students feel like part of a community, it helps promote student well-being. When students act out, disrupting the rhythm of the community, individual and community well-being is also disrupted. Such a disruption can lead to increased use of mental health and health services on campus. For example, a privately run off-campus housing complex devoid of RA staff may not be as well-equipped to manage roommate and apartment-to-apartment conflict successfully, as well as other inappropriate behaviors. As a result, students use campus counseling services in greater numbers.

Finally, the collegiate experience is about holistic learning. Residence life professionals serve as educators inside and outside the classroom. They teach students about choices, consequences, and impact on others. They demonstrate teamwork, community engagement, and appropriate behavior daily for students. Through educational conversations and role modeling, they equip students with the skills to be great employees, community members, friends, and spouses/partners.

Peer Conduct Boards

Residence life goals should include promoting student learning throughout the collegiate experience, supporting student and community well-being, co-defining and teaching the values of community, and restoring community when inappropriate behavior affects others. Like most campus missions, learning, well-being, and community are foundational parts of what college provides. It is the role of residence life professionals to provide students with the tools to resolve conflict as individuals and a community.

Using students to provide the campus response to student conduct matter has a history dating back nearly 200 years. Marc Shook, associate provost and dean of student affairs at LaGrange College, as well as a regular presenter on the subject of conflict resolution (2013), traces the involvement of students in the adjudication of student conduct matters from the colonial colleges to the present day. In 1825, Thomas Jefferson was the first to propose the use of student-run student conduct panels at the University of Virginia. This failed after less than a year, and several other colleges and universities attempted to use student panels to no avail. Eventually, ongoing student conflict gave way to assault and other destructive behavior.

As time has evolved, so have campuses' use of students in addressing peer behavior, with the entire community engaging more deeply with peers who violate community norms. The British model of higher education gave way to the Germanic model, with faculty more focused on research, and some institutions created honor systems for managing student behavior (Shook, 2013). Into the early 1900s, many institutions found success with such systems, but most student-run judicial tribunals or panels were abject failures (Shook, 2013). As an increasingly more-diverse and older student body arrived at college, there was a greater push for student self-governance, which gained increased momentum well into the 1950s (Shook, 2013). In the 1960s, faculty governance in higher education gave way to the selection of the first student affairs professionals, with responsibility for student life and behavior allowing faculty to focus on research, not student behavior.

"Courts of law, however, may be more responsible than any of the student protest movements for the vast proliferation of peer-review hearing boards" (Shook, 2013, p. 43); a perspective worth noting. In particular, *Dixon v. Alabama* (1961) addressed certain rights for students in disciplinary proceedings, including due process, when students were dismissed without notice or opportunity to share their side of what occurred. During the 1960s, this focus on legalism and the fear of being sued led to many colleges developing peer-led behavioral standards boards.

Today, the organization of hearing boards often varies based on types of offenses being adjudicated, potential penalties that may be assigned, and the focus of the particular board on all or part of campus. Boards made up of faculty, staff, or students tend to hear cases at the campus level, while student-led boards hear cases in the residence halls or among student organizations. For example, at Texas Tech University, the members of academic integrity case boards are students and faculty only. Behavioral case boards are one student, one faculty, and one staff member. For Title IX cases, three administrative hearing officers are assigned to the board. Finally, elected student members belonging to Interfraternity Council organizations can serve on the board for Greek-related matters (Texas Tech University, 2017).

+ Peer Conduct Boards

The role, structure, and responsibilities of a peer conduct board can be as varied as the campuses that host them. Regardless of how they manifest themselves, what is important is that the boards reflect the campus conduct philosophy and mission. These statements from conduct board descriptions illustrate the variety of approaches used.

- "Peer Conduct Board hearings are formal hearings by a student panel to determine the responsibility of a student (hereafter called the respondent) for violating the Code of Conduct and to recommend sanctions for responsibility" (Peer conduct board, 2017).

- "[Students serve] on average, two hours per week depending on your involvement with the council. During recruitment and Creed activities, involvement can be as much as 5-7 hours per week. Members may sit on hearings whenever they are available" (Carolina Judicial Council, 2017).

- "The Peer Conduct Board, composed entirely of students, is trained and supported under the auspices of the Office of the Dean of Students in hearing student conduct matters of low severity and serves as the Parking Appeal Board for the Department of Public Safety" (Peer conduct board-Fairfield, 2017).

- "The purpose of the Residence Hall Peer Conduct Board is to provide a student voice in the judicial process. The hope of the board is that students would see themselves as part of a greater community and understand how their actions affect others. As peers of the involved students, the Residence Hall Peer Conduct Board students bring a unique perspective to the process and can help the involved students to better understand the impact of their actions on other students and the greater Winona community" (Peer conduct board, Olcott, 2017).

The Carolina Judicial Council at the University of South Carolina is a student organization, the school's description of which reads:

> A unique student organization at the University of South Carolina, the Carolina Judicial Council, is a recognized honors society and as such attracts some of the University's elite students. The Council serves a dual purpose; as campus role models, we personify the tenets of our guiding philosophy, the Carolinian Creed, and we function as a peer conduct review board acting with the Office of Student Conduct and Academic Integrity (Carolina Judicial Council, 2017).

The Ohio State University at Mansfield branch campus and North Central State College, like many community colleges and two-year campuses, do not use peer judicial boards, due to an inability to select and adequately train a student board with enough tenure to provide some continuity for the process. When the Ohio State University Council needs students to serve on academic misconduct hearings on a regional campus, a student leader is chosen, even though they have not received any training to serve.

The greater the impact and the greater the consequences that may be levied, the more likely faculty and staff are to be members of such a board. For example, if a student may be expelled for a behavior in offense affecting the greater community, like a violent attack, faculty and staff are more likely to be members of the board. Typically, solely student-run peer conduct boards exist in residence and Greek life, probably due to the belief student behavior in these settings most-significantly affects only other students. At many small community, technical, and non-residential colleges, it may be challenging to have a student-run board, since students leave after a year or two to attend other campuses. As a result, these campuses may lean toward using conflict resolution or restorative justice processes run by an administrator to restore community, or administrator or faculty boards, if any boards at all.

The responsibilities of peer conduct boards can vary from campus to campus. Some may require intense and regular training; some may require no training. Some may be involved in proactive educational opportunities based on community values and decision-making; some may not. Board members may serve in other capacities, such as reviewing parking appeals; others may not. Some may serve the entire campus; others may serve only residence life or the fraternities and sororities. Boards may decide the outcome for inappropriate behavior and recommend an outcome to an administrator who renders the final decision, which may or may not be the decision of the peer conduct board.

Many pros and cons have been outlined regarding the administration of campus discipline by students.

The pros include:	The cons include:
• There are educational benefits for the students who serve on the boards. • The campus community benefits due to student self-governance. • Students learn best from other students or their peers. • An impartial jury of one's peers provides justice (Shook, 2013).	• The time involved with selecting and training peer conduct boards may make them ineffective. • Peers are more likely to deliver harsher and potentially unfair sanctions. • Peer conduct boards may fail to abide by the institution's rules and procedures, creating a threat of legal action (Shook, 2013).

Some institutions, based on size and the time students remain at the institution, may influence whether a campus uses peer conduct boards or elects to use conflict resolution and restorative practices to resolve incidents of inappropriate behavior.

THE ROLE OF THE RESIDENT ASSISTANT

While all housing and conduct staff members have a role to play in the building of community, the bulk of the responsibility on many campuses falls to the resident assistants. The resident assistant is critical to the development of community in residence halls. There are multiple student employment and leadership opportunities in residence life — desk attendants, program planning, residence hall councils, or governing groups like a residence hall association — but the role of the RA is different: "The role of the resident assistant in developing a socially just community is paramount" (Cook & McCoy, 2017, p. 69).

RAs are empowered to provide leadership, set tone, and influence positive social change in the community where they have responsibility. RAs communicate the values of the institution and the residence life department through their work every day. They use meetings, bulletin boards, and floor programs to communicate behavior expectations, as well as safety and security procedures; celebrate special occasions and college traditions; and emphasize educational priorities. RAs identify and support individual residents with door decorations, sociograms, and meeting with each student one-on-one or in small groups.

They may have job requirements for educational programming and team building that should result in building a sense of trust and connectedness between the RA and the resident. A number of studies and books stress the important contribution RAs make to students' sense of belonging, coping with the transition, and creating community on the floor (Chambliss & Takacs, 2014; Collins, Dolly, Leonard, & Whitaker, 2016; Erb, Sinclair, & Braxton, 2015).

RAs and Community-building

As has been discussed throughout this section, paraprofessionals influence the experience of all residents of campus housing. Student staff members are on the front line of student development, and their interaction with residents influences the sense of community and connection to the institution and other people. As a result, RAs must understand their role in building the foundation for community.

One of the primary areas where RAs must be prepared to build community involves equity, diversity, and inclusion. Student staff must understand their role in working effectively with students from different cultures. They need to learn to listen to their residents, to observe, to reflect, and to be prepared to admit when they make a mistake. RA training should include self-reflection exercises, sharing personal experiences, and role-playing.

The second area of concern is trust and support. Consistency and accountability are incredibly important. RA training can include establishing expectations for visibility, the value of similarly confronting issues, and sharing potential conduct situations. While personal style is always going to be a part of any RA's interactions with residents, role play and review of conflict resolution activities are important to building their competency and confidence. Actions such as sharing a status on Facebook such as "Another long night on duty in ABC Hall" or comparing horror stories over lunch in the dining center with staff from other halls are detrimental to the community because they do not build trust and support. Encourage debriefing, but keep it within the hall staff or to the hall director.

One of the most visible RA initiatives will be creating and managing programs and activities. In community-building, programs that engage residents can be valuable resources. Some of those programs are passive in nature (i.e., bulletin boards), while others are active (i.e., events on campus or in the residence hall). Educational programming is paramount and should be coordinated with professionals in health, counseling, local police or campus safety officers, and others with content expertise. The RA role should take the lead in social programming and building community by creating interactions where students can get to know themselves and one another, in addition to learning new skills and information.

Community Development Activities

RAs can use activities to create, enhance, and foster the development of community. Some activities, like those at Missouri State University, can be completed early in the semester (i.e., floor/wing meeting, use of roommate/suitemate agreements, completing floor diagram/names test), while others can be planned throughout the semester (i.e., sociogram activity and success chats). Successful development of community can help the RA feel more confident when addressing residents, since they already have a connection. When RAs know their residents, they can connect students who have similar interests to each other. A strong community is one where residents feel more comfortable addressing issues directly with each other rather than through the RA. The development of communication skills ideally will be an outcome of participating in community development activities.

The following examples are some of the many ways the RA can create a community on a floor. RAs need to be prepared to deal with conflict that may occur when the needs of the individual collide with the needs of the community. Consistent, effective conflict resolution can lead to and can be evidence of a sense of community in residence life.

Floor and wing meetings. A meeting scheduled within the first few days of checking in can establish the tone for the community. During this meeting, the RA can outline expectations of how residents should conduct themselves in terms of following rules or talking to each other. Policies can be explained, and the RA can describe how inappropriate behaviors will be addressed. The RA can also explain how programs/activities will be planned and how residents can get to know each other.

Asking residents to brainstorm ideas for things to do and engaging them in the planning process demonstrates the RA wants residents to be actively involved in community development, which encourages them to listen to each other and work together, and creates an opportunity for the RA to learn more about the members of the floor.

Roommate/suitemate agreements. During floor meetings, the RA can introduce the concept of roommate/suitemate agreements. These documents are starting points for residents to discuss their needs and ideas with fellow roommates/suitemates. Many students never shared a room before coming to college. These agreements assist students in discussing the various aspects of living with another person. Who cleans the bathroom when, how food is shared (if at all), and who can visit at certain times are just a few of the areas covered by the agreement. Students often assume living together will work out just fine;

however, they quickly discover others do not do things the same way as they do. By offering the agreement as an option for students or requiring all residents to complete it, the RA can head off conflicts that may disrupt the community or become policy violations.

Floor diagram and names test. After a few weeks of living together, the RAs, either individually or as a staff, can be asked to participate in a floor diagram or names test. In this exercise, the RA receives a blank floor chart or diagram of the floor or building wing and is challenged to enter names of their residents in the rooms where they live. Sometimes only first names are required, but supervisors can ask RAs to provide one specific detail (e.g., Joe played on his high school

✚ Balancing Rights

In any housing system, situations will occur where the needs and rights of one student will conflict with the needs and rights of other residents on a floor or in a residence hall. When this occurs, it is important to give careful attention to the due process rights of the student who violated the code of conduct while considering the potential impact on other residents. For example, if a student is disruptive to the community (e.g., violent or threatens another resident), the student still will be entitled to due process under the university's code of conduct. However, while due process is being followed, the other residents may be fearful remaining in their living environment. Consultation with the conduct office, dean of students, and possibly legal counsel, can result in methods, specific to the college or university, to manage the situation.

One option could be to move the violating student to a new residence temporarily while the investigation and conduct process is completed. Many colleges do not promise a specific assignment to a student; rather, the housing contract only agrees to provide a space in a residence hall. In these and all conduct hearings, it is important to address the concept of respect toward and from the student and staff. Assure students that any complaints regarding their treatment will be heard, and be intentional and direct in discussing disrespectful comments or behaviors reported by staff.

basketball team) about each resident as well. If the test is given again later in the semester, the supervisor can expect the RA to know more about the residents.

Sociogram. Sociograms can be completed mid-semester after the RA has time to get to know the residents and observe patterns that develop on the floor. The RA draws a diagram of the floor and enters the names of all the residents in their specific rooms. Then the RA selects ways to represent areas of pride on the floor visually, who interacts with whom, organizations in which students are involved, etc. RAs can be as creative as they choose, but the point is to describe the community to the RA's supervisor. After the RA sees a visual representation of the community, he or she can hold conversations and set goals to address identified concerns.

Success chats. One-on-one conversations or success chats can take place at certain times during the semester to create opportunities for touchpoints with residents. At some schools, the RA meets with students twice during the semester. Together, they identify and address three topic areas depending on the time in the semester (e.g., adjusting to university life is the topic for the first chat of the fall semester). These short discussions allow RAs to discover how students are adjusting, what needs they have, and how they are doing. They help staff members assist students in ways that may have been overlooked. At first, RAs may think the amount of time needed to complete the chats would be overwhelming, but they should discover the time spent is worthwhile because they are able to connect with each resident and help as needed, which could keep problems from escalating.

CONCLUSION

According to Blimling (2003), "The development of community in a residence hall is enhanced when people have mutual respect for one another, respect one another's rights, trust one another, and have a commitment to the group as a whole" (p. 292). Consider this quote in the context, once again, of the conflict between the RA and the music-playing student. Is the student acting respectfully? Is the staff member? What actions by the student could be seen as disrespectful? Does the student view the RA as disrespectful?

Each of the specific populations and concepts discussed here brings a different view to the idea of respect. Some students feel it is disrespectful to be told what to do in their home. Others feel challenged by instructions given by a peer. Consider, also, the RA's identity and experiences. Someone used to being listened to and cooperated with will see it as disrespectful when a student does not comply. Conversely, if the RA was brought up to be accommodating and not challenge others, students may view this as a weakness and exploit it, resulting in disrespectful attitudes and behaviors.

In this light, it is easy to see why it is important staff members (students and professionals) be proficient in using consistent, assertive (not aggressive) confrontation methods, as well as tactics to de-escalate situations. It shows the value of having discussions during one-on-one and staff meetings about the issues unique to student employees and peer accountability or confrontation. Staff should understand the concept of earning — rather than expecting — respect and of setting expectations about respect for the community. Recognizing and establishing this notion of respect can be instrumental in building the sense of community that should be a priority for residence life professionals. It is the foundational component of a successful experience for students. It creates a safe environment for learning and growth for students, as residents and as paraprofessionals. A sense of community is the environment residence life and student conduct professionals believe shapes student behavior and positively influences decision-making and interpersonal communications.

The familiar scenes of college life illustrate a sense of community — eating pizza well into the morning hours, watching television or playing video games with roommates, sporting school colors to attend a football game, studying for finals fueled by a pile of snacks in the lounge. These scenes are created by design, not default. They are the result of established practices, training resident assistants and other staff to effectively support diverse populations, implementing conflict resolution as a tool for student development, and using peer conduct boards and restorative justice techniques to rebuild the floor's or hall's sense of community if it is damaged.

Poor choices and bad behaviors are also familiar scenes of college life. Many of the poor choices and bad behaviors are evidence of developmental stages experienced by college students — testing authority, trying something new, caving to peer pressure. Student conduct, again by design, helps transition students in their development. An insistence on accountability for behaviors can provide the optimum balance of challenge and support for growth. Does the sense of community influence the behavior? Although there may not be a definitive answer, residence life and conduct professionals certainly must work toward that end.

REFERENCES

Blimling, G. (2003). *The resident assistant* (6th ed.). Dubuque, IA: Kendall/Hunt Publishing Company.

Boyer, E. (1990). Campus life: In search of community. A Special Report on the Carnegie Foundation for the Advancement of Teaching. Princeton, NJ: Princeton University Press.

Carolina Judicial Council. (2017, October 16). Retrieved from http://www.housing.sc.edu/studentengagement/plocjc.html.

Chambliss, D. F., & Takacs, C. G. (2014). *How college works.* Cambridge, MA: Harvard University Press.

Clemons, S. A., McKelfresh, D., & Banning, J. (2005). Importance of sense of place and sense of self in residence hall room design: A qualitative study of first-year students. *Journal of the First-Year Experience, 17*(2), 73–86.

Cook, K., & McCoy, D. L. (2017). Messages in collusion: Resident assistants and white racial identity development. *Journal of College and University Student Housing, 43*(3), 68–79.

Collins, B., Dolly, D., Leonard, M. B., & Whitaker, J. L. (2016). Bridging the gap: Building meaningful connections after the groups scholars program. *Journal of the Student Personnel Association at Indiana University,* 71–83. Retrieved from https://education.indiana.edu/graduate/programs/hesa/iuspa/2016%20Bridging%20the%20Gap.pdf.

Dixon v. Alabama State Board of Education, 294 F.2d 150 (5th Cir. 1961).

Erb, N. M., Sinclair, M. S., & Braxton, J. M. (2015). Fostering a sense of community in residence halls: A role for housing and residential professionals in increasing college student persistence. *Strategic Enrollment Management Quarterly, 3*(2), 84–108. doi: 10.1002/sem3.20063.

Gardner, J. (1996). Building community. *Community Education Journal 23*(3), 6–9.

Hotchkins, B., & Dancy, T. (2017). A house is not a home: Black students' responses to racism in university residential halls. *Journal of College and University Student Housing, 43*(3), 42–53.

Kriesberg, L. "De-escalation Stage." *Beyond Intractability.* Guy Burgess and Heidi Burgess, (Eds.) University of Colorado, Boulder: Conflict Information Consortium. Posted September 2003 at: http://www.beyondintractability.org/essay/de-escalation-stage.

McMillan, D. W., & Chavis, D. M. (1986). Sense of community: A definition and theory. *Journal of Community Psychology, 14,* 6–23.

Merriam-Webster Online. (2017a). Retrieved from https://www.merriam-webster.com/dictionary/conflict.

Merriam-Webster Online. (2017b). Retrieved from https://www.merriam-webster.com/dictionary/de-escalate.

Pascarella, E. T,. & Terenzini, P. T. (2005). *How college affects students: A third decade of research.* San Francisco, CA: Jossey-Bass.

Peer conduct board. (2017, October 16). Retrieved from https://aurora.edu/student-life/residence/judicial-affairs/disciplinary-hearing-process/peer-conduct-board.html#.WeO34DBrxPY.

Peer conduct board-Fairfield. (2017, October 16). Retrieved from https://www.fairfield.edu/undergraduate/student-life-and-services/office-of-the-dean-of-students/peer-conduct-board.

Peer conduct board Olcott. (2017, October). Retrieved from http://www.winona.edu/asf/media/peer_conduct_board-olcott.pdf.

Reaves, B. A., & Goldberg, A. L. (1996). Campus law enforcement agencies, 1995. Retrieved from https://www.bjs.gov/content/pub/pdf/CLEA95.pdf.

Schrage, J. M., & Giacomini, N. G. (Eds.). (2009). *Reframing campus conflict: Student conduct practice through a social justice lens.* Sterling, VA: Stylus Publishing.

Shook, M. H. (2013). The historical evolution of student participation in disciplinary proceedings. *Journal of the Association of Student Conduct Administrators, 5,* 37–60.

Texas Tech University (2017). *Texas Tech student handbook.* Retrieved from http://www.depts.ttu.edu/dos/docs/StudentHandbook_2017-2018.pdf.

Tinto, V. (1993). *Leaving college: Rethinking the causes and cures of student attrition* (2nd ed.). Chicago, IL: University of Chicago Press.

University of South Carolina. (2017). Carolinian Creed. Retrieved from https://www.sa.sc.edu/creed/creedhistory.

1. Think about your residence hall community. What evidence do you have that there is a strong sense of community? What evidence do you have to suggest that there is a need for improvement? For the areas of improvement, what steps would you take to implement positive change?

2. Reflect upon a recent conflict among residents that was not resolved well after staff intervention. Could components of the training program have been enhanced to improve the knowledge, skills, and abilities of the staff to better deal with conflict?

3. Think about the interactions you have observed between staff and students from underrepresented groups in your residence hall community. Are there areas for improvement? What training or interventions with staff could help build understanding and inclusiveness?

4. Think about your experiences with peer conduct boards. Talk about scenarios where this system has been positive and where the outcomes have created challenges. If you were the director, would you keep the model of peer conduct boards or explore other options?

5. If you had the opportunity to serve on a planning committee for a new residence hall, what suggestions would you make to the architects to assist with building a sense of community for the residents?

DETERMINING CONDUCT PHILOSOPHY

Shana Warkentine Meyer and Lyn Redington

"There are people who view conduct as a terrible thing; the worst part of our job. I will never be one to tell you conduct is fun; I don't get joy out of working with conduct or seeing people in pain. But I do find it to be the most humbling and privileged work I do. When students get to my desk, they are usually facing consequences that are very serious. They've made some choices that are very damaging. To be in a position to walk next to somebody who is, at that moment, experiencing what can feel like a real life-changing crisis; the privilege to be the person that gets to — that gets to — make that right? I think that's humbling. I am aware of the gift we as professionals give to the field when we do conduct work, and I am humbled by that."

— Dr. Carrie Petr, vice president for student affairs,
Doane College (Personal communication, November 2, 2017)

FORBIDDEN CANDLES. Underage drinkers. Violated quiet hours. Disgruntled roommates. Vandalized walls. Undocumented pets. These are only a few of the many reasons why college and university student residents may find themselves a part of the student conduct process. These also are only a few of the reasons why many campus housing and residence life professionals — even if the word "conduct" isn't part of their job title — must be well-versed in the student conduct process.

The intersection of student housing and student conduct is filled with challenges and opportunities. The approach residence life and conduct professionals take toward meeting both of these is guided by their institutional and personal conduct philosophy. For most people in higher education today, that philosophy puts more focus on developmental outcomes than punitive sanctions. In this approach, conduct is an educational process with a focus on changing student behavior, not the student.

It is shortsighted to believe the conduct process begins only when a student violates residence hall or campus policies. More broadly speaking, the philosophy of conduct opens by setting behavioral expectations in the residence halls and campus communities. It includes establishing traditional events, campus climates, and accepted behaviors, as well as acknowledging when students express behaviors at odds with these accepted and understood guidelines.

By examining conduct holistically, residence life professionals begin to shape student conduct by establishing written and unwritten guidelines and strategies that create a sense of community among students. Most housing professionals would agree on an underlying philosophy that residence halls should be living and learning communities where students feel safe in their growth and development, diversity is accepted, and mistakes can be learning opportunities. These values help shape a positive experience and sense of belonging for students.

When a conduct process follows such a philosophy, incidents such as those listed above are no longer just red flags on a report, but chances to educate students about personal safety, the dangers of alcohol, consideration for others, conflict resolution, restorative acts, individual responsibility, and much more, while leaving room to repair any damage to the residence hall's sense of community. To accomplish this, though, requires a commitment. Most housing and conduct professionals would agree it would be far easier if conduct violations simply were handled like transactions: Break a rule, face the corresponding punishment. To elevate the conduct process requires the foundational cornerstone of an agreed-upon conduct philosophy upon which individual staff members, departmental teams, and entire institutions can build their practice, policy, and strategy to reach their desired outcomes.

CONDUCT PHILOSOPHY THROUGH THE YEARS

The novelist James Baldwin urged people to "Know from whence you came. If you know whence you came, there are absolutely no limitations to where you can go." When looking at the history of higher education and how college and university campuses serve as microcosms of society as a whole, it is certainly easy to see how the areas of student housing, residence life, and student conduct track with the key occurrences that have influenced the mission and focus of higher education.

This evolving context serves as the basis for campus philosophies and practices, from university missions to campus cultures. Understanding history helps demonstrate how each institution responded to changes in its unique fashion and, in turn, why they may display variations (some slight, some dramatic) in their missions and their approaches to conduct processes.

In Brubacher and Rudy's *Higher Education in Transition, An American History: 1636–1956,* the authors noted how the earliest American campuses were inspired by British colleges where the residence halls "were designed to bring the faculty and students together in a common life which was both intellectual and moral" (1968). These residential colleges focused on learning in and out of the classroom, since faculty often lived in the residence halls with the students and provided tutoring to them.

Philosophically, this view remains alive today and is a core component of housing conduct: residence halls should be living and learning environments. While morality may be an outdated term, behavior that has a negative effect on students being able to live in their residences is taken seriously and adjudicated through campus conduct processes.

As the United States grew, so did its higher education footprint. In 1862, the Land Grant College Act was passed, creating 69 new colleges and beginning to separate colleges from their traditional religious or spiritual connections and influence. These new institutions began revising previously accepted rules and regulations, including those associated with residential living. In the 1880s, universities chose to concern themselves less with the behaviors of students in their homes or their social lives and more with classroom learning. However, entering the 1900s, this trend began to change again, spurred by campuses such as Yale University that had "an adherence to the English philosophy that the communal life of students has high educational value" (Blimling, 1995, p. 26). Residence halls became integral to providing extracurricular campus activities for their residents.

As campus facilities shifted from a place to live to a place where extracurricular activities and interactions were encouraged, campus administrators recognized the need to organize formally and address campus behavioral issues. *The Student Personnel Point of View* was published in 1937 after a two-day American Council on Education (ACE) conference. This seminal document clarifies the field of student personnel work and the relationship of those in the field to other administrative and academic functions on the university campus. The concept of educational officers was first created in response to a need to assist in the ever-growing arena of campus disciplinary matters.

> These officers were appointed first to relieve administrators and faculties of problems of discipline; but their responsibilities grew with considerable rapidity to include a large number of other duties: educational counseling, vocational counseling, the administration of loans and scholarship funds,

part-time employment, graduate placement, student health, extracurricular activities, social programs, and a number of others. The officers undertaking responsibility for these educational functions are known by many names, but during the past two decades, they have come as a group, to be called personnel officers. (*Student Personnel Point of View*, 1937, p. 3)

Beyond establishing student affairs as a profession, this was the first time student personnel staff, like housing officers, were organized and recognized for their efforts, as well as the importance of what occurs in a student's life outside the classroom. In 1949, ACE revisited the Student Personnel Point of View and issued an updated report, charging student personnel workers to focus on many facets of students' lives, including development of individuality and responsibility. This update further defined student affairs' role in campus conduct as beyond that of a disciplinarian.

Progressive emancipation from the restrictions of childhood is a major challenge to every adolescent. Reveling in his newfound freedoms, for which he may not yet be prepared by adequate self-discipline, the college student may find himself in conflict with accepted social patterns and standards. Other students, whose domination by their families may extend to the college campus, may voice their rebellion in actions offensive to their fellow students or embarrassing to the college family to which they now belong. In such situations, preventive therapy may be accomplished by enlisting parental cooperation in counseling in such personal problems when they are discovered and diagnosed. When the need for social discipline does arise, the college should approach the problem as a special phase of counseling in the development of self-responsibility for behavior rather than in a spirit of punishment of misbehavior. (*Student Personnel Point of View*, 1949, p. 6–7)

While these changes in how staff members were perceived occurred, there also was a change in the collective student body on campuses across the country as thousands of World War II veterans enrolled, spurred by the G.I. Bill. In fact, "sixty percent of those veterans who were eligible to enroll in institutions of higher education after World War II enrolled within approximately two years of the end of the war" (Blimling, 1995, p. 36). The older students altered the traditional student demographics, which led to changes in previous beliefs and practices, such as in loco parentis (in place of a parent). This influx also led to rapidly increasing enrollment numbers, generating a construction boom, forcing colleges and universities to expand in size, scope, and capacity. The federal government also became increasingly involved in the administration of colleges and universities through the Higher Education Facilities Act and the Higher Education Amendments Act of 1962.

Societal changes also affected campus life. In 1961, the case of *Dixon v. Alabama* "was the first time that any American court recognized that students at a state university have due process protection under the Fourteenth Amendment" (Lee, 2014). The case grew out of an incident where Alabama State College students who had protested a segregated lunch counter were expelled outright from their school without a hearing. Six students filed suit and, after initially losing their trial, won on appeal. "Instead of allowing state universities to discipline their students without regard to their constitutional rights as they were permitted to do during the *in loco parentis* era, the Fifth Circuit mandated that state universities had to abide by constitutional restrictions. Specifically, it held that state universities must provide notice and some opportunity to be heard before they could expel their students for misconduct."

This acknowledgment by the courts had an even greater impact in that "other student activists for racial justice across the country were afforded constitutional due process protections during the height of the civil rights movement."

Changes continued to affect campuses. Along with taking up the case of civil rights, students worked to improve women's and LGBTQ rights. The change in the legal voting age from 21 to 18 spurred students to claim their new freedoms of choice and expression. The Federal Educational Right to Privacy Act of 1974 granted students additional protection and privacy. The Clery Act in 1986 changed rules regarding safety information that campuses needed to divulge. One after another, states raised the legal drinking age from 18 to 21 in the 1980s.

As the 21st century began, more changes occurred, with an increased awareness of mental health issues and the growing diversity of students. There was a new focus on mandates such as Title IX and the Violence Against Women Act, as well as an increased awareness of decolonization, freedom of speech, and social justice.

Each step of the changing times, cultures, and student demographics had corresponding changes that influenced campus philosophies on all matters, including campus conduct. The division between public and private, religiously affiliated institutions of higher education that began more than 150 years ago can still be felt because they can apply differing codes of conduct and beliefs, tying the university's mission to what student behaviors are expected. Residence halls — no longer just a place to sleep — focus on the whole student, providing a place where students can grow and develop through social and educational programming. Residence life professionals develop ways to create resident interactions, establish community standards, and address negative behaviors that may occur behind closed doors. "Due process" and other terminology reminiscent of judicial language is now part of the campus conduct lexicon. Housing and conduct policies and practices are amended to support students' inalienable rights as their interpretations change. They address new realities such as legalized marijuana, concealed carry laws, and support animals.

The world changes. The philosophies of student housing and student conduct change with it.

FOUNDATIONAL PHILOSOPHY

A college or university's conduct philosophy is like a fingerprint: unique to the institution. Still, virtually all of them can be traced back to a larger foundational philosophy. Much of the philosophy behind student conduct processes is based on Karen S. Kitchener's article "Intuition, Critical Evaluation, and Ethical Principles: The Foundation for Ethical Decisions in Counseling Psychology" (1984). In it, Kitchener identifies five moral principles. When investigating a campus conduct violation, each of these principles should be examined to help in identifying the "why" behind case resolution.

- **Autonomy** addresses the individual's freedom of choice and action; independence that can be explored to help a student understand how their actions have consequences when those actions go against community values.
- **Justice,** as a concept, prescribes "treating equals equally and unequals unequally but in proportion to their relevant differences" (p. 49).
- **Beneficence** relates to the well-being of the student and considers that, at times, a student facing conduct consequences is seen as being in trouble or acting up. Treating a student respondent with beneficence reflects on the overall welfare of the student, being proactive, and preventing harm.
- **Non-maleficence** is the concept of doing no harm to others. When sanctioning a student for their conduct, the concept of not inflicting intentional harm is an important one.
- **Fidelity** refers to the notion of loyalty, faithfulness, and honoring commitments.

Each of these principles plays a part in developing the educational, restorative, community-based, holistic, and punitive philosophies instrumental in the conduct process. Rarely can a system be focused purely on one philosophy; components of other philosophies may bleed into each other. Campus philosophies are developed over time, based on student demographics, university mission, history, staff experiences, beliefs, and other factors. The following is an overview of influential philosophies.

Educational Philosophy

In student conduct, an educational philosophy is one in which students have the opportunity to reflect on their actions, relate them to their goals at their institution (and beyond), and determine how their actions affect these goals. In examining departmental missions for many housing and residence life communities, a common thread is that of developing and supporting students to become strong citizens and scholars. Students are welcomed into vibrant communities that foster their personal growth and that enhance their student experiences. Minimally, the goal of a university experience is to learn. Within an educational philosophy, sanctions should be related to the action and provide an opportunity to reflect, learn, and grow from the experience.

Mandy Hambleton, Title IX director at Florida State University, explains how she approaches conduct cases with an educational philosophy.

> My philosophy centers around education, empowerment, and encouraging behavior change. I educate students about community expectations, ways to resolve conflict, and resources that are available to them to avoid policy violations; empower students to take ownership of the resolution of their conflicts; and encourage them to make positive, sustainable behavior changes that will help them better achieve their goals and be successful students and citizens. (Personal communication, October 30, 2017)

Restorative Philosophy

A restorative philosophy of conduct is based on the larger concept of restorative justice, a process by which those who have caused harm meet with those who have been affected by their actions (see Chapter 6). The goal of this facilitated process is to allow the parties to explore the actions, what harm was caused, and how the offending party can begin to repair the harm. Sanctions may be in the form of a mutually agreed-upon agreement that details obligations of the offending party in an attempt to restore peace, fix what was broken, and take steps to move forward. This model attempts to increase understanding, connection, and healing among those affected by behaviors or actions.

Carrie Petr, vice president for student affairs at Doane University in Crete, Nebraska, is one who practices restorative justice in her approach to conduct. She states:

> Everyone wants to live in harmony; when you're out of harmony, that hurts. People want to find a way to restore harmony without losing things they cannot afford to lose. I often ask, What are the things you need to do

in order to restore trust and harmony in your community, your relationship, your personhood? What will feel like success for you? What will allow you to wake up tomorrow and have this be a memory? I have never gone wrong in that conversation. It always feels better. Always. (Personal communication, November 2, 2017)

Community-based Philosophy

A system built around a community-based philosophy seeks a balance between the individual rights of students and the responsibility to the greater living community. This philosophy is particularly applicable in a residence hall, where individual health and safety factors may put the greater community at risk, property loss or damage can affect all members of the community, or personal and academic success no longer will occur if the educational living environment is compromised.

Kevin Carmody, associate dean of student life and Title IX coordinator at Ferris State University, defines his philosophy as a combination of community-oriented, educational, and holistic. He explained:

> While I love restorative justice practices and to be educational, safety for the community must come first. I often think of Maslow's Hierarchy: if we don't first establish safety, then nothing else that we attempt will matter. Secondly, I believe that behavior can be changed when the right intervention can come into play. I think that being educational is much more than just assigning reflection papers. I actively assess interventions to find out if they're making an impact on behavior, I seek to understand what the core issue is and attempt to tailor educational interventions specific to that thought process, belief, or misperception that informed the behavior. (Personal communication, October 27, 2017)

Holistic System

A holistic system views the whole student in a conduct process. This type of system takes the whole person, including experiences, traumas, and backgrounds, into account when evaluating the conduct case and, if appropriate, in assigning sanctions.

S. Nicole Ferguson, director of the Office of Student Conduct and Case Management at Colorado State University-Pueblo, has drawn from her counseling background to influence her conduct practice:

> My philosophy stems from a counseling background and the knowledge

that a student is likely to act out when some other aspect of their life is out of their control. I believe that all students have the potential to learn from their mistakes, but we have to encourage that learning more than others encourage the violations. Breaking the rules can be fun! We have to remember the cost of fun sometimes. (Personal communication, October 24, 2017)

Anthony Ungaro, a former residential community educator at Oklahoma State University, addresses his sanctioning philosophy, which goes beyond traditional sanctioning rubrics and focuses on the whole person.

Most sanctions are set and are given to multiple people when it might not match the deeper issue. With alcohol, there is often one blanket sanction, but the remaining need to be used based on individual need, not a matrix. All students come into the meeting with different backgrounds; the same sanctions will not work for everyone and will start to inhibit learning rather than aid it. (Personal communication, October 24, 2017)

Punitive System

A punitive system views the process as a "punishment," and fines may be levied for violations (beyond restitution). Few, if any, conduct systems will openly state their processes are punitive; however, upon examination of terminology, many codes of conduct processes have a punitive feel even when their language is more subtle. Purposeful language and reflection on the words used may be helpful in changing this culture if desired. Doane University's Petr explained, "You have to be able to execute the philosophy that speaks to you. When I have been in a position where I'm supposed to 'punish' somebody, it doesn't speak to me, and so I'm not selling it very well. I like to handle conduct in a way that is educational and developmental, but not permissive." (Personal communication, November 2, 2017)

INSTITUTIONAL MISSION, VALUES, AND CULTURE

In constructing a conduct philosophy, institutions can begin to personalize it after considering foundational strategies, based on the influences of institutional mission, values, and culture.

Conduct and housing work and the way it is done will differ based on the wide variety of available institutions. According to the IES – National Center for Educational Statistics, there are 4,352 degree-granting universities in the U.S.

➕ Additional Thoughts

Those who work in student housing and student conduct often must face the misperception that they are only rule-makers or enforcers. The insights from the following professionals, as well as others quoted in this chapter, demonstrate how the work goes beyond that.

Kevin Carmody is associate dean of student life and Title IX coordinator at Ferris State University, a public university of approximately 15,000 students in Big Rapids, Michigan.

> I believe that any time you have an intervention, you have opportunities to address more than just the negative behavior. I can't tell you how many students I would see for alcohol or noise [violations], and also find out that they're homesick, or struggling with a decision about a major, or were recently dumped.
>
> At one of my previous institutions, we looked at students who were referred for alcohol violations and their retention with the institution. They shocked everyone when those who were referred to student conduct retained at higher rates than other students. I believe firmly that this is because those students made a connection with a professional who cared about them, who asked them how they were doing, and hopefully helped to connect them with other resources. That's why I fell in love with student conduct. Because we get to have those types of conversations with students who aren't typically getting those types of contact with other areas of the institution. (Personal communication, October 27, 2017)

Bryan Hinnen, director of Headington Hall at the University of Oklahoma, holds a unique position in that he works in housing, yet his employer is the athletics department.

> I always give the students the opportunity to do the right thing, take ownership, and learn from their mistakes. When it comes to student-athletes, we have our conduct meeting and discuss the choices they have made, the consequences of their decisions, and how their influence [affects] the community around them. We emphasize they are leaders whether they chose to be or not, the second they sign their national letter of intent. My favorite thing to do, though, is after we have completed their conduct meeting, [we] give the student 24 hours to tell their coach, before I do. It's a great lesson that the information

will be better coming from them, than me. (Personal communication, December 1, 2017)

Michelle L. Boettcher is an assistant professor of higher education student affairs and educational and organizational leadership development at clemson university.

When the assistant director and I started at the same time in the Office of Judicial Affairs (OJA), we had an opportunity to review the ways in which we did our work. I often tell newer hearing officers that at some point, they will have to determine for themselves whether they focus on fairness or consistency because these are not the same thing. Consistency is easier because it basically comes down to "If you violate A, you get sanction 1. If you violate B, you get sanction 2."

Fairness is the more challenging and more than just approach to the work. Were there other factors in a particular situation? What were the factors in the lives of the students involved? This takes more time and a willingness to ask probing questions to understand the big picture.

When we started our work, the office was more focused on consistency. It took us years to transform that culture. We did it in hearing cases fairly quickly, but the larger project was to change the ways in which OJA engaged with the larger community. Some things we did to transform the culture included:

· We expanded outreach efforts, including training for faculty, staff, student organizations, and offices across campus.

· We set up meetings with all new faculty on campus to introduce ourselves and talk about how we could support academic work and how the judicial processes at the university worked.

· We significantly increased our proactive efforts related to student conduct, specifically reaching out to groups and organizations with histories of conduct issues to introduce ourselves and provide opportunities for ongoing dialogue.

· We worked intentionally to develop a good relationship with a variety of areas on campus that do not historically have great issues with student conduct offices in higher education, including athletics, fraternity and sorority life, LGBTQ student organizations, etc.

Ultimately, our work focused on relationships and we worked intentionally to connect with key collaborators on campus. And, as mentioned, it took years to make any sort of significant change on campus. (Personal communication, October 28, 2017) (as of 2008), accounting for 22.4 million people (students, faculty, and staff). Thousands more exist around the world and most of these can be placed into some category. While not an exhaustive list, some of the various types of higher education institutions include liberal arts, Hispanic serving institutions (HSIs), religiously affiliated, comprehensive, tribal, historically Black colleges and universities (HBCUs), graduate schools, professional, for-profit, women's colleges, research-intensive, community colleges, open enrollment, highly selective, land grant, regional campuses, and much more. Each will have differing missions, values, and cultures; however, a solid personal philosophy of campus conduct can be successful in a multitude of institutional types.

How does a conduct officer develop a solid personal philosophy? One way to start is by undertaking some campus research to see how the campus's philosophy blends with the individual's perspective. Reviewing the institution's mission is a valuable first step.

Mission statements should summarize the essence of an institutional philosophy and typically are used in strategic planning and accreditation processes. In outlining what is valued or different about an institution, the mission statement describes what the institution stands for and why the institution focuses on this stance. In short, it answers the question, "Why do we exist?" By understanding what is important to the institution as a whole, housing professionals may be able to apply these values in creating a conduct philosophy.

Many institutions have moved toward shortening their mission statements to simplify the message. The University of Rochester revamped its mission statement in 2009 and ended up with a 10-word mission statement: "Learn, Discover, Heal, Create — and Make the World Ever Better" (Kiley, 2011). One can see the connection between this campus mission statement and the decision to use restorative circles as part of campus conduct processes. According to the University of Rochester Standards of Student Conduct:

> Restorative circles provide parties involved in a dispute with an opportunity to discuss the issue(s) that lead to the conflict in a safe, non-adversarial environment. Trained facilitators assist the participants in communicating about the dispute and help the participants to create an agreement regarding how to repair the harm that was caused. Practically, a restorative circle is a gathering of individuals who are involved (directly or indirectly) in a dispute with the purpose of talking about what happened and making a plan for resolving the issue. The circle typically meets twice, once to discuss the issues that lead to the conflict and once again to review the agreement that was developed during the first circle. (Office of the Dean of Students, 2017)

Colorado Christian University's mission is only one sentence: "Colorado Christian University cultivates knowledge and love of God in a Christ-centered community of learners and scholars, with an enduring commitment to the integration of exemplary academics, spiritual formation, and engagement with the world" (Colorado Christian University's Vision and Mission, n.d.). In turn, its mission alignment continues with CCU's community living expectations, which state, "Colorado Christian University expects you to uphold a high standard of behavior and personal values. We define these standards by aligning our expectations with the University's mission and its Christ-centered heritage." (Community Living Expectations, n.d.)

McMaster University, in Hamilton, Ontario, Canada, has a mission statement that is five sentences long:

> At McMaster, our purpose is the discovery, communication, and preservation of knowledge. In our teaching, research, and scholarship, we are committed to creativity, innovation, and excellence. We value integrity, quality, inclusiveness, and teamwork in everything we do. We inspire critical thinking, personal growth, and a passion for lifelong learning. We serve the social, cultural, and economic needs of our community and our society. (President's Office — Mission and Vision, 2017)

McMaster demonstrates its values of inclusiveness and teamwork by operating under a restorative justice model; offering an option for voluntary resolution (in which the complainant and respondent both agree to a resolution); and allowing an option of having the case heard by a peer conduct board (Code of Student Rights and Responsibilities, May 18, 2016).

Sometimes the mission can come from an entity even larger than the institution. For example, the Colorado State University System Board of Governors adopted a set of values to be shared by both CSU-Pueblo and Colorado State University in Fort Collins. These values dictate the institutions will:

- Be accountable
- Promote civic responsibility
- Employ a customer focus
- Promote freedom of expression
- Demonstrate inclusiveness and diversity
- Encourage and reward innovation
- Act with integrity and mutual respect
- Provide opportunity and access
- Support excellence in teaching and research

S. Nicole Ferguson, director of student conduct and case management at Colorado State University-Pueblo, recognizes how this mission and her institutional type influence her conduct practice:

> At my current institution, we have around 5,000 students. It is easier to take the time to schedule an entire hour for a student than at a larger institution and to take that time to really meet them where they are and attempt to elicit change. Getting to better know my particular student population has made a vast difference. We are an HSI so I frequently stay abreast of what is happening in the government and in the media that could be causing the violations I see with my particular student population. I definitely seek to first understand, and then sanction as needed. (Personal communication, October 24, 2017)

As professionals expected to support the institutions conduct mission, it is important for student affairs professionals to consider whether the institutional mission and campus conduct philosophy align with their philosophy. As Vinay Patel, assistant director for housing and residence life, upper-class experience, at Tulane University, explains:

> It's important to find out; does your philosophy fit within the context of the institution? Or, how can you make it fit? The culture of the institution matters. Some of the questions I ask are, "Is the institution selective?" "What is the focus of the institution and the department?" That may affect how conduct and sanctions play out. Previously, I enforced a departmental policy regarding smoke detector tampering. A likely sanction was the student's removal from housing. While I found enforcing this policy difficult, there was context [for] why the institution had those policies in place. You can have your personal philosophy and opinions, but they have to fit the overall culture of the institution, too. If they don't, it is time to move on. At the end of the day, my personal philosophy cannot be bigger than that of the department or university. (Personal communication, February 20, 2018)

LANGUAGE AND PHILOSOPHY

As an institution's conduct philosophy develops, it will shape — and be shaped by — the language used to express or present it. Ensuring the words in the campus or departmental code of conduct match the institution's philosophy creates the foundation for building the system. This is particularly noteworthy because language evolves over time, and if the language used in the campus or departmental conduct code has evolved as well, it must be noted. Karen Yin, founder of the *Conscious Style Guide,* writes about "conscious style," or "the art of using words effectively in a specific context" (About Conscious Style, 2017). In reviewing language used in campus conduct processes, it is important to note institutional and departmental mission, audience, tone, and level of formality. Depending on departmental and campus size and type, the answers to these questions will vary, and thus, the language used at various campuses will vary.

Ensuring the student code of conduct includes all members of the student population is an important dynamic that enables individuals to feel respected and valued, as well as included. Departmental discussions may include the use of inclusive language that eliminates gendered terms and acknowledges the gender identities of all people, removing assumptions. This may manifest itself through use of gender-inclusive pronouns such as they, them, themselves; sie, hir, hir, hirs, hirself; zie, ze, zir, zirs, zirself; or other options. It may also feature gender-inclusive titles such as chairperson, chair, or moderator rather than the less-inclusive terms of chairman or foreman. Hearings and processes may be scripted to ask participants what their gender pronouns are. If forms include gender descriptors, non-binary options should be included.

Caley Logsdon, an area coordinator at the Rhode Island School of Design, shared her perspective on gender identity in the conduct process:

> The student/respondent agency should be allowed to define their gender identity instead of selecting a box. If they have to click a box, the box can say, "Please provide your gender identity" with a text box. I think it is truly important in the conduct process for students to have some degree of agency at all levels. What might we say or how might we make a student feel if they are not adequately represented in the code of conduct in self-disclosing gender identity and forcing them to click a box? The ability to select multiple boxes is important because many trans* folx may identify with multiple gender identities, such as non-binary and masculine of center. Many times, our systems in higher education use legal names. In the conduct process, I think it is important to think about chosen names and how people need to be addressed, beyond trans students, but also international students who have Anglicized names. (Personal communication, February 22, 2018)

While student conduct documentation and hearings have similarities to a judicial process in a court of law, many campuses intentionally use language that separates campus conduct systems from the criminal justice system. Instead of campus judicial systems, the more-common vernacular is campus conduct systems that address the student's behavior. Rather than terms like "plaintiff" and "defendant," substitutions like "reporting party" and "respondent" are often used. Instead of "judging," terminology like "reviewing" may seem less condemnatory and more objective in its interpretation.

Ferguson had the opportunity to rewrite her campus code when she began her position at Colorado State University-Pueblo. She remembers:

> The language definitely did not match my philosophy. It felt very punitive and negative. The prior code used words like victim, perpetrator, hearing, and disciplinary action. These words do not have much of a therapeutic tone, which better aligns with my philosophy. It is hard to come into a meeting with someone automatically feeling like they are against you. I have softened this language to call hearings meetings and call reporting parties and responding parties by name. This seems to be resulting in a less defensive tone when students meet with me or when their parents call to ask questions. (Personal communication, October 24, 2017)

Beyond the code and conduct processes, terminology is a factor in the communications sent to students. Nathan Roberts, director of residential life at Missouri Western State University, explains he prefers to use the term "in violation" rather than "responsible" as a post-hearing finding. He states, "Students don't often think they are 'responsible.' The term seems to set up barriers for a discussion. Speaking of being 'in violation' seems to be a bit more antiseptic and opens up the conversation" (Personal communication, November 29, 2017).

On the other hand, Jerrid Freeman, vice president for student affairs at Northeastern State University, says, "I have changed my terminology to 'responsible' to further engage students in an educational discussion about their responsibility" (Personal communication, November 17, 2017).

For campuses with a large number of students who do not consider English as their primary language, it may be prudent to translate the code of conduct into different languages or provide interpreters during campus hearings. In reviewing and rewriting campus terminology, a word of caution: Kevin Carmody, associate dean of student life and title IX coordinator at Ferris State University, reiterates words mean different things to different people, so no one person should attempt to revise conduct codes on their own.

> When looking at policy, I think it's sometimes more difficult to match up with a personal philosophy because those efforts are often done in a team. I have never revised policy by myself, nor would I. I often consult with legal, do focus groups with students and other stakeholders, consult with colleagues, read tons of other sample policies to find other ways

of saying that. I think that they become more of a conversation with a number of different philosophies that are hopefully in harmony with one another. (Personal communication, October 27, 2017)

PHILOSOPHY AND PRACTICE

Buoyed by an established conduct philosophy and an understanding of institutional characteristics, housing and conduct professionals can craft, implement, and enforce specific policies and practices. While some standards certainly have near-universal acceptance, this is again an opportunity to identify an institution uniquely. Consider again the wide range of descriptors that could be applied to a campus. Each one of them could have an impact on the conduct process.

As an example, community colleges or four-year schools that follow open enrollment would most likely not enforce "no tolerance" policies, since those policies could go counter to their mission of access for all. Another example is professionals who work at smaller schools can be more likely to interact with students regularly on campus and have an opportunity to develop a relationship with those as they go through the conduct process, while someone at a larger campus may only have one brief interaction with those involved. Even campus occupancy rates can influence conduct decisions. For example, a housing department with a waiting list of students who need a room may be more strict in their conduct violation tolerance and be more likely to remove a student from the residence halls permanently than one without such pressure.

The responsibility to enforce specific policies, and champion the overall conduct philosophy, will fall to almost every housing and conduct staff member on campus. They are charged with holding students accountable to campus rules, policies, and expectations. Student conduct administrators themselves are employed by departments with a varying set of names, including residential education, campus conduct, residential conduct, community standards, student conduct, student rights and responsibilities, student integrity, dean of student's office, and more. With so many sub-systems, it is important to know where conduct operates on a college campus and residence halls. Who hears which cases? What is the synchronization between parties? How can all parties remain consistent in their philosophies?

Understanding and adhering to the conduct philosophy is important to ensure consistency throughout the system. Michelle Boettcher, assistant professor of higher education student affairs at Clemson University, was a hall director before she became a professor. In her various campus positions, she saw how residence life professionals and conduct officers' roles intersect and how those intersections could create different experiences for students.

✚ Application of Theory

Student development theory has numerous applications, including helping to create a personal conduct philosophy. By understanding these theories, practitioners can have a better understanding of why students behave as they do. By knowing a student's stage in personal development and cognitive thinking, practitioners can understand their motivations for behaviors.

These student development theories can help conduct officers develop and solidify a conduct philosophy (Evans, Forney, Guido-DiBrito, 1998).

- Chickering's Theory of Identity Development - The Seven Vectors
  Application: creating residential learning contracts.

- The Cross Model of Psychological Nigrescence
  Application: improving environmental climate, understanding White privilege.

- Helm's White Identity Development Model
  Application: improving environmental climate, understanding White privilege.

- Phinney's Model of Ethnic Identity Development
  Application: improving environmental climate, understanding White privilege.

- Cass's Model of Homosexual Identity Formation
  Application: providing support.

- Schlossberg's Transition Theory
  Application: self-help.

- Perry's Theory of Intellectual and Ethical Development
  Application: reviewing policies, training RAs, mediating roommate conflicts.

- King and Kitchener's Reflective Judgment Model
  Application: role modeling for RA training, understanding diverse populations, questioning beliefs.

- Kohlberg's Theory of Moral Development - Stages of Moral Reasoning
  Application: creating socially just communities, personal development, self-reflection.

As a hall director at institutions where there were lots of hearing officers across campus, I had concerns about fairness from one hearing officer to the next. It's tough to have systemic adherence to a conduct philosophy when you have more than 20 hearing officers managing different communities. No matter where conduct is adjudicated, it is helpful to focus on the institutional mission to ensure all groups are adhering to a similar conduct philosophy. (Personal communication, October 28, 2017)

The following shows some of the many campus responsible parties when it comes to campus and housing conduct. There may be additional responsible parties on campus and within residence halls.

Office/ Individual	Role	Considerations	Relation to Housing
President/ Chancellor	Ultimately responsible for entire campus, including all students and student conduct.	Important to report up campus chain of command. They should not read something in the newspaper or hear it from a parent, alumni member, or board member that they have not first been told by campus staff.	Varies based on campus size. Most likely informed of high-level housing cases. Likely not concerned with day-to-day conduct cases. Interest in how conduct and recidivism affect student retention.
Senior Student Affairs Officer/ Dean of Students/Vice President/ Chancellor of Administration and Finance	Oversees conduct process. May set designee to oversee conduct processes. Appeals may come to this office.	Title varies from campus to campus. Maintains clear documentation from responsible parties to triangulate behavior patterns.	Varies based on campus size. Second-highest-level administrator, ultimately responsible for oversight of housing.
Academic Departments/ Honor and Integrity Offices	Adjudicates honor code violations such as cheating.	Standards vary based on department (e.g., law school may have stricter student standards).	Housing programs may host academic programs within the department. Build relationships with academic affairs. Programs may involve residents in processes as hearing board members or respondents.
Residence Life	Oversees and enforces policies and procedures that apply to student residents.	Wide range of staff involved, from RAs and hall directors to director of residence life.	

continued on next page

Office/ Individual	Role	Considerations	Relation to Housing
Appellate Board	Reviews appeals.	Specific allowances for appeals should be included as part of code of conduct.	May exist at the housing and university level. Staff members may be involved as advisors. Residents may be involved as board members, complainants, or respondents.
Peer Hearing Boards/Student Government Judicial Branch	Hears cases and appeals of lower-level violations, such as parking citations or student voting issues.	May not be appropriate for all cases.	May exist at housing and university level. Residents may be involved as hearing members, complainants, or respondents.
Student Organization Conduct Board	Investigates and hears cases of violations committed by student organizations.	Individual members most likely heard through a student conduct process.	Housing organizations that have committed violations may have their case heard through this process.
Fraternity/ Sorority Hearing Panel	Investigates and hears cases of violations committed by student organizations.	Alumni and national headquarters of fraternities and sororities may be involved.	Processes may vary depending on whether fraternities or sororities reside in campus housing, own their own chapter houses, or if the violation occurs in home privately owned or rented by group member.
Human Resources/ Student Employment Office	Investigates and hears cases of violations committed by student organizations.	Documentation throughout any conduct situation is important.	If student is employee of housing department, conduct code violations may affect employment.
Coaches/ Athletic Teams	Investigates and hears cases of violations committed by student organizations.	While student-athletes are as accountable to conduct systems as any other student, may face additional sanctions from coaches or overseeing bodies.	Residence life staff works with athletics staff to understand housing conduct processes. Athletics department should not have input into sanctioning process, and athletes should not receive special treatment.
International Student Services	Investigates and hears cases of violations committed by student organizations.	In addition to government standards, international students may receive study-abroad scholarships that include additional standards they are expected to uphold.	Residence life staff works with ISS staff to understand housing conduct processes. ISS department should not have input into sanctioning process, and international students should not receive special treatment.

Office/ Individual	Role	Considerations	Relation to Housing
Early Alert/ Student Success Office/ Behavioral Intervention Team	Investigates and hears cases of violations committed by student organizations.	Early-alert systems do not always equate with conduct issues; open with communication helps student receive services and resources before a behavioral issue occurs.	When possible, housing staff member should serve on Early Alert and Behavioral Intervention teams to triangulate housing information.
Title IX	Oversees cases of sexual assault, harassment, and other Title IX violations.	A student may face Title IX and student conduct processes simultaneously.	Residents may be involved as witnesses, complainants, or respondents. Staff members may be trained to serve as university investigators.
University Police/ Campus Security	Supports campus through community policing, emergency response, investigations, police reports, tickets, and arrests.	University police partner with housing office for relationship-building and community policing.	Residence hall crimes are reported to campus police.
Mandatory Reporters/ Campus Security Authorities (CSAs)	Required by the Clery Act to file reports of certain crimes.	Clery-reportable cases may be investigated by university police and local authorities, as well as residence life or conduct offices. Because campus processes are not criminal in nature, accountability in two systems is not considered double jeopardy.	A number of staff in housing roles are CSAs. Important that conduct documentation is done in a Clery-compliant manner.
University Legal Counsel/Risk Management	Many campuses employ lawyers either on a full-time basis or contractually.	Legal counsel not likely to be involved in day-to-day residence hall conduct issues. Contacted, when necessary, by department directors.	Policy revision or creation, particularly in response to mandates or laws. Guidance in criminal cases. Assistance when staff operates outside standard operating procedures, creating risk. Evaluates programming risk and liability waivers.

CONCLUSION

As the statements included throughout this chapter illustrate, and as reinforced daily by all who work in conduct, it is not an easy path to walk. The work is a mixture of emotion and by-the-book decisions. It is filled with difficult conversations as well as tales of redemption. It can show individuals at their most cruel and also their most vulnerable. Having a philosophy to lean on and refer to when facing these conditions is valuable.

Vinay Patel, assistant director of housing and residence life, upperclass experience, at Tulane University in New Orleans, could only begin to see how a conduct philosophy shaped his work when he looked back on his career.

> When I started out, my conduct philosophy wasn't very developed. In my first job, our staffing was stretched so thin, we focused on functioning. Only when I could later track cases through an online conduct system did I start to see the bigger picture and develop my own philosophy. I started by using common sense and talked to students about what spoke to their experiences. When I moved to a different institution, I learned there were other ways of conducting conduct meetings. Now I use my intuition to figure out what is going on in a student's world that would lead them to the decisions they made. As much as I'd like to follow one over-arching conduct philosophy, sometimes that isn't possible, especially within the context of the university philosophy or when there is not a developed departmental philosophy. (Personal communication, February 20, 2018)

As with housing systems, conduct philosophy is continually morphing. New federal mandates, changing cultures, generational traits, updated university missions, and the hiring of new staff members all may affect a department's philosophy over time. It is essential staff members take time to review conduct terminology in the greater scope of these changes, and that they use appropriate terms in discussions and hearings to keep up with changing times.

It also is vital to remember a conduct philosophy, as well as specific policies and practices, is worthless if there is no commitment from staff to comply with them. Ensuring policies and procedures are known and followed is critical to the success of students, staff, and institutions. One of the biggest mistakes made by institutions is when staff members do not follow their own policies. Personal philosophy should not override campus policies; instead, personal philosophy should fit into the realm of campus policies. When policies do not fit an institutional conduct philosophy, those policies should be revamped, rather than the conduct officer overriding them with a personal philosophy.

Ensuring policies and procedures are aligned with institutional missions, abiding by those policies and procedures, and supporting the development and education of our students are critical to ensure the success of our respective programs.

REFERENCES

About Conscious Style (2017). Retrieved November 29, 2017, from http://consciousstyleguide.com/about/.

Alea, P. (August 2010). Women create new rules for campus leadership. *Women in Higher Education,* 19, 8. p. 1(2). Retrieved October 4, 2010, from Academic OneFile via Gale: http://find.galegroup.com.proxy.lib.uni.edu/gtx/start.do?prodId=AONEanduserGroupName=uni_rodit.

American Association of University Professors (AAUP). (2006). AAUP faculty gender equity indicators 2006. Retrieved September 9, 2010, from http://find.galegruop.com/gtx/printdoc.do?contentSet+IAC-DocumentsanddocType=IACandisl.

Becoming a leader: Preparation meets opportunity. (Jan 2010). *Women in Higher Education,* 19, 1. p.20(2). Retrieved October 4, 2010, from Academic OneFile via Gale: http://find.galegroup.com.proxy.lib.uni.edu/gtx/start.do?prodId=AONEanduserGroupName =uni_rodit.

Biddix, J. P. (Sept 2010). So you want to be chief of student affairs? *Women in Higher Education,* 19, 9. p. 19(2). Retrieved October 4, 2010, from Academic OneFile via Gale: http://find.galegroup.com.proxy.lib.uni.edu/gtx/start.do?prodId=AONEanduserGroupName =uni_rodit.

Blimling, G. (1995). *The resident assistant* (4th ed.). Dubuque: Kendall/Hunt.

Branch-Brioso, K. (2009). Keeping pace, but not catching up. *Diverse: Issues in Higher Education,* 26(2), 14–16. Retrieved from UNI Xerxes, September 16, 2010.

Caton, M. (2007). Common trends in U.S. women college president issues. Forum on *Public Policy: A Journal of the Oxford Round Table,* NA. Retrieved from UNI Xerxes, September 16, 2010.

Clery Center, About. (2018). Retrieved February 18, 2018, from https://clery-center.org/about-page/.

Code of Student Rights and Responsibilities. (May 18, 2016). Retrieved December 1, 2017, from http://www.mcmaster.ca/policy/Students-AcademicStudies/Code_of_Student_Rights_and_Responsibilities.pdf.

Colorado Christian University's Vision and Mission. (n.d.). Retrieved November 30, 2017, from http://www.ccu.edu/about/mission/.

Colorado State University-Pueblo (n.d.). Retrieved December 1, 2017, from https://www.csupueblo.edu/about/vision-and-mission.html.

Community Living Expectations, (n.d.). Retrieved November 30, 2017, from http://www.ccu.edu/campuslife/community/conduct/.

Cook, S. G. (2010). Shattered glass ceiling still leaves jagged edges. *Women in Higher Education,* p.19(3). Retrieved October 4, 2010, from Academic OneFile via Gale: http://find.galegroup.com.proxy.lib.uni.edu/gtx/start.do?prodId=AONEanduserGroupName =uni_rodit.

Dominici, F., Fried, L., and Zeger, S. (2009). So few women leaders. Academe, 95(4), 25-27. Retrieved from UNI Xerxes, September 16, 2010.

Dukes, C. (2010). Women's leadership in the community college sector. *On Campus with Women, 38*(2). Retrieved from UNI Xerxes, September 16, 2010.

Easterly, D. (2008). Women's ways of collaboration: A case study in proposal development. *Journal of Research Administration, 39*(1), 48. Retrieved from UNI Xerxes, September 16, 2010.

Evans, N. J., Forney, D. S., and Guido-DiBrito, F. (1998). *Student development in college: Theory, research, and practice.* San Francisco: Jossey-Bass.

Hall, C. (2010). Learning from number two: Diversity in community college leadership. *On Campus with Women, 38*(2), NA. Retrieved from UNI Xerxes, September 16, 2010.

Henking, S. (2008). I am a leader. I am also a woman. *On Campus with Women, 37*(1), NA. Retrieved from UNI Xerxes, September 16, 2010.

Images from the chronicle reflect women as leaders. (2007). *Women in Higher Education, 16*(7), 1. Retrieved from UNI Xerxes, September 16, 2010.

Jefferson, T. (1822, November 2). Letter to Dr. Thomas Cooper. Electronic Text Center, University of Virginia Library, http://etext.virginia.edu/etcbin/toccernew2?id=JefLett.sgmandimages=images/modenganddata=/texts/english/modeng/parsedandtag=publicandpart=268anddivision=div1.

June, A. W. (2010, September 15). In hiring and promoting female faculty members, it may help to have a union. *Chronicle of Higher Education.* Retrieved from https://www.chronicle.com/article/In-HiringPromoting-Female/124424.

Keim, M. (2008). Chief student affairs officers in 2-year colleges: Their demographics and educational backgrounds. *Community College Journal of Research and Practice, 32*(4–6), 435–442. Retrieved from UNI Xerxes, September 16, 2010.

Kiley, K. (2011, June 20). Saying more with less. Retrieved November 30, 2017, from https://www.insidehighered.com/news/2011/06/20/colleges_pare_down_mission_statements_to_stand_out.

Kitchener, K.S. (1984). Intuition, critical evaluation and ethical principles: The foundation for ethical decisions in counseling psychology. *Counseling Psychologist, 12*(3), 43–55.

Lee, Philip, The Case of Dixon v. Alabama: From Civil Rights to Students' Rights and Back Again (December 23, 2014). *Teachers College Record, 116,* 1–18. Available at SSRN: https://ssrn.com/abstract=2542343.

Lorden, L. (1998). Attrition in the student affairs profession. *NASPA Journal,* *35*(1), 207–216. Retrieved from WilsonWeb, September 10, 2010.

Madsen, S. (2008). *On Becoming Women Leaders.* San Francisco: Jossey-Bass.

Office of the Dean of Students. (2017). Retrieved December 01, 2017, from http://www.rochester.edu/college/odos/policies/student-conduct.html.

Panel recounts history of women leading student affairs. (2010). *Women in Higher Education, 19*(4). p. 17(2). Retrieved October 4, 2010, from Academic OneFile via Gale: http://find.galegroup.com.proxy.lib.uni.edu/gtx/start.do?prodId=A ONEanduserGroupName =uni_rodit.

Pepple, C. (Sept 2010). Dean Norma Burgess: 'life is a journey for me.' *Women in Higher Education, 19*(9). p. 23(1). Retrieved October 4, 2010, from Academic OneFile via Gale: http://find.galegroup.com.proxy.lib.uni.edu/gtx/start. do?prodId=AONEanduserGroupName =uni_rodit.

President's Office – Mission and Vision. (2017). Retrieved from https://www. mcmaster.ca/presidentsoffice/mission.html.

Reason, R. D., Walker, D. A., and Robinson, D. C. (2002). Gender, ethnicity, and highest degree earned as salary determinants for senior student affairs officers at public institutions. *NASPA Journal, 39*(3), 1–4. Retrieved from WilsonWeb, September 10, 2010.

Renn, K. A. and Jessup-Anger, Eric R. (2008). Preparing new professionals: Lessons for graduate preparation programs from the national study of new professionals in student affairs. *Journal of College Student Development, 49*(4), 319–335. doi: 10.1353/csd.0.0022.

Rosser, V. J., and Javinar, J. M. (2003). Midlevel student affairs leaders' intentions to leave: examining the quality of their professional and institutional work life. *Journal of College Student Development, 44*(6), 1–12. doi: 10.1353/ csd.2003.0076.

Rudolph, F. (1990). *The American College and University: A History.* Athens and London: University of Georgia Press.

Street, S., and Kimmel, E. Gender role preferences and perceptions of university administrators. *NASPA Journal, 36*(3), 222–39, 1–7. Retrieved from Wilson-Web, September 10, 2010.

The Student Personnel Point of View (1937). Retrieved November 29, 2017, from https://www.naspa.org/images/uploads/main/Student_Personnel_Point_of_ View_1937.pdf.

Solomon, B. M. (1985). *In the company of educated women.* New Haven, CT: Yale University.

Schroeder, C., and Mable, P. (1994). *Realizing the educational potential of residence halls.* San Francisco: Jossey-Bass.

1. Consider the history of your campus. What historical milestones may have influenced philosophies reflected in current conduct practices? Have these practices evolved to reflect new ways of thinking?

2. How do practices and philosophies change when new professionals are hired by the institution? Do they?

3. What information would you include in an RA training session to help RAs understand the campus conduct philosophy? What information should be provided regarding the conduct process, why it operates the way it does, and how the conduct should be approached?

4. How would you best explain the philosophy of the department's conduct system to parents and families during move-in?

5. Personal philosophy and policy compliance are often put to the test. Discuss possible approaches to the following scenarios:

   a. There may be mitigating factors for the student who has allegedly violated the code of conduct that would deem typical sanctions inappropriate. How does this situation change if these factors are ones of ability? Poverty? Mental illness? What if it was a well-liked student leader or a high-profile student-athlete?

   b. What options are available if you believe a supervisor is pressuring you to resolve a conduct situation in a way you believe is inappropriate for the nature of the facts and type of case?

   c. An external constituent has contacted the institution and is applying pressure to resolve a conduct situation in a manner inconsistent with past practices. How does this situation change if the constituent is a parent? A donor? A board member? A coach? An elected official?

UNDERSTANDING STATE AND FEDERAL LAWS

Eric Nestor and John Wesley Lowery

While every college and university has its policies and regulations, those rules were informed by and are beholden to the laws of its state and federal jurisdictions. These laws dictate not only student legal behaviors, but how schools hear and handle their conduct cases. Some of these laws may speak to highly specific actions, while others apply to deeply held constitutional rights. They can vary from state to state, and all of them have the potential to be amended quickly and suddenly. As a result, the legal landscape of higher education in general and student conduct individually can change with relatively little notice.

As student conduct and student residential life are shaped by how the courts and regulatory agencies interpret and enforce constitutions and legislation, professionals in student conduct and housing must remain informed of appropriate laws and any proposed changes to those laws.

CONSTITUTIONAL LAW AND STUDENT RIGHTS

Federal and state constitutions are arguably the most significant sources of law shaping practice and policies in student conduct and student housing. Constitutions establish limits on governmental action and articulate student rights. The U.S. Constitution does not mention education specifically, but state constitutions often establish specific institutions or governance structures. The aspects of the U. S. Constitution that affect student conduct and student housing practice most directly are the First Amendment, Second Amendment, Fourth Amendment (particularly search and seizure), and the Fourteenth Amendment's guarantee of due process. Meanwhile, states are free to afford more rights through a state constitution, but cannot take away or limit rights guaranteed by the federal constitution.

A college or university's control — that is, whether it is a private or a public institution — will affect its relationship to constitutional control. For example, private colleges and universities are not required to afford students the rights guaranteed by the U.S. Constitution, unless they are engaged in state action. Also, private universities may be required to comply with the U.S. Constitution when acting under state law. However, in many situations, it can be difficult to ascertain those differences. As the Supreme Court observed in *Burton v. Wilmington Parking Authority* (1961), "Only by sifting facts and weighing circumstances can the non-obvious involvement of the State in private conduct be attributed its true significance" (p. 722).

Consider the example of *Powe v. Miles* (1968), where Alfred University, a private institution in New York, administered the New York State School for Ceramics, a public entity. The court ruled that, in terms of discipline, students in the School for Ceramics were protected by due process under the Fourteenth Amendment, but students enrolled in other programs did not enjoy those constitutional rights. Beyond state action, the courts will also consider whether private universities have contractual obligations to afford rights similar to those for public college and university students.

Freedom of Expression

Since the 1960s, the courts have considered a number of issues under the First Amendment that first established and later clarified students' rights and shaped the practice (Bird, Mackin, & Schuster, 2006). In the student affairs context, the First Amendment rights of greatest significance include freedom of speech, free exercise of religion, and implicit right of association. In *Tinker v. Des Moines* (1968), the Supreme Court observed, "it can hardly be argued that either students or teachers shed their constitutional rights to freedom of speech or expression at the schoolhouse gate" (p. 506). When difficult disputes arise around issues of freedom of speech, student affairs professionals are well-served by remembering the field's primary role as educators, as well as the Supreme Court's observation.

> [F]reedom to differ is not limited to things that do not matter much. That would be a mere shadow of freedom. The test of its substance is the right to differ as to things that touch the heart of the existing order. If there is any fixed star in our constitutional constellation, it is that no official, high

or petty, can prescribe what shall be orthodox in politics, nationalism, religion, or other matters of opinion or force citizens to confess by word or act their faith therein. If there are any circumstances which permit an exception, they do not now occur to us. (*West Virginia State Bd. of Educ. v. Barnette*, 1943, p. 642)

As institutions work to create inclusive campus environments, they balance their efforts against First Amendment obligations. The use of specific policies to address hate speech first arose in the late 1980s (see *Doe v. University of Michigan*, 1989; *Iota Xi Chapter of Sigma Chi Fraternity v. George Mason University*, 1993; *UWM Post, Inc. v. Board of Regents of the University of Wisconsin System*, 1991). During this early period, every challenged policy was declared unconstitutional (Chemerinsky & Gillman, 2017). Over the past decade, many institutions have sought to use broader institutional harassment policies to prohibit or punish speech was viewed as racist, sexist, or homophobic (see *DeJohn v. Temple Univ.*, 2008; *McCauley v. Univ. of the Virgin Islands*, 2010); however, the outcome for institutions was the same (Chemerinsky & Gillman, 2017).

These policies were voided most often for vagueness or overreach, meaning the policy prohibited speech outside the protections of the First Amendment, such as *true threats,* that the Supreme Court has defined as, "those statements where the speaker means to communicate a serious expression of an intent to commit an act of unlawful violence to a particular individual or group of individuals" (*Virginia v. Black*, 2003, p. 343), as well as speech protected by the First Amendment (Chemerinsky & Gillman, 2017).

Freedom of speech is not restricted to the spoken word. Issues often arise in student housing due to speech communicated through materials some students may find offensive hanging on other students' doors, on their walls, and in their windows. It is worth remembering Justice Samuel Alito's observation, made while he was serving on the U.S. Court of Appeals for the Third Circuit, that the free speech clause protected a "wide variety of speech that listeners [or readers] may consider deeply offensive, including statements that impugn another's race or national origin or that denigrate religious beliefs" (*Saxe v. State College Area School District*, 2000, p. 206).

In response, institutions can adopt viewpoint-neutral policies that ban all postings or displays on the exterior of doors and windows. Chemerinsky and Gillman (2017) noted, "a campus could have a rule preventing students from affixing anything to the windows of their dormitory rooms, but a campus could not prohibit just the display of Confederate flags" (p. 129). Furthermore, institutions must be prepared to consistently and vigorously enforce such policies and also consider what might be lost as a result.

Another speech-related issue that arises in the residential context is sexually explicit and lewd speech. In housing, this typically occurs in the form of posters and other pictures students post on their walls or doors. While the courts have not addressed this issue directly, the Supreme Court's consideration of a broader array of cases involving public nudity clearly indicates blanket prohibitions are unlikely to survive legal challenge (*City of Erie, et al. v. Pap's A. M., tdba 'Kandyland,'* 2000; *Erznoznik v. City of Jacksonville*, 1975). These decisions are not to suggest public institutions cannot place narrow limits on public displays of nudity, but this issue is far more complex than it might appear at first blush. With regard to displays within their residences, institutional actions are even more constrained when roommates do not object.

While the First Amendment does not require institutions to register or recognize student organizations, public institutions with such a system, however, cannot deny a group recognition or the associated benefits because of disagreements with the group's beliefs (*Healy v. James,* 1972; *Widmar v. Vincent*, 1981). In *Widmar v. Vincent* (1981), the Supreme Court ruled the University of Missouri Kansas City (UMKC) must afford religious student groups the same access to a meeting room in the residence halls as granted non-religious student groups. The court rejected UMKC's claim the establishment clause of the First Amendment prevented the university from allowing student religious groups to hold religious services in the residence halls.

A related issue that arises in the residence halls is specific religious practices that violate institutional policies. One example of this could be smudging, a ritual burning of sage or other sacred plants by American Indian or Alaska Native students. Institutions must balance the religious exercise requests of students against legitimate safety concerns of the university to avoid establishment clause problems (Lee, 2010). For example, institutions could choose to identify limited spaces on campus for students to observe religious practices safely. However, institutions also could take reasonable steps to develop smudging policies in the residence halls while still prohibiting all other non-religious instances of burning.

In *Board of Regents of the Univ. Wis. System v. Southworth* (2000), the Supreme Court upheld mandatory student activities fees to fund student organizations as long as campuses distributed funds in a manner that was viewpoint-neutral. This includes funding the programs of student religious groups when other groups are eligible for funding for similar activities (*Badger Catholic v. Walsh*, 2010; *Rosenberger v. Rector and Board of Visitors of the University of Virginia*, 1995). However, the courts have allowed public colleges and universities to deny recognition to student religious groups that refused to comply with an all-comers policy (*Christian Legal Society v. Martinez*, 2010) or the institution's non-discrimination policy (*Alpha Delta Chi-Delta Chapter v. Charles Reed*, 2011). While *Widmar v. Vincent* (1981) provides access to space, these student religious groups must enjoy recognition for that decision to apply.

The courts begin their analysis of students' right to protest on campus with a consideration of the nature of the forum in which the protest takes place. Public colleges and university campuses include both public and non-public forums (Kaplin & Lee, 2014). Residence halls also include both public forums and private forums. The lobby and meeting rooms are often limited public forums, but hallways and student rooms are viewed as private forums. As a result, institutions can limit door-to-door solicitations in the residence halls (*Chapman v. Thomas*, 1984). The courts have allowed public institutions some flexibility in terms of time, manner, and place to restrict students' protests or, by extension, distributing literature on campus. However, these restrictions must be shaped to serve substantial and content-neutral governmental interests (*Ward v. Rock Against Racism*, 1989).

Institutions may discipline students for protests that materially disrupt the institution's operation (*Shamloo v. Mississippi State Board of Trustees*, 1980). Some institutions have sought to manage student speech and protests through the identification of free speech zones, but the courts have overturned those policies when the zones are too restrictive (*Roberts v. Haragan*, 2004; *University of Cincinnati Chapter of Young Americans for Liberty v. Williams*, 2012).

Public institutions have greater flexibility when establishing the rules governing off-campus speakers. In *ACLU v. Mote* (2005), the court noted a university could "constitutionally exclude outsider speech as long as the exclusion is viewpoint[-]neutral and reasonable" (p. 446). In a series of recent cases often brought by traveling preachers, the courts have considered specific aspects of outside speaker policies for reasonableness, upholding different policies for outside speakers (*Gilles v. Blanchard*, 2007), requirements for some advance notice, and limitation to specific parts of campus for assemblies (*Sonnier v. Crain*, 2010). However, those restrictions must be content-neutral (*Orin v. Barclay*, 2001).

One area of campus First Amendment jurisprudence that remains unsettled is the extent to which students can be disciplined for their speech on social media. In cases where the courts have sided with institutions, there has been a clear link between the student's academic major and the online speech, combined with clearly defined academic policies (*Tatro v. University of Minnesota*, 2012; *Yoder v. University of Louisville*, 2013). Another clear exception would be when students engage in speech that falls into a clear exception under the First Amendment, such as true threats.

Possession of Firearms

The issue of campus safety and the right to possess firearms has seen a great deal of attention in recent years, particularly since there have been multiple efforts, both successful and non-successful, to expand concealed carry permit-holders' rights to carry firearms legally on public college campuses. Legislation has been introduced in more than a dozen states in each of the past few years to expand concealed carry on college campuses. These efforts to expand concealed carry have been successful in a number of cases. For example, the legislatures in Arkansas, Georgia, Idaho, Kansas, Texas, Mississippi, and Wisconsin have passed laws expanding the right to concealed carry on public college campuses (National Conference of State Legislatures, 2017).

While these state laws vary, most have prohibited concealed carry in campus buildings, particularly residence halls. Institutions in Texas, where the law is most expansive, were left with far fewer options to restrict concealed carry inside campus buildings. The University of Texas elected to allow carrying firearms in public areas of the residence halls, but generally not in student rooms (University of Texas, 2016). By contrast, Texas A&M University placed even fewer restrictions on concealed carry in student residence halls, only requiring handguns stored in a student's residence hall room be kept in a university-approved safe (Texas A&M University, 2016).

Another contentious issue several states encountered after passing concealed carry legislation was associated with football stadiums. Under pressure from multiple groups, including the Southeastern Athletic Conference, the University of Arkansas had to consider almost immediately amendments to its law to exclude sporting events.

Furthermore, state courts in Colorado (*Regents of the Univ. of Colo. v. Students for Concealed Carry on Campus*, 2012), Oregon (*Oregon Firearms Education Foundation v. Board of Higher Education*, 2011), and Utah (*University of Utah v. Shurtleff*, 2006) have interpreted existing state laws to prevent public colleges from banning concealed carry on campus. By contrast, the Virginia Supreme Court upheld George Mason University's policy, which prohibited concealed carry in buildings and at large outdoors events (*Digiacinto v. Rector and Visitors of George Mason University*, 2011). It is clear both the courts and state legislatures will continue to address these issues.

Search and Seizure

The Fourth Amendment to the U.S. Constitution protects individuals against unreasonable searches and seizures by government officials or those acting on the government's behalf. While commonly associated with searches of homes, the Fourth Amendment also applies to a variety of types of searches on campus, including residence halls, lockers, backpacks, and purses, as well as individual people and individual drug-testing. The courts have distinguished between searches by the police, campus or otherwise, for the purpose of law enforcement and searches by public campus officials other than police to enforce campus rules without encouragement or involvement by the police.

The courts typically have not required warrants for searches by campus officials for enforcing campus rules, or in response to emergencies when acting independently of the police (*Commonwealth v. Neilson*, 1996; *Piazzola v. Watkins*, 1971; *State v. Hunter*, 1992). However, the courts still demand these searches be reasonable when conducted by campus officials, even if the standard used to judge reasonableness is lower than that for law enforcement (Jones, 2007). For searches by the police in residence halls, the courts have typically limited their analysis to the student's room. The outlier case in this area is *State v. Houvener* (2008), in which a Washington state appellate court treated hallways just like residence hall rooms. Searches by private college employees are not governed by the Fourth Amendment unless those individuals are acting on behalf or behest of police or other government officials (*New Hampshire v. Nemser*, 2002).

Several other exceptions to the Fourth Amendment are particularly relevant to student housing. The first is the plain view exception, which applies in circumstances where officials are within a private space legally and are able to see evidence of illegal activity (*Washington v. Chrisman*, 1982). Another issue is "legitimate health and safety inspections conducted pursuant to college rules" (Pavela, 2004, p. 6). Pavela (2004) cautioned searches should be announced in advance or be on a routine schedule, and be limited in both purpose and scope.

The last exception worthy of mention here is consent. With the freely given consent of students, their property can be searched without reasonable cause (Pavela, 2004). However, a resident of a room can only give consent to search their own property or shared property, not the property of a roommate.

O'Leary, Lapp, and Wintner (2009) offered this summary of the issues with searches conducted by college officials: "With limited exception, courts support the rights of college and university officials to enter and search rooms in order to serve institutional purposes, which include protecting the health and safety of students and enforcing college rules and regulations." However, institutions should consider the framework for these searches carefully, as well as who should be responsible for those searches.

Due Process

The Fourteenth Amendment also requires federal or state governments to provide due process before denying "any person of life, liberty, or property" (U.S. Const. Amendment XIV, § 1). In *Dixon v. Alabama State Board of Education* (1961), the U.S. Court of Appeals for the Fifth Circuit was the first to employ the Fourteenth Amendment to define the relationship between colleges and students. The court noted "due process requires notice and some opportunity for [a] hearing before students at a tax-supported college are expelled for misconduct" (*Dixon*, p. 151). However, the courts have not consistently established the exact standards of due process that must be met (Kaplin & Lee, 2004; Silverglate & Gewolb, 2003; Stoner & Lowery, 2004). The Supreme Court in *Goss v. Lopez* (1975) required only that students "be given some kind of notice and afforded some kind of hearing" (p. 579) before a suspension of 10 days or more. While the *Goss* case involved K–12 students, these standards apply in higher education as well.

Regarding the institution's rules themselves, the courts have required rules not be vague and must avoid violating the First Amendment rights described earlier. Kaplin and Lee (2014) noted the courts have seldom rejected college rules for vagueness, citing *Soglin v. Kauffman* (1969) as one of the few cases to reach this result. Silverglate and Gewolb (2003) noted the more obvious it would be to the average student the behavior was in question would be prohibited, the less likely the court would be to overturn a rule for vagueness.

The courts have also articulated a set of procedural protections for students facing suspension or expulsion for behavioral violations, including allegations of academic dishonesty. The Supreme Court in *Goss v. Lopez* (1975) required a student have prior notice "of what he is accused of doing and what the basis of the accusation is" (p. 582). The lower courts have not consistently held a specific number of days of notice must be provided — only that the notice be provided in advance (Kaplin & Lee, 2014; Stoner & Lowery, 2004). The notice requirement has varied from just a few days (*Nash v. Auburn University*, 1987) to as many as 10 days (*Esteban v. Central Missouri State College*, 1969). Because these requirements vary by the federal circuit, institutions should consult with legal counsel to determine the appropriate time frames in their jurisdictions.

In a hearing, the fundamental right students must be afforded is "an opportunity speak in their own defense and explain their side of the story" (Kaplin & Lee, 2009, p. 594). Students have sought to have the courts recognize additional due process claims regarding the conduct of hearings, and the courts have reached a variety of decisions. Students have claimed the hearing body or decision-maker was biased against them, or complained administrators played multiple roles, but the courts have rejected these claims unless there is clear proof of bias (*Gorman v. University of Rhode Island*, 1988; *Nash v. Auburn University*, 1987).

A more-difficult question occurs when a student enjoys a right to consult with an attorney during the hearing, and what role the attorney may play (*Osteen v. Henley*, 1993). The courts have "never recognized any absolute right to counsel in school disciplinary proceedings" (*Donohue v. Baker*, 1997, p. 146).

The situation most likely to give rise to a right to seek the advice of legal counsel during a disciplinary hearing is when students face concurrent criminal charges. However, the attorney's role is quite limited. The court in *Osteen v. Henley* (1993) concluded:

> Even if a student has a constitutional right to consult counsel … we don't think he is entitled to be represented in the sense of having a lawyer who is permitted to examine or cross-examine witnesses, to submit and object to documents, to address the tribunal, and otherwise to perform the traditional function of a trial lawyer (p. 225).

Direct cross-examination is also not generally acknowledged as a constitutional requirement (Kaplin & Lee, 2014). The U.S. Court of Appeals for the 11th Circuit concluded: "There was no denial of appellants' constitutional rights to due process by their inability to question the adverse witnesses in the usual, adversarial manner" (*Nash v. Auburn*, 1987, p. 664). A related issue is the use of visual barriers between the accused student and a complainant or witness, which are most commonly used in sexual assault cases to prevent direct visual contact, not hiding the identity of the witness (Stoner & Lowery, 2004).

The courts have not imposed any specific standard of proof colleges and universities must use in reaching decisions at a hearing. The most commonly used standard of proof in a campus student conduct system is a preponderance of the evidence, or a *more-likely-than-not* standard. After the hearing is concluded and a decision is reached, the courts expect the accused student be notified in writing, at least in serious cases, of the decision. The courts have not generally required any specific content in that notice beyond a brief explanation of the reasons for its decision (*Jaksa v. University of Michigan*, 1984). The courts also have not required public institutions offer any form of appeal after the decision is reached (Kaplin & Lee, 2014; Silverglate & Gewolb, 2003). Although not required, many commenters recommend the institution offer an opportunity to appeal (Stoner & Lowery, 2004).

These requirements of due process apply to cases in which students face suspension or expulsion. The courts have not outlined the process required in less-serious cases. In fact, the courts have even suggested some cases are so minor they require "very little or no process" (Silverglate & Gewolb, 2003, p. 22). For example, the notice and hearing requirements outlined by the courts do not apply in the same way in these less-serious cases, with both steps happening at the same meeting. Many institutions go well beyond the minimal procedural due process requirements established by the courts. In fact, Gehring (2001) worried institutions relied on "unnecessarily formalized … procedures" (p. 477), while Dannells (1997) warned this excessive focus on procedural rights had "undermined the informal and uniquely educational element of college student discipline" (p. 69). This is not to suggest institutions should only provide, with exacting precision, the minimal due process rights outlined by the courts. In fact, Pavela and Pavela (2012) argued for an ethical and educational imperative of procedural due process.

FEDERAL STATUTES AND GUIDANCE AND STATE LAWS

While constitutional law applies directly to public colleges and university, federal statutes commonly apply to all institutions that are recipients of federal financial assistance, either directly or indirectly in the form of federal student aid. These can largely be traced back to the Higher Education Act of 1965 (HEA). Signed into law by President Lyndon Johnson, the HEA vastly expanded the amount of federal money provided to institutions of higher education, establishing numerous loans, grants, and scholarships. It has been reauthorized, renewed, or amended eight times since it was first signed into law. This occurred most recently in 2008, when the Higher Education Opportunity Act reauthorized an amended version of HEA 1965. Along with having a dramatic impact on the Clery Act, it also addressed issues related to memoranda of understanding between institutions and law enforcement, information about emergency response and evacuation plans, student speech, fire safety information, and peer-to-peer file sharing.

It is invaluable for higher education professionals, and particularly those in housing and conduct who are highly involved in students' lives, to have a fundamental understanding of the significant federal statutes and guidance, as well as state laws, that affect the student community. The following explanations of laws and regulations, grouped into similar topics, are not designed to be an all-encompassing resource, but should provide a foundation for understanding the impact of key legislation in this area.

Inclusion and Equity

Along with student safety, one of the primary roles of campus housing and residence life is to provide an inclusive and equitable living environment. This mission is supported by a number of legislative acts established at both the federal and local level.

Title VI. Title VI of the Civil Rights Act of 1964 states: "No person in the United States shall, on the ground of race, color, or national origin, be excluded from participation in, be denied the benefits of, or be subjected to discrimination under any program or activity receiving Federal financial assistance" (Civil Rights Act of 1964. Public Law No. 88-352, Sec. 601, 1964). Among the programs under Title VI are admissions, academic programs, student services, counseling, discipline, classroom assignment, athletics, and housing.

This law requires institutions to provide services and opportunities to all students, regardless of protected identities, and such participation must not discriminate. This means all students must receive the same rights, services, and support when charged with violating institutional policy and institutions may not sanction or discipline students of a particular protected class differently when such a decision would be based on that protected class (i.e., race, color, or national origin) alone. Equally, students may not be denied housing based on race, color, or national origin. The U.S. Department of Education's Office for Civil Rights investigates and enforces such violations (2015c).

Fair Housing Act. Originally signed into law under Title VIII of the Civil Rights Act of 1968, the Fair Housing Act (FHA) prohibits discrimination based on race, color, religion, sex, or national origin in the sale and rental of real estate, including the related items of homeowner's insurance and mortgage lending. Residence halls and apartment complexes are covered under the FHA, since they are identified specifically in the definition of a "dwelling unit" within the act. The 1968 act was expanded to prohibit discrimination based on disability or on familial status through the Fair Housing Act Amendments of 1988.

Of particular note to housing professionals is that the FHA (1968), by having provisions for emotional support animals, creates a broader range of assistance animals that must be accommodated by college housing programs than the Americans with Disabilities Act does. To qualify as an emotional support animal, the animal does not require training and does not have to be a dog. However, the person and animal must pass a three-part test: (1) the person must have a disability; (2) the animal must be necessary for the person with a disability to use and enjoy a dwelling; and (3) there must be a nexus between the disability and the assistance the animal provides (Pet Ownership, 2008).

Sometimes, state laws and regulations will expand federal protections. For example, in *Levin v. Yeshiva University*, 2001 (*Levin v. Yeshiva University*, 691 N.Y.S.2d 280 (Sup. Ct. N.Y. 1999) affirmed, 709 N.Y.S. 2d 392 (N.Y. App. Div. 2000), affirmed and modified in part, 96 N.Y.2d 484 (N.Y. 2001)), a same-sex couple wanted to live together in on-campus housing held for married students with their spouses and children. As part of the requirement, students applying to live in these accommodations had to provide proof of marriage to the institution. The students were denied the opportunity to live in this housing because they were not legally married. They argued their denial violated their right to live together, since they had been in a relationship for a significant amount of time, and the policy discriminated against them based on their marital status and sexual orientation. Their argument was based on the New York State Roommate Law (N.Y. Real Prop. Law § 235-f), New York City Human Rights Law (N.Y.C Admin. Code § 8-197(5), and New York State Human Rights Law (N.Y. Exec. Law §§ 296(2-a), 296(4), 296(5).

While their arguments were rejected in court, including through the appeals process, the court stated an argument might have existed for the plaintiffs based on a disproportionate impact based on their sexual orientation. The New York State Court of Appeals, while upholding the lower courts' findings, indicated the process the lower courts used to determine whether a disproportionate impact existed was flawed (*Levin v. Yeshiva University*, 2001). It is important to recognize that claims based on a housing requirement for marriage no longer apply in states where same-sex marriage is legal. However, housing officials have to be familiar with both state law and local laws/ordinances as they affect the legality of an institution's housing policy.

A case involving gender identity recently challenged whether the Fair Housing Act protected individuals who identify as transgender. While transgender people are not explicitly stated as a protected class in the FHA, such protections were applied in *Smith v. Avanti* (2017). In his opinion, Judge Raymond Moore wrote:

> In this case, the Smiths contend that discrimination against women (like them) for failure to conform to stereotype norms concerning to or with whom a woman should be attracted, should marry, and/or should have children is discrimination on the basis of sex under the FHA. The Court agrees. Such stereotypical norms are no different from other stereotypes associated with women, such as the way she should dress or act (e.g., that a woman should not be overly aggressive, or should not act macho), and are products of sex stereotyping. (Retrieved from Lambda Legal, 2017).

This ruling was notable as the first time the courts applied legal protections under the FHA to individuals identifying as transgender. Institutions must ensure their housing policies provide housing options that do not discriminate against transgender students.

Age Discrimination Act of 1975. Similar to other federal acts, the Age Discrimination Act prohibits discrimination on the basis of age in any program or activity that receives federal funding. Again, participation in housing programs, residence hall activities, and student conduct processes must be handled in a non-discriminatory manner. However, there are approved exceptions to the Age Discrimination Act when age is a normal factor in the ordinary operation of the program or activities. A key aspect of the exceptions is that age must be used with another characteristic to demonstrate the exception applies. For example, if an institution has an academic program specifically designed for older, non-traditional students that includes a living-learning community as a component, then the students in the program could be placed together in on-campus housing. While age is a factor due to their non-traditional status, the required additional characteristic is enrollment in the program that includes the living-learning community experience. Therefore, such housing program would not discriminate on the basis of age.

The Rehabilitation Act of 1973 and the Americans with Disabilities Act. The Rehabilitation Act of 1973 and the Americans with Disabilities Act (ADA) are prime examples of federal laws that originally may not have been created with higher education in mind, but certainly intersect with student conduct and campus housing. The Rehabilitation Act prohibits discrimination on the basis of disability in programs receiving federal financial assistance, including federal agencies and contractors. Section 504 of the Rehabilitation Act states, "no qualified individual with a disability in the United States ... shall, solely by reason of her or his disability, be excluded from, denied the benefits of, or be subjected to discrimination under any program or activity receiving Federal financial assistance." In regard to campus housing, Section 504 requires,

> housing [for] non-handicapped students shall provide comparable, convenient, and accessible housing to handicapped students at the same cost as to others ... such housing shall be available in sufficient quantity and variety so that the scope of handicapped students' choice of living accommodations is, as a whole, comparable to that of non-handicapped students. (Rehabilitation Act, 2000)

The United States Supreme Court was challenged to interpret Section 504 in *Southeastern Community College v. Davis*, 442 U.S. 397 (1979), when it ruled, "Section 504 imposes no requirement upon an educational institution to lower or to effect substantial modifications of standards to accommodate a handicapped person." However, as stated in Title 34 of the United States Code of Federal Regulations, institutions must make modifications to existing facilities to accommodate students with documented disabilities. Housing professionals have to work with design and construction when planning new facilities or renovations to existing ones. When a student with a disability has provided proper notice to the institution, the institution is obligated to ensure the parts required for use by the student are "readily accessible to handicapped persons" (Rehabilitation Act, 2000).

Congress passed the ADA in 1990; it was the first major civil rights legislation to address the needs of individuals with disabilities. Similar to other civil rights legislation, the ADA prohibits discrimination in the areas of employment, public services, accommodations, and telecommunications. Institutions are only obligated to accommodate a student with a disability when the institution has been provided with confirmation of a disability through diagnosis. Students with disabilities who fail to provide proper diagnoses are not entitled to receive accommodation. Additionally, institutions would not be required to make accommodations even when such proper diagnosis has been provided when such accommodations would "fundamentally alter the nature of a service, program, or activity, or that would result in an undue financial or administrative burden" (U.S. Department of Education, 2015b).

The ADA also requires institutions to have processes and policies in place to allow service animals for students with documented disabilities. Under the ADA, service animals are defined as "dogs that are individually trained to do work or perform tasks for people with disabilities." The work performed by the dog must be directly related to the disability (U.S. Department of Justice, 2011). (Emotional support animals, which are not covered under the ADA, are discussed in more detail in the section related to the Fair Housing Act.)

Just as institutions may have to make housing accommodations, their conduct processes also must allow students with disabilities to participate. For example, conduct offices should include language in appointment letters addressing the process for students to follow should they require accommodations for conduct meetings. Conduct offices are encouraged to reach out to their disability services offices to explore the opportunity of training disability services staff as conduct procedural advisors. This would allow students to seek accommodations from staff trained in the conduct process, enabling the student to receive more-complete service. It is important for a conduct office to have a strong working relationship with its student disability services office to ensure systems are in place to assist students when an accommodation is warranted.

Privacy and Transparency

In the areas of both campus housing and student conduct, institutions and individuals are responsible for maintaining a significant amount of data related to students and the campus as a whole. Some legislative acts have been established through the years to guide this responsibility regarding what is to be protected and what must be made available to the general public.

Family Educational Rights and Privacy Act. Enacted as part of the Educational Amendments Act of 1974, the Family Educational Rights and Privacy

Act (FERPA), also known as the Buckley Amendment, protects the educational records of students by granting them the right to inspect their educational records, request corrections to their records when such records are inaccurate, a formal hearing when such correction is not made, and to restrict access of their records to other individuals except when a specific exception exists (U.S. Department of Education, 2015a).

FERPA (1974) gives institutions the right to make any information public about students considered "directory information." This includes a student's name, address, telephone number, date of birth, place of birth, honors and awards, and dates of attendance. On the other hand, students have the right to request institutions *not* disclose such information. Institutions also can restrict further what they consider directory information. In some cases, this may include campus addresses and phone numbers.

FERPA identifies several exceptions for the release of information without student approval. Institutions may release student information to another institutional official if that official has a "legitimate educational interest" in the information. This may relate to performing a job function or providing a service to the student and, the student's family, or both. Institutions also may release such information to other institutions to which the student has applied, to comply with a subpoena or judicial order, in cases of health or safety emergencies, or for financial aid eligibility and determinations, among other purposes. Each institution must have and publicize a policy document that addresses its compliance with FERPA, which must include the conditions under which the institution may release records without student consent.

Where FERPA often enters the discussion related to student conduct is when and how information can be shared with parents or guardians. If information to be shared with third-party individuals (such as parents or guardians) is not covered by one of the exceptions identified in FERPA, then the institution must have a written release on file signed by the student, documenting the student's approval to share such records. For example, an institution should have a FERPA release form to allow verbal disclosure of a student's conduct record. By signing this form, a student provides authorization for the institution to discuss their conduct case or history with a specific individual(s). Institutions must also have a process for students to request access to their conduct records. Institutions do not have to provide actual copies to the student; rather, they must provide access to those records. Once a student makes such a request, FERPA regulations give the institution 45 days to comply with the request. A student's conduct record is an official educational record that must be made available to the student through this process.

Campus Security Act/Clery Act. The Campus Security Act originally was passed by Congress and signed into law by President George H.W. Bush in 1990.

Renamed in 1998 as the Jeanne Clery Disclosure of Campus Security Policy and Campus Crime Statistics Act, or more simply, the Clery Act, it was a response to the murder and rape of a college student, Jeanne Clery, at Lehigh University in 1986. After her death, Clery's parents advocated for increased campus crime reporting to provide more information to prospective and current students, as well as their families, on the types and number of crimes that occur on a college campus. The Clery Act amended the Higher Education Act of 1965 to require this additional reporting. Since 1990, the Clery Act continued to evolve and be amended to respond to contemporary safety and security concerns on college campuses in the United States (Clery Center, n.d.).

As detailed in *The Handbook for Campus Safety and Security Reporting*, 2016 edition, the Clery Act requires higher education institutions to:

- Collect, classify, and count crime reports and statistics.
- Issue campus alerts and timely warnings for ongoing threats and issue emergency notifications when the health and safety of campus constituents is at stake.
- Provide prevention and awareness programming on the topics of dating violence, domestic violence, sexual assault, and stalking.
- Have established conduct procedures in place to address alleged dating violence, domestic violence, sexual assault, and stalking.
- Publish an annual security report by October 1 that includes crime statistics for the prior three years, policy statements related to crime reporting, law enforcement authority, and drug and alcohol use; distribute the report to all current students and employees, and make it available to all to prospective students and employees.
- Submit annual crime statistics to the U.S. Department of Education.
- Maintain a daily crime log, if the institution maintains its own security or police department, available for public review. (U.S. Department of Education, 2016)

The Higher Education Opportunity Act of 2008 (HEOA) amended the Higher Education Amendments and the Clery Act by expanding these requirements. The HEOA required institutions to disclose missing student notification procedures, publish annual fire policy statements and fire statistics reports, and submit fire statistics to the U.S. Department of Education annually.

In 1992, the Campus Sexual Assault Victim Bill of Rights passed as part of the Higher Education Amendments of 1992 and amended the Clery Act to require higher education institutions receiving federal funding to provide basic rights to victims of sexual assault, including notifying victims of their options to report the alleged sexual assault to law enforcement. It also included a requirement both parties be notified of the outcome of any disciplinary proceeding. The Campus Sex Crimes Prevention Act of 2000 amended the Clery Act to require an institution to provide information, in an annual security report, about where information on state-registered sex offenders can be found.

The *Handbook* provides detailed descriptions of the types offenses that must be counted, classified, and reported to the Department of Education. However, specific rules must be followed when determining how to classify certain incidents, as well as how to work within the hierarchy rules. This level of understanding requires a deep understanding of the *Handbook*. An excerpt provides a glimpse into how specific violations are to be reported:

> When preparing an institution's statistics for the annual security report, it is imperative the proper definitions are used when determining if an incident is to be reported for a specific category. Specifically, the Clery Act states the following: "Under the Clery Act, for the purposes of counting and disclosing Criminal Offense, Hate Crime, arrest and disciplinary referral statistics you must do so based on definitions provided by the Federal Bureau of Investigation's (FBI's) Uniform Crime Reporting (UCR) Program. The definitions for Murder, Rape, Robbery, Aggravated Assault, Burglary, Motor Vehicle Theft, Arson, Weapons Carrying, Possessing, Etc. Law Violations, Drug Abuse Violations, and Liquor Law Violations are from the Summary Reporting System (SRS) User Manual from the FBI's UCR Program. The definitions of Fondling, Incest and Statutory Rape are from the FBI's National Incident-Based Reporting System (NIBRS) Data Collection Guidelines edition of the UCR. Hate Crimes are classified according to the FBI's Uniform Crime Reporting Hate Crime Data Collection Guidelines and Training Manual. Note that, although the law states that institutions must use the UCR Program definitions, Clery Act crime reporting does not have to meet all of the other UCR Program standards.
>
> For the categories of Domestic Violence, Dating Violence and Stalking, the Clery Act specifies that you must use the definitions provided by the Violence Against Women Act of 1994 and repeated in the Department's Clery Act regulations. (U.S. Department of Education, 2016)

While many of the reportable crimes may be tabulated by a campus security or law enforcement department, the housing or conduct office may maintain disciplinary referrals without arrests related to alcohol, drugs, and weapons either partially or solely. The total number of students referred to the institution's conduct process must be included in the annual security report. It is important to understand this number is not to be based on a finding of responsibility; rather, the total number of students referred when the alleged behavior is what fits the Clery reportable definitions. Housing and conduct officials should work closely with the designated Clery reporting agents on their campuses to ensure all of the correct information is shared and tabulated correctly. For staff new to Clery reporting, training sessions available across the country can serve as an educational foundation.

While the Clery Act reporting requirements do not relate only to the type of incident, they also define the geographic reporting locations for institutions. As the *Handbook* states, "[C]rimes that don't occur within your Clery Act geography are not included in your Clery Act statistics, even if your students or employees are involved" (U.S. Department of Education, 2016). Thus, it is important for campus housing professionals to be familiar with how Clery categorizes geographic locations for reporting purposes.

Depending on how data are maintained at an institution, either campus housing or conduct officials may be required to send Clery-reportable information to the person responsible for maintaining Clery statistics on campus. Clery-reportable crimes must be broken down as occurring either on-campus, on public property, or off-campus. Within these broad categories are specific definitions and subcategories. For example, an on-campus facility is defined as one the "institution owns or controls," is "reasonably contiguous to one another," and "directly support[s] or relate[s] to the institution's educational purposes."

More specifically, the *Handbook* states, "Generally speaking, it is reasonable to consider locations within one mile of your campus border to be reasonably contiguous within your campus" (U.S. Department of Education, 2016, pp. 2-3–2-4). Within on-campus is a subcategory of on-campus student housing that includes fraternities and sororities, and requires reporting for the following: "the total number of crimes that occurred on campus, including crimes that occurred in student housing facilities," as well as "the number of crimes that occurred in on-campus student housing facilities as a subset of the total" (U.S. Department of Education, 2016, pp. 2-9–2-10). It also includes a requirement for reporting information from housing facilities "owned by a third party that has a written agreement with your institution to provide student housing," regardless of who pays the rent.

The Clery-reportable offenses were expanded by the passage of the Violence Against Women Reauthorization Act (VAWA) of 2013. Section 304 of VAWA, known as the Campus Sexual Violence Elimination Act (Campus SaVE), amended the Clery Act by expanding institutions' reporting requirements to include incidents of domestic violence, dating violence, and stalking. It also added the categories of national origin and gender identity to the categories that must be included in hate crime reporting. It also expanded institutional requirements related to sexual violence to include that:

- Institutions must inform victims of their options to either notify and seek assistance from law enforcement/campus authorities or not; and
- Institutions must inform victims of their rights regarding the issuance of interim measures, such as no-contact orders, restraining orders, and protective orders, as well as any obligations the institution may have to issue them.

For cases involving domestic violence, dating violence, sexual assault, and stalking, VAWA requires the following: a statement of the standard of evidence to be used in resolving disciplinary complaints; specific education and training of staff and students; a list of possible sanctions or protective measures an institution may impose; simultaneous notification of the outcome, appeal process, final resolution to both the complainant and respondent; and institutional policy on maintaining victim confidentiality.

Institutions must follow specific guidelines when reporting offenses in an institution's annual security report. The Clery Act defines specific individuals on each campus as campus security authorities (CSAs) who have the responsibility to report Clery violations through the process identified by the institution. These individuals are described in the *Handbook*. In general, a CSA is someone with "significant responsibility for student and campus activities." This includes:

- Campus police and security;
- "An individual or individuals who have responsibility for campus security but who do not constitute a campus police department or a campus security department";
- "Any individual or organization specified in an institution's statement of campus security policy as an individual or organization to which students and employees should report criminal offenses";
- "An official of an institution who has significant responsibility for student and campus activities, including, but not limited to, student housing, student discipline and campus judicial proceedings. An official is defined as any person who has the authority and the duty to take action or respond to particular issues on behalf of the institution." (U.S. Department of Education, 2016)

A crime is considered to have been reported once it has been reported to a CSA, the institution's campus safety/police department, or local law enforcement agencies. Therefore, an institution's annual Clery data must include information about crimes reported to local law enforcement when such crimes match a Clery-reportable offense and occur within the Clery-defined geographic boundaries.

The Clery Act specifically identifies student resident advisors and assistants, as well as students who monitor access to residential facilities "that are owned by recognized student organizations." Individuals identified as CSAs, which includes all housing staff, are required to report knowledge of any Clery-reportable crime reported to them when they act in a CSA capacity. Housing and conduct professionals need to understand the federal government has identified them as employees of an institution who have an ability to take action and respond to safety concerns. They have an obligation to understand their requirements under Clery and to report such violations. For staff in multiple roles, which might include serving as a point person for collecting Clery-reportable data, it is vital to become familiar with the *Handbook*.

Criminal Law

College and university students are not exempt from laws that govern the countries, states, and municipalities where their campuses reside. However, campus conduct regulations, policies, and procedures may intersect with these laws and must be navigated carefully on those occasions.

Drug-Free Schools and Communities Act Amendments of 1989. Any higher education institution receiving federal funds must certify to the U.S. Department of Education it has established a program to prevent the use of illicit drugs and abuse of alcohol by its students and employees. The Drug-Free Schools and Communities Act Amendments of 1989 (DFSCA) also requires institutions to provide information about laws related to illicit drugs and alcohol, health risks of substance use/abuse, treatment and counseling programs available, and sanctions the institution will impose for violations of its drug and alcohol policies.

This act is particularly relevant with regard to the changing legality of marijuana use in various states. While use of marijuana, including recreational, may be legal in some jurisdictions under certain conditions (such as age of the user), the DFSCA requires institutions comply with its requirements to receive federal funding. Students, faculty, and staff must be informed of their institution's obligations under DFSCA. (It should be noted that Clery Act reporting has been updated to reflect the decriminalization of marijuana. The possession of marijuana that would result in a decriminalized offense should not be included in Clery Act reporting [U.S. Department of Education, 2016]). Students living on campuses and employees working in jurisdictions where marijuana use is legal likely will be attending an institution at which such use, while legal off campus, is prohibited on campus. As part of the DFSCA, institutions are also required to undergo a biennial review to "(A) determine the effectiveness and implement

➕ Related Cases

As is its nature, the legal landscape of higher education can shift quickly. Along with the cases cited in this chapter, refer to these additional cases for insight into other emerging legal issues.

- See *J.A.M. v. Nova Southeastern University,* U.S. Ct. of App., 11th Cir. (April 6, 2016) for a recent example supporting previous decisions on the need to focus on the behavior of the student rather than the student's disability.

- For case law examples of ADA and Section 504 as it relates to campus housing, see *Fleming v. New York University,* 865 F.2d. 478 (2d Cir. 1989) and *Fialka-Feldman v. Oakland University Board of Trustees,* 678 F.Supp. 2nd 576 (E.D. Mich. 2009).

- For case law related to children and married students in college housing, see *Bynes v. Toll,* 512 F.2d 252 (2d Cir. 1975).

- For a case law example where The Americans with Disabilities Act (ADA) was challenged, see *Buescher, et al. v. Baldwin Wallace University,* U.S. Dist. Ct. N.D. Ohio (March 18, 2015).

- For case law related to student contract law, see *Russell v. Salve Regina College,* 938 F.2d 315, 316 (1st Cir.1991); *Giles v. Howard University,* 428 F.Supp. 603, 605 (D.D.C.1977); *Walker v. President and Fellows of Harvard College,* U.S. Ct. of App., 1st Cir. (October 24, 2016); *Fellheimer v. Middlebury College,* 869 F. Supp. 238 (D. Vt. 1994); *Mangla v. Brown University,* 135 F.3d 80 (1st. Cir. 1998).

---

changes to the program if they are needed; and (B) ensure that the sanctions [developed by the institution] are consistently enforced."

Housing officials, particularly those at institutions where first-year students are required to live on campus, are uniquely positioned to play an important role in educating students about their institution's expectations related to substance use. Some students have difficulty understanding the reasons certain behavior is permitted or legal in certain areas but not others. Housing staff, in partnership with conduct staff, should design educational initiatives to help students comprehend their responsibilities. For example, students may be able to consume alcohol legally, but still live on a dry campus that prohibits alcohol; or they may have a legal conceal/carry license for a firearm, but are not permitted to have firearms on institutional property.

Title IX. Originally passed as part of the Education Amendments of 1972, Title IX is a civil rights law that prohibits discrimination on the basis of sex in any program that receives financial assistance from the federal government. While most commonly thought of as the law that requires gender equity in sports, the understanding of what Title IX covers has been expanded over the last 10 years, particularly since the release of the Office of Civil Rights 2011 Dear Colleague Letter (2011 DCL). This 2011 DCL reinforced information included in a 2001 Dear Colleague Letter and further specified requirements of institutions regarding sexual violence.

First, every institution must distribute a "notice of non-discrimination." Second, an institution must designate a specific employee to address complaints related to Title IX. Third, institutions must "adopt and publish grievance procedures providing for prompt and equitable resolution of student and employee sex discrimination complaints" (Ali, 2011, p. 6). The grievance procedure is to be "easily understood, easily located, and widely distributed" (Ali, 2011, p. 10). Investigations are to be conducted impartially and not be delayed until any criminal investigation is finished — institutions should begin their own investigations and take any interim protection measures necessary. All parties must be included in each step of the process equally and have the same rights in the process. For example, if one party can present witnesses, the other party must also have that opportunity.

The 2011 DCL also defined "prompt and equitable" timeframes. Specifically, institutions are expected to conduct full investigations of complaints of sexual violence, both parties should receive a written outcome of the investigation concurrently, and both parties have the right to appeal the decision. The 2011 DCL also indicated such investigations should conclude within 60 calendar days. Finally, the 2011 DCL specified specific education requirements for engaging in proactive and preventive education about sexual violence.

It took three more years for the Office for Civil Rights to provide clarifying information about its 2011 DCL. In April 2014, the OCR released the "Questions and Answers on Title IX and Sexual Violence," commonly referred to as the FAQ document, which addressed 52 commonly asked questions about how the 2011 DCL should be implemented (Lhemon, 2014). One year later, the OCR also clarified the role of each institution's Title IX coordinator in another DCL (Lhemon, 2015).

The White House also released "Not Alone: The First Report of the White House Task Force to Protect Students from Sexual Assault," the first of two reports designed to address sexual assault on college campuses. It provides recommendations for campus climate surveys, preventive educational programs, sample policy languages, and training (Not Alone, 2014). The Second Report of the White House Task Force to Protect Students from Sexual Assault (2017) differs from the 2014 report in that it is more of a summary of accomplishments and list of resources than a list of recommendations.

✚ Clery Act Reportable Offenses

The Campus Security Act, originally passed in 1990, was renamed in 1998 as the Jeanne Clery Disclosure of Campus Security Policy and Campus Crime Statistics Act, or more simply, the Clery Act. The act advocated for increased campus crime reporting. Under the act, the following offenses must be reported by all United States campuses that receive federal funds.

Clery-reportable offenses

- Criminal homicide: murder and non-negligent manslaughter, manslaughter by negligence
- Sexual assault: rape, fondling, incest, statutory rape
- Robbery
- Aggravated assault
- Burglary
- Motor vehicle theft
- Arson
- Hate crimes specifically related to:
  - Larceny-theft
  - Simple assault
  - Intimidation
  - Destruction/damage/vandalism of property
- Arrests and disciplinary referrals related to:
  - Weapons law violations
  - Drug abuse violations
  - Liquor law violations
- VAWA-related offenses
  - Domestic violence
  - Dating violence
  - Stalking

(U.S. Department of Education, 2016)

These Dear Colleague Letters, the FAQ document, and the First Report, combined with the various resolutions the OCR made with institutions found in violation of Title IX, served as the primary guidance for institutions in instituting their Title IX investigative and resolution processes as it relates to campus sexual violence. However, in September 2017, Education Secretary Betsy DeVos announced new interim guidance on the investigation and adjudication of sexual misconduct cases on college campuses (Jackson, 2017a). This announcement also withdraws the 2011 DCL and the subsequent 2014 FAQ, stating that the release of those documents as guidance ignored the public notice and comment period.

While some of the same requirements from the 2011 DCL are included in the interim guidance, it also includes some changes. For example, the 60-day requirement to complete an investigation was replaced with no time limit as long as the investigative process is a good faith effort that is fair, impartial, and timely. The standard of proof was modified to permit both "preponderance of the evidence" and "clear and convincing" in deciding responsibility. Further, if institutions permit appeals of a final adjudicated outcome, they may permit appeals only by the responding party or both parties (Jackson, 2017b).

Given this new interim guidance, the final investigative and adjudication requirements for institutions are unknown at this time. Since this is a developing process, institutions and individuals should maintain close communication with their institution's general counsel and government relations offices; follow proposed laws through their congressional representatives' and senators' websites; and attend professional higher education conferences with a focus on law and policy.

Conduct and housing professionals should be sure to adjust any current practices to meet the needs of federal law and guidance, as well as any specific state requirements. For example, New York's Enough is Enough law, passed in 2015, places specific expectations on all institutions in the state, both public and private. Some of these expectations include the requirement all institutions in New York have the same definition of affirmative consent and the same bill of rights, and provide amnesty to individuals in the area of alcohol and drug violations when reporting sexual violence. New York's law also requires specific notations in academic transcripts if a student has been suspended or expelled for a crime of violence as defined by Clery (N.Y. Education Law, 2015).

In 2014, California enacted Senate Bill 967, known as California's Yes Means Yes law. It requires institutions in the state that receive state financial assistance use affirmative consent as the definition for consent to sexual activity (California Senate Bill 967, 2014).

Attorneys in Student Conduct Meetings. In recent years, several states have passed laws that require institutions to permit attorneys to be present in student conduct meetings. The first state to enact such a law was North Carolina, through the Students and Administration Equity (SAE) Act (2013). The SAE Act applies only to state institutions; gives students and officially recognized student organizations the right to have attorneys present in non-academic conduct proceedings; and allows for a "licensed attorney or non-attorney" advocate to "fully participate during any disciplinary procedure."

Arkansas followed in 2015 with HB 1892, "To Provide a Right of Counsel for Students during Disciplinary Appeal Proceedings at State-supported Institutions of Higher Education," as did North Dakota through SB 2150. The Arkansas law is similar to North Carolina's SAE Act in that the right to have an attorney does not apply to proceedings involving academic dishonesty. However, it differs significantly from the SAE Act in that a student may only have an attorney represent them and fully participate in appeal hearings when the student "has received a suspension of ten (10) or more days or expulsion."

North Dakota's SB 2150 (2015) permits attorneys to participate fully in all disciplinary proceedings, except in cases involving academic dishonesty. The law also allows students to "seek a review of the institution's decision in the district court for the jurisdiction in which the institution is located" when a student has been "suspended for more than ten days or expelled from an institution" or when an official student organization is found to be responsible through the institution's disciplinary process. Like North Carolina and Arkansas, the North Dakota law only applies to institutions under state control.

Contract Law

Students' contract rights have come a long way since *Anthony v. Syracuse University*, 231 N.Y.S. 435 (N.Y. App. Div. 1928), where the court permitted the institution to dismiss a student for virtually any reason it deemed appropriate, as long as it adhered to campus policy: In recent years, the courts have generally viewed the relationship between an institution and the student as a contractual one.

Institutions engage in many different contracts with students, some of which are implied and others that are express. Implied contracts are not explicitly written or stated, but customs or assumptions assume their existence (Kaplin & Lee, 2014). An example of an implied contract can be found in *Carr v. St. John's University*, 187 N.E.2d 18 (N.Y. 1962). While not about housing contracts per se, the court applied contract theory in the university setting in this case. *Carr v. St. John's University* focused on students who were dismissed from the institution after they participated in a civil marriage ceremony. The court ruled when a student is admitted to the institution, an implied contract exists that the student will earn a degree if they follow all the expectations of the institution. While the *Carr v. St. John's University* case involved a private institution, the court stated such an application could also apply to public institutions in *Healy v. Larson*, 323 N.Y.S.2d 625, *affirmed*, 318 N.E.2d 608 (N.Y. 1974).

Express contracts are those whose terms are stated or written explicitly and agreed to by all parties (Kaplin & Lee, 2014). Housing and food service contracts are two of the most-common express contracts in higher education. A housing contract can be viewed as a landlord-tenant lease agreement, identifying the expectations and obligations of students while they live in campus housing and the responsibilities of the institution. More specifically, housing contracts typically include the following components: definitions, eligibility for and duration of housing, charges and utilities, payments/refunds, an institution's right of entry and inspections, restricted or permitted behavior/modifications, room assignments and changes, and termination of occupancy processes. Housing contracts also often include statements on local laws, codes, and ordinances; subletting; rights to legal action; withdrawal from a housing unit; and changes to the lease agreement.

Students living in campus housing are subject to the terms of the housing contract as well as the institution's code of student conduct. Many housing contracts also state failure to follow the code of student conduct or any other institutional policy may be a breach of contract. Housing contracts often identify actions that may be taken by the institution if a breach of contract occurs. However, these contracts are not limited to actions on the part of the institution; they also include the rights afforded to the student. Typical contracts include a reasonable right to privacy for the student, with requirements for advance notice of entry, except in cases of emergency, and regularly scheduled health and safety inspections.

Specific provisions in housing contracts can allow institutions to take action against a student for failure to follow the contract and sometimes allow the institution to side-step the student conduct process. For example, a standard component of college student housing contracts often includes prohibiting damage or alterations to the housing unit. The contract may state if significant damage is found during an inspection, the institution may relocate the student to a different housing unit or cancel the housing contract, requiring the student to find alternate living accommodations. Because the contract specifies prohibited and allowed actions, the institution can use the terms of the contract to enforce expectations as opposed to sending the student through the student conduct system. However, institutions have to be careful to follow the rights of the student as expressed in the contract. Furthermore, possible institutional responses will be quite limited under the housing contract.

CONCLUSION

It is imperative for individuals working in housing and student conduct to understand and value the importance of legal issues in their work. Every aspect of the housing and student conduct experience, whether it is the ability to put a specific housing program into place, allow or not allow certain speech to occur, search a student room, permit guns on campus, take action against a student, or provide rights to students, is affected by guidelines; legal precedent, or case law; and federal, state, and local laws. Drafting housing policies and student conduct systems requires knowledge in these areas to ensure the institution does not violate students' rights or fail to follow the law, either of which would open the institution to a potential lawsuit.

While some laws have been in place for a long time and may go through reinterpretation, such as those addressed in the U.S. Constitution, other laws, such as Title IX, are constantly in flux as institutions attempt to align their processes with new federal guidance and statutes. To be an effective and informed administrator requires studying legal issues in higher education and remaining abreast of potential changes in the legal landscape that could affect student housing and conduct.

The cases cited in this chapter are by no means an exhaustive list. Maintaining relationships with general counsel, professionals, and faculty in the field is vital to staying up-to-date on the most-salient issues, as are professional conferences that offer sessions focused on legal issues and case law. These all are invaluable resources of information that can help administrators be knowledgeable and keep their institutions compliant.

Finally, administrators and their professional staff should also review their work regularly through a legal lens and consider the applicability of these topics to their institution. Only by envisioning the real-world application and effect of these laws can we use them fully as a community-shaping resource.

REFERENCES

ACLU v. Mote, 423 F.3d 438 (4th Cir. 2005).

Age Discrimination Act of 1975. Public Law No. 94-135, 1975.

Ali, R. (2011). Dear Colleague Letter. Washington, DC: U.S. Department of Education, Office for Civil Rights. Retrieved October 3, 2017, from https://www2.ed.gov/about/offices/list/ocr/letters/colleague-201104.pdf.

Alpha Delta Chi-Delta Chapter v. Charles Reed, 648 F.3d 790 (9th Cir. 2011).

Badger Catholic v. Walsh, 620 F.3d 775 (7th Cir. 2010).

Bird, L. E., Mackin, M. B., & Schuster, S. K. (2006*). The First Amendment on campus: A handbook for college and university administrators.* Washington, DC: NASPA.

Board of Regents of the Univ. Wis. System v. Southworth, 529 U.S. 217 (2000).

Burton v. Wilmington Parking Authority, 365 U.S. 715 (1961).

California Senate Bill 967. (2014). An Act to Add Section 67386 to the Education Code, Relating to Student Safety. Retrieved October 10, 2017, from https://leginfo.legislature.ca.gov/faces/billNavClient.xhtml?bill_id=201320140SB967.

Campus Sex Crimes Prevention Act of 2000. Public Law No. 106-386.

Campus Sexual Assault Victims' Bill of Rights. Higher Education Amendments of 1992. Public Law No. 102- 325, section 486(c).

Carr v. St. John's University, 187 N.E.2d 18 (N.Y. 1962)

Chapman v. Thomas, 743 F.2d 1056 (4th Cir. 1984).

Chemerinsky, E., & Gillman, H. (2017). *Free speech on campus.* New Haven, CT: Yale University Press.

Christian Legal Society v. Martinez, 561 U. S. 661 (2010).

City of Erie, et al. v. Pap's A.M., tdba 'Kandyland,' 529 U.S. 277 (2000).

Civil Rights Act of 1964. Public Law No. 88-352.

Civil Rights Act of 1968. Public Law No. 90-284.

Clery Center. (n.d.). Retrieved November 04, 2017, from https://clerycenter.org/policy-resources/.

Commonwealth v. Neilson, 666 N.E.2d 984 (Mass. 1996).

Dannells, M. (1997). *From discipline to development: Rethinking student conduct in higher education.* ASHE-ERIC Higher Education Report, 25(2). San Francisco, CA: Jossey-Bass.

DeJohn v. Temple Univ., 537 F.3d 301 (3d Cir. 2008).

Digiacinto v. Rector & Visitors of George Mason Univ., 704 S.E.2d 365 (Virginia, 2011).

Dixon v. Alabama State Board of Education, 294 F.2d 150 (5th Cir. 1961).

Doe v. University of Michigan, 721 F. Supp. 852 (E.D. Mich. 1989).

Donohue v. Baker, 976 F. Supp. 136 (N.D. NY 1997).

Drug-Free Schools and Communities Act Amendments of 1989. Public Law No. 101-226.

Education Amendments of 1972. Title IX. Public Law No. 92-318.

Educational Amendments Act of 1974. Public Law No. 93-380.

Erznoznik v. City of Jacksonville, 422 U.S. 205 (1975).

Esteban v. Central Missouri State College, 415 F.2d 1077 (8th Cir. 1969).

Fair Housing Act, Title VIII of the Civil Rights Act of 1968. Public Law No. 90-284, 1968.

Fair Housing Amendments Act of 1988. Public Law No. 100-430, 1988.

Family Educational Rights and Privacy Act of 1974. 20 U.S.C.S. § 1232g.

Gehring, D. D. (2001). The objectives of student discipline and the process that's due: Are they compatible? *NASPA Journal 38*, 466–481.

Gilles v. Blanchard, 477 F.3d 466 (7th Cir. 2007).

Gorman v. University of Rhode Island, 837 F.2d 7 (1st Cir. 1988).

Goss v. Lopez, 419 U.S. 565 (1975).

Healy v. Larson, 323 N.Y.S.2d 625, affirmed, 318 N.E.2d 608 (N.Y. 1974).

Higher Education Act of 1965. Public Law No. 89-329.

Higher Education Opportunity Act of 2008. Public Law No. 110-315, 2008. Retrieved October 21, 2017, from https://www2.ed.gov/policy/highered/leg/hea08/index.html.

Iota Xi Chapter of Sigma Chi Fraternity v. George Mason University, 993 F.2d 386 (4th Cir. 1993).

Jackson, C. (2017a). Dear Colleague Letter on Sexual Violence. Washington, DC: U.S. Department of Education, Office for Civil Rights. Retrieved October 14, 2017, from https://www2.ed.gov/about/offices/list/ocr/letters/colleague-title-ix-201709.pdf.

Jackson, C. (2017b). Q&A on Campus Sexual Misconduct. Washington, DC: U.S. Department of Education, Office for Civil Rights. Retrieved October 14, 2017, from https://www2.ed.gov/about/offices/list/ocr/docs/qa-title-ix-201709.pdf.

Jaska v. University of Michigan, 597 F. Supp. 1245 (E.D. Mich. 1984) aff'd 787 F.2d 590 (6th Cir. 1986).

Jones, E. O. (2007). The Fourth Amendment and dormitory searches. *Journal of College and University Law, 33*, 597–624.

Kaplin, W. A., & Lee, B. A. (2014). *The law of higher education* (5th ed., Student version). San Francisco, CA: Jossey-Bass.

Lambda Legal. (2017). Smith v. Avanti. Retrieved November 5, 2017, from https://www.lambdalegal.org/in-court/cases/co_smith-v-avanti.

Lee, B. A. (2010). Fifty years of higher education law: Turning the kaleidoscope. *Journal of College and University Law 36*, 649–690.

Levin v. Yeshiva University, 691 N.Y.S.2d 280 (Sup. Ct. N.Y. 1999) *affirmed*, 709 N.Y.S. 2d 392 (N.Y. App. Div. 2000), *affirmed and modified in part*, 96 N.Y.2d 484 (N.Y. 2001). Retrieved October 12, 2017, from https://www.law.cornell.edu/nyctap/I01_0089.htm.

Lhamon, C. E. (2014). Questions and Answers on Title IX and Sexual Violence. Washington, DC: U.S. Department of Education, Office for Civil Rights. Retrieved October 18, 2017, from https://www2.ed.gov/about/offices/list/ocr/docs/qa-201404-title-ix.pdf.

Lhamon, C. E. (2015). Dear Colleague Letter. Washington, DC: U.S. Department of Education, Office for Civil Rights. Retrieved October 18, 2017, from https://www2.ed.gov/about/offices/list/ocr/letters/colleague-201504-title-ix-coordinators.pdf.

McCauley v. Univ. of the Virgin Islands, 618 F.3d 232 (3d Cir. 2010).

Nash v. Auburn University, 812 F.2d 655 (11th Cir. 1987).

National Conference of State Legislatures. (2017). *Guns on campus: Overview.* Retrieved from http://www.ncsl.org/research/education/guns-on-campus-overview.aspx.

New Hampshire v. Nemser, 807 A.2d 1289 (N.H. 2002).

North Dakota SB 2150. (2015) Retrieved October 15, 2017, from http://www.legis.nd.gov/assembly/64-2015/documents/15-0596-05000.pdf?20150421194937.

Not Alone: The First Report of the White House Task Force to Protect Students from Sexual Assault. (2014). Washington, DC. Retrieved from October 21, 2017, on https://www.justice.gov/ovw/page/file/905942/download.

N.Y. Education Law, Article 129-b §§ 6439-6449, July 7, 2015. Retrieved October 20, 2017, from https://www.nysenate.gov/legislation/bills/2015/s5965.

O'Leary, K., Lapp, D. J., & Wintner, T. H. (2009, January 21). Whose room is it anyway? Lawful entry and search of student dormitory rooms. *NACU-ANotes, 7*(3). Retrieved from http://counsel.cua.edu/studlife/publications/dormsearch.cfm.

Oregon Firearms Educ. Found. v. Bd. of Higher Educ., 264 P.3d 160 (Oregon, 2011).

Orin v. Barclay, 272 F.3d 1207 (9th Cir. 2001).

Osteen v. Henley, 13 F.3d 221 (7th Cir. 1993).

Pavela, G. (2004, July 29). The law of search and seizure for residence life staff members. *ASJA Law and Policy Report, 150,* 1–4.

Pavela, G., & Pavela, G. (2012). The ethical and educational imperative of due process. *Journal of College and University Law 38,* 567–627.

Pet Ownership for the Elderly and Persons with Disabilities. 24 C.F.R. § 5 (2008).

Piazzola v. Watkins, 442 F 2d 285 (5th Cir. 1971).

Post-9/11 Veterans Educational Assistance Act of 2008. Supplemental Appropriations Act of 2008. Public Law No. 110-252, 2008.

Post-9/11 Veterans Education Assistance Improvements Act of 2010. Public Law No. 111-377, 2011.

Powe v. Miles, 407 F.2d 73 (2d Cir. 1968).

PsychArmor Institute: The Premier Free Online Training for Engaging the Military Community. (n.d.). Retrieved November 05, 2017, from https://psycharmor.org/.

Regents of the Univ. of Colo. v. Students for Concealed Carry on Campus, LLC, 271 P.3d 496, (Colo., Mar. 5, 2012).

Rehabilitation Act of 1973. 34 C.F.R. Part 104. (13 November 2000). Retrieved November 04, 2017, from https://www2.ed.gov/policy/rights/reg/ocr/edlite-34cfr104.html.

Roberts v. Haragan, 346 F. Supp. 2d 853 (N.D.Tex 2004).

Rosenberger v. Rector and Board of Visitors of the University of Virginia, 515 U.S. 819 (1995).

Saxe v. State College Area School District, 240 F.3d 200 (3d Cir. 2000).

Shamloo v. Mississippi State Board of Trustees, 620 F.2d 516 (5th Cir. 1980).

The Second Report of the White House Task Force to Protect Students from Sexual Assault (2017). Washington, DC. Retrieved October 22, 2017, from https://www.whitehouse.gov/sites/whitehouse.gov/files/images/Documents/1.4.17.VAW%20Event.TF%20Report.pdf.

Silverglate, H. A., & Gewolb, J. (2003). *FIRE's guide to due process and fair procedure on campus.* Philadelphia, PA: Foundation for Individual Rights in Education.

Smith v. Avanti. WL 1284723, 2017 U.S. Dist. LEXIS 5477 (D. Colo. Apr. 5, 2017).

Soglin v. Kauffman, 418 F.2d 163 (7th Cir. 1969).

Sonnier v. Crain, 613 F.3d 436 (5th Cir. 2010).

Southeastern Community College v. Davis, 442 U.S. 397 (1979). Retrieved from https://www.law.cornell.edu/supremecourt/text/442/397.

State v. Houvener, 186 P.3d 370 (Wash. Ct. App. 2008).

State v. Hunter, 831 P.2d 1033 (Utah App. 1992).

Stoner, E. N. II, & Lowery, J. W. (2004). Navigating past the "spirit of insubordination": A twenty-first century model student conduct code with a model hearing script. *Journal of College and University Law 31*, 1–77.

Students & Administration Equality Act. Regulatory Reform Act of 2013. N.C. Gen. Stat. § 116-40-11 (2013).

Tatro v. University of Minnesota, 816 N.W.2d 509 (Minn. 2012).

Texas A&M University. (2016). *Carrying concealed handguns on campus.* Retrieved from http://rules-saps.tamu.edu/PDFs/34.06.02.M1.pdf.

Tinker v. Des Moines Independent Community School District, 393 U.S. 503 (1968).

To Provide a Right of Counsel for Students during Disciplinary Appeal Proceedings at State-supported Institutions of Higher Education. Arkansas HB 1892. Act 1194. 2015.

U.S. Const. Amend. I.

U.S. Const. Amend. II.

U.S. Const. Amend. IV.

U.S. Const. Amend. V.

U.S. Const. Amend. XIV.

U.S. Department of Education, FERPA for Students. (2015a). Retrieved November 05, 2017, from http://www2.ed.gov/policy/gen/guid/fpco/ferpa/students.html.

U.S. Department of Education, Office for Civil Rights. (2015c). Education and Title VI. Retrieved October 21, 2017, from https://www2.ed.gov/about/offices/list/ocr/docs/hq43e4.html.

U.S. Department of Education, Office of Postsecondary Education. (2016). *The Handbook for Campus Safety and Security Reporting*, 2016 Edition, Washington, DC (2016).

U.S. Department of Education, Office for Civil Rights. (2015b). Students with Disabilities Preparing for Postsecondary Education. Retrieved November 04, 2017, from https://www2.ed.gov/about/offices/list/ocr/transition.html.

U.S. Department of Justice. Civil Rights Division. (2011). Service Animals. Retrieved November 4, 2017, from https://www.ada.gov/service_animals_2010.htm.

University of Cincinnati Chapter of Young Americans for Liberty v. Williams, 2012 U.S. Dist. LEXIS 80967 (S.D. Ohio, 2012).

University of Texas. (2016). *Campus carry information for students.* Retrieved from https://utexas.app.box.com/v/cc-info-sheet-students.

Univ. of Utah v. Shurtleff, 144 P.3d 1109 (Utah, 2006).

UWM Post, Inc. v. Board of Regents of the University of Wisconsin System, 774 F. Supp. 1163 (E.D. Wis. 1991).

Violence Against Women Reauthorization Act of 2013, Public Law No. 113-4 (2013).

Virginia v. Black, 538 U.S. 343 (2003).

Ward v. Rock Against Racism, 491 U.S. 781 (1989).

Washington v. Chrisman, 455 U.S. 1 (1982).

West Virginia State Bd. of Educ. v. Barnette, 319 U.S. 624 (1943).

Widmar v. Vincent, 454 U.S. 263 (1981).

Yoder v. University of Louisville, 2013 U.S. App. LEXIS 9863 (6th Cir.2013).

DISCUSSION QUESTIONS

1. Review your campus policies with an eye toward whether they are inclusive and respectful of different student populations. For example, how do your policies address married students in campus housing? What are your policies related to students who identify as transgender or LGBTQ? Does your policy have provisions to address students with children?

2. Under what conditions does your contract permit the institution to cancel a student's housing? Are there specific behaviors for which you would refer the student to the student conduct process as opposed to taking action through the housing contract? What are the benefits of allowing the student to go through the conduct process as opposed to taking action through the housing contract? Is your institution consistent in how it addresses behavior that violates the housing contract?

3. What role are attorneys allowed to play in your institution's student conduct process? Are the roles of attorneys clearly defined in the conduct system handbook? Has legislation been proposed in your state that would permit attorneys to participate in student conduct meetings? What type of training does your institution provide to conduct boards/panels and individual hearing officers on the role of attorneys in the process? Do staff members who resolve the lowest-level cases understand what to do if an attorney accompanies a student to a conduct meeting?

4. Are staff aware of who tabulates Clery data for your office and your institution? How are Clery-reportable offenses shared with the point person for all Clery data on your campus?

5. For housing officials who also resolve conduct cases, where do students complete a FERPA release to gain access to records or grant permission to speak with a third party?

continued on next page

6. How would you handle receiving a FERPA release granting permission to speak to a student's parents/guardians? How and where is the release filed? Who would talk with the third party? Does the identity of the third party determine with whom to speak (e.g., attorney versus parent/guardian)?

7. Do your appointment or hearing notices to students provide information regarding accommodations for registered disabilities? Do your website and handbooks address accommodations directly in policy and process statements?

8. For accommodations related to housing, can students easily find information related to service or emotional support animals? Is it cross-referenced in places such as the housing or residence life website, disability services, and health services?

9. Does your state have a universal definition of consent for sexual activity on college campuses or is one likely to be passed? How do you disseminate the definition of consent used by your institution? Are your investigative processes for allegations of sexual violence/misconduct in compliance with current federal and state law? Are they widely accessible and written in a manner your student population can comprehend?

10. As you revise your code of student conduct, do you have a working relationship with either your general counsel's office or a retained outside counsel to help ensure your processes are compliant?

11. For colleagues working in states where marijuana is legal, what initiatives are in place to help students understand the requirement to prohibit the use of illicit drugs on campus? Are there ways conduct and housing officials at your institutions can partner in educating students on alcohol abuse and illicit drug use?

PREPARING HOUSING AND CONDUCT STAFF

Patience Bryant, D. Matthew Gregory, and Virginia Albaneso Koch

FACILITATING THAT initial floor meeting can be a milestone moment for most housing and residence life professionals. The resident assistant (RA) or some other live-in student staff member stands at the front of the room to conduct an icebreaker exercise to introduce residents to each other. Next on the agenda is promoting all the events during welcome week and then, perhaps most importantly, a discussion of the rules and policies students will be expected to adhere to throughout the rest of the year.

During RA training, it has probably been emphasized that this first meeting with residents will be an opportunity to set a foundation for the semester. For the RA to assume a dismissive attitude may seem to welcome challenging behaviors throughout the year. To come across as overly strict may invite defiance from residents looking to flex their independence. Neither approach will set a positive tone for the floor or help build community. To find that happy medium and maintain it throughout the ups-and-downs of a school year is a lot to ask of an individual.

Preparing staff — both students and professional staff — to nurture community while being asked to manage conduct and behavioral interventions is not an easy task, but it is one of the most important that housing and residence life supervisors may have. This task can be made easier by understanding overarching training considerations regarding adult learning and sound foundational principles for professional and paraprofessional training. In addition, it is important to recognize each campus is unique and there are differences the staff training should address. This goal can be achieved by developing and implementing training topics and methods that recognize these factors while adhering to the overarching outcomes and learning objectives of community-building.

Much has been written about the importance and development of community in higher education. Considerable research focuses on the interaction of a student with the surrounding environment (Astin, 1993; Chickering & Reisser, 1993; Pascarella & Terenzini, 1991). The development of a safe and healthy community that supports academic achievement is closely related to the degree to which the residents or students embrace living on the floor. Whether residents want to belong or feel they belong to a given community is indicative of the degree to which they embrace living on the floor (Block, 2008; Strayhorn, 2012).

One must first understand the definition and make-up of community to help begin to understand what a community entails, and when it is fully formed and poised to promote a positive environment for its members. Boyer (1990) identified six principles of community: (1) educationally purposeful, (2) open, (3) just, (4) disciplined, (5) caring, and (6) celebrative.

When considering the concept of community from the vantage point of Boyer (1990), it becomes apparent how both housing and residence life staff and student conduct staff can build and maintain a positive campus community. An educationally purposeful community is an environment where students are supported and allowed to focus on academic goals and educational pursuits, and where learning is encouraged. An open community promotes free thought and free speech in accordance with a civil regard for fellow community members. A just community fosters an appreciation for the individual and actively values diversity between and among community members. From a social justice lens, this is present in communities that recognize each person can add value to the group and discussion.

In a disciplined community, policies and rules are written clearly, are easy to understand, and serve the common good. Individual community members are aware of and accept their responsibility to the community. Caring community members are sensitive to the welfare of each other and value the service done to benefit others. Finally, celebrative communities involve the celebration of traditions, rituals, and shared values that are conducive to a positive communal experience for current and future members.

The responsibility to follow these six principles lies with a wide variety of staff in a college or university campus. When identifying the staff roles involved in community-building and maintenance, it is easy to first think of orientation staff and live-in housing and residence life staff. However, defining community more broadly, to include residential, academic, and campus communities, helps colleagues begin to understand that many more staff members are likely to be involved.

The *ACUHO-I Standards & Ethical Principles for College and University*

Housing Professionals (2017) identifies functional areas of campus housing from which one can discern a basic staffing pattern. Depending on the size of the residential community, one or more staff members may work in each of the specific areas identified: business/management, student learning and development, residential facilities, dining services, emergency preparedness, and public /private partnerships. For many campus housing departments, the live-in staff members are likely to be housed in the student learning and development area, often referred to as residence life.

However, creating and maintaining the residential community should not be viewed as solely the responsibility of the residence life or live-in staff. At times, other professionals, such as members of the maintenance or housekeeping staff, may identify a potential policy violation and bring the concern to the attention of staff responsible for student conduct. Staff in all functional areas must have a fundamental knowledge of community, community-building, the impact of community on the student experience, and the maintenance of a community. Staff outside residence life need an awareness of resources and reporting mechanisms to meet residents' needs. The training for housing staff as a whole depends on an institution's mission and expectations set forth for employees.

The responsibility for developing and maintaining the campus community can stretch even further. While certainly not an exhaustive list, the admissions office, orientation programs, parent and family offices, security or police departments, and faculty all contribute to the campus community. Social media and communication before the student's arrival on campus create online communities where peer groups share information related to the campus and housing. In prepping staff for successful behavioral interactions with residents, it is important to recognize the reputation of the housing operation and the institution. Campus partners, such as orientation, can be integral in framing conduct processes in a positive or negative light. Expecting staff to nurture relationships and role model this across campus can help staff later on during challenging situations.

The student conduct office can be one of the most helpful partners in addressing student behavior. In any community, there are expectations of the community as a whole, expectations of community members, and collective rules or governance structures, often articulated in campus codes of conduct and handbooks for residential students. These documents further define the community and provide a shared identity of a given community. The student conduct office is most often the keeper of these policies. It is easy for the student conduct office and staff to be reactionary by design and not feel a responsibility for creating a community.

While student conduct staff often have a limited or narrow opportunity to engage with individual community members, the impact is significant, given how integral communal governance is to the overall health of a community

(Boyer, 1990). Campus-wide conversations about campus community, the campus brand, traditions, governance, and rules will promote the desired communal identity and must involve efforts before the students' arrival, during the collegiate experience, and after graduation. The student conduct office as a campus partner can help train hearing and resolution officers, as well as student staff resident assistants. This partnership allows them to share their expertise and creates a collaborative approach between the housing and the conduct office. While the saying has become cliché, it does indeed take a village to create a community.

COMPETENCIES AND STANDARDS

Residence halls are the site of community, development, learning, and growth. By upholding established standards and competencies, staff members can provide a community foundation. Residents rely on housing staff to take the lead in setting community standards for their areas and look to their staff members to be the model they should follow.

"The RA is critical in the community standards model (CSM) because he or she promotes dialogue among students that allows for free expression yet affirms civility. The RA is also instrumental in creating a caring community, one that values and recognizes each member's experiences and promotes his or her participation in the CSM" (Piper & Buckley, p. 193, 2004). Piper and Buckley said residents look to their closest staff member — their RA — as someone who will help them define what their community is, help them see how they can relate to each other, and assist them in deciding what they want in their particular community.

This approach is modeled through the ACUHO-I Core Competencies (2007). The 12 listed competencies reflect the wide range of responsibilities that fall to a campus housing and residence life department. Each also includes specific function competencies and knowledge needed at different stages of a professional's career. Among these, Student Behavior is the competency that discusses student conduct and conflict resolution. These competencies require the staff members to not only know how to identify, document, and uphold any established rules and policies, but to educate students about the student conduct process. Staff must work to provide transparency in the student conduct process; develop partnerships with other offices and agencies to bring in necessary expertise when necessary; and create or update codes and regulations that provide residents with safe and effective living and learning environments. For these efforts to be successful, there must be established community standards, student development theory when executing policies, and alternative methods of resolution.

Conflict resolution is included under this competency because it provides staff with the opportunity to use other methods to address cases where the community is disrupted. Alternative methods of resolution give staff the opportunities to work with their residents to create community even in the middle of a conflict. Using conflict resolution as an option when dealing with student conduct allows a chance to hold peers accountable and gives housing staff a chance to express how they, as a member of the community, have been affected by their resident's actions. Conflict resolution identifies and repairs the harm as well as heals the community.

The changing demographics in higher education are not limited to the classroom and it is important for staff members to acknowledge what each person brings to their team. Building a community means staff members must learn how to work together despite differences and model the same behavior for their residents in hopes they will follow suit. Each member of the community comes from an environment that influences the way they think, act, and function. Culturally competent staff members possess and bring to the community cultural knowledge, cultural awareness, and cultural sensitivity.

The *ACUHO-I Standards & Ethical Principles for College and University Housing Professionals* (2017) addresses the value of community by including, among its tenants, a declaration that an ethical housing program:

- Strives to establish a residential environment that promotes the appreciation, understanding, and respect for differences.

- Fosters a residential environment that encourages members of that environment to consider the impact that their behaviors can have on larger environmental, social, and economic systems.

- Develops and maintains staff relationships in a climate of mutual respect, support, trust, and interdependence while recognizing the strengths and limitations of each colleague.

- Is aware of the political implication of housing as an integral part of higher education and is obligated to maintain effective relationships with the global community so programs, policies, and procedures are fully understood.

These standards set the tone for the department and community. Staff members are expected to model the behavior they would like to see amongst their residents and other staff members, carrying themselves in such a way that promotes integrity, dignity, and competence. These ethical standards are not only necessary for staff members when working together, but for establishing what a community is among their residents.

✚ Educational Outcomes for RAs

L. Dee Fink is a professional consultant in higher education who, in 2003, established a taxonomy that included six categories to be used in assessing educational outcomes: (1) foundational knowledge; (2) application; (3) integration; (4) human dimension; (5) caring; and (6) learning how to learn. Supervisors can use these designations as a framework for developing learning outcomes for staff training exercises. The following example shows possible considerations for what RAs should be able to accomplish within a year of completing the Behind Closed Doors exercise.

Foundational Knowledge

- Know the responsibilities of the RA position.
- Remember campus resources and be able to refer people appropriately.
- Respond to a variety of crisis and emergency situations appropriately.
- Identify a variety of safety and security concerns, and address them in a manner appropriate to the circumstances.

Application

- Hold oneself and others accountable for actions.
- Respond effectively to unexpected experiences.
- Analyze the needs of community members.
- Identify inappropriate behaviors and respond accordingly.
- Adapt one's behaviors, including verbal and nonverbal communication, appropriately to interact with diverse community members.

Integration

- Make decisions that are congruent with personal values and beliefs while considering the perspectives of others.

Human Dimension

- Influence others in making positive and healthy choices.
- Interact respectfully and compassionately with others.
- Become more comfortable with the ambiguity of the RA role.

Caring

- Value and demonstrate care and concern for others.
- Listen to others with respect.

Learning How to Learn

- Exhibit self-reliant behavior, resilience, and persistence.
- Learn from mistakes and experiences.

Foundational Skills

Beyond these specific competencies and expectations, professionals should possess a number of foundational skills. These are often a focus of professional development opportunities presented to student staff to assist them in preparing for life after college. Residential staffs encourage personal development by providing opportunities for educational programs and environments that promote mental, physical, and spiritual wellness. In these types of environments, staff can assist students in gaining a sense of identity and an appreciation for diversity, inclusion, and differences. A residential setting lets students set community expectations to allow them to learn how to foster respect for other peoples' opinions and property, and encourage their development of conflict resolution skills. When students begin to feel a part of their community, they develop a sense of responsibility for that community.

However, staff members rarely arrive at their positions as fully formed individuals. Staff have to be taught these skills just like their peers in the community. Taking the lead in the personal development and community development of residents will allow residential staff members to practice and refine them. A number of these skills can be developed in the role of a staff member, including, but not limited to, collaboration, communication and interpersonal skills, problem-solving, time management, organization, teamwork, and leadership (Holmes, 2014). These skills combine attributes such as people, social, and communication skills, as well as social intelligence, to help individuals navigate their environment, work well with others, perform well, and achieve their goals (Klaus, 2008). They can be beneficial to the residential experience and enable staff to deal effectively with confrontations and differences.

Such collaboration will allow staff to learn how to work with others, including other staff members in a variety of situations. Increasing communication and interpersonal skills will be beneficial for staff members to acquire in their roles, allowing them to work with challenging residents and assist residents in learning how to connect with others. Gaining experience in problem-solving will help student staff members, who may rely on external authority figures to assist them in solving their problems, learn how to develop solutions on their own, since their residents will look to them for help. Professional staff members will be able to increase their problem-solving skills, since they will become the authorities over their areas and will help guide other staff members and their residents in resolving issues.

Time management is a skill staff will need, because they have to learn how to manage multiple projects and responsibilities while maintaining a connection with other staff members and their residents. Time management will also assist in helping them set priorities for the communities they oversee.

As important as it is for staff members to be able to work with others and in groups, they will also need to learn how to be leaders. Their residents will often turn to them for assistance, so they will have to be able to take charge when the community needs it.

These skills will allow residential staffs to learn how to work effectively with others and to confront conflict. "Members of healthy communities acknowledge their differences, seek to understand each other's perspectives, clarify roles and responsibilities, participate in group decision making, and authentically communicate their needs" (Piper & Buckley, 2004, p.188).

Training residential staff members to address student behavior by using conflict resolution will allow for reframing approaches to common campus issues while recognizing the changing demographics of campus populations. The skills the staffs learn will then transfer to the residents. Learning how to use various conflict resolution styles, such as mediation and restorative practice dialogues, when confronted with issues and disagreements will help students while they work on maintaining and building their on-campus communities.

Mediation skills give staff members the opportunity to learn how to negotiate confrontation, among not only dissenting residents but dissenting colleagues as well. Mediation skills give staff members the opportunity to learn how to listen objectively and how to empower residents to work with each other when dealing community problems. Restorative practice allows staffs to respond to policy violation, community issues, and conflict by focusing on repairing the relationships and reintegration into the community (Mahnke, 2016).

TRAINING TECHNIQUES

It has been asserted that "what differentiates high-quality housing and residence life (HRL) programs from poor-quality programs is the quality of the HRL staff" (Blimling, 2015, p. 135). Training staff about their role in student conduct and community development involves challenging them to integrate multiple skill sets, discern which skills to apply across a wide variety of scenarios, and commit to a fair and just process from confrontation to resolution.

Blimling points out that "qualified people with good judgment and clear understandings of how to respond to students can make the difference between minor roommate squabbles and major conflicts in [residence halls]" (p. 177). Preparing paraprofessionals and housing professionals at all levels of their careers for success with student conduct and community is a critical task that requires thoughtful curricular design, attention to evidence-based training methods, and consistent evaluation and learning assessment to inform future practices. Practitioners charged with training and educating housing staff on student conduct are wise to involve staff with an educational background in curriculum development.

Identifying qualified staff to serve as designers of staff training programs may require some effort. For instance, in a survey of 338 housing professionals in the United States responsible for coordinating RA training programs, Koch (2012) found while 82% of respondents had master's degrees (p. 134), 35% of respondents had not completed any coursework or professional development in curriculum design (p. 137). Koch noted housing professionals who lack sufficient preparation might resort to replicating staff training programs similar to those they participated in, thus failing to serve the needs of learners or match content to the institutional context.

Educational Design

In considering best practices in staff training, it is wise to revisit the fundamentals of educational design. Fink (2013, p. 25–27) identified four components of teaching: knowledge of subject matter, educator-student interaction (lecturing, leading class, communicating in-person and electronically), course management (administrative tasks including grading and providing prompt feedback), and design of instruction (identifying learning goals, developing learning activities, integrating feedback and assessments, sequencing, and scaffolding lessons).

Fink and other curricular design experts agree that "rather than focusing on content to be covered, curriculum design needs to emphasize larger goals, essential questions, and key performance tasks, which become the blueprint for design" (Cullen, Harris, & Hill, 2012, p. 107). Guided by this blueprint, staff members responsible for training paraprofessional and professionals should develop curricula consistent with their institution's mission, vision, values, philosophy toward student behavior, community, and engagement on campus. The curricular blueprint dovetails with and builds upon existing onboarding processes, providing staff members with an approach that considers and builds upon the experience of learners, their beliefs about how to resolve conflict and build community, and institutional expectations of their role.

Evidence-based Training

Ruth Colvin Clark (2015) provides training professionals with a detailed and research-based guide to evidence-based training methods, which she defines as "the application of data-based guidelines as one factor when making decisions regarding the requirements, design, development, and delivery of work and instructional environments designed to optimize individual or organizational goals" (p. 26). Clark notes that academic research evidence is drawn from experimental comparisons, correlation studies, meta-analysis, and qualitative research. It differs from practitioner evidence, which stems from program evaluation and assessment, observation, and performance metrics (p. 29). Clark's

TABLE 4.1 Strategies to Improve Practice During Staff Training Programs

Evidence-based Guideline	Practice Strategy
"Incorporate the context of the job to build practice exercises that require application rather than recall of content." (p. 206)	Develop campus-specific BCD scenarios that require multiple skills (relationship skills, problem-solving skills, helping skills, administrative skills) to address the issue successfully.
"Adjust the amount of practice in your training based on: • "Consequences of error: If serious, requires more rather than less practice. • "Acceptability of a job aid: If yes, then fewer practice exercises might suffice. • "Complexity of the work: If high, drill and practice might be needed to automate requisite sub-skills." (p. 210)	Addressing bias-related interpersonal conflicts in a residential community is complex and may have negative consequences if not handled appropriately. When there is little opportunity to correct missteps, and/or nuanced or expert responses are critical to success (i.e., sexual assault or other violent behavior), it is better to over-prepare and practice to ensure an appropriate response is delivered at the onset. When addressing student conduct and supporting community development, staff rarely get a second chance to make a lasting and positive first impression.
"Distribute practice within your lessons and throughout your course rather than lumping them together. Convert learning events into learning processes." (p. 213)	When teaching content-dense subjects such as residence hall policies and procedures, begin training with assigned readings. Reserve in-person, instructor-led sessions for interactive role plays, case studies, and problem-based learning. If using an online learning management system, follow up with discussion board entries or reflective learning prompts to extend the learning experience and encourage learners to share their perspectives.
"When it is important to respond differently to different categories of problems, mix practice items rather than grouping similar practice types together." (p. 215)	Mixing categories of skills or problems presents a realistic and authentic picture of a housing staff member's day. Within a matter of hours, a housing staff member may shift focus from implementing community programs to confronting an alcohol-related situation, addressing a roommate issue, or filing an online report. Enabling learners to practice shifting their focus throughout a learning experience will prepare them to be nimble and accustomed to the unpredictable nature of the work.

Evidence-based Guideline	Practice Strategy
"Assign comparison practice exercises to build relevant prior knowledge, to correct flawed or incomplete mental models, or to reflect on decisions made in a training scenario." (p. 218)	Housing staff members often must confront students whose behavior is based on their misunderstanding, misinterpretation of, or disregard for campus policies. Creating interactive training scenarios that challenge learners to compare their flawed mental models with those rooted in institutional or departmental philosophies will help them build confidence and learn more deeply.
"Provide detailed task-specific feedback to practice exercises that explains why a response is correct or incorrect. Give feedback not only on outcomes but also on techniques and processes. For procedural tasks, provide step-by-step immediate feedback." (p. 222)	Adults learn more effectively and grow personally when provided with corrective, detailed, and informative feedback regarding the task at hand. Whether it is by teaching a student employee how to complete an incident report or helping professional staff resolve a complex roommate issue, providing performance feedback strengthens opportunities for improved and consistent performance in the future.

Source: Adapted by the authors, based on Ruth Colvin Clark's Evidence-Based Training Methods: A Guide for Training Professionals (2nd edition).

guidance on workplace learning strategies applies to all adult learners from undergraduate staff members to seasoned professionals.

For example, Clark maintains that "for the most part[,] we underestimate the role of focused practice in building competence" (p. 202). Clark defines practice as "a deliberate assigned activity designed to promote behavioral and psychological response that will build goal-relevant knowledge or skills" (p. 203). Like Wiggins (1998), who promoted the use of authentic tasks and performer-friendly feedback, Clark maintains while learners must be able to repeat or recognize lesson content, it is perhaps even more important to be able to apply one's knowledge to a job-related task.

For housing professionals, opportunities to engage in skill development can occur in many forms, such as Behind Closed Doors (BCD), an interactive role-play activity widely used in RA training programs. A deliberately designed BCD experience includes opportunities for the behaviorally-based feedback provided by experienced coaches (i.e., returning RAs and professional staff) who help "learners to bridge performance gaps" (p. 203).

Table 4.1 provides additional guidelines related to practicing skill development in student conduct and community development, along with examples of evidence-based strategies.

Information Delivery

Along with Clark's evidence-based guidelines for designing staff training experiences, it is also important to consider approaches that, if applied in part or whole, will improve the learning experience for adult learners at all levels of housing and student conduct departments. As these examples illustrate, there is much to consider when developing a curriculum to train staff to perform their responsibilities competently. Training professionals must shape the training around the unique situational factors of their institutions, the experience of their learners, and the external and internal expectations of staff. Building competency and keeping skills sharp requires ongoing training, not only for staff new to their positions but also for seasoned staff members.

Focus on the learner's level of prior knowledge, rather than their learning style. Professionals may be surprised to learn there is no evidence that learning styles exist (Clark, 2015, p. 7). Clark acknowledges that learning style inventories and resources are popular and fueled by a "charismatic intuitive appeal" (p. 5), and is quick to emphatically implore training instructors to stop using learning style inventories and resources. Instead, Clark encourages training professionals to focus on learners' prior knowledge with the subject matter and tailor a training curriculum to the learner's level (i.e., novice/rookie, skilled/intermediate, proficient/advanced, expert/senior). When educators leverage prior knowledge to establish a baseline for learning, they ensure learners are not talked down to or presented with information that is over their heads.

Cornell University's Center for Teaching Innovation (2018) suggests educators can assess learners' background knowledge by incorporating a variety of discussion, self-assessments, and structured activities. Some examples of these include exercises that explore commonly held misconceptions about a particular topic.

Select active learning techniques that promote psychological engagement with the content. Active learning is used widely in educational settings as "a response to the pervasive use of non-interactive lectures" (Clark, 2015, p. 16). Active learning is "anything that involves students in doing things and thinking about the things they are doing" (Bonwell & Eison, 1991, p. 2), but it is not enough to have learners physically moving or interacting with one another. Clark emphasizes the research says "it is psychological engagement rather than physical engagement that counts" (p. 19).

Some effective strategies to improve learning and psychological engagement include using clickers or polling technology with multiple choice questions and follow-up explanations (p. 69–70); asking learners to self-explain content verbally or in writing (p. 70); and incorporating "collaboration when problems or assignments are challenging and/or will benefit from group synergy" (p. 73).

Users of Fink's taxonomy for significant learning have found psychological engagement across a variety of disciplines is higher when curricular design includes at least one of these learning goals: learning about oneself and others (human dimension); developing new feelings, interests, or values (caring); or becoming a self-directed learner (learning how to learn) (Fink & Fink, 2009).

Fink (2013) maintains deep and lasting learning occurs when educators mix these affective learning goals with traditional goals of understanding and remembering information and ideas; application of skills and knowledge; and connecting ideas, learning experiences, and other realms of one's life (pp. 31–38). Additionally, Fink (pp. 169–172) points out that when educators match learner's skill level effectively to the proper level of challenge with a supportive curricular design, the learners are more likely to achieve a "flow experience" (Csikszentmihalyi, 1997) in which they are fully engaged, motivated, and focused in ways that transcend time and energy (Figure 4.1). Fink notes that rich learning experiences — those "in which students are able to simultaneously achieve multiple kinds of significant learning" (p. 123) — produce flow experiences and lasting learning.

Encourage instructors to be psychologically open and available. Effective teaching is an art more than a science, and having a social presence embedded with positive social cues may be outside the comfort zone of some individuals. Whether delivering a lesson to an entire department, a small staff, or an online platform, some instructors may rely on a more-formal tone to project greater credibility or professionalism.

This approach may be counterproductive, since research indicates instructor use of conversational language and other social cues promotes deeper learning (Clark, 2015). In fact, researchers found that instructors who projected a more-relaxed, friendly persona received higher satisfaction ratings and their instructional materials were perceived by learners as easier to understand (p. 131). Researchers have found that instructors are more effective when they use conversational language that includes polite phrases, first- and second-person terms (e.g., I, you, we), and offer their own relevant experiences and perspectives on the content (p. 144). Using these strategies enables instructors to build a reputation for being approachable and relatable, and deepens the learning experience.

Limit the use of personal anecdotes. All housing and conduct professionals have their own stories of dealing with extreme roommate conflicts or out-of-control parties. While instructors use personal stories "to attract attention, generate interest, illustrate a point, dramatize a lesson, [and] add spark to dry

FIGURE 4.1 Flow Experiences in Relation to Challenges and Skills

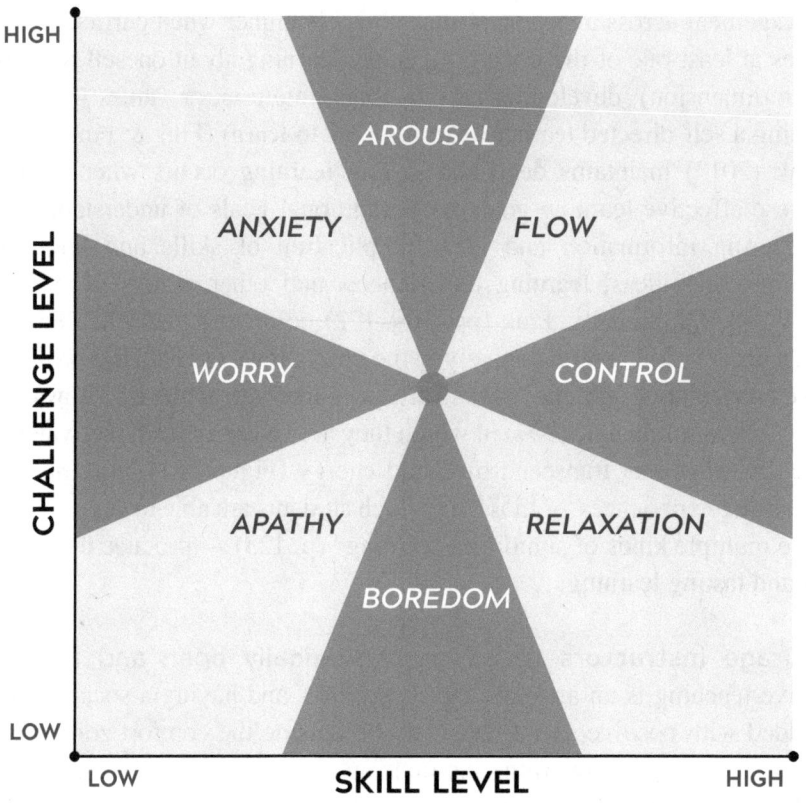

Source: Csikszentmihalyi, 1997, p. 31. © 1997 Mihaly Csikszentmihalyi. Reprinted by permission from Basic Books, a member of Perseus Books, LLC.

content" (Clark, 2015, p. 151), and relevant stories can help instructors be more relatable, there is a risk of overusing such stories. It is important to remember that, in some cases, less is more. Clark notes how research indicates adding irrelevant details impedes learning and recommends instructors should "keep stories that are relevant to [the] learning goal, discard stories that are tangential, and avoid placing any stories in the middle of an explanation where they might disrupt the mental processing needed for understanding" (p. 156).

Use experts to create problem-based scenarios. Problem-based, or authentic, learning scenarios include case studies and interactive role plays, such as the popular Behind Closed Doors program used by many housing professionals as a capstone experience in RA training. In problem-based scenarios, learners are presented with realistic work-based tasks that are resolved using critical thinking, creative problem solving, and integrated application of knowledge in a supportive and guided environment.

When designing staff training workshops, few instructors can deny having reused old scenarios or borrowed scenarios from other campuses due to time constraints or other limitations. While this approach may not hurt on occasion, instructors are encouraged to take the time to develop real-world or authentic scenarios with experts such as selective groups of returning staff members or de-identified scenarios from the actual events on campus, rather than use scenarios that have not been updated or tailored to specific sets of learners.

Clark (2015) noted that not only does scenario-based learning help learners understand the relevance of their training, is also enables individuals to learn from their mistakes and provides a memory repository for later use as well as opportunities to receive memorable instructive feedback (p. 289).

Performance Feedback

Much in the way that a program or initiative should not be considered complete until its outcomes have been assessed, so should staff training not be considered complete until participants have received feedback on their performance. Feedback can be delivered by a variety of means, but all should contribute to the learning process.

Educative assessment promotes learning (Fink, 2013, p. 106) and has four components: (1) forward-looking assessment, (2) criteria and standards, (3) self-assessment, and (4) FIDeLity feedback. To illustrate this educative assessment, consider a group of RAs as they participate in the Behind Closed Door exercises. While new RAs participate in BCD, they receive verbal and written feedback that helps them understand what they are doing well and what abilities they should continue to develop. The first-year RAs will assess their own performance as well as receive feedback from others with more experience who also are observing the BCD scenario (i.e., the actors and the facilitators, as well as campus partners from other offices such as counseling services, health and wellness, the women's center, campus police, and others).

Forward learning assessment. Behind Closed Doors is an excellent example of forward learning assessment or authentic assessment (Wiggins, 1998, pp. 22, 24). The scenarios are realistic and require students to use their RA knowledge and skills wisely, and demonstrate sound judgment to resolve the scenarios successfully. Through direct participation and indirect, or vicarious, peer observation, new RAs rehearse and practice their knowledge and skills in a safe and nurturing learning environment.

Criteria and standards. If asked, almost every housing and residence life professional would be likely to say they have an intuitive understanding of approaches and strategies they feel work with students, as well as those that are not as successful. It is when the professional tries to state these ideas concisely that problems can develop. Sometimes, providing feedback to RAs in a meaningful way can feel more subjective than objective. To prevent feedback from becoming personal, provide staff with rubrics that describe what constitutes high-quality performance.

Self-assessment. "To be powerful performers in life as well as self-directed learners, students must learn how to assess the quality of their own work" (Fink, 2013, p. 103). Before beginning a BCD scenario, the facilitator should review and discuss with new RAs the appropriate rubric so performance expectations are clear. The incoming RAs will then evaluate their own work, as well as the work of their peers, after each scenario. These insights can be a valuable part of the debriefing session that follows a BCD scenario.

FIDeLity feedback. "FIDeLity" is an acronym referring to feedback that is Frequent, Immediate, and Discriminating (that is, based on clear criteria and standards), as well as delivered Lovingly (or supportively). HRL staff members will be called on to use this ability throughout the academic year. The expectation of providing feedback in a supportive or loving manner cannot be overstated. "When there is empathy, personal understanding, and love, students are more likely to open up and internalize the multiple meanings of feedback in a fuller way" (Fink, 2013, p. 106).

As training continues throughout the school year or a professional's career, there will be time to see individuals strengthen their abilities. This growth should be encouraged through appropriate levels of challenge and support. Fink adds, "when other students, the teacher, or external assessors compliment learners on their success in learning, they provide a powerful incentive to continue learning and to continue improving" (p. 108).

COMPLIANCE TRAINING

Recent years have shown an increase in required training from governmental, legal, and institutional authorities. Some of these expectations come from federal regulations, such as (in the United States) the Clery Act and Title IX, and others come from case law. While residence life staff have understood longstanding legal responsibilities such as duty to report, they are now challenged with the additional task of providing preventive education and resources for residents. This focus on compliance and risk management training, such as reporting crimes or sexual harassment, and performing facilities checks, can be viewed by some professionals as extra responsibilities that disrupt the residence life training schedule at the expense of time that could be spent on community-building and student development. Regardless, those feelings, do not relieve housing and conduct professionals of their liability and risk management responsibilities. Legal and liability issues must be incorporated as part of regularly occurring training for housing and residence life, as well as student conduct staff.

Legal and Liability Challenges

Housing and residence life staff members largely understand they are responsible for the students who reside on their floors or in their buildings. Consider the role in comparison to a lifeguard: The lifeguard does not necessarily live with the patrons of the pool and does not necessarily know many of the people in the pool, but both housing staff and lifeguards have responsibility for the people they supervise, based on a position description or job agreement. Both must be familiar with the facility and with rules and policies, and enforce those rules and policies for the safety of the patrons. For student conduct staff, the relationship and responsibility to the community may resemble those of law enforcement personnel and the citizens they serve.

Campus housing staff often know the occupants of the floor and will become acquainted with guests who frequent the floor. The proximity of staff to students might suggest staff who live and work on a floor or in a building on a daily basis may have greater responsibility and therefore, potential liability, for their residents. It is reasonable to conclude the live-in staff members are more aware of facility issues, more familiar with potential disciplinary concerns surrounding residents of the floor, and first to know of emergencies on the floor.

While the live-in staff may be the closest to a potential liability concern, other housing and residence life staff are not immune to liability. Conduct staff work with students daily, but rarely meet with the same students more than once. Unlike housing staff, conduct staff will not be likely to know students who appear before them personally or develop personal relationships with the majority of students they encounter. From a cursory review of court cases related to campus housing, the list of possible defendants includes building staff, area staff, and central housing administration, and can extend to upper university administration. The list of defendants stands as a testament to the need for training in legal issues and liability for a wide range of staff.

As Donald Gehring asserts in *Administering College and University Housing: A Legal Perspective*, society has become more litigious, monetary awards for damages have increased, and it has become essential for housing staff to be aware of legal issues relevant to their work (1992). Gehring says legal issues can originate from a variety of sources, including a contractual relationship between staff and resident, federal and state laws, housing and campus policies, and case law.

More recently, Peter Lake introduced the notion of a facilitator university (Lake, 2013), which can be understood by considering the context of the relationship between the student and the university: Lake characterizes the facilitator university as a shared responsibility between institutional staff and the student's parents. This shared responsibility is largely based on the student being an adult and on the reality that parents do not absolve themselves of the responsibility for their student when the student graduates from high school. The shift from responsibility as a surrogate parent to one of shared responsibility with the parents has not necessarily resulted in fewer legal challenges against institutions.

An understanding of tort law is valuable in understanding the legal responsibility staff may have for campus housing. William Kaplin and Barbara Lee (1995) define a tort "as a civil wrong, other than a breach of contract, for which the courts will allow a damage remedy" (p. 98). From relevant case law, specific training topics associated with tort law can be identified to prepare housing staff adequately. The element of a tortious claim, which can include but is not limited to breach of contract, duty, and education malpractice, that frequently appears in lawsuits against institutions is that of negligence. Negligence means that an institution "owed a duty to the injured party but failed to exercise due care to avoid the injury" (Kaplin & Lee, p. 193).

In *Kleinknecht v. Gettysburg College*, 989 F.2d 1360 (3rd Cir. 1993), potential negligence was analyzed by whether a "special relationship" existed between the student and the university, and the proximate cause of an injury was "foreseeable" by the university. For example, consider a case where an RA is notified a resident was injured on the floor as a result of stepping on shards of glass from a broken window. Through further exploration, supervising staff learned the window was broken the previous day and the RA knew about the breakage. The RA failed to contact maintenance staff to report the broken window before the injury occurred. In training, it may be emphasized that because there was a connection between the university (through the RA) and the injured student constituting a special relationship, and that the RA had prior knowledge that the window was broken, the potential for injury was foreseeable and could have been prevented through a timely maintenance request.

In campus student conduct administration, notice to the student of an alleged violation of policy and the opportunity to be heard are essential elements of the campus process to respond to concerning behavior. A seminal case is *Dixon v. Alabama State Board of Education*, 294 F.2d 150 (5th Cir. 1961). In *Dixon*, the federal Fifth Circuit court concluded students may not simply be expelled or removed from school at the discretion of the school administration, even in the best interest of the campus community (*in loco parentis*), without some form of notice and hearing.

Later, a U.S. Supreme Court case, *Goss v. Lopez*, 419 U.S. 565 (1975), provided more specificity on due process minimum standards, including oral or written notice of charges, an explanation of the allegations and evidence, an opportunity for the student to respond to the allegations, and the evidence in a hearing. Other courts have addressed due process and the degree to which institutions afford due process that does not violate the due process clause of the Fourteenth Amendment of the U.S. Constitution.

In a litigious climate, lawsuits against campus-based professionals are filed more often and regularly name individual administrators in such suits. To reduce liability, student conduct administrators must ensure their respective campus and housing processes include and adhere to minimal due process elements. Many full-time and graduate residence life staff also serve as conduct resolution officers. A strong foundation in student rights and institution responsibility is necessary for any staff who will have to hold residents responsible for behavior.

Another way for student conduct and housing professionals to reduce the potential risk of being on the receiving end of a lawsuit is to know, rigidly follow, and regularly review campus conduct and campus housing policies, since one sure way to be named individually in a lawsuit is to step outside published campus policies and procedures. This includes published rules and regulations, residence hall handbooks, and anything on the institution's website. If informal policies are part of the campus culture, they should be formalized in a documentable form for annual review.

In short, staff must follow the policies without deviation. For live-in staff and campus conduct staff, training must include a mechanism to ensure these staff fully know and understand established institutional policies. Some of these training sessions have included online courses and quizzes, experiential case studies such as Behind Closed Doors, and policy trivia nights.

Case Law Training

A valuable approach to understanding the liability and responsibilities of a housing professional is to review legal precedents. Existing case law may have the power to directly affect the work of a given housing and residence life program, depending on whether the institution is in the jurisdiction of the court that heard the case. However, even when the institution is not in the same jurisdiction as the case, the outcome of the case may still be helpful as a way to inform staff training by providing real-life examples of tort liability.

While professionals should take steps to remain aware of relevant cases through environmental scanning, professional publications, conference sessions, and the like, supervisors may also maintain a collection of useful examples. The nuances associated with the law enforcement and housing staff roles also may present an opportunity for collaborative, scenario-based training with campus law enforcement officers.

Facility or property injury. Another area of potential liability for housing departments is the safety of the physical structure itself. In *Williamson v. Long Island University*, 2017 NY Slip Op 06100 (N.Y. Sup. Ct. 2017), a resident of an on-campus residence sued her institution after sustaining injuries related to an unsecured light globe in her room. The globe fell from the ceiling and struck the resident in the head, causing an injury. The university prevailed on the grounds the university did not create the dangerous condition and was not reasonably aware the light fixture condition existed.

Housing staff can be trained to recognize potential environmental concerns to prevent injury. Some mechanisms to incorporate in staff training may include routine health and safety inspections, regular reporting of maintenance concerns and defects, training residents on how to submit maintenance requests, and conducting rounds to ensure the common areas of the building are safe and free from defect. Framing the facilities responsibilities as part of the community-building process can help supervisors connect the dots for resident assistants. A caring community is one that is safe and where residents want to live.

Duty to protect. In addition to the potential responsibility for the physical facility, case law alleges the institution has a duty to protect the safety of a resident from third-party criminal activity. In *Boyd v. Cebalo*, 2015-CA-1085, 2016 WL 1061064 (La. Ct. App. 2016), a resident was sexually assaulted by a guest of a suitemate while asleep in her own bed. The bathroom door of the shared suite bathroom had a lock on the inside of the door to deny entrance to others while the bathroom was in use, but there was not a lock on the outside or room-side of the bathroom door to prevent people from entering the room through the shared bathroom.

The resident sued the university on a negligence claim that involved failure to properly secure the room, failure to protect students from criminal activity, and foreseeability. The appeals courts found the trial court wrongly dismissed the negligence claim on the notion it may be reasonable for the institution to have known a lock on the outside of the door could have increased student safety. Citing an earlier case, *Williams v. State*, 786 So.2d 927 (La. Ct. App. 1981), the appeals court remanded the case back to the trial court, finding the locking mechanism referenced by the resident did not constitute an unreasonable or sophisticated security modification. Cases such as these serve as a reminder that in addition to amenities, a top priority for renovations and new construction should also be resident safety.

Contractual claims. A contract claim is another source of litigation facing housing and residence life departments. A standard practice among institutional housing departments is to have a housing contract — a document, much like a private landlord lease, that articulates the agreed-to services, length of stay, and behavioral expectations of the contracting student. It is also common for this document to contain a clause that states the contract may be rescinded for good cause.

In *Doe v. Devonshire*, No. 16-10458-NMG, 2016 WL 1555682 (D. Mass. 2016), the institution terminated Doe's housing contract after the conduct process found a documented pattern of behavior deemed by the institution to be disruptive, creating a sexually hostile environment and demonstrating conduct of a lewd nature. After multiple conversations, a relocation, investigations, and disciplinary action, the institution terminated Doe's housing contract. Doe filed suit to ask the court for preliminary injunctive relief to lift the instituted ban from housing and a breach of contract claim that he was removed before the stipulated contract end date. The court sided with the institution and disagreed with the "everybody is doing it" defense, or that the institution's decision to terminate the housing contract was arbitrary and capricious.

The courts regularly address the designation of whether something is arbitrary and capricious. "Arbitrary" has been shown to represent a decision that was made without any reason or support from policy. A "capricious" decision is a decision or judgment made on impulse and without more in-depth consideration. Ultimately, Doe's motion for preliminary injunctive relief of the contract cancellation was denied and the contract cancellation was upheld.

In the case of more-serious violations, campus housing professionals and student conduct administrators often must explain why an alleged violator is allowed to continue living in the residence halls. While it may be tempting and contractually permissive, a more-robust approach lessens the potential for contractual claims. Policies such as an administrative move policy that will allow a resident to remain in campus housing pending adjudication or issuing an interim restriction that may limit contact by a student with others are both approaches that address community concerns, while ensuring a resident's minimum due process rights.

Search and seizure. Questions regarding routine room inspections and the laws concerning search and seizure occur regularly during housing and residence life staff training. Case law has established select, agreed-upon conditions when it comes to the ability of housing staff to enter a room and the degree to which housing staff may be acting as agents of law enforcement. Most public university housing contracts allow housing staff to enter a room after specified notice of entry that was well-published on the floor or building, and to conduct routine inspections to ensure the health and safety of residents. Private institutions may have more latitude for when staff enter a resident's room.

Law enforcement agents may not conduct these inspections nor address suspected criminal activity without either consent of the resident or a valid warrant issued by a judge or magistrate, nor may housing staff act as an extension of law enforcement for the purpose of responding to criminal activity when law enforcement officers are present but do not enter the residence in question.

An example of such a scenario is *State v. Rodriguez*, No. PD-1391-15, 2017 WL 2457441 (Ct. Crim. App. Tex. 2017). In this case, the Court of Criminal Appeals of Texas reasoned RAs could contractually conduct in-person, routine health and safety inspections of resident rooms. The question arose after the RAs found a substance consistent with marijuana after opening a closed trunk in a student's room. Following the direction of supervising housing staff, the RAs then found unknown pills believed to be drug contraband and a pipe known to be used to smoke marijuana. The items were collected and the RAs took a picture of them. The senior housing staff member then contacted the campus police to report the discovered items.

Sometime after the police had arrived, entered the room in question, and witnessed the reported items believed to be consistent with drug contraband, the resident of the room arrived on scene. The officers did not secure a search warrant for the room nor did they ask for or receive consent to search from the resident. After a conversation with the resident, the police read the resident her Miranda rights. After being read her rights, the resident admitted the pills were ecstasy.

Negligence and duty to supervise. In *Furek v. University of Delaware*, 594 A.2d 506 (Del. 1991), the university became aware of the potential for ongoing hazing concerns and imposed regulations in response to control hazing activity thought to be occurring among Greek chapters (Kaplin & Lee, p. 105). For the university to demonstrate awareness of possible acts of hazing by instituting regulations intended to curb that behavior created a duty to supervise participating students between the institution and the students. Because it was foreseeable hazing was a problem and was known to the university, the university had a responsibility to protect students from potential harm.

On the notion of duty to supervise, most tort-based cases cite *Bradshaw v. Rawlings*, 612 F.2d 135 (3rd Cir. 1979), and *Baldwin v. Zoradi*, 176 Cal. Rptr. 809 (Cal. Ct. App. 1981), as examples of when an institution did not have a duty to supervise or a duty to care for injured students (Kaplin & Lee, p. 107–110). In *Bradshaw v. Rawlings*, two students were returning from a university-sponsored event for the sophomore class. Alcohol was served at the event, even though many of the attendees were not of legal drinking age. Flyers advertising the event were posted around campus advertising alcohol at the event and it was later discovered a faculty advisor for the class bought beer for the class president. The court found since *in loco parentis* was no longer in place, the university did not owe a duty to protect students from possible harm.

CONCLUSION

The challenges facing residence life professionals and paraprofessionals working in residential settings continue to mount as campus leaders face concerns such as increases in bullying and violence, declines in student mental health, and an increasingly litigious society. In additional, the need for a strong and inclusive sense of community has never been greater. As residential communities become more diverse by race, ethnicity, religion, sexual orientation, and gender expression, helping students manage their interpersonal relationships with those different from them also becomes more complex.

Residence life staff today must hone and sharpen a long list of skills and abilities. Many of those skills related to student conduct must be implemented precisely and consistently to keep from putting the institution at risk of non-compliance or violation of federal or state laws. For staff training to be effective and long-lasting, staff members responsible for developing and implementing training curricula must incorporate evidence-based strategies and proven design methods, such as Fink's (2013) integrated course design, into their training programs. The resulting high-impact training programs will not only prepare staff for their paraprofessional or professional roles, but also enhance their abilities in a broad set of soft skills that will help them be successful in all aspects of their lives.

REFERENCES

ACUHO-I (2017). *ACUHO-I Standards & Ethical Principles for College and University Housing Professionals*. Columbus: Association of College & University Housing Officers - International. Retrieved from http://www.acuho-i.org/knowledge-resources/standards/acuho-i.

Angelo, T., & Cross, P. (1993). *Classroom assessment techniques: A handbook for college teachers*. San Francisco: Jossey-Bass.

Astin, A. W. (1993). *What matters in college: Four critical years revisited*. San Francisco: Jossey-Bass.

Baldwin v. Zoradi, 176 Cal. Rptr. 809 (Cal. Crt. of Appeals 1981).

Boyd v. Cebalo, 2015-CA01085, 2016 WL 1061064 (La. Ct. App. 2016).

Blimling, G. S., (2015). *Student learning in college residence halls: What works, what doesn't, and why*. San Francisco, CA: Jossey-Bass.

Block, P. (2008). *Community: The structure of belonging*. San Francisco: Berrett-Koehler.

Bonwell, C. C., & Eison, J. A. (1991). Active learning: Creating excitement in the classroom. ASHE–ERIC Higher Education Rep. No. 1. Washington, DC: George Washington University, School of Education and Human Development.

Boyer, E. L. (1990). *Campus life: In search of community.* Princeton, NJ: Carnegie Foundation for the Advancement of Teaching.

Bradshaw v. Rawlings, 612 F.2d 135 (3rd Circuit 1979).

Council for the Advancement of Standards in Higher Education (2009). *CAS self-assessment guide for housing and residential life programs.* Washington, DC: Author.

Clark, R. C. (2015). *Evidence-based training methods: A guide for training professionals* (2nd ed.) Alexandria, VA: ATD Press.

Chickering, A. W., & Reisser, L. (1993). *Education and identity* (2nd ed.). San Francisco: Jossey-Bass.

Dixon v. Alabama State Board of Education, 294 F.2d 150 (5th Cir. 1961).

Doe v. Devonshire, No. 16-10458-NMG, 2016 WL 1555682 (D. Mass. 2016).

Fink. L. D. (2013). *Creating significant learning experiences: An integrated approach to designing college courses*, Second Edition. San Francisco, CA: Jossey-Bass.

Fink, L. D., & Fink, A. K. (2009). *Designing courses for significant learning: Voices of experience.* Hoboken, NJ: Wiley and Sons.

Gallagher, D. M., Meagher, P., & Vander Velde, S. (2014). Motivation and Outcomes for University Students in a Restorative Justice Program. *Journal of Student Affairs Research and Practice. 51*(4), 364.

Gehring, D. D. (1992). *Administering College and University Housing: A Legal Perspective* (2nd ed.). Asheville, NC: College Administration Publications.

Goss v. Lopez, 419 U.S. 565 (1975).

Holmes, B. (2014). Hone the top 5 soft skills every college student needs. *U.S. News and World Report.* https://www.usnews.com/education/blogs/college-admissions-playbook/2014/05/12/hone-the-top-5-soft-skills-every-college-student-needs.

Howell, M. T. (2005). Students' Perceived Learning and Anticipated Future Behaviors as a Result of Participation in the Student Judicial Process. *Journal of College Student Development 46*(4). Retrieved from https://muse.jhu.edu/article/184914/summary.

Janosik, S. M., & Stimpson, M. T. (2017). The influence of the conduct system and campus environments on student learning. *Journal of Student Affairs Research and Practice 54*(1), 28 41.

Kaplin, W. A., & Lee, B. A. (1995). *The Law of Higher Education* (3rd ed.). San Francisco: Jossey-Bass.

King. R. H. (2012). Student Conduct Administration: How Students Perceive the Educational Value and Procedural Fairness of Their Disciplinary Experiences. *Journal of College Student Development 53*(4). Retrieved from http://www.tarleton.edu/housing/documents/educationalroleincollegestudendhousing.pdf.

Klaus, P., Rohman, J. M., & Hamaker, M. (2007). *The hard truth about soft skills:*

Workplace lessons smart people wish they'd learned sooner. New York, NY: HarperCollins.

Kleinknecht v. Gettysburg College, 989 F.2d 1360 (3rd Circuit 1993).

Koch, V. A. (2012). *An exploration of current practices in curricular design of resident assistant training programs.* Dissertations. Paper 360.

Lake, P. F. (2013). *The Rights and Responsibilities of the Modern University: The Rise of the Facilitator University* (2nd ed.). Durham, NC: Carolina Academic Press.

Livingston, W. G., Scott, D. A., Rush, S. B., Watson L. A., Neiduski, M. L., & Pinkenburg, S. J. (2013). When Community and Conduct Collide: Residents with Invisible Disabilities and the Student Conduct Process. *Journal of College and University Student Housing 40*(1), 214–227.

Mahnke, Carla. (2016). *Restorative practices: Student conduct administrator staff development* Arizona State University. ProQuest Dissertations Publishing. 10107734.

Pascarella, T., & Terenzini, P. (1991). *How college affects students.* San Francisco: Jossey-Bass.

Piper, T. & Buckley, J. (2004). Community Standards Model: Developing Learning Partnerships in Campus Housing. In M. B. Magolda & P. M. King (eds.). *Learning Partnerships: Theory and Models of Practice to Educate for Self-Authorship* (pp. 185-212). Sterling, VA: Stylus Publishing.

Stimpson, M. T. & Janosik, S. M. (2015). The Conduct System and Its Influence on Student Learning. *Journal of College Student Development 56*(1), 61–66.

State v. Rodriguez, No. PD-1391-15, 2017 WL 2457441 (Ct. Crim. App. Tex. 2017).

Strayhorn, T. L. (2012). *College students' sense of belonging: A key to educational success for all students.* New York: Routledge.

Truitt, John W., & Indiana State Univ., Terre Haute. (1969). *Factors Underlying the Need for In-Service Development Programs in Student Personnel Work.* Washington, D.C.: Distributed by ERIC Clearinghouse, http://www.eric.ed.gov/contentdelivery/servlet/ERICServlet?accno=ED022203.

Williams v. State, 786 So.2d 927 (La. Ct. App. 1981).

Williamson v. Long Island University, 2017 NY Slip Op 06100 (N.Y. Sup. Ct. 2017).

Yussman, H. (2016, September 22). Conduct change eases burden on ResLife staff. Retrieved April 11, 2018, from https://kenyoncollegian.com/news/2016/09/conduct-change-eases-burden-on-reslife-staff/.

1. What is your housing department's philosophy regarding training? How does this affect how you prioritize time in the training schedule? Do you find yourself focusing more on compliance issues and mandates or on community-building? How can you strike a balance between many topics?

2. How do you plan for continual training and development of staff at all levels regarding conduct, conflict, and confrontation of behavioral issues? What would you include in a comprehensive, year-long plan?

3. Consider how technology has affected our work and how our students learn. What are some ways to integrate technology in your training with student staff? With hearing officers?

4. How does your housing department train live-in staff to remain safe while engaging in behavioral confrontations? Knowing that panic buttons cannot realistically be installed everywhere, what is the safety plan for hearing officers who may have a meeting with an aggressive residents?

5. Peer conduct boards serve an important role in community accountability. How do you continue to motivate volunteers on a peer board? With more-complex conduct processes, how do you train and retain board members?

6. How do you discuss risk management issues with your live-in staff? How can you best explore protocols to determine the why between many policies and procedures?

CRAFTING AND REVISING CONDUCT PROCESSES

Jennifer Forry, Nicole DiBartolo, and Derrick Dixon

THROUGHOUT THE history of higher education, college campuses have faced the challenge of managing student conduct. As far back as 1822, after student riots on campus, Thomas Jefferson, founder and president of the University of Virginia, wrote a letter to a fellow college president stating "the article of [student] discipline is the most difficult in American education" (Jefferson letter of November 2, 1822, Note 1). Later, in 1870, a small coeducational college published a booklet outlining conduct expectations in college buildings and residence halls that detailed:

- Students are expected to be kind and respectful to others.
- Students, while connected with the college, are strictly forbidden the use of intoxicating liquors and tobacco, profanity, or indecent language on the college premise, or so far as the college has any jurisdiction.
- Students must refrain from all improprieties in the halls, boisterous talking, or scuffling.
- Young men and women are not allowed to take rides or walks without permission.
- No student will fire gunpowder in college buildings, or on the premise, or engage in card playing or any other form of gambling in college, or in the city, or commit injuries upon the person or property of any student.
- The faculty shall have the authority to visit and search any room in college, using force as necessary to enter, and assess all damages occasioned by the violation of the offender. (Cowley, 1937)

Campuses today are far different from those of the past, but managing behavior and developing a healthy sense of community among student residents remains an important part of the work done by residence and conduct professionals. The 1870 rules may seem antiquated, but have parallels to issues common today. They show how student conduct must evolve to meet the ever-changing campus environment while retaining the fundamentals of the earliest residential conduct processes. Almost two centuries later, through all the widespread and dramatic changes colleges and universities have experienced, student conduct practitioners are still refining how to create processes that meet the needs of a particular community at a particular time.

INFLUENCING FACTORS

According to Simon Sinek, an author and motivational speaker, "All organizations start with *why*, but only the great ones keep their *why* clear year after year" (Sinek, 2009). While he may have been discussing corporate marketing strategies when he said this, the logic applies to establishing student conduct processes as well. Before an organization can create or revise its processes related to conduct, it must firmly understand the outcomes it hopes to achieve. It must know the *why*. As housing and conduct professionals create and revise their processes, they discover myriad factors will influence their decisions.

Professional Standards

Conduct processes do not have to be created from whole cloth. Over the years, a number of associations have established and revised accepted best practices and guidelines to help lead the work. Familiarity with these standards through publications, conference presentations, and the like is one of the best ways for housing and conduct professionals to stay abreast of current trends and issues. While these standards don't provide specifics of a campus policy, they do provide the foundation for constructing processes and policies.

Council for the Advancement of Standards in Higher Education. Since 1979, the Council for the Advancement of Standards in Higher Education (CAS) has promoted standards for student affairs in 45 functional areas, including both student housing and conduct. Among its statements is, "[W]hen we rely on established student learning and development theories to tailor an appropriate institutional response to student conduct and conduct issues, we can advance the overall academic mission" (Schrage & Giacomini, 2009, p. 34). To that end, CAS (2013) outlines a comprehensive approach to residence life and conduct in which residence life staff members:

- Document institutional and residential living policies, procedures, and expectations, including the potential consequences for violation.
- Involve students in programming, policy development, and self-governance.
- Promote and provide education about the effects and risks of drug and alcohol use and other high-risk behaviors.
- Encourage residents to exercise responsibility for their community through confronting inappropriate or disruptive behavior.
- Encourage residents to participate in mediating conflict within the community.
- Encourage residents to learn about their rights as students, tenants, residents, and consumers.

Association of College and University Housing Officers - International. Similarly, the *ACUHO-I Standards and Ethical Principles for College and University Student Housing* says ". . . the formal education of students, consisting of the curricular and the co-curricular, must promote student learning and development, contribute to students' realization of their potential, and prepare students for life after college" (Association of College and University Housing Officers-International, 2017). Since this relates to policies and procedures concerning community development, the document goes on to detail how an ethically performing department will:

- Provide students a clear protocol for reporting incidents or concerns through a code of standards and conduct.
- Promote and demonstrate an educational response to the impact of illegal substances, prescription or other drugs, and alcohol use and abuse.
- Ensure policies and procedures are in place to respond to students exhibiting behaviors related to psychological distress and work to limit the impact of such behaviors on the community.
- Formulate codes, policies, regulations, and standards to ensure a safe and secure living and learning environment for residents.
- Develop appropriate appeals/grievance processes for students and staff per community standards, student handbook, human resource policies, unions, etc.
- Ensure that the safety and security of residents and their property is demonstrated in an occupancy agreement/residence contract.
- Promote and demonstrate proactive educational opportunities regarding sexual violence prevention and response.

Association for Student Conduct Administration. The *ASCA Ethical Principles and Practices in Student Conduct Administration* posits "a primary purpose for the enforcement of standards of conduct is to maintain and strengthen the ethical climate and to promote the integrity of institutions of higher learning" and "clearly articulated and consistently administered standards of conduct form the basis for behavioral expectations within an academic community" (Association for Student Conduct Administration, 2017). The document goes on to describe the following principles of ethical practice.

- **Autonomy.** In practice, the principle of autonomy compels ASCA members to support both the mission and goals of the employing institution and the rights, privileges, and responsibilities of the students within that institution.
- **Non-malfeasance.** In practice, ethical codes do not define what constitutes harm to others or under what circumstances harm is justifiable. An ethical dilemma occurs whenever a professional has to choose among competing "goods," some of which may involve potential discomfort or some degree of harm to the individual. Any such rules, procedures, and standards shall reflect the commitment to equity, fairness, respect, honesty, trustworthiness, and responsibility.
- **Beneficence.** In practice, the principle of beneficence obligates ASCA members to treat others courteously and accept students as individuals, each with rights and responsibilities, as we seek to create and maintain a campus climate in which we work towards positive learning and personal growth.
- **Justice.** The principle of justice commands ASCA members to treat others with respect and fairness, preserving their dignity, honoring their differences, and promoting their welfare.
- **Fidelity.** The principle of fidelity instructs ASCA members to act in a manner that demonstrates the intention of fidelity (loyal, faithful, honoring commitments) and therefore builds trust among community members.

State and Federal Law

Adequate knowledge of underlying laws is an essential element of the professional practice of any student affairs administrator, since these laws shape policies, practices, and everyday decision-making. While Chapter 3 of this book provides a thorough overview of the state and federal laws that affect student housing and conduct, these factors can influence the creation of a conduct process.

Contract law. It is well-established there is a contractual relationship between a student and the university. The common law contract assumes the student and the university are parties to binding agreements, each giving certain benefits and detriments to fulfill the arrangement (Stoner & Lowery, 2004).

College students are adults in almost every phase of institutional life. According to McClellean and Stringer (2009), it is unrealistic for institutions to expect to control all the actions of all its students. Until the mid-1960s, colleges and universities functioned much like parents, exercising extensive control over students and their behavior. During the 1960s, courts began to move away from the concept of *in loco parentis*. Challenges to the broad exercise of authority and control led to a reduction in institutions' power and contributed to the demise of *in loco parentis* as a basis of liability for colleges and universities (McClellean & Stringer, 2009). Institutions entered into contracts with their students to provide educational services in exchange for students obeying certain policies (Stoner & Lowery, 2004). In this regard, a student-university contract must satisfy the same requirements that apply to contracts in general. Therefore, a student claiming a university breached its contract with the student must show there was a valid contract, the university breached its duties under its contractual agreement, and the breach can cause the student damage (McClellan & Stringer, 2009).

In addition to a university conduct code, many university housing programs will have additional policies specific to the residents of the community, such as establishing noise levels during certain dates and times. When students sign their housing contracts, they are acknowledging these policies and agreeing to abide and follow the expectations of the community where they reside.

Due process. Alexander and Alexander (2011) explain "a student's constitutional interests in higher education are in large part defined by the legal concept of due process of law." The landmark case *Dixon v. Alabama State Board of Education* (1961) defines the relationship between a public institution and its students, indicating "due process requires notice and some opportunity for [a] hearing before students at a tax-supported college" (Dixon, p. 151). Under the Fifth Amendment (through the Fourteenth Amendment), public colleges and universities may not deprive a student of life, liberty, or property without affording that student due process of law (Lancaster & Waryold, 2008). Lancaster and Waryold (2008) further explain both liberty and property interests are at stake for the student when institutions are managing cases of suspension or expulsions. Silverglate and Gewolb (2003) further explain that the courts have largely and consistently addressed the process institutions are required to follow in cases where students face suspension or expulsion.

These guidelines for due process do not necessarily hold true for situations with less-serious legal consequences. Some courts have even indicated that some cases are so minor, they may not require much of a process at all (Silverglate & Gewolb, 2003). These types of cases may be more prevalent in student housing communities where hearing officers are managing housing-specific policy violations. Although hearing officers in a department of residence life are not typically charged with suspending or expelling a student from college housing, the residence life conduct process should be consistent with the college or university process. Staff also must remain aware that the due process rights afforded to students in the housing process are consistent with the overall college or university process.

Due process of law is broken down into procedural due process and substantive due process (Alexander & Alexander, 2011). Procedural due process is due to an individual before a constitutional right can be taken away (Alexander & Alexander, 2011). It focuses on the institution's process for responding to incidents (Lancaster & Waryold, 2008). On the other hand, substantive due process focuses on the nature of the institution's policies and procedures to ensure there are no problems related to vagueness and overbreadth (Lancaster & Waryold, 2008). Alexander and Alexander (2011) say that "procedural due process prescribes what formal process is required of government before it can take away a substantive right of an individual. Property and liberty are substantive rights. A state can deprive a person of liberty and property, but it cannot do so without employing the proper legal procedures." Regardless of new policies or codes, public or private institutions should always follow the general requirements of minimal procedural due process (Stoner & Lowery, 2004).

Search and seizure. The legal boundaries of search and seizure in colleges and universities have become increasingly defined in recent years, as drugs and weapons have become more common on university and college campuses. When addressing university and student property in campus residential communities, warrantless and unreasonable search and seizure are illegal, but government officials can conduct *reasonable* searches (Alexander & Alexander, 2011). However, the law on search and seizure of a student's possessions differs legally, depending on the circumstances of the housing.

The Fourth Amendment of the U.S. Constitution specifically protects people in their "persons and houses," but it does not protect against searches by private entities (such as private colleges) and those for the purposes of institutional safety, conduct, and decorum not intended to be used for prosecution in a criminal proceeding (Alexander & Alexander, 2011). Therefore, residence life professionals must have policies on how to conduct an inspection and what appropriate steps staff should follow if a policy violation occurs in a residence.

Many U.S. Supreme Court decisions have given university officials the legal prerogative to enter residence hall rooms to determine any action occurring that may be harmful to the health and safety of the residential community and is against the conduct guidelines of the department, college, or institution. Housing professionals also have the authority to enter residence hall rooms to check maintenance issues, such as plumbing or heat, and evaluate whether damage may have been done to university property (2011). In addition, residence hall staff may make searches with valid reason if students have pets in their residence hall room against residence policy.

Most residential campuses have fire safety policies that prohibit students from using open heating element appliances in their residence hall room. The health and safety of students require housing and university programs to be able to enter and monitor residence hall rooms, and should be an important consideration when crafting or updating residential policies and the student code of conduct. However, residence life professionals must follow all procedures as set forth by their departmental expectations. For example, when conducting health and safety inspections in a residence hall, the university staff may be required to notify residential students of the time and place the inspection will take place.

University officials also will be required to report to the university police items discovered while conducting routine health and safety checks that violate criminal or institutional policy (Alexander & Alexander, 2011). In *People v. Kelly* (1961), a student tried to suppress evidence obtained from his residence hall room without a search warrant. The court upheld the search because the residence hall room permitted the house master to enter any room in an emergency. The court did not attempt to define "emergency," but stated that when a student accepted residence in the hall, it implied to the university a promise to respect and abide by all its rules (Alexander & Alexander, 2011). Court cases support the institution's right to search residence hall rooms because they are school property and merely used by the student (Alexander & Alexander, 2011).

Institutional and Departmental Fit

A code of conduct should be used to establish the department's educational values and create a positive living-learning environment on campus (Paterson & Kibler, 1998). As a result, many issues requiring consideration will be identified throughout an evaluation of the student conduct process. However, administrators have developed student conduct codes that fit the unique environments of their individual campuses and respond to the needs of their students by addressing issues that have a profound impact on the living and learning environment (Stoner & Lowery, 2004).

The relationship between university policies and how they affect student behavior and campus norms are as varied as the institutions in higher education. While laws protect people, they cannot foresee how students in the residence halls will experience such laws and the implementation of such policies (Poullard, 2011). Therefore, drafting new policies should be framed with the sociopolitical context of the campus in mind (Poullard, 2011).

Campus norms and expectations, past incidents, and current events dictate how a department creates and enacts policy. For example, the issue of allowing animals to live in residence halls has been challenging for most residential campuses. Within the past several years, residential campuses with no-pet policies have received an increasing number of requests from students who claim the need for a companion or emotional support animal as an accommodation for a mental, psychiatric, or emotional disorder. Due to the American Disabilities Act of 1990 (ADA) and numerous U.S. Supreme Court decisions, university administrators are required to accommodate a student's request, asserting having an animal living with them in their residential community provides them therapeutic benefit (Von Bergen, 2015). While new laws create new policies, residence life departments have the power to address the responsibilities of people with animals. Residence life professionals can set expectations the student must comply with, such as being responsible for cleaning up of the animals' waste and complying with other community policies (Von Bergen, 2015).

A student conduct process is not a one-size-fits-all proposition. While some facets of conduct policies and practices are common from campus to campus, the institution can amend them to fit the nuances of their particular needs in the process of creating those policies and practices. This flexibility can be invaluable. Here are details of some of the internal and external factors that help shape a conduct process.

Mission. A community standards process defines the expectations a campus housing community has for student behavior. For generations, these expectations have been that higher education administrators will provide educational and intentional learning to students who strive to develop into good citizens, while responding appropriately to student behaviors that damage the living and learning environment (Stoner & Lowery, 2004). To achieve this, institutions employ residence life staff for a variety of housing-specific responsibilities that include overseeing and administering student conduct matters. Before crafting or revising a conduct process to meet the needs of a residential community, residence life practitioners need to understand the current policy, legal requirements for updating and or altering the policy, how the policy aligns with the institution's mission statement, and how the process affects the residential and college community.

Institutional control. In considering desired outcomes, it is important to remember campus communities are answerable to a variety of authorities. "For instance, private colleges and universities are not required to provide the same due process rights because the institutions are not agencies of the government[,] but are more akin to private corporations. Private institutions, therefore, have much more latitude in determining their conduct procedures than those in the public sector" (Association of Student Conduct Administrators, 2006). Using federal and state laws, along with considering the institutional mission and identity, will give student conduct professionals direction as they develop residence hall processes and procedures that will be used to enforce those policies.

Institutions of higher education have the authority to regulate student conduct in and outside the classroom. This includes both academic and personal behaviors that violate a student code of conduct or honor code. As outlined by Kaplan and Lee (2009), "within the confines of constitutional law, public institutions may create rules for student conduct, and develop systems to determine whether a student has violated one or more rules, and if so, what punishment should be meted out. Private institutions have a little more leeway than public institutions, but the rules of private colleges must comport with state law and any state constitutional protections that may exist" (p. 441).

Public institutions also must ensure their policies and sanctions are equitable, clearly written for general understanding, and compliant with both local law and federal requirements. Private institutions have more flexibility in their processes since they do not fall under federal constitutional constraints. However, they are still required to demonstrate good administrative practices and provide fundamental fairness for students.

Institutional type and affiliation. Along with higher education institutions identifying as public or private, colleges and universities also will have intersected identities that align to their types and affiliations. These may include, but not be limited to, a religious affiliation, gender-specific student populations, or a professionally focused curriculum. Campuses also may benchmark their procedures against common or aspirational institutions based on geography, athletic conference membership, or other factors. As a result, when crafting a code of conduct, student conduct professionals must pay close attention to meet all institutional expectations.

For example, a student who violates the policy on drug possession of a medical or pharmacy institution may face greater professional or personal consequence than someone who violates the same policy at a liberal arts institution. Students enrolled in professional programs or career specialties are often held to different standards of conduct due to the professional standards of their chosen careers. A medical student who was a repeat drug offender, for example, would raise significant concerns about their ability to practice or prescribe medicine.

A campus housing program may decide that certain substance violations can result in severe sanctions, including removal from campus living. This is usually determined by the university administration and its community expectations. Some residence life programs may decide a first-time marijuana violation, for instance, would result in a possible removal from the residential community, while a similar institutional type and size may require a counseling assessment or an educational sanction after a first-time drug offense.

The conduct processes of religiously affiliated and faith-based institutions may be crafted to align with the principles and values of the institution and how they connect to the identified faith, traditions, and teachings. As one example, a Jesuit institution may address parietals differently from how other campuses would. Parietals are visiting guidelines that include the expectation of forbidding members of the opposite gender as overnight guests. While this community standard aligns directly with a Jesuit institution's mission and Catholic teachings, it can be difficult to execute and uphold. However, it gives residence life professionals a unique opportunity during the student conduct process to educate the students about their institutional values and the reasons behind institutional policies. A residence life professional working with a student through the conduct process should ask the student to relate their actions and behaviors to the institution's values.

Program-specific needs. Other contributing factors that must be considered when creating or updating policies in a residential community include whether that campus' residence halls include academic initiatives, such as themed housing, specialty floors, and living-learning communities. Such programs have gained in popularity as research has shown that students who live in these communities have higher grade point averages, are more connected to campus, are retained more easily, and have an increased persistence to graduation (Buch & Spaulding, 2008). Specifically, student involvement in the residence hall community may have an influence on learning and development that is different from in-class or other out-of-class experiences (Arboleda, et al., 2003).

Student conduct professionals should consider whether these communities require altered or community-specific policies due to their connection to specific skills or academic departments. A leadership-themed floor, for example, may receive the opportunity to designate and make recommendations for policy changes in their community. Providing this type of opportunity encourages the students to use the leadership skills they are acquiring by applying them to their everyday experiences. Similarly, a wellness floor may have higher standards for students who violate a drug or alcohol policy than a floor without such a focus. Consider offering students the opportunity to work together as a team to develop a higher standard of behavior that outlines different expectations for floor accountability.

Learning Outcomes

As part of the educational mission of the student conduct process, it is important when crafting and administering the process to understand that it is not a criminal process, nor should it be used as a substitute for a law code (Paterson & Kibler, 1998; Lancaster & Waryold, 2008; Alexander & Alexander, 2011). Educating students should always be the priority for any process. Violating institutional policy would never result in an outcome where the student would be subject to criminal conviction or federal adjudication (Paterson & Kibler, 1998). Therefore, hearing officers should not treat students as if they are going through a criminal proceeding and should avoid using criminal language writing the code of conduct.

Paterson & Kibler (1998) further explain the value of a hearing officer viewing everyone as a student as opposed to a defendant or prosecution witness. Making the distinction between the criminal and university process is necessary for residence life and student conduct professionals, due to the emphasis housing departments place on building community and developing responsible citizens. As outlined by appellate court judge Justice Blackmun, "School regulations are not to be measured by the same standards which prevail for criminal law and for criminal procedures" (*Esteban v. Central Missouri State College*, 1969). Similarly, in a case decided in 2000 in a United States District Court, the judge noted that student disciplinary proceedings "are not criminal in nature as they only regulate the relationship between the student and the university and have no bearing on a student's legal rights or obligations under state or federal criminal laws" (*United States v. Miami Univ.*, _F.3d._, Case No. 2-98-0097 (S.D. Ohio, 2000) (Smith, J.). A well-designed policy respects the important differences between student discipline and the criminal process.

Student conduct professionals should acknowledge that students may possess limited knowledge of what their experience will be as they go through the conduct process. It may be a natural response for students and parents to prepare to enter the hearing the same way they would prepare to go through the criminal process. Students and parents often mirror the language of a criminal process as opposed to that used in a student handbook. Some even consider hiring legal representation. Students and parents should be educated about the process to provide information on how to navigate the process and make informed decisions.

In addition to ensuring students understand the distinction between the conduct process and the criminal process, the hearing officer should also have a thorough understanding (Paterson & Kibler, 1998; Alexander & Alexander, 2011). When a student is documented for violating the code of conduct, there should never be a presumption that the student violated the code until the student has had an opportunity to be heard (Paterson & Kibler, 1998; Alexander & Alexander, 2011). This is critical in upholding the promise the institution has made to the student to maintain a safe and positive living environment where they will be treated with fairness and dignity despite their presumed actions

(Paterson & Kibler, 1998). To ensure ongoing student development, the conduct process should always seek to be educational and not punitive.

Finally, student conduct can not only educate students, but also can help retain them. "There is no other area in student affairs that offers a greater opportunity to make an impact on the growth and development of students than in student conduct" (Waryold & Lancaster, 2013, p. 5). Residence life practitioners can directly influence and affect the residence life community positively through the student conduct process.

As can be imagined, it is not easy to develop and administer a process that includes each of the components. However, as outlined by Paterson and Kibler (1998), developing such a process is one of the most important things a student conduct administrator can do for the campus community. How a student conduct professional crafts a code of conduct will have a direct impact on the living environment for students.

CREATING STUDENT CONDUCT PROCESSES

The purpose of creating community standards is to create the best environment in which students can live, learn, and grow into productive role models of the community. As Lancaster and Waryold (2008) summarize, "misconduct shows that the offending student is not getting the full benefit from the opportunity to develop in a positive living and learning environment" (p. 48).

The process of drafting and assessing a student conduct code allows all members of the community and the university administration to evaluate what choices they believe are educationally appropriate. Since a student conduct process can be a powerful instrument for encouraging an environment in which students live and learn successfully (Stoner, 2000), crafting such a conduct process should be done in a manner that preserves the dignity of each member of the community. When making an effort to create the best living environment, it is the obligation of students to treat all other members of the community with dignity and respect (Stoner, 2000). Although the process is designed to hold students accountable, some students will fail to live up to the community expectations; the process should be designed to protect the individual and every student's liberties and property rights as afforded by the Constitution and Fair Housing Act (Alexander & Alexander, 2011).

Residence life professionals have a responsibility to craft and develop conduct processes that are educational and developmental, and provide students with the ability to acquire new skills and a deeper sense of their ethical and moral selves. A code of conduct is not simply "rules and regulations" for students to follow. It establishes how the community will govern, provide accountability to its members, and let all residents have a positive living experience. College and university administrators should identify important principles about their processes when drafting their own student disciplinary codes (Stoner & Lowery, 2004).

When reviewing the conduct process, the institution will need to remember basic student affairs concepts that include treating all students with equal care, fairness, and dignity. Tamara L. King, associate vice chancellor for student support and wellness at Washington University in St. Louis, 2009 ASCA president, and an acknowledged leader in the field of student conduct, offers several recommendations when reviewing and crafting a conduct process. First, she suggests being thoughtful and critical about new processes and procedures while considering multiple viewpoints when learning about new developments and promising practices in the field. Knowing the campus's student body is key. Second, processes should consider any campus-specific contextual dynamics, campus culture, or institutional political climates while recognizing that not every new idea, program, or policy is applicable, transferable, or appropriate for that campus. Finally, the department should engage in continuous, ongoing assessment to know if processes are effective or a revision is needed. Having these elements in mind will ensure any policy creation or revision is appropriate and meets the institutional mission.

Conduct Process Committees

When beginning the process of developing or reviewing the student conduct process, a committee that includes members from the campus community should be formed. Members could include, but are not limited to, key stakeholders in the divisions of student affairs, residence life, student conduct, athletics, faculty, and the student body (Stoner, 2000). In the process of identifying members of the community, ask, "Who are the right people sitting around the table to manage this process effectively?" Participation from a diverse group of community members will provide an opportunity for feedback and internal guidance while offering a collaborative approach to shared community expectations. Dawn Eades, associate dean of students at Massachusetts College of Pharmacy and Health Sciences University in Boston, Massachusetts, recommends:

> When developing a code of conduct task force, include student affairs staff, faculty members, non-student–affairs staff, and students. Invite an outside student affairs leader to come in as a guest speaker to discuss the importance of the task force and what goes into revising the conduct process. It was through these task force meetings [that] I realized how little the university community knew about the code of conduct and discipline process. Much time was spent discussing student development and having an educational process that aligns with the mission of the university. From there, we spent two semesters making revisions

for senior-level leadership to review and accept or reject recommended changes. (Eades, 2018)

Keep in mind that the group should be relatively small for it to work effectively. Setting goals and objectives for the group will assist in crafting a vision and timeline.

Before starting a review process, student affairs practitioners should request to meet with the chief student affairs officer to review community expectations, deadlines, and objectives for the working group. The chief student affairs officer at the university has ultimate authority on code and conduct revisions, and will provide expectations and feedback about the revision process. A student conduct administrator should consider inviting the following community members to serve on the review committee.

Legal staff members. Understandably, the law and legal requirements for the student code of conduct should play a significant role in the review process. According to Stone (2000), legal counsel must be involved in reviewing disciplinary policies because students who have been sanctioned through the university or residential process could bring lawsuits against the institution. Requesting legal counsel to participate in the code review will provide a deeper understanding of the institution's policies and enables practitioners to be more effective in communicating about the process if challenged by outside counsel. Involve legal counsel when reviewing recent Clery Act reports and institutional policy violations from the past three years. This will provide guidance on conduct trends and the legal obligations that the institution must follow.

Student affairs directors. The directors of the residence life, student conduct, and public safety offices should all be invited to work with the committee directly or indirectly. Each of these departments has responsibilities that align directly with the student code of conduct and how the institution will address policy violations.

Faculty members. Engaging faculty in this type of committee work is often rewarding and can lead to stronger campus partnerships between academic and student affairs.

Health and wellness staff members. A member of the health and wellness department or the counseling center will assist in guiding committee discussions centered about drugs, alcohol, and mental health concerns.

Title IX coordinator. Due to the sensitive nature of sexual misconduct incidents, the committee should have the Title IX coordinator or designee sit on the committee.

Institution-specific positions. While almost all institutions fall under private or public, it is important to consider institutional identity when selecting committee members. A clergy member, faculty-in-residence, or alumnus who is knowledgeable about student conduct should be sought out strategically to work with the review committee.

Student representatives. Great committees are ones that afford opportunities for students to provide feedback and recommendations on light of their student experiences. Student conduct professionals should consider asking two to three students to participate in the process and may want to consider inviting a student who has gone through the conduct process. There is no better feedback than direct feedback.

Student athletes. The NCAA has many rules and regulations centered around student behavior. A member of the athletic administration team or a coach will enable the committee to learn how some teams and coaches set higher expectations for their student-athletes — in many cases, student-athletes can be held accountable not only by residence life but also by athletics or their coach.

Process Elements

When creating or revising the student conduct code, one of the first places for the committee to start is deciding what elements will make up the process and how the process will be laid out. This is important because anyone who reads the code should get a sense of what the process entails, the general order the process will take, and what it will potentially feel like to be a participant or supporter of a participant in the process. Being transparent about the process can also give students, faculty, staff, families, and other key stakeholders a sense of security and fairness about the process as a whole.

A sound code of conduct should describe the elements of the conduct process accurately. While each institution's code of conduct can and should differ, some aspects of the student conduct process are considered universal and should factor into the policy creation and revision process.

While residence life professionals may not be an active part of each stage of the student conduct process, they do need to understand each element of the process. Understanding the conduct process in full ensures professionals can fully engage in a code creation or revision process, answer stakeholder questions regarding the process, and — depending on the campus — potentially serve as a hearing or appellate officer. Here several common elements to many codes of conduct.

Official notice. One fundamental element includes providing students with written notice when an incident is documented and an alleged policy violation has occurred. Written notice should include both physical and electronic communication. The notice should include a summary or description of what occurred, details of how the process works, and potential charges resulting from the incident. The notice should also identify a date, time, and location for the student to meet with a residence life professional regarding the incident. This meeting generally is referred to as a pre-hearing or information session.

Pre-hearing. Many campuses, either formally in their code of conduct or informally in their practice, allow students to conduct a pre-hearing or information session meeting regarding their incident. At this meeting, the student receives more information regarding the incident, reviews all associated incident documentation or information in the student's case file, and receives an outline of the conduct process, along with their rights and responsibilities as a participant in the process. These meetings generally are held to calm student fears regarding the process; help students understand its purpose; and address logistical issues, such as when, where, and with whom their hearing will take place. Before the meeting adjourns, the student should receive a physical or electronic record of the pre-hearing or information session meeting and any other information needed before the actual hearing occurs.

Hearing. The hearing is the setting for students to address any concerns and violations of policy alleged to have occurred during the incident. Students should be afforded an opportunity to be heard, dispute information, and present supporting documentation (Alexander & Alexander, 2011). Hearings can be both formal and informal in nature.

The committee should discuss if and under what circumstances residence life professionals adjudicate alleged policy violations through formal and informal hearings, and codes of conduct with both options should be clear on the distinctions between the two. For policy violations considered less egregious, an institution may wish to offer an informal resolution mechanism for students to quickly and efficiently accept responsibility for the violation(s) while still protecting students' rights. The code of conduct should also address whether an informal resolution to a case is an option, and if so, under what circumstances an informal resolution is available and what that process entails.

A solid understanding of due process rights afforded to the students will provide a baseline of how to craft and administer the process to ensure students and their property rights are protected. Protecting students from violations of due process will also provide students with the freedom and ability to maximize their experience in going through the conduct process. When students feel comfortable about participating in the process, it allows the hearing officer a chance to develop a solid understanding of the incident. Then, if the student accepts responsibility or is found responsible, the hearing officer will be in the best position to identify the education or sanction needed to help repair the harm caused to others, the community, and the student who allegedly violated policy.

Sanctions. If a student is found responsible for violating the code of conduct or honor code, the hearing officer or body should assign sanctions appropriate for the incident that support student learning and institutional expectations. While a student code of conduct or honor code usually does not name specific sanctions, some violations may be codified depending on institutional mission, culture, or values. Sanctions should be designed and assigned with the education of the student in mind. (Chapter 8 discusses approaches to and development of sanctions in greater detail.)

Advisors. At most institutions, students do not have the right to be represented by an attorney as they navigate through the conduct process; however, most colleges do permit students to have an advisor present at a hearing. Typically, an advisor provides support to the student as they prepare for their hearing and can attend all relevant meetings with the student and hearing officer. Katie Collins, director of student involvement and seasoned conduct advisor at Newbury College in Brookline, Massachusetts, offers:

> An advisor can help support and bring equity to a process for students who do not know how to advocate for themselves. Talking with an advisor before a hearing can help a student think more thoroughly through the process and how to communicate information in a way that is honest and respectful. When students have a person who is in their corner during the process, it assists in setting the student up for success and can diminish the fears and anxiety that can occur during conduct hearings. (Collins, 2018)

The advisor may also support the student through the appeals process (when applicable), provided the advisor does not participate on behalf of the student during their hearings and meetings. Institutional advisors should be trained annually on the institution's conduct process so they can assist students in navigating it. Residence life professionals should consult with departmental supervisors and other campus student conduct personnel before serving as an advisor in a student's conduct process to ensure avoiding the perception of bias or conflict of interest.

Today, publicity concerns and increased involvement of attorneys in the conduct process can complicate already-difficult situations. In many discipline situations, such as those involving allegations of sexual misconduct, discipline outcomes correlate to negative institutional visibility. For professionals in residence life, it is no longer uncommon for attorneys to threaten lawsuits challenging student conduct regulations and policies (Stoner, 2000). Often, the interpretations of events may not reflect the reality of the situation, but still may put pressure on the student discipline process. Residence life professionals should work with departmental supervisors, campus conduct professionals, and campus general counsel to address any concerns appropriately that are presented by attorneys during the conduct process.

Appeal. A reliable code of conduct should include information about how and under what circumstances a student can appeal a first-level hearing decision. Common reasons used as grounds for appeals in student conduct include errors that violate a student's due process rights; demonstrated bias or prejudice by the hearing officer or body precluding an impartial hearing; new information not reasonably available at the time of the first-level hearing that would have substantially affected the outcome; assigning sanctions disproportionate to the violation committed; and the information presented at the first-level hearing not supporting a finding of responsibility.

The code of conduct should include a description of the appellate process; how decisions are reached; what, if any, decisions are recommendations as opposed to final decisions; and what constitutes final agency action. That is when the institution reaches its conclusion with a case and any further appeals or remedies sought for would have to be pursued through the criminal or civil court process.

Most housing conduct cases follow the same appellate process as non-housing cases; any institution wanting a separate appellate process for housing conduct cases should describe that process thoroughly and accurately. While most residence life professionals are likely to have little if any involvement in the appellate process, staff should be aware of what the process is in case they serve as an appellate officer or have to answer student questions regarding the process.

Conduct Process Implementation

In addition to crafting and administering a conduct process that preserves individual dignity, protects individual property rights, and fosters learning and development, it is equally as important to ensure the details of the process are communicated effectively to the college and university community (Lancaster & Waryold, 2008). This implementation process should be modified to identify the most-effective method for the particular campus community needs. However, a few steps should be consistent across campuses.

Review. To promote a good residential environment, institutions should review their student conduct process and policies regularly. Regular reviews of the student conduct process and policies can ensure these are relevant and continue to support the institution's educational mission (Stoner, 2000). One critical best practice is to review the department's policies either annually or bi-annually to keep the conduct code relevant to the latest innovative misbehaviors by college students (Lancaster & Waryold, 2008).

According to Stoner (2000), conducting an institutional review every three years is an ideal review model for student conduct processes. This will ensure the code of conduct is relevant and timely, and includes updated laws, legislation, and current national misconduct trends. The student discipline policies resulting from a systematic review will help nurture the living and learning environment on campus, while still preserving students' rights and reinforcing their responsibilities. Policies and procedures consistent with best practices and legal requirements will enable student conduct administrators to create and enforce sanctions consistent with local and federal laws protecting the institution from liability. It may be helpful to gather a list of comparison schools to benchmark and review their overarching codes of conduct. The review committee may also find other similar institutions have standards that reflect the current process in place (Stoner, 2000).

Before releasing the process to the overall community, the process should be reviewed and approved by members of the relevant departments, as well as the institutional administration (Lancaster & Waryold, 2008). One common way to ensure an updated code of conduct has been thoroughly vetted is by hosting open forums on campus, including in residence halls. This allows any interested institutional community stakeholders to voice concerns, support, or ideas before the final code of conduct is adopted. Members of the code of conduct committee can visit student organization meetings, such as the Residence Hall Association, National Residence Hall Honorary, Student Government Association, Student Activities Board, fraternity and sorority chapters and councils, or identity-based student groups, to share information, answer questions, and address potential issues. Effectively communicating the process to the institutional administration will ensure staff has the support needed when or if there is pushback from other members of the community (e.g., faculty, staff, or students).

Training. Although it is time-consuming, effectively training every level of staff (residential learning student and professional staff, operations and assignments staff, and facilities and maintenance staff) both in housing and across campus (faculty and staff in residential colleges, university police, student conduct office, etc.) will provide a consistent message to the students in relation to the housing conduct process.

This training process should occur annually and include every individual serving as a hearing officer or support person in the process (Lancaster & Waryold, 2008). It should include an in-depth discussion of the guiding philosophy of the conduct process, what the conduct process means in the context of on-campus housing, the staff's role in implementing the process, and how the student conduct process can be used as an effective community-builder.

While it could be easy to fall into the trap of only using a lecture format to facilitate training on the student conduct process, numerous learning styles should be engaged in teaching staff about the student conduct process. Videos, hands-on demonstrations, shadowing staff opportunities, and printed or electronic learning manuals can all help staff learn how to administer the student conduct process properly.

At Florida State University, for example, residence life professionals and graduate assistants engage in role playing to give new staff a chance to learn and practice in a safe, friendly environment before facilitating cases on their own. The new staff receive scripted documentation and fictitious incident information before the role plays. At the role plays, new staff members are paired with returning staff, some of whom take the role of the charged student while others portray coaches for the new staff. New staff members facilitate the practice hearings, and both the returning staff actor and coach give suggestions and offer feedback to help the new staff learn and grow. To close, all of the staff share thoughts, tips, and advice for being effective hearing officers.

Residence life student conduct hearing officers will only be as successful as the training they receive. The more hands-on training opportunities staff get to learn and improve, the more likely they are to serve as effective hearing officers for residential students.

Communication. Once the staff has been properly trained, evaluate the most effective ways to distribute information to the community. Communicating the student code of conduct to the campus community can take many forms, including flyers, posters, advertisements around campus and at athletic events, social media, email, campus videos, pamphlets, and handbooks.

One advantage of campus housing is staff has direct access to the students they serve. Ideally, the standards of the community should be communicated to students *before* their arrival on campus. Student conduct professionals should work with campus partners such as residence life and housing, student affairs, and new student orientation to identify opportunities to present community expectations to incoming students and parents. Another way to communicate

✚ Using Information Technology

Today's student affairs professionals should never underestimate the role that information technology plays in the student conduct process and how online resources can be used effectively and efficiently. Lancaster and Waryold (2008) defined information technology as a tool for managing information using computers and computer software to convert, store, protect, transmit, and retrieve information. Nearly 10 years ago, they painted a picture of an office of student conduct from the future in which reports of misconduct would be sent electronically through a secure website, record-keeping would be completely paperless, and all correspondence would be sent through electronic mail.

That vision has largely come true as information technology has been ingrained in the work of residence life professionals. For the most part, there are hardly any institutions not using some form of information technology in their conduct process, whether it is using e-mail to communicate with students and colleagues, managing a website that provides resources to community members related to their department, social media pages, or some form of a program designed to manage data.

One of the crucial applications of student conduct administration is data management. The enactment of the Family Educational Rights and Privacy Act of 1974 (FERPA) stated as the condition of federal funds that institutions comply with prescribed procedures in keeping and releasing students' educational records. Disciplinary files maintained in the context of the university setting are protected under FERPA. The word "maintained" suggests FERPA records are stored in a filing cabinet in a records room on campus or a permanent secure database. Over the years, though, the field has transitioned from using paper-based systems to electronic data management systems to assist in managing the significant amounts of disciplinary records required to be maintained in accordance with campus, state, and federal privacy laws (Lancaster & Waryold, 2008).

Lancaster and Waryold also say that regarding record retention, an electronic record is considered no different from a physical record. An electronic student conduct database should be considered a resource shared in the department or with other institutional units where multiple administrators can access the same student information instantaneously. However, there must be expectations about which data should and should not be included in the case file.

continued on next page

➕ Using Information Technology

continued from previous page

Within student housing, information technology comes in various forms, including but not limited to housing management systems, access control systems (student/staff access to buildings and rooms, electronic key boxes, key cards and scanners, check-in and checkout process), housing work order systems, departmental computers, display boards, interface software with various campus partners, and a host of other resources that have changed the way in which housing practitioners function in their day-to-day work. As a result, when crafting your process, consider the way these resources (or lack thereof) will affect the work that housing hearing officers will do.

In addition to housing data, most online databases include mechanisms that allow departments to run reports specific to their campus. Having this information can help the department better understand trends or issues within their campus community and pinpoint specific education to address those trends. If a hearing officer notices an increase in the amount of vandalism occurring in their community, they could execute educational programming geared toward addressing this issue. To help the hearing officer gain support from the department and building staff, the hearing officer can use information generated during an analysis of the caseload to show there has been a shift in the specific behavior. The hearing officer can also highlight whether a specific type of vandalism, for instance, is more prevalent. Developing community-specific education is important in helping individuals understand the challenges the community is facing, since no two communities are the same.

In the near and farther future, student conduct professionals will find themselves using information technology in their daily work, whether it involves checking camera footage to identify students involved in an incident or reviewing sign-in logs to identify whether an alleged policy violator was in the building. That means residence life professionals should work to ensure staff members are aware of and appropriately trained in how to use the resources available to them on campus.

this material to students is through educational programming or learning plans facilitated by building-level student and professional staff. Signage should be used to help students understand community expectations and ways to identify resources. By engaging multiple modes of communication, residence life professionals can support promoting student understanding of the code of conduct.

Published code of conduct. It is now common practice for colleges and universities to have a published student code of conduct, either online, in print, or both. Having a written student code of conduct, such as in a pamphlet or handbook, enables the university to educate students about how to behave appropriately as members of an academic and residential community, as well as highlighting community expectations (Lancaster & Waryold, 2008; Stoner & Lowery, 2004).

A well-defined handbook is one of the best methods of communicating the expectations an institution has for community standards. A student conduct professional should consider the following common content areas when developing or updating a student handbook.

- **Institutional and residence life mission statements.** The mission statement provides a basis for accountability and institutional and departmental direction. The values of the institution and department should be clearly defined.
- **Institutional and departmental policies.** Policies serve as the foundation for how the community is defined and what its conduct parameters are. Definitions of conduct terms should be included in the section to provide transparency and a greater understanding of how the policies are defined.
- **Students' rights and responsibilities.** These provide a general notice to students of their rights and responsibilities as members of the community. This area should include the role of advisors (when applicable), notice of charges, the role of pre-hearings, the assigned conduct officer or hearing board, and the level of offense.
- **Length of process and expected timeline of events.** A prompt and efficient process plays a significant part in providing due process and fairness to students. "A good goal is to try and complete the large majority of matters in 7 days and all matters (including the appeal) within 30 days" (Lancaster & Waryold, 2008, p. 49). While some cases may require additional time, carefully consider the reason for a delay before extending the process.
- **Sanctions.** Refer to the definitions of conduct terms. This area should describe possible sanctions for different outcomes. When possible,

choose sanctions that provide opportunities for students to repair the harm done by their behaviors.
- **Appeals process.** All students should be afforded the right to an appeal, regardless of what type of sanction has been imposed. How a student can file or write an appeal should be clearly described and reviewed with the student in person, and identify the appellate officer.

No matter how the message is communicated, it should be relayed intentionally with attention to tone and how the message will be heard and understood in mind. When communicating the student code of conduct process, remember to explain how the department will respond to a case. This information should also include the due process rights afforded to a student if who is charged as potentially violating the code of conduct. From the development phase through communication of the finished product, avoid being vague and overly broad in content — community members should have specific guidance on university policy, so policies should be drafted with the appropriate degree of specificity. *Woodis v. Westark Community College* (1998) notes that "the more obvious it would be to the average person that one's behavior is prohibited, the less likely the court would be to void a rule of vagueness." Including as many members of the campus community as possible in the crafting and revision process can ensure community safety is highlighted; the student conduct process is easily understood; and the positive, educational environment of the residence halls is promoted.

CONCLUSION

Think back to the example from 1870, when desired conduct could be summed up in six straightforward rules. Where students then were asked to be "kind and respectful to others," now institutions need to concern themselves with cyber-bullying. Forbidden use of "profanity, or indecent language" has turned into free speech issues involving posters and signs. Today, not only are young men and women allowed to walk together, policies must account for gender-inclusive housing and co-ed floors. The worlds are wholly different, yet, in many ways, the processes institutions use today to create their policies and procedures are not that different. The process adapts and changes to evolve with the times.

As Lancaster and Waryold (2008) summarized, "misconduct shows that the offending student is not getting the full benefit from the opportunity to develop in a positive living and learning environment" (p. 48). Residence life and conduct professionals are responsible for crafting and developing conduct processes that are educational and developmental, and that provide students with the ability to acquire new skills and a deeper sense of their ethical and moral selves.

For these professionals, crafting or revising the conduct process and codes of conduct can provide a unique educational opportunity for students to learn from their behaviors and how it impacts their community. A code of conduct is not simply rules and regulations for students to follow. It establishes how the community will govern, provide accountability to its members, and allow for all residents to have a positive living experience.

REFERENCES

Alexander, K. W., & Alexander, K. (2011). *Higher education law: policy and perspectives.* New York, NY: Routledge, 2011.

Arboleda, A., Wang, Y., Shelley, M. C., & Whalen, D. F. (2003). Predictors of residence hall involvement. *Journal of College Student Development 44*(4), 517–531.

Association for Student Conduct Administration. (2017). *Ethical principles and practices in student conduct administration.* Retrieved from http://www.theasca.org/files/Governing%20Documents/ASCA%20Principles%20and%20Practices%20-%20Feb%202017.pdf.

Association of College and University Housing Officers-International. (2017). *ACUHO-I standards and ethical principles for college and university housing professionals.* Retrieved from http://www.acuho-i.org/Portals/0/doc/res/2017-acuhoi-standards.pdf .

Bowen, W., & Tobin, E. (2015). *Locus of authority.* Princeton, NJ: Princeton University Press.

Buch, K., & Spaulding, S. (2008). A longitudinal assessment of an initial cohort in a psychology learning community. *Teaching of Psychology, 35,* 189–193.

Donaldson, J. N., & Steyer, S. (1997). Discipline in the halls: Perceptions of the residential judicial program. *Journal of College and University Student Housing, 26*(1), 39–44.

Hustoles, C., & Palmer, L. (2015). Through the eyes of higher education attorneys: How department chairs are navigating the waters of legal Issues and risk management. *Journal of Law and Education. 41*(1), 118–146.

Kaplan, W., & Lee, B. (2009). *A legal guide for student affairs professionals.* San Francisco, CA: Jossey-Bass.

Lancaster, J., & Waryold, D. (2008). *Student Conduct Practice the Complete Guide for Student Affairs Professionals.* Sterling, VA: Stylus Publishing.

McClellan, G. S., & Stringer, J. (Eds.). (2009). *The handbook of student affairs administration (sponsored by NASPA, Student Affairs Administrators in Higher Education).* San Francisco, CA: John Wiley & Sons.

Patterson, B. G., and Kibler, W. L. (Eds.). (1998). *The administration of campus discipline: Student, organizational and community issues.* Asheville, NC: College Administration Publications.

Poullard, J. (2011). What is the relationship between changing university policy and changing student norms?: Where policy meets student behavior. In J. Baxter Magolda, M. B., & Magolda, P. M. (Eds.), *Contested Issues in Student Affairs: Diverse Perspectives and Respectful Dialogue,* 142–153. Sterling, VA: Stylus Publishing.

Nikolaevna, M., and Alexandrovna, N. (2016). On using the results of the SWOT analysis for Academic Writing Syllabus Design. *GESJ: Education Science and Psychology. 5*(42).

Schrage, J., & Giacomini, N. (2009). *Reframing Campus Conflict.* Sterling, VA: Stylus Publishing.

Sinek, S. (2009). *Start with why how great leaders inspire everyone to take action.* New York, NY: Penguin Group.

Sokolaw, B. (2004). *Crafting a Code of Conduct for the 21st Century College* White Paper. Berwyn, PA: National Center for Higher Education Risk Management.

Stoner, E. N. (2000). *Reviewing Your Student Discipline Policy: A Project Worth the Investment.* United Educators.

Stoner, E., & Lowery, J. (2004). Navigating past the spirit of insubordination: Twenty-first century model student conduct code with model hearing script. *Journal of College and University Law, 31*(1), 1–78.

University of Mississippi Case Study. (n.d). Retrieved from https://www.badgepass.com/wp-content/themes/badgepass2017/resources/brochures/case-studies/ole-miss.pdf.

Von Bergen, C. W. (2015). Emotional support animals, service animals, and pets on campus. *Administrative Issues Journal: Education, Practice & Research, 5*(1), 15–34. doi:10.5929/2015.5.1.3.

Waryold, D. M., & Lancaster, J. M. (2013). *The good, the bad, and ugly of student conduct administration: Tips on working wisely.* Boone, NC: Appalachian State University.

Notes

1. Jefferson's letter of November 2, 1822, was to Thomas Cooper, second president of South Carolina College (now called the University of South Carolina) (1884). *The Works of Thomas Jefferson*, Vol. VII, 268.

2. Cowley, W.H. (1937). "The disappearing dean of men." Paper presented at 19th annual conference of the National Association of Deans and Advisers of Men, Austin, TX (reported in the verbatim transcript of the conference proceedings, 85–102).

1. In what ways can the conduct process be educational for the students involved?

2. How should conduct administrators use local and federal laws to guide the development of a student handbook?

3. What are some common conduct process concerns students have shared? How can housing and conduct professionals take feedback and put it into action?

4. In what way do the goals and outcomes of your department's conduct process promote a positive living experience for students?

5. It what ways does your department work to restore justice to the community once a violation has occurred?

6. In what ways does your conduct process currently support students' moral and ethical development? What, if anything, can be updated, modified, or changed to better support that development?

6

CONNECTING CONDUCT AND SOCIAL JUSTICE

Mallory Martin-Ferguson, Delmy M. Lendof, and Denise Balfour Simpson

CAMPUS CONDUCT is not simply about misbehavior followed by punitive reactions. Conduct professionals — those who operate both within residential environments and across entire campuses — have a unique role in establishing campus community and addressing student behaviors in a way that furthers student development and learning.

In building community, housing and conduct professionals are encouraged to balance the needs of the community with the needs of those *in* the community. However, maintaining the balance between community and individual is not always an easy task. This challenge can be clear particularly when housing and conduct professionals must respond to incidents that address human rights and equality, such as cases related to bias, hate crimes, freedom of speech, bullying, and other topics involving what is considered to be fair and just among the individuals in a society.

This is the importance of framing campus conduct in a social justice lens. As housing and residence life professionals pursue their primary charge to create and maintain a sense of community in the residential environment, the tenets of social justice are a valuable resource. While colleges and universities generally have policies and procedures for managing basic issues of student misconduct, incidents involving diversity and social justice needs tend to be more complex and sometimes require additional efforts.

As colleges and universities look to elevate their student service systems, the staff must consider the intricacies of connecting conduct and social justice even for incidents that do not meet the standard for a policy violation. With this approach, student conduct processes can serve as a tool to engage in dialogue, foster inclusion, and support learning.

UNDERSTANDING SOCIAL JUSTICE

Social justice is defined as the distribution of advantages and disadvantages, opportunities, resources, and privilege in society (Martin & McLittle, 2016). These elements and their availability are linked to social identities that affect individuals' personal lives, their worldviews, and their interactions with others.

In discussing social justice, resources can be physical (owning a home or receiving a consistent paycheck), as well as accessible (a stable transportation system and awareness of how to navigate in society via social capital). While these straightforward definitions are easy to grasp, a broader concept to define is that of privilege. Within the social justice framework, privilege is a term used to describe unearned access to resources only readily available because of one's social group membership (Adams, Bell, & Griffin, 1997).

Society grants privilege to certain individuals based on their social identities. Those in a position of privilege can use their positions to benefit others with more or the same level of privilege or they can oppress those with less privilege. For example, those who belong to dominant social groups (e.g., male, heterosexual, Christian, Caucasian, middle- or upper-class socioeconomic standing) experience privileges in society because of the existing social structures.

To discuss social justice better, some other terms must be understood. Particularly in efforts in building a unified community, definitions are beneficial for a shared understanding and common language.

- **Culture** is reflected as learned and shared values, beliefs, and behaviors in a community of people; "a dynamic process, not a reified construct, and is based on the notion that culture continually undergoes transformation" (Bennett, 2015, p. xxiii). Culture often includes diverse aspects of identity, such as nationality, ethnicity, gender, age, physical characteristics, sexual orientation, economic status, education, profession, religion, and organizational affiliation.
- **Diversity** is used in student affairs to discuss staff demographics, student enrollment, and campus offerings (Martin & McLittle, 2016). At its base level, diversity means difference. People are all different, and those differences are to be recognized and celebrated. Society places value on differences, which affect how the more mainstream, common, or accepted people feel and operate in the world. Student interactions centered on the diversity in housing communities can foster relationships and a sense of belonging.
- **Inclusion** is a feeling of belonging and connection to spaces and individuals (Martin & McLittle, 2016). Inclusion is about ensuring people feel comfortable being who they are, have the space to be who they are, and see themselves within a community. This is an important frame-

work for housing and residence life professionals to ensure students feel belonging and can succeed within the residential environment. Inclusivity is no easy feat, since it requires intentional planning and recognition of identities other than the majority or dominant identity. Inclusion is about moving from a stance of invitation to one where the inherent value and presence of people is already recognized and built into processes and places. Examples of this include, but are not limited to, access to bathrooms and buildings; visual representations of students, faculty, and staff in the community; resources to support underrepresented groups; names used on campus buildings; and languages used in policies and documents.

- **Equality** and **equity** are concepts rooted in power, privilege, and oppression (Martin & McLittle, 2016). Equality seeks to promote fairness and justice as it aims to ensure everyone gets the same thing and starts at the same place. Equity, on the other hand, aims to give everyone what they need to be successful; in other words, equal opportunity for all regardless of social identity. An oft-used analogy is tequity means everyone gets a pair of shoes while equality means everyone gets a pair of shoes that fit.

- **Power** is defined by access to the resources that enhance chance of having what they need to live a safe, productive, enriching life (Adams, Bell, & Griffin, 1997). Examples of power are found in social structures (e.g., media, education, criminal justice systems, government, and societal values) and can be allocated, determined by a level of authority, or based on personal morals and beliefs.

- **Intercultural competence** is defined by Bennett (2015) as "knowledge, attitudes, and skills that enhance the effectiveness and appropriateness of interaction in a range of intercultural contexts" (p. 53).

- **Intercultural communication** is "the interactive process of negotiating shared meanings across cultures" (Bennett, 2015, p. xxiii). Furthermore, intercultural communication "involves an exchange between people who are different culturally. People can be perceived as culturally different because of gender, race, ethnicity, sexual orientation, religion, disability, or mental health status" (Bennett, 2015, p. 32). Intercultural communication "focuses on patterns of interaction between people from different cultures as they engage in mutual meaning-making, including the process of developing intercultural competence as bridging differences." A similar term, cross-cultural communication, "compares one culture with another among a pair of cultures (or a variety of cultures)" (p. 157).

Bennett's distinction between intercultural and cross-cultural communication informs the choice to use the word *intercultural* in this chapter. Intercultural communication expands the dialogue to include connectedness through interaction, which creates a climate of learning and shared understanding, and reinforces the concept of building community through conduct.

Social Justice and the Housing Mission

Addressing student behavior, upholding campus and community values, and ensuring student safety are accepted outcomes of student conduct and campus housing systems across institutions. The housing and residence life community is uniquely poised to address each of these aspects of a student's growth. The physical structures provide safety and security; the staffing presence offers care and support; and the multitude of programs, events, and opportunities offered in the community give residents the ability to engage and develop along with diverse community members.

The connection between conduct and social justice forms in addressing behavior in these multifaceted communities. Institutions such as the Council for the Advancement of Standards (CAS) in Higher Education accept and support these standards, which provides a foundation for administrators involved in the conduct process. The CAS (2009) statement of shared ethical principles, Principle IV – Justice, states that:

> We actively promote human dignity and endorse equality and fairness for everyone. We treat others with respect and fairness, preserving their dignity, honoring their differences, promoting their welfare. We recognize diversity and embrace a cross-cultural approach in support of the worth, dignity, potential, and uniqueness of people within their social and cultural contexts. We eliminate barriers that impede student learning and development or discriminate against full participation by all students. We extend fundamental fairness to all persons. We operate within the framework of laws and policies. We respect the rights of individuals and groups to express their opinions. We assess students in a valid, open, and fair manner and one consistent with learning objectives. We examine the influence of power on the experience of diversity to reduce marginalization and foster community. (p. 24)

However, it cannot be assumed conduct and housing systems in all institutions share this belief or are structured for and have allocated the proper resources to support this connection. For example, following up on a student's behavior is important to ensure proper educational measures are in place and staff members are performing their due diligence to mitigate risk for the institution. Housing and residence life conduct officers work to follow up on resident behavior, yet also have the added layer of addressing residential community needs in ways campus conduct officers are not be poised to do.

As a result, housing and residence life conduct officers engage with conflict in a fluid way, considering the needs of the student, other residents, the floor, their student staff, and the larger residential community in its context or relationship to the university.

All of this work requires a commitment from both the department and the college or university. One way to advocate for that commitment is to ensure that those values — care, respect, safety, engagement, inclusivity, development, etc. — are incorporated and expressed in the organization's mission. Consider the following public mission statements from a variety of housing and residence life departments.

> **Howard University.** "The Department of Residence Life at Howard University, in support of the division of Student Affairs mission, is committed to creating and supporting a rich learning environment in a community of care and mutual respect that will empower students to be engaging citizens through fostering their development of lifelong skills. HU Housing & Residence Life will provide safe, inclusive, and secure residential communities where a diverse and innovative team of professionals encourages students to pursue academic excellence, personal growth, civic leadership, and responsibility." (*Residence Life and University Housing*, 2017)

> **Georgetown University.** "Georgetown University embraces its inclusive tradition [of] valuing the diversity present in our community and treating all with dignity. Living in a community calls each individual to challenge, support and encourage one another in a relationship of mutual trust and respect." (*Mission, Values, and Vision: Residential Living*, 2017)

> **Loyola University Chicago.** "In partnership with our residents, the Department of Residence Life enhances the Loyola Experience by providing safe and supportive living communities where students can engage with others, explore their personal identity, and develop a deeper understanding of their impact on the world." (*Residence Life, Mission*, 2017)

> **Florida International University.** "The diversity of our residential community takes many forms. It includes differences related to race, ethnicity, national origin, gender, socioeconomic status, sexual orienta-

tion, religion, age and ability. We believe that any form of discrimination against any individual or group is a threat to the welfare of the entire community. We are guided by the belief that celebrating diversity enriches and empowers the lives of all people. Therefore, everyone who chooses to live in or visit our residential communities must understand that we will not tolerate any form of bigotry, harassment, intimidation, threat, or abuse, whether verbal or written, physical or psychological, direct or implied. Our residential communities are rich, alive and dynamic environments that are designed to enable all individuals to develop and grow to their full potential. All members of the community are encouraged to live by these principles so that we can foster a successful learning environment." (*Housing and Residential Life Diversity Statement*, 2017)

University of California Santa Barbara. "UCSB is a distinguished university recognized for its leadership by state, national, and world academic communities. Housing, Dining, & Auxiliary Enterprises exists as an integral part of the educational program and academic services of UCSB. Inherent in the operation of Housing & Residential Services is the formation and support of an atmosphere that is conducive to living and learning for our residents and for those who use our services. Housing & Residential Services promotes the academic mission of UCSB and creates through support services and developmental programs a sense of community among students, faculty and staff." (*Housing, Dining, and Auxiliary Enterprises*, 2017)

It is easy to see how these statements strive to balance the needs of both the individuals and the community, as well as the unique identities that comprise both. By recognizing the impact identities have in how individuals interact with the world (and how others interact in return), the importance of understanding these identities within oneself and others becomes clear. Social justice is about social group identity — simply having a shared identity does not equate to a shared experience with said identity. However, systems of power, privilege, and oppression are carried out and enacted in groups, which then influence an individual's experience. The residence community can offer a safe, supportive, and structured place to engage in diversity; indeed, this is the hope of residential programs. Furthermore, the housing and residence life conduct process can offer the opportunity to respond in just and inclusive ways when negative behaviors occur. This adaptive response is what connects conduct and social justice, since no student or community has the same needs.

Housing and residence life programs serve multiple students who have varying needs, backgrounds, experiences, and identities. This can be exciting for students without exposure to diversity in their home communities and, at the same time, jarring as diversity confronts students in new ways. As a result, students may feel increasingly connected to their community because they feel an immense sense of belonging — or extremely isolated or further marginalized in a community that does not recognize their identity. Thus, it is critical housing and residence life conduct professionals know how to navigate identity and diversity when it shows up through conflict in the community.

One helpful response in this effort is to normalize how conflict occurs and share how conflict is a part of life. By the nature of living in a community of individuals who have differences among them, one can expect conflict to arise at times. It might help to remind community members that "conflicts represent a potential for activity, for participation" (Christie, 1977, p. 7). Social identities and lived experiences inform an individual's response to conflict. Common examples of conversations in differences in the residential experience could include waking and sleeping hours, different verbal cadence and tone in conversations, identifying shared versus individual items in the room, individual study habits, navigating the acceptance of visitors to the shared space or overnight guests, cleanliness, and individual faith practices such as prayer or dietary restrictions.

Incorporating social justice principles into the conduct process invites students to the conversation and ensures they have a voice. Because colleges and universities have historically benefited people with power and privilege, a social justice focus serves to shift power to the student and works to ensure current systems or policies do not further oppress or marginalize them. Acts such as changing a process, amending language, engaging with a student, naming a concern, and more all help break current oppressive systems down in both small and large ways. Through these actions systems can be dismantled and changed.

BUILDING A SOCIAL JUSTICE FOUNDATION

Conduct officers have the responsibility to uphold fairness and objectivity throughout the conduct process, especially in decision-making and sanctioning, since these aspects of the process can significantly change the trajectory of a student's life (Lopez-Phillips & Trageser, 2008). While housing and residential life conduct officers may not play a direct role in creating and revising campus policies and practices, they can work at the intersection of several student development theories. This work can assist students in forming their identities, move them forward in their development, and lead efforts in furthering residence and campus communities through socially just sanctions.

To encourage learning, reflection, and meaning-making in students, conduct officers must have a greater foundation of these tenets, typically encompassed as personal values, of their own, but how do they balance maintaining personal values with working at educational institutions? Sometimes the missions and objectives of colleges and universities can cause people to abandon, albeit unintentionally, their core values and judgment to meet an end. It takes practice and self-awareness to act according to personal ethics while achieving institutional goals and expectations.

Karen Strohm Kitchener's seminal article, "Ethical Principles and Decisions in Student Affairs" (1985), defines five principles of ethical student affairs practice, which also provide guidance for effective student conduct practice, especially when it comes to socially just decision-making and sanctioning. These principles are:

- **Respect autonomy.** Allow individuals the freedoms to determine how they live their lives if their actions do not interfere with the welfare of others.
- **Do no harm.** Avoid physical or psychological harm to others.
- **Benefit others.** Strive to improve and enhance the welfare of others, even when this benefit appears as an inconvenience.
- **Be just.** Provide fair treatment, although fairness may not always be equal, and student affairs practitioners should use caution in approaching the difference.
- **Be faithful.** Act in an honest, straightforward manner while maintaining respect and civility toward others and remain trustworthy through positive interactions with others.

Other student development theories also intersect with social justice principles as they relate to decision-making and sanctioning processes.

Kohlberg's Theory of Moral Development offers six stages of moral development on three levels. They can be used to ask how student behavior in an incident informs decision-making regarding behaviors in a future incident, and the response can be used to develop sanctions to enhance their moral judgment for the future (Kohlberg & Mayer, 1972).

Gilligan's Theory of Moral Reasoning features three levels with three transitions and focuses on moral development for women. The transition to each stage centers on a sense of self and morality, and concepts of justice and care for others. They can be used to ask how a student's behavior was driven by care for self rather than care for others (Gilligan, 2016).

Kolb's Theory of Experiential Learning states learning is a transformative process that comes through experiences, reflection, and application of learning to create new or different experiences. It can be the basis of asking a student to reflect on or develop an action plan related to how future behaviors could change the trajectory of a future incident (Kolb & Kolb, 2005).

Dewey's Concepts of Experience and Education say education is a reflective process based on experiences and learning. It can help focus on asking a student to reflect on a current incident to learn about what they might change about their behavior to prevent a recurrence (Dewey, 1921).

Harro's Cycle of Socialization provides a process for individuals to understand and make sense of the world around them by understanding they are socialized to play certain roles, and either change or maintain a cycle of oppression through their actions. It can be used to ask how a student's behaviors in an incident were due to socialization and how these behaviors strengthen or weaken their identity (Harro, 2000).

Grace's Four "V" Model of Ethical Leadership encourages a lifelong commitment to learning and core values through values, vision, voice, virtue, and renewal (Grace, 2001).

Kidder's Ethical Template posits five ethical principles to guide ethical decision-making that aligns with personal values: obeying the law, the front-page test, the regard test, the gut test, and considering the Golden Rule (Kidder, 1996).

Social Group Identity

Colleges and universities must introspectively examine how social group identities influence the conduct process. Social group identities are salient and indiscernible, and permeate interactions with others, whether consciously or unconsciously.

Most individuals carry at least one dominant identity, and this identity intersects with and influences how they experience — or are perceived by others to experience — the world at any given moment. Messages related to social group identities, and perceptions of those identities are developed at birth and reinforced through social systems (e.g., education, family and friends, religious and government institutions) and lived experiences (Harro, 2000) related to power, privilege, and oppression. In addition to social identities, students possess a unique culture in the personal experiences, peer influences, and cultural orientations they present during a conflict (Giacomini & Schrage, 2009), which also confounds students' relationships with codes and processes.

Just as encouraging students to explore their identities throughout the college experience is essential, so it is essential for conduct officers to reflect on their individual social group identities. This reflection is key to improving how the identities of conduct officers shape interactions with students during the conduct process and how these interactions, or perception of these interactions, contribute to or collude with oppressive acts on campus. Important questions to consider are "How do social group identities intersect with how someone implements the process?" and "How is a social group identity perceived by participants in the process?" For instance, a student who attends a conduct meeting in sweatpants might be perceived as unprepared or insincere because of messages the conduct officer has received about the importance of attending such a meeting in more-formal attire. This perception could intentionally change how the conduct officer interacts with the student during the meeting, or the conduct officer may not even be aware of how this messaging influences actions toward the student.

Consider how a student of color might perceive a White conduct officer when discussing an incident involving racially charged speech. How a conduct officer who identifies as a person of color facilitates the process when dealing with the same incident may be different from how a White person facilitates the process, but the conduct officer of color may also send certain messages, whether intentional or unintentional, based on other salient identities or their lived experiences. Failure to look introspectively at identity can negatively influence interactions with students. It might not be possible to recognize differences related to diversity, power, and privilege, and this can lead to stereotyping, minimizing student experiences or perpetuating oppression.

Systems of Oppression

In considering how social group identities influence power and privilege in conduct codes processes, it also is important to acknowledge how these identities lead to systems of oppression. Oppressing others can be conscious and unconscious, and individual, institutional, and societal (Holmes, Edwards, & DeBowes, 2009). For example, if a student cites a religious difference as the reason for a conflict with another student, and the conduct officer does not identify with said religion, how might this influence the conduct officer's response to the conflict? The conduct officer's response may also be shaped, whether consciously or unconsciously, by how the college or university supports and makes resources available for the student's stated religious beliefs. Is this a religion widely accepted by societal values and beliefs? How do these values and beliefs reinforce certain messages to the student? On a day-to-day level, what messages do staff and faculty send through the setup and characteristics of their offices? What do these messages perpetuate in relation to dominant social group identities, power, or privilege, and what do these messages tell students?

Restorative Justice

The principles that form the foundation of restorative justice are closely connected to the concepts of conduct and social justice. Practiced in New Zealand, Australia, and in the Mennonite religious tradition (Costello, Wachtel, & Wachtel, 2010), restorative practices have been widely used outside the United States for decades. Juvenile offender programs, elementary and secondary schools, and, more recently, colleges and universities have begun to adopt restorative practices in student conduct and sanction determinations.

Restorative practices touch on four core principles: inclusive decision-making, active accountability, repairing harm, and rebuilding trust (Karp, 2013). These values relate directly to the goals and missions of residential communities and their work toward social justice.

The relationship between restorative justice and social justice can be thought about through the lenses of respect, relationships, and responsibility. For example, people in a community deserve and want to be respected in their spaces and for who they are (recall the definitions of diversity and inclusion). They lose trust in that relationship when disrespect toward them manifests through harmful behaviors. Restorative justice seeks to address the harm and restore the relationship.

The restoration could be education about the impact of the behavior or interaction, or more formal and require the offender to complete a program or use other learning opportunities, such as a dialogue or apology. Restorative justice also asks offenders to take responsibility for their actions and behaviors. Someone who causes harm in the community has an obligation to others to acknowledge the impact and work to make it right.

Concurrently, restorative justice practices parallel the obligation to address harm and community accountability through student conduct policies and practices. Rather than a process coming from authority and historical power structures, restorative principles work first from the community to understand individual needs and harms (many of which are rooted in longstanding isms such as racism, sexism, etc.). Simply stated, infusing restorative practices into student conduct systems can help create the type of communities colleges and universities aspire to become.

The overall philosophy of restorative practices focuses on moral concern, citizenship, and emotional intelligence. Such a philosophy lends itself to a different type of engagement from the student (Karp & Sacks, 2014). The model code approach tends to focus on facts and procedures (e.g., did the student violate the code? did the student understand the rules?). On the other hand, the restorative practice approach relates to personal

responsibility, acknowledging hurt from behaviors, and reintegration into the community (e.g., in what ways was identity involved in
the conflict? what dynamics were at play for the student at the time
of incident? what actions could the student take to reassure the
harmed party that they will be a responsible member of the community now?). By asking students affected or harmed what needs they
have and inviting the student who caused that harm to participate in
the process, accept responsibility, and work to address those needs,
the dynamics of power in a traditional conduct process shift from the
conduct officer to the participants involved in the incident.

A premise of restorative practices related to conduct and social
justice is that "people are happier and more likely to make positive
changes when those in authority do things *with* them, rather than to
or for them" (Costello, Wachtel, & Wachtel, 2010, p. 8). One significant
indicator of how building community in the housing and residence life
conduct process that infuses a social justice approach is how much
students feel involved or accepted in the process. When conduct
officers, whether within the housing and residence life department or
campus-wide, share the process with students, they give students a
voice and provide a sense of inclusion. Conversely, when the conduct
process merely dictates a student's behavior with little to no input
from the student, the implication is a student conduct process that
values adjudication over community and perpetuates a system of
oppression over others.

The difficulty with addressing systems of oppression is that they are deeply
ingrained in society, thus permeating campus communities. This can be especially
evident to housing and residence life conduct officers because residence halls
are, in many ways, microcosms of the world, and these professionals are likely to
witness systems of oppression both in and beyond the student conduct process.
However, conduct officers still have the responsibility to create fair and equitable
student conduct systems for everyone, regardless of living arrangement.

As stated earlier, reflecting on personal social group identities allows conduct
officers to understand better how biases and prejudices show up in their daily
work. Nevertheless, it is not enough just to reflect on how personal identities
preserve systems of oppression. Rather, a residence life professional must also
take steps to address systems of oppression when they occur. Sometimes conduct officers have the best intentions in attempting to remain neutral or take
no action. However, this approach can be equally damaging, because remaining
silent in the face of oppression reinforces the oppression. Developing a personal

critical consciousness, then using this knowledge to construct, revise, and facilitate student conduct codes and processes through a social justice lens, is one step conduct officers can take to ensure their colleges and universities are working against perpetuating oppression.

When addressing the creation or revision of campus policies and practices, campus conduct officers may be most familiar with the Model Student Conduct Code (Stoner & Lowery, 2004). However, each institution has its particular version of a document that outlines community expectations for student residents' behavior. Consider the following questions when creating or revising codes and practices to ensure those codes are conceived and put into operation in an inclusive and just manner.

- Who is involved in the process? In what ways?
- Who has a voice in the process? In what ways?
- Who is affected or may be affected by the policy or practice? What evidence exists for this?
- What educational measures or sanctions are written into the code?
- How might those measures or sanctions rebuild harm in a community or unknowingly affect a student?

While the policies of a single campus may not reflect the model code, or demonstrate inclusion of all the students who came to the campus from diverse backgrounds, residence life professionals can still provide justice and care toward students through the decision-making and sanctioning process. Asking illuminating questions during the process of policy and practice creation and revision can lead to expanding campus policies and processes that include a spectrum of resolution options.

Sanctions, while an intrinsic part of the conduct process, can contribute, although inadvertently, to campus systems of oppression. While determining consistent outcomes is a priority for conduct officers, they also will be called to review cases holistically and provide outcomes that consider individual student needs.

Consider the implications of sanctions in accordance with the definitions of equity and equality provided earlier. Sanctions should be fair, but they do not always have to be equal. Conduct officers should keep student development in mind, consider the impact of sanctions (e.g., financially, culturally, etc.), and discuss this impact with students before applying sanctions. This is not to suggest the students determine their own sanctions and implementation of them. Rather, the ideal is for students to partner with the conduct officer to develop sanctions, and for the impact of different sanctions to be weighed up front as part of the outcome.

This approach also allows conduct officers to raise greater awareness of the impact of sanctions in consideration of social justice concerns, which works against systems of oppression inherent in sanctioning processes. For illustration, the Family Rights and Privacy Act (FERPA) allows, but does not require, colleges and universities to notify a parent or guardian of a student's alcohol or drug violation. When the college or university expects a conduct officer to include calling the student's parent or guardian as a sanction, this potentially has an unjust impact on the student. Depending on the policy violation, a parent or guardian may withdraw the student from the campus for reasons related to social identity or cultural values, regardless of the severity of the incident. Considering the impact of sanctions is important when developing inclusive policies and practices, particularly when implementing certain sanctions may not be the most socially just choice of action. Remember that sanctions should be designed to educate about and stop harmful and unsafe behaviors on campus, and these outcomes can be produced in a variety of ways.

CONNECTING SOCIAL JUSTICE AND CONDUCT

As stated by Bickel and Lake (1999), "safe campuses begin with simple steps designed to institute a sense of community with shared values and meaningful responsibility" (p. 14). These steps are typically embodied in a set of university policies (e.g., code of student conduct, student rights and responsibilities, etc.), processes, and practices.

Codes of conduct address a myriad of behaviors, and "few individuals on the college campus have the conduct officer's positional power to significantly change a student's reality" (Lopez-Phillips & Trageser, 2008, p. 121). While student conduct codes and processes should balance the needs of individual students with the needs of campus communities, foundational challenges of student conduct work still permeate student conduct processes today.

Historically, cases before the 1960s rarely involved protecting students' rights, fairness, due process, or implementing appropriate sanctions (Lake, 2009). Student discipline at that time related to the power, privilege, and prerogative of the sanctity of college, rather than campus life itself. A collegiate education was reserved for the few and privileged, primarily White males in positions of power, financial prosperity, or religious motivation. They only possessed the protection of economic interests and property. In today's campus climate, though, the diversity of college students provides unique opportunities for personal growth and development to occur, and student conduct processes have become more educational and less legalistic. However, the perception of codes and policies from students with identities historically excluded from higher education (e.g., race, gender, class, ability) is not always supportive.

In framing student conduct policies and practices through a social justice lens, it is important to recognize the power and privileges still inherent in codes and practices, and to identify what has to shift to create and maintain inclusive climates of accountability. When constructing, revising, and facilitating student conduct codes and processes through a social justice lens, it is important to consider how social group identity and systems of oppression permeate codes and processes.

One way to institute a social justice framework in the conduct system is with a conduct letter (or another method of communication) a student may receive in documenting an incident. Student conduct letters often appear formal to students and may create fear or concern if the student is being asked to meet with a conduct officer or person of authority regarding the incident, not to mention how they may be feeling after being confronted by a security officer, campus police, or housing staff member. Using language that educates and encourages thinking and reflection, rather than using language that places blame, can remove barriers between the accuser and accused.

Blame comes from a position of authority and power, since someone is often accused of behavior before being asked what occurred or what their role may have been in the allegations. It presumes fault and offers judgment, both aspects that perpetuate oppression. Providing the purpose of the meeting and its general overview also offers transparency about the process and an opportunity for the student to arrive prepared to engage in dialogue, rather than participate solely from the receiving end of a decision. Because housing and residence life conduct officers operate as agents under oppressive systems, such as institutions, and work with mandates and policies via federal and state laws, there is a need to use the roles (and interactions with students) in ways that combat accusation, blame, and oppression because "the application of institutional policies and procedures in an oppressive society run by individuals or groups who advocate or collude with social oppression produces oppressive consequences" (Adams, Bell, & Griffin, 1997, p. 18–19).

An example of this practice occurs at the University of Michigan. There, housing conduct letters (2016) ask students to reflect on the following questions before attending a meeting about an issue and explains how their responses to the questions will drive the content of the meeting: What level of involvement or responsibility they might have had in the incident; who may have been harmed in this incident and in what ways; and what can be done to address and repair the harm that may have been caused in the community.

Educating the Community

As mentioned earlier, CAS has developed standards for advancing student conduct practice. A closer look at the standards related to diversity and inter-cultural communication provides clear guidance related to equity, access, and diversity. Further, student conduct programs and services should align with institutional policies as well as state and federal regulations. Programs should be fair, equitable, and non-discriminatory; maintain an environment free from discrimination; not discriminate on the basis of age, cultural heritage, disability, ethnicity, gender identity and expression, nationality, political affiliation, race, religious affiliation, sex, sexual orientation, economic, marital, social or veteran status, and any other bases; ensure physical and program access for people with disabilities; and be responsive to the needs of all students and other populations served. Student conduct programs and services:

> must promote environments that are characterized by open and con-tinuous communication that deepens understanding of one's own iden-tity, culture, and heritage, as well as that of others ... recognize, honor, educate, and promote respect about commonalities and differences among people within their historical and cultural contexts ... address the characteristics and needs of a diverse population when establishing and implementing policies and procedures. (CAS, 2009, p. 364)

It is imperative to understand how diversity and intercultural communication affect student conduct work related to the educational needs of students while protecting the safety and welfare of the residential community. Individual actions, institutional policies, and practices should be welcoming, accessible, inclusive, equitable, and free from harassment. Many factors related to ethical decision-making, diversity, and intercultural communication should be consid-ered when approaching campus policies, processes, and sanctions. Residence life professionals should examine whether these will affect students differently because of their socioeconomic status, race or ethnicity, culture, faith or reli-gious affiliation, physical ability, gender or gender identity, immigration status, or veteran status.

These examples outline how ethical decision-making, diversity, and intercul-tural communication can play out in different student conduct scenarios.

Identity. In consideration of the history of racism and practices of discrimi-nation in the United States, the student experience differs drastically based on personal experiences and individual identities, including but not limited to race, religion, gender identity, and immigrant status. To not unintentionally con-tribute to exclusive practices, one must recognize the ways discrimination and prejudice have played out, not only in society but also through the processes in place, since they may also unintentionally contribute to oppressive acts.

For instance, some marginalized students are either not aware of their rights, too afraid to speak up, or have given up because colleges and universities have historically failed to respond to their needs and concerns in an equitable and inclusive manner. While student conduct policies and practices can survive a review that looks for obvious signs of oppression, students are not always concerned about inclusion and, sometimes without realizing it, display racist, prejudiced, and discriminatory language and actions toward others based on social identity.

It also is important to acknowledge the unique experiences of international students and how their personal norms and experiences differ from campus norms, including housing communities. Residence life officers must consider how to engage international students in such discourse while meeting them where they are. Given the ongoing increase of international students attending college, it is essential to explore how ethical decision-making, diversity, and cross-cultural communication approaches pertain to the experience of a diverse student body. For example, around the world campus alcohol policies can range from alcohol being prohibited entirely to those that allow alcohol consumption by those of legal drinking age as well as several variations in between. While the legal drinking age in the United States is 21, the legal drinking age is 18 or younger in many other countries. Plus, drinking or touching alcohol in some countries, religions, and cultures is prohibited altogether. This knowledge should be used to shape conduct policies, processes, sanctions, educational programming, and preventive measures.

Socioeconomic status. Several conduct processes have fines associated with the sanctioning process. A fine, regardless of how big or small, is likely to affect students based on their socioeconomic status — this can raise concern about the potential for public humiliation of a student who cannot pay the fine. While some colleges and universities consider community service as a sanction instead of paying a fine, this has the potential to minimize the value of others typically employed to do the work required by the student's community service. For instance, does it devalue the work of custodial staff when students are ordered to complete custodial projects as a punishment?

Another example of how differences in socioeconomic status permeate student conduct occurs with institutional response to a student found smoking marijuana or using an illegal drug and how the consequences vary when addressed by a housing staff member as opposed to a member of the police department. Depending on the severity of the incident, and the details of the report, the student could lose federal financial aid if arrested. Moreover, if the police are involved, the next steps may drastically change based on the student's ability to have access to an attorney or guidance from family members knowledgeable of the court system. It is important to consider the short- and long-term implications of the process in such an example and how this may differ for students based on their socioeconomic status.

Cultural Constructs in Authority and Dispute Resolution

Student conduct processes focus on the safety and welfare of students and the campus community. Conduct processes are often perceived as educational and not as punitive as the criminal justice system. In fact, most higher education institutions dislike references to their processes as criminal courts. Nevertheless, the process itself is authoritative in nature. In most instances, either a person (conduct officer) or a group of people (conduct board) reviews cases and makes decisions that ultimately have a direct impact on students' ability to remain enrolled at their college or university. While conduct officers, including housing and residence life conduct officers, often receive educational and practical training to manage the responsibilities of their positions, this does not always include discussions of oppression inherent in the process.

Here are examples of how cultural constructs of language, communication style, and interactions with the police play out in the conduct process as it pertains to positions of authority.

Language. Conduct policies and practices, whether applicable to the entire institution or specifically the housing and residence life system, are often filled with words not always familiar to all students. Some of these include, but are not limited to, bullying, sexual misconduct, affirmative consent, harassment, bias, hate speech, academic dishonesty, and freedom of speech. In addition, students may not have a language or cultural framework to understand the role of a campus support office or the support it can offer throughout the student conduct process.

In addition to the student's ability to understand terminology related to conduct, it is important conduct officers understand language that includes the student experience. An example could be the complexities related to inclusive language in dealing with issues of identity and orientation. It is essential for conduct officers to be aware of language and its role in conduct process, from the forms students complete at the onset of the process to the words used to describe an incident. Conduct officers can use inclusive language as a means to educate students and the campus community about the diverse needs of the community, which can lead to larger discussions related to social justice on campus and maintaining an environment that respects the identities of everyone in that environment.

Communication Style

Understanding communication style in its relation to social identity is important. For instance, if the conduct officer's communication style is linear, direct, or emotionally restrained, how might that affect interactions with someone who communicates in a circular, indirect, and emotionally expressive manner?

Another question would be how communication styles can be used to demonstrate power over, or oppress, others. For example, in some cultures, students are taught not to question or make eye contact with a person of authority. What are the unwritten expectations for students to engage verbally in a discussion about an incident? Should a student's ability to actively discuss and make eye contact influence how the case is addressed?

These questions point to what Ikeda (2015) defines as low-context and high-context communication styles. With low-context communication, "most of the information is given and received through explicit verbal or nonverbal messages," while "in high-context communication, much of the message is already in the minds of the people; therefore, people do not give and receive explicit messages. In this communication style, people are expected to behave appropriately without much explanation about the situation" (p. 77).

Police and public safety officers. Most colleges and universities have public safety officers, police officers, or other law enforcement staff. These roles are authoritative in nature, but to assume that all students perceive these representatives of the institution the same way is misguided. For instance, some students arrive on campus with a distrust of people in such roles and, even when their safety is at risk, may opt against asking for help or reporting an incident from fear of how they may be treated.

Consider, for example, undocumented students on college campuses across the United States who fear campus police could arrest them and have them deported to their countries of origin, although they have no connection to those countries or were never raised there. Many Muslim students living on college campuses fear they are being followed or profiled by police in light of the current political climate toward terrorism in the United States. Students who have been previously incarcerated may avoid seeking services, accessing buildings, or interacting with certain people or offices out of fear they will be asked for a form of identification or have to disclose information about their incarceration. Transgender students may avoid reporting an incident because of concerns about mistreatment or harassment based on gender identity.

This perception of the police and public safety officers has implications for students' response to conduct processes, since many students view student conduct officers as an extension of law enforcement. Some colleges and universities attempt to bridge the gap between public safety and police, student conduct offices, and the campus community. They strive to build rapport and trust, educate stakeholders, and reframe themselves as collaborative offices designed to enforce safety and accountability who also protect students' needs and support students' human rights.

Examples of colleges and universities with positive partnerships between police/campus safety units abound. Some have developed collaborative programming with hopes of increasing communication and trust between police, public safety, and the community. Others have police and campus safety officers wear informal uniforms in similar attempts to break down barriers and misconceptions about their role.

In focusing on cultural constructs involved in dispute resolution and intentionally working to make the process inclusive, it is also essential for conduct officers to consider the perspectives of and resources available to students.

Student perspectives. It is essential to take the time to meet with students and hear their perspectives on an incident. There is a story, and the student may be the best person to share it. Regardless of whether the case involved one or several students, conduct officers should meet with each student individually, even if the conduct officer decides to meet with the group later. Sometimes meeting with all students involved requires a lot of time and energy, but it also allows individual perspectives to be heard in a private and caring way, and to include pertinent campus resources to resolve a case accordingly. When applicable, hearing individual perspectives also allows the conduct officer to gauge whether other forms of resolution options could be more appropriate than formal adjudication processes, which can also lead to resolving incidents in a more socially just manner.

Access to resources. The ability to access resources that support students within the conduct process can be determined by the amount of social and cultural capital the student and their parents or family members possess. Failure to address this inequality contributes to instances of power misuse and oppressive action on campus. For example, it is often assumed students are aware of their options to consult with or engage a lawyer, advisor, or another support individual in the conduct process. This assumption could adversely affect the student's outcome in a conduct case, if it means a student did not use those resources and indicates having an advisor present during a conduct meeting would have been helpful. Is it possible to simply assume the student knew how to ask for the resource and the benefits of receiving support? Should a student's ability to obtain legal counsel affect the outcome of the conduct process?

While some students have easy access to attorneys, this is not the case for all students. Should the involvement of highly engaged parents or family members

➕ Additional Readings

These titles, as well as others cited in this chapter, are valuable resources to further one's understanding of social justice as it continues its growth as an emerging practice in student affairs and higher education.

- *Advancing Social Justice: Tools, Pedagogies, and Strategies to Transform Your Campus*
  Tracy Davis and Laura M. Harrison (2013)

- *Disability in Higher Education: A Social Justice Approach*
  Nancy J. Evans, Ellen M. Broido, Kirsten R. Brown, and Autumn K. Wilke, (2017)

- *Law and Social Justice in Higher Education*
  Crystal Renée Chambers (2017)

- *Leadership, Equity, and Social Justice in American Higher Education: A Reader*
  C. P. Gause (2017)

- *Little Book of Restorative Justice for Colleges and Universities: Repairing Harm and Rebuilding Trust in Response to Student Misconduct*
  David Karp (2013)

- *Promoting Diversity and Social Justice: Educating People from Privileged Groups*
  Diane Goodman (2011)

- *Readings for Diversity and Social Justice*
  Maurianne Adams, Warren J. Blumenfeld, Heather W. Hackman, Madeline L. Peters, and Ximena Zuniga (2013)

- *Reframing Campus Conflict: Student Conduct Practice Through a Social Justice Lens*
  Jennifer Meyer Schrage and Nancy Geist Giacomini (2009)

- *Transgender Issues on College Campuses*
  Brett Beemyn, Billy Curtis, Masen Davis, and Nancy Jean Tubbs; part of New Directions for Student Services series (2005)

- *University Ethics: How Colleges Can Build and Benefit from a Culture of Ethics*
  James F. Keenan (2017)

(who may even be alumni or institutional donors) as support individuals influence the outcome of the process? It is essential for conduct officers to ensure students are aware of the resources available to them, particularly before the student conduct meetings, and the ability or inability to obtain certain resources does not influence the case outcome. The same is true when making accommodations related to ADA, Title IX, and other state, federal, and local laws and policies, which may require collaboration with other campus offices.

CONCLUSION

Today's media headlines are filled with coverage of incidents involving police brutality, gender identity and inequality, and immigration status, to name just a few issues that could affect campus communities. The worldwide political climate has brought issues of social justice more to the forefront of debate and dialogue as well. College and university campuses are not exempt from these issues. In response, some colleges and universities have been quick to implement inclusive practices and social justice initiatives in support of their diverse student populations. However, other colleges and universities may be slow to change and lag in acknowledging or responding to such issues.

Conduct officers, both residential and campus-wide, are not always positioned to respond to these societal issues in socially inclusive ways. In some cases, the institutions cannot or will not acknowledge how these issues include or isolate students within the campus community. This also places conduct officers in difficult situations when making decisions, addressing incidents of misconduct, and striving to create and maintain educational and inclusive communities. This charge is especially challenging for housing and residence life professionals, whose primary charge is to create and maintain these communities within the residential environment.

Because of their wide-reaching impact on campuses, student housing departments are positioned uniquely to lead the charge for social justice approaches to conduct. Housing and residence life programs ensure the educational success of students and create opportunities to learn and develop within safe, supportive, and inclusive living communities. The applicable conduct policies and practices can either include students in shared learning and understanding, thereby maintaining the student's sense of community, or exclude students and continue to reinforce oppressions historically inherent to university conduct systems.

As residential communities become more diverse, and incidents involving conduct matters become more complex, housing professionals have the responsibility to be receptive of new conduct practices that incorporate a social justice lens. It is essential to be reflective of how identity is viewed, both by oneself and by students. Institutional student conduct norms that oppress students instead of viewing them as partners in the process must be challenged, not only at the level of revising codes and practices but also in day-to-day interactions with students. This requires conduct officers to be willing to challenge oppressive behaviors and educate the campus community on social injustices when they occur. This also requires conduct officers to develop and advocate for practices that embrace equality and acceptance toward all students.

When students experience policies and practices that do not support their social identities and receive conduct outcomes that oppress them, they view conduct officers as the adversary, rather than as their education and support system. Some may argue that a socially just student conduct process is an aspirational, utopian standard. However, it also has been shown to be an achievable one that infuses a social justice ethic into conduct policies and practices that move the processes toward a more inclusive community, not only within residential spaces but across entire campuses and throughout society.

REFERENCES

Adams, M., Bell, L. A., & Griffin, P. (Eds.). (1997). *Teachings for diversity and social justice.* London, UK: Routledge.

Bickel, R. D., & Lake, P. F. (1999). *The rights and responsibilities of the modern university: Who assumes the risk of college life?* Durham, NC: Carolina Academic Press.

Bennett, J. M. (Ed.). (2015). The sage encyclopedia of intercultural competence. Retrieved from https://ebookcentral.proquest.com.

Christie, N. (1977). Conflicts as Property. *The British Journal of Criminology 17,* 1–15.

Costello, B., Wachtel, J., & Wachtel, T. (2010). *The restorative circles in schools: building community and enhancing learning.* Bethlehem, PA: International Institute for Restorative Practices.

Council for the Advancement of Standards. (2009). *CAS professional standards for higher education* (7th Ed.). Washington, DC: Author.

Dewey, J. (1921). Democracy and education. New York, NY: Macmillan.

Florida International University. *Housing and Residential Life Diversity Statement.* Retrieved November 9, 2017, from https://studentaffairs.fiu.edu/campus-services/housing-and-residential-life/about/index.php.

Georgetown University. *Mission, Values and Vision: Residential Living.* Retrieved November 15, 2017, from https://studentliving.georgetown.edu/mission.

Gilligan, C. (2016). *In a different voice: psychological theory and women's development.* Cambridge, MA: Harvard University Press.

Giacomini, N. G., & Schrage, J. M. (2009). Building community in the current campus climate. In J. Schrage & N. Giacomini (Eds.), *Reframing campus conflict: Student conduct practice through a social justice lens,* 50–64. Sterling, VA: Stylus.

Grace, B. (2002, October). *Ethical Leadership Institute training material.* Seattle: Center for Ethical Leadership.

Harro, B. (2000). The cycle of socialization. In M. Adams, W. J., Blumfield, R. Castañeda, H. W. Hackman, M. L. Peters, & X. Zúñiga (Eds.), *Readings for diversity and social justice: An anthology on racism, antisemitism, sexism, heterosexism, ableism, and classism,* 15–21. New York, NY: Routledge.

Holmes, R. C., Edwards, K., & DeBowes, M. M. (2009). Why objectivity is not enough: the critical role of social justice in campus conduct and conflict work. In J. Schrage & N. Giacomini (Eds.), *Reframing campus conflict: Student conduct practice through a social justice lens,* 50–64. Sterling, VA: Stylus Publishing.

Howard University. *Residence Life and University Housing.* Retrieved November 9, 2017, from https://residencelife.howard.edu/about-us.

Ikeda, K. (2015). Communicating across cultures with people from Japan. In J. Bennett (Ed.), *The SAGE encyclopedia of intercultural competence,* 77–80. Thousand Oaks, CA: SAGE Publications Ltd. doi: 10.4135/9781483346267.n35.

Karp, D. R. (2013). *Little book of restorative justice for colleges and universities: Repairing harm and rebuilding trust in response to student misconduct.* Intercourse, PA: Good Books.

Karp, D. R., & Sacks, C. (2014). Student conduct, restorative justice, and student development: Findings from the STARR project: a student accountability and restorative research project. *Contemporary Justice Review 17*(2), 154–172. http://www.tandfonline.com/doi/abs/10.1080/10282580.2014.915140.

Kidder, R. (1996). *How good people make tough choices: Resolving dilemmas of ethical living.* New York, NY: Fireside.

Kitchner, K. S. (1985). Ethical principles and decisions in student affairs. In H. J. Canon and R. D. Brown (Eds.), *Applied ethics in student services,* 17–20. San Francisco, CA: Jossey-Bass.

King, F. (2017). *Social Identity Worksheet.* Adapted by the University of Michigan's Housing Diversity and Inclusion Office.

Kohlberg, L., & Mayer, R. (1972). *Development as the aim of education. Harvard Educational Review 42*(4), 449–496.

Kolb, A. Y., & Kolb, D. A. (2005). Learning styles and learning spaces: Enhancing experiential learning in higher education. *Academy of Management Learning & Education 4*(2), 193–212.

Lake, P. F. (2009). *Beyond Discipline: Managing the Modern Higher Education Environment.* Bradenton, FL: Hierophant Enterprises, Inc.

Lopez-Phillips, M., & Trageser, S. P. (2008). Development and diversity: A social justice model. In J. M. Lancaster, & D. M. Waryold (Eds.), *Student conduct practice: The complete guide for student affairs professionals*, 119–134. Sterling, VA: Stylus Publishing.

Loyola University Chicago. (2017). *Residence Life, Mission, Vision, Outcomes.* Retrieved November 9, 2017, from https://www.luc.edu/reslife/about/mission/.

Martin-Ferguson, M., & McLittle, A. L. (2016). *Conversation on Diversity, Equity and Inclusion* (PowerPoint slides). Retrieved from Martin and McLittle Consulting, LLC.

Stoner II, E. N., & Lowery, J. W. (2004). Navigating past the "spirit of insubordination": A twenty-first century model student conduct code with a model hearing script. *Journal of College and University Law 31.*

University of California, Santa Barbara. (2017). *Housing, Dining and Auxiliary Enterprises.* Retrieved November 9, 2017, from http://www.housing.ucsb.edu/about-us.

University of Michigan. (2016). *Housing student conduct and conflict resolution office.* Initial charge letter.

1. In looking at your housing and residence life policies or mission, what does inclusion look like at your institution?

2. Can housing and residence life staff work to effectively balance conduct compliance (such as federal laws and standards) and address student equity in an incident?

3. What training does your institution provide for housing conduct officers regarding social justice, inclusion, power, and privilege in the conduct process? Is this training valuable? If not, what changes should occur? If your training does not cover these areas, what can you do to begin conversations about this topic?

4. Which campus partners (e.g., campus safety or law enforcement, campus conduct office, bias incident response team, identity-focused support offices, etc.) are on your campus to support training, outreach, and dialogue on your campus about community and conduct? What can you do in your role to encourage collaborative dialogue and action on this topic?

5. Reflect on your professional values and ethics. How do you act according to your values and ethics while also achieving institutional goals and expectations? How do you respond to a situation that challenges your values and ethics?

6. How does your housing and residence life conduct process serve the various identities of your student population? What can you do in your role to ensure students feel included and heard in the process?

7. What steps do you have in place for determining whether an incident should proceed as an educational conversation, the formal conduct process, or both? Which campus partners, if any, do you consult in making these decisions?

7

CONNECTING CONDUCT AND MENTAL HEALTH

Mary Anderson, Heidi Anderson-Isaacson, and Douglas Bell

> *Madison and Jasmine were first-year students at a small, private university. One evening, as they walked into the community bathroom at the end of their hall, they found Madison's roommate, Jennifer, sitting on the bathroom floor, cutting her forearm with a razor. Shocked, Madison asked Jennifer what she was doing, and if she was okay. Jennifer started to cry as she replied, "I just don't think I can take it anymore. Sometimes I feel like it's pointless for me to be here. I just want to die."*
>
> *While Madison sat and talked with Jennifer, Jasmine ran down the hall to find Amy, their resident assistant, for help. As the two of them made their way back to the restroom, they couldn't help but remember how, earlier in the semester, Jennifer had been transported to the hospital after she took a handful of her antidepressants, saying she just wanted to "sleep for a long time."*

UNFORTUNATELY, scenarios like these are all too familiar at colleges and universities around the world today as students face disorders such as anxiety, depression, psychosis, eating disorders, schizophrenia, and many others. Such scenarios illustrate the challenges residence life staff face as they work with students who navigate their college experience while coping with a variety of mental health concerns. The staff, from undergraduate students who serve as resident assistants to seasoned student affairs professionals at all levels of the department, must be prepared to address not only the mental health concerns that may severely affect the day-to-day life of individual students, but also the conduct issues that may result from their living and learning environment.

Although the desire is to create a culture of care, there is likely to be a time where a student with mental health issues must be charged with disrupting the community, and some sanction or intervention will have to be levied. For campus housing and conduct professionals to manage such situations successfully requires a knowledge of mental health issues as well as a willingness to address them with proactive policies that are educational, just, and compassionate. This puts practitioners in the role of both counselors and disciplinary agents. Nonetheless, Gerald Amata, in his book *Mental Health and Student Conduct Issues on the College Campus* (2015), argues for separating these two roles: "it is critically important that the [counseling] service be administratively neutral" (p. 2). Professionals must separate the behavior from the action, and the mental health diagnosis cannot have an impact on the outcome of a conduct case. It is not illegal to have a mental health diagnosis, and students should not be treated as if it is.

STUDENT MENTAL HEALTH

Helping students develop and succeed was the primary consideration for campus counseling centers throughout most of the 20th century. Since the 1990s, though, increasing resources have been dedicated to addressing student mental health issues (American Psychological Association, 2018). Not only are more students arriving on campus with diagnosed mental illnesses, but the severity of their psychological problems also has increased during the last 30 years (Gallagher, 2012).

This issue is illustrated in the responses to the 2017 National College Health Assessment II survey. Among the findings, 88% of students reported feeling overwhelmed by all they had to do, 85% felt exhausted, 64% reported feeling very lonely, and 53% said they experienced feelings of hopelessness in the previous 12 months (American College Health Association, 2017). Students reported their feelings of stress made life difficult to handle in the areas of academics (49.8%), finances (32.7%), sleep (31.4%), intimate relationships (31.7%), family matters (28.6%), personal appearance (29.9%), and career-related issues (25.5%).

In addition to these self-reported challenges by students, the Association for University and College Counseling Center Directors 2016 Annual Survey reported the most prevalent concerns of students presenting at college counseling centers included anxiety (50.6%), depression (41.2%), relationship issues (34.4%), taking psychotropic medications (26.1%), suicidal thoughts/behaviors (20.5%), extensive or significant prior treatment histories (16.2%), self-injurious behaviors (14.1%) alcohol abuse/dependence (9.5%), ADD or ADHD (9.3%), sexual/physical assault (8.8%), issues of oppression (8.3%), substance abuse/ dependence other than alcohol (7.5%), eating disorders (7.4%), learning disabilities (7.2%), and being a victim of stalking (2.2%) (Reetz, Bershad, LeViness, & Whitlock, 2016). The Center for Collegiate Mental Health (CCMH) said in its 2017 annual report that depression and anxiety are the most-frequent mental health conditions on college campuses, with a clear increase over the past four years. With students experiencing more stress and mental health issues becoming more common, residence life staff need to be better trained and more prepared to work with distressed students.

Research continually emerges about college students and mental illness, at least partly because early adulthood is the time many conditions such as depression, anxiety, bipolar disorders, and schizophrenia are uncovered (Hollingsworth, Dunkle, & Douce, 2009). This rise in mental health concerns among college students also may be attributed to student experiencing an increase in violence in their homes, living during times of war, and growing up with more frequent terrorist attacks (Hollingsworth, et al., 2009). Self-destructive behaviors such as cutting, scratching, and burning are being more widely studied in college-aged students.

The increase in students who attend college while experiencing a mental illness is also attributable to the advancement of treatment options available (Pena, 2008). While mental illness has, in the past, been considered a barrier to college success, students who may not have considered higher education in the past have been able to enroll in and maintain their academic status in college (Gallagher, 2015; Pena, 2008) thanks to earlier diagnoses, the help of medication (about 34% of students have taken medications as a result of a mental health concern [Center for Collegiate Mental Health, 2017]), and increased counseling and psychiatric services on college campuses.

Despite this progress, though, barriers to success continue to exist. Stigma is still one of the most-common reasons students are not willing to disclose mental illness and receive help (Angermeyer, van der Auwera, Carta, & Schomerus, 2017; Gruttadaro & Crudo, 2012). Gruttadaro and Crudo (2012) reported only 50% of respondents in their study had disclosed their mental health conditions. The number-one reason that students failed to disclose their conditions was due to the fear of how others — including faculty, staff, and other students — would perceive them. Almost 40% of respondents also indicated they did not know how to gain access to accommodations on their campus, and 64% reported no longer attending college due to their mental health conditions (Gruttadaro, & Crudo, 2012).

Pathological behaviors also have, in recent years, become a focus of institutions of higher education (Dannells, 1997). The evolution of student social behaviors occurring on college campuses has moved beyond relatively benign cases of underage drinking to an increase in more-severe behaviors, such as sexual assaults, domestic violence, and homicide. The American College Health Association found 41% of students reported feeling overwhelming anger within the last 12 months (2017), with 8.4% reporting they considered seriously hurting another person (Center for Collegiate Mental Health, 2017.

These behaviors are proving to be a new challenge for campus administrators in the area of controlling student misconduct on campus. Although disruptive student social behaviors were once seen as ordinary in adolescents, the awareness of mental illness has brought new light to why students behave as they do and how campus policies are structured to work with these students.

The issue of pathological behaviors cannot be ignored when examining the changing behaviors of students in the university setting. The situations administrators face have not only made student affairs professionals change the way they work with student behavior after an incident occurs, but have also changed the way universities implement proactive strategies to prevent significant incidents from occurring. Several trends to address these behaviors commonly seen on campuses include developing threat assessment teams; hiring case managers not only for counseling centers but also for student affairs offices; and creating programs to train students, faculty, and staff to become more aware of and adept at recognizing the signs of students in distress.

Mental Health Conditions

The Centers for Disease Control and Prevention (CDC, 2018) defines mental illnesses as "disorders generally characterized by dysregulation of mood, thought, and/or behavior, as recognized by the *Diagnostic and Statistical Manual*, 4th edition, of the American Psychiatric Association (DSM-IV)" (para 1). According to the National Alliance on Mental Illness (NAMI), mental illness can affect mood or feelings and may affect social relationships with others.

Mental illness can be caused by a variety of factors, or a combination of factors, such as trauma, genetics, environment, lifestyle, or biochemical reactions, with 75% of psychiatric conditions developing by the time a person is 24 years old (NAMI, 2017, para. 4). Osfield and Junco (2006) highlight many mental health conditions as described in the DSM-IV higher education professionals are most likely to encounter.

Student affairs professionals often struggle when a behavior is "viewed by some as disturbing (but not disruptive)" and that "most likely will not even reach the threshold of a violation of the institution's code of conduct" (Dickstein, 2011, p. 35). Still, residence life staff should be aware of these conditions with which students within their halls may be living. It is not the expectation for staff to diagnose or label students, but to be sensitive to the needs of the residents in crisis or care outreach situations. These conditions include:

- **Autism spectrum disorder.** Includes challenges with social interactions, communication, and repetitive behaviors.
- **Bipolar I and Bipolar II disorders.** Experiencing manic episodes, as well as major depressive episodes. Manic episodes include a feeling that the student can accomplish great things that may result in risky behaviors that the person would not otherwise take. Bipolar I Disorder includes greater frequencies and intensities of mania than Bipolar II Disorder, which mainly includes depressive episodes accompanied by at least one manic episode.
- **Borderline, histrionic, and narcissistic personality disorders.** Results in an inability to adapt to environmental and cultural expectations, which may cause major depressive episodes and anxiety disorders.
- **Generalized anxiety disorder.** Excessive worry and anxiety that usually lasts for at least six months and is not a result of a specific event.
- **Major depressive disorder.** A prolonged period (at least two weeks) of depressed mood or loss of interest. Other symptoms may include a change in weight, loss of sleep or sleeping too much, trouble with concentration, restlessness, or thoughts of death.
- **Obsessive-compulsive disorder (OCD).** Manifests through intrusive anxious thoughts or repetitive behaviors in which one engages to reduce anxiety
- **Panic Disorder without Agoraphobia.** Caused by a sudden onset of acute fear, accompanied by physiological symptoms such as a racing heart rate, difficulty breathing, and chest pains.
- **Post-traumatic Stress Disorder (PTSD).** Features symptoms related to a previous traumatic event that may cause flashback-like experiences which produce a great deal of anxiety.

Mental Health Considerations

Along with specific mental health disorders, it is valuable for housing and conduct professionals to be familiar with larger, overarching considerations related to student mental health.

Threat to others. Due to the potentially devastating consequences, one of the most-important considerations when examining mental health conditions is identifying a student's threat to self and/or others. While student safety has always been a consideration, an increase in awareness as well as time, energy, and resources directed toward protecting campus communities evolved after the 2007 event when a Virginia Polytechnic Institute and State University (Virginia Tech) student shot and killed 32 people and injured 17 others. After this tragedy, Virginia Governor Tim Kaine appointed a review panel to investigate the incident and make recommendations on their findings. After conducting more than 200 interviews and an extensive review of records and reports, the panel discovered the student had a history of psychological problems since childhood. In 1999, some of his teachers reported suicidal and homicidal ideations he revealed in some of his writings after the mass shooting at Columbine High School (Mass Shootings at Virginia Tech Review Panel, 2007). The student had been referred to — and participated in — several mental health treatment programs. In addition, his behavior had been monitored by various campus faculty, staff, and administrators. Still, the tragedy was not avoided.

Threat to self. Although violence against others has been a factor in some of the tragic acts on college campuses involving the mental health of students, most instances of harm feature a threat to self. This may entail alcohol and drug abuse, risky sexual behavior, or criminal activity, as well as severe eating disorders or self-injurious behavior such as cutting. However, in terms of students being a threat to themselves, it is the most severe self-harm that is usually considered: that of suicide.

Suicide is the second-most common cause of death among college-age students in the United States (Jed Foundation, 2017). CCMH stated in its 2017 annual report 27% of respondents engaged in self-injurious behaviors and 34.2% of students seriously considered suicide, indicating a rise in students seeking mental health support for these two concerns. Suicide attempts are also on the rise, with 10% of students reporting they have attempted to end their lives (Center for Collegiate Mental Health, 2017). Between 1,100 and 1,400 college students take their own lives each year and 10% of college students experience suicidal ideation (Jed Foundation, 2017).

In the past, completed suicides by self-inflicted gunshot wounds were most-common among college-aged students, but suffocation, including hanging, and poisonings have been on the rise for this age group (CDC, 2017). Although attempts by females are more frequent, males complete suicide more often (CDC, 2014). Because people with depression face a greater risk of committing suicide, colleges and universities must have a heightened sense of how to work with students at risk of harming themselves (Pena, 2008).

Communities of care. Although decades have passed since the elimination of *in loco parentis*, the ability for colleges and universities to regulate student behavior through student codes of conduct is still a right of residence life programs, as well as an expectation, not only from students but their families. The belief is residence hall staff will create and provide safe environments for all students to live and learn, free not just of hostility but of disruption. To provide these environments, residence life staff must create communities of care to support the mental health needs of their residents. Staff must be adequately trained to address all types of behaviors appropriately, no matter the root of the behavior.

Residence life staff at all levels must know how to identify signs of student distress and understand how that distress may manifest as different types of behavior. Staff must be comfortable with intervening and making appropriate referrals before the behavior disrupts the community.

Although colleges and universities have added crisis intervention teams and case managers to their campuses to better support students in the campus community in recent years, barriers to students with mental health issues receiving help remains a challenge. Whether it is a lack of resources to support increasing student mental health needs, stigma discouraging disclosure, or an unwillingness for students to seek the necessary assistance to learn positive coping mechanisms and skills to aid in resiliency, student behavior that results from a psychological diagnosis must be addressed by residence hall staff to maintain an educational environment. Staff must be well-equipped to provide educational interventions that aid in maintaining a safe community, as well as support students in their developmental growth and academic success.

It is hoped that residence hall communities will be built on acceptance and inclusiveness of all, providing students a safe place to disclose their mental health challenges so they can get support early. However, when residents are unwilling to self-disclose, mental health conditions must be considered and recognized by student affairs staff as early as possible to enable support and intervention to avert behavior unacceptable to community standards of living.

Mental health in under-represented groups. When addressing behavior in the residence halls, staff should consider possible cultural differences. Although students with mental health issues from varying backgrounds should be held to the same standards of conduct, cultural differences need to be considered in the conduct conference with the accused student to understand their perspective better. Specific barriers and challenges may exist that keeps students from accessing resources. As an example, individuals from under-represented groups, including international students, are less likely to get access to treatment due to cultural stigmas, receive lower qualities of care, face culturally insensitive healthcare systems, experience language barriers, and have lower rates of health insurance. In addition, students from under-represented groups may face racism, bias, homophobia, or discrimination in treatment settings (NAMI, 2017).

INSTITUTIONAL RESPONSE

For many, if faced with the scenario described at the start of the chapter, the response may not extend far past their immediate concern for Jennifer. Is she okay? Will she get the help and counseling she needs? While tending to Jennifer is the primary concern, residence life and student conduct professionals must also turn their concern to other affected students. Behavior such as Jennifer's can be disruptive to a residential community (Dickstein & Christensen, 2008). To address these types of behaviors, as well as the possible fallout from them, it is important for administrators to have appropriate policies and procedures in place.

Sanctions

When a student is found in violation of a campus or housing department's code of conduct, administrators must think about the appropriate conditions or sanctions to address the student's behavior. When a student's behavior is influenced by their mental health, however, sanctioning becomes more challenging. "The goal of [sanctioning is to help] students understand how their behavior affects themselves and others while motivating the student not to repeat the inappropriate behavior in the future are the two outcomes of the sanctioning process" (Dickstein & Christensen, 2008, p. 229). While sanctions should be tailored to an individual student, they must reflect the norms of the local campus community, and be consistent and fair (Ragle & Paine, 2009).

One of the foundational elements of student conduct is that sanctions address the action taken and remain separate from the underlying causes of the action. In practice, this means that although charging a student with a conduct violation should be based on behavior alone, mental health can be considered when administering sanctions. To that end, sanctions may include a mandatory assessment by a mental health professional. Seeking an assessment by a mental health professional will provide a conduct administrator with a professional diagnosis and opinion from which the administrator can decide appropriate actions.

For example, if a university wishes to implement a mandatory withdrawal policy because it is concerned a student is psychologically unstable and poses a risk to self or others, it is highly recommended the university "conduct a direct threat assessment" (Dickstein, 2011, p. 38). The assessment must be based on medical training, best judgment, and evidence-based best practices (U.S. Department of Justice, 42, U.S.C. 12111 (3)).

Access to a licensed professional trained in threat assessment, such as a forensic psychologist, could help a university avoid a potential lawsuit. Although residence life and conduct professionals may be aware of possible mental illness affecting students in higher education, it is important to have an assessment from a trained mental health professional who will be able to provide information regarding the ability of the student to be successful in the university setting. For example, in the scenario previously outlined, one of Jennifer's sanctions may be to receive a mental health assessment for the conduct administrator to review. Although the goal is to keep the student enrolled at the university, a mental health assessment may reveal it is in the student's immediate best interest to withdraw from an institution until their condition stabilizes.

A voluntary withdrawal allows the student to leave the institution for a period to address any mental health concerns affecting their involvement in the campus community. Involuntary withdrawal policies give an institution the ability to separate a student from the institution so the student can receive needed medical attention (Wei, 2008). To legally complete an involuntary withdrawal, campus administrators are required to make an individualized and objective assessment of a student's ability to participate safely in an educational community (Jed Foundation, 2008). Any involuntary withdrawal policy must include information that ensures due process. In addition, the policy should be clear whether, if an involuntary withdrawal is implemented, the evidence supports the student engaged in conduct that poses a risk to the student and/or the university community.

Intervention

While sanctions address behavioral violations, there may also be times when housing officers are motivated to intervene in the interest of the health of the student or others, even if a violation has not occurred. The value of this was illustrated in a presentation to the St. Catherine University behavioral intervention team (2009) by John Nicoletti, a national expert in police psychology, violence risk assessment, workplace and school violence prevention, and crisis intervention and trauma recovery. He explained that, when a student is not behaving appropriately, the campus should put up a roadblock to stop the behavior. Staff should speak with the student and explain how the behavior is inappropriate. If the behavior does not stop, a larger roadblock is needed to try to resolve the behavior. If that does not work, that is when the student could be considered a risk.

Although Nicoletti shared his information in the context of a mass shooting, it can be applied to other low-level issues such as students who are on the autism spectrum and unable to take social cues, or a student who is exhibiting concerning behaviors. Consider an example where a student at a small liberal arts university creates a video of herself engaged in cutting activity and then shares it on social media. Such behavior could be considered harm to self (for engaging in the cutting) and harm to others (for the emotional trauma experienced by her peers), even though it failed to reach the level of violating any existing rules. The institution, in this case, could create that roadblock by having an intentional discussion with the student and explain to her why the behavior had to stop or that she might find herself in the conduct process.

The Assessment Intervention of Student Problems (AISP) model (Delworth, 1989/2009) represented an early model of intervention with students of concern. It incorporates three components: "a) the formation of a campus assessment team; b) a general assessment process for channeling students into the most appropriate on-campus and off-campus resources; and c) intervention with the student of concern" (Dunkle, Silverstein, & Warner, 2008, p. 590).

The first element of this model is creating a campus assessment team as the basis for providing a coordinated, campus-wide system for dealing with students of concern. This may involve a case management team that includes key personnel from various areas, including counseling, residence life, and the student conduct or judicial office (Deisinger et al., 2008; Delworth, 1989/2009; Dunkle et al., 2008; Van Brunt, Reese, & Lewis, 2015). Effective communication, collaboration, and coordination are necessary for collecting, evaluating, and responding to critical information (Deisinger et al., 2008). The use, membership, responsibilities, and processes of case management teams vary from institution to institution. Threat assessment, behavioral intervention, case management teams, student conduct office, and residential life staff all assist institutions in addressing concerning behaviors.

Code of Conduct

For a college or university to assist students successfully by using sanctions and interventions, they must be supported by well-crafted and comprehensive policies. To create such policies can be challenging, since there are several considerations for addressing the behavior of students whose behavior may be influenced by their mental health. It is crucial the institutional code of conduct includes language to address the behavior of a student regardless of whether their behavior is due to a mental health crisis.

As mentioned previously, the Title II/Direct Threat Standard influences the institutional policies that address students who are a threat to themselves. Based on the Title II/Direct Threat standard, it is important for both residence life staff and conduct administrators to focus on a student's behavior rather than the cause of that behavior. Enacting policies focusing strictly on behavior rather than on disability limits the legal risk when the Title II regulation is in question. Focusing on the student's behavior and how it violates the code of conduct will ensure administrators are not engaging in discriminatory practices.

Many institutions address student self-injurious behavior influenced by mental issues through the code of conduct. Amada (2015), in *Mental Health and Student Conduct Issues on the College Campus,* argues it is important not only to have a code of conduct in place; it is also important for universities to have "clear, coherent, comprehensive, mutually compatible, and enforceable" codes of conduct. However, he found this not always the case for colleges and universities (p. 100). He highlights the importance of, when developing the code of conduct, including disruptive behaviors in the code. In addition, an annual review of the code of conduct by a variety of administrators is warranted.

In the example that opened the chapter, if that incident had occurred at the University of Houston, Jennifer would allegedly have violated the code of conduct and received notice regarding information about the conduct process. This is because the University of Houston's Student Code of Conduct (2017) lists a variety of prohibited conduct that includes "intentionally inflicting mental or bodily harm upon any person" as well as "taking any reckless, but not accidental, action from which mental or bodily harm could result to any person" or "communicating a threat to cause mental or bodily harm to any person." In addition, it stipulates the term "any person" as used in the code of conduct "may include oneself."

Campus Housing Contracts and Service Agreements

Along with codes of conduct created by colleges and universities, campuses may also refer to university housing contracts and service agreements to regulate student behavior. Administrators must ensure their contracts and service agreements comply with Section 504 of the Americans with Disabilities (ADA) as well as the Title II regulation, when providing language regarding removing students from the residential community. For example, the University of Georgia's housing contract (2017) provides information in its contract that outlines the authority of the residence life staff if a student poses a danger to themselves or others. "Behaving in a manner that may create the appearance of and/or pose a danger to the student or to others" may allow the university to revoke the student's ability to remain within the residence hall.

Again considering the earlier example, Jennifer's behavior could warrant her removal from the campus's housing and residence life system due to the "danger to the student or to others." That portion of the contract must be reviewed by the institution's legal representatives to ensure nondiscriminatory practices.

Additional emerging issues related to students' mental health now must be addressed in campus housing contracts. In addition to language regarding a university's authority to revoke a student, the contract or service agreement must also outline information regarding emotional support animals. Emotional support animals (ESAs) "provide support, well-being, comfort, aid, or a calming influence through companionship, non-judgmental positive regard, affection, and a focus in life simply by being close to their handler." (Von Bergen, 2015, p. 21). ESAs may help reduce psychological or emotional issues that affect a student's well-being in the residential community (Von Bergen, 2015). While pets are not permitted in most residential facilities, service animals have access to all campus locations.

Administrators must give students information about the policy and procedures to properly receive approval of an ESA. Students must be allowed an ESA after going through the proper channels and receiving approval by the institution.

STUDENTS' RIGHTS

Student affairs practitioners, as well as the institutions for which they work, often must navigate a gray area of legal issues and student accountability when working through the conduct process. Students' rights are protected by overarching laws such as Section 504 of the Rehabilitation Act and Title II of the Americans with Disabilities Act. Complicated rulings and regulations are part of the challenge that university administrators will find themselves sifting through to protect their campuses, their students, and themselves.

Increased concern and awareness of legal liability also can affect how campuses address their treatment of mental illness. As one example, a Syracuse University student sued the university after she jumped from the eighth floor of her residence hall in a failed suicide attempt. She said that the university negligently handled her suicidal condition when they sent her a conduct letter for her refusal of treatment with a local mental healthcare provider (Cohen, 2007). Cases such as this demonstrate how vital it is for professionals in the residence life and conduct fields stay informed about the ever-changing legal issues that affect their work. When institutions establish policies and procedures to address student behaviors, administrators must be aware of applicable disability laws and ensure the regulations they create focus on behavior, regardless of what is causing the behavior. Knowledge of disability laws can assist administrators in developing policies and procedures that balance legal liability while avoiding discriminatory practices.

Also challenging are the multiple interpretations of the law. Although this book and this chapter will serve as a useful tool to help guide professionals in decision-making and policy implementation, consulting with legal counsel is encouraged. Taking that extra step is necessary to protect the institution from liability issues.

Multiple pieces of legislation have been implemented to protect students with disabilities from being denied acceptance to, or being removed from, an

✚ Addressing Student Conduct and Mental Health

Balancing the needs and rights of an individual with those of the community at large is a difficult proposition that becomes more so when also considering a student's mental health. The following steps are a foundation upon which to build policies and practices.

- Identify the behavior(s) and how the behaviors are affecting the community.

- Separate the mental health issue from the specific behavior(s) and determine whether the behavior(s) violate university policy.

- If an alleged policy violation exists, send the student written notice of the alleged charges and explain next steps.

- Allow the student the opportunity to respond to the charges in person.

- Follow regular conduct protocol as outlined in the student code of conduct.

- Depending on the severity of the incident, consider putting interim measures in place, such as an interim suspension or interim housing removal, until the case is resolved. Use interim measures only when necessary to protect the student of concern and/or the community. Remember that the decision to impose this expectation must be based only on the behaviors exhibited, not the mental health diagnosis. It is also recommended to outline this step in the student code of conduct.

- Consider mental health conditions and the impact they have on behavior when administering sanctions. For example, having a student complete a mental health assessment and follow the recommendations of a therapist could be an appropriate sanction.

---

educational setting solely based on disability. At the forefront of these in the United States are the Americans with Disabilities Act and the Rehabilitation Act of 1973, Section 504. These two pieces of legislation directly inform campus housing and conduct when supporting students struggling with mental health illness, and the behavior issues that may be present. Although they do serve as a guide, legal ambiguity can lead to professional uncertainty.

Americans with Disabilities Act

Campuses have long abided by the ADA to respond to those with impaired mobility, vision, or hearing. The act states "no qualified individual with a disability shall, by reason of disability, be excluded from participation in or be denied the benefits of services, programs, or activities of a public entity, or be subjected to discrimination by any entity" (42 U.S.C. 12131, (Sec. 203), 1990/2008). Title II of the ADA prohibits "discrimination on the basis of disability in all services, programs, and activities provided to the public by State and local governments, except public transportation services" (U.S. Department of Justice, Civil Rights Division, 2016).

An exception to this regulation comes into play when an individual poses a threat to others. Before 2011, colleges and universities based standards of safety on the interpretation of Title II's direct-threat standard, which included threat to self as well as threat to others; however, the Department of Justice (DOJ) eliminated information related to the risk of self-harm that year (National Association of College and University Attorneys, 2014). "Although, as written, Title II of the ADA applied only to public institutions, the OCR has historically interpreted Title II and Section 504 as being similar in intent and informed private colleges and universities that they will be held to the same standard" (Grace, 2014, Para. 2). Therefore, private and public university administrators must ensure they are not removing students from residence halls or universities based on their disabilities alone, but rather are addressing self-harming behaviors based on the student code of conduct and appropriate due process.

Many institutions have struggled with the ADA because of the ways it protects people with both visible and invisible disabilities. College campuses are seeing an increase in the number of students reporting invisible disabilities, such as "anxiety, attention deficit, hyperactivity disorder, dyslexia, autism spectrum disorder, and food or environmental allergies" (Barger, 2016). "The law defines a disability as a physical or mental impairment that lasts longer than six months, and substantially limits one or more major life activity, including learning, eating, sleeping, seeing, hearing, walking, standing, communicating, or concentrating" (Barger, 2016).

What can be a challenge for student affairs and residence life professionals is that colleges are only required to support students who report their disabilities to the university. Even when a student does disclose a disability, typically to a disability resources office on campus, the information often is shared with other departments only on a need-to-know basis to support the student's academic success. In many cases, it is not considered necessary to alert the residence life staff to a student's invisible disability and, as a result, those staff are not aware the invisible disability could be a source of conduct exhibited by a student.

In *Bhatt v. the University of Vermont*, "Rajan Bhatt, a former medical student, falsified an evaluation for a surgery rotation" (McKendall, 2010, p. 2). The student claimed it was an honest error and a one-time incident. The university allowed Bhatt to remain in school, but the student later forged other documents. Bhatt revealed in a subsequent hearing he suffered from "Tourette's syndrome and a related obsessive-behavior disorder" (McKendall, 2010, p. 2). After the university dismissed Bhatt, the student sued the university for an ADA violation. The case was dismissed, with the court citing that "medical schools are not required to alter their policies or programs in such a way as would compromise the integrity of their programs" (McKendall, 2010, p. 2). In this case, the university separated the behavior from the disability and identified the behavior (document forgery) as harmful to patients.

Invisible disabilities such as mental health conditions should be considered and accommodated as required by law. Because it is difficult to know whether a student has a disability, conduct officers should include language in communications to students specifically outlining the steps they must take to request reasonable accommodations for both conduct conferences and hearings. The Rehabilitation Act of 1973, Section 504, states in part, "no otherwise, qualified handicapped individual … shall solely, by reason of his handicap, be excluded from the participation in, be denied the benefits of, or be subjected to discrimination under any program or activity receiving federal financial assistance" (29 U.S.C. 794, (A) 1982).

The law illustrates the importance of colleges and universities basing decisions solely on an individual's behavior. It is also important for campuses to have clear codes of conduct that help guide them through the conduct process to ensure a fair outcome for all involved. Just as with any other student involved in the conduct process, it is important to follow the process exactly as outlined in the code of conduct, which includes all written notices about meetings and hearings. In addition, when working with any student, but particularly a student with a diagnosed mental health condition, it is important to "carefully document observations and concerns" (Amada, 2015, p. 70).

The case of *Doe v. Hunter College of the City University of New York* illustrates the importance of following the process outlined in the code of conduct. In this case, a student who had overdosed on Tylenol was hospitalized. When she returned to campus, she found the locks on her door had been changed and she no longer had access to her room. The university had not provided any written notice of their intent to change the locks on her doors, so they were sued for violating their own outlined process (Judge David L. Bazelon Center for Mental Health Law, 2006). As illustrated in this example, the action was taken before the student was notified of a potential code of conduct violation and, more importantly, before the student had a fair conduct hearing.

Family Education Rights and Privacy Act

When working with students who experience mental health and conduct issues, partnering with parents can be beneficial. However, involving parents cannot always be the first step toward resolution of an issue. Before contacting parents, it is recommended practitioners consult their institution's interpretation of the Family Education Rights and Privacy Act (FERPA). Most institutions use the parameters of "harm to self or others" as the guide for when to initiate family involvement.

If this is the threshold a campus plans to use for parental involvement, it is also recommended to discuss what constitutes a threat to self or others. In the past, campuses have taken a student-centered approach to FERPA and were conservative about the choice to involve parents. This conservative approach has shifted in recent years, however, after several legal cases addressed a parent's right to know.

One of the most high-profile cases related to this subject occurred in the spring of 2000, when Elizabeth Shin, a residential student at Massachusetts Institute of Technology (MIT), completed suicide by setting herself on fire in her residence hall room. Before her death, Shin had engaged in self-harming behaviors such as cutting, overdosed on Tylenol with codeine, and threatened to stab herself with a knife. Shin had informed other MIT students, including ones living with her in her residence hall, of her depression and suicidal thoughts (*Shin v. MIT*, 2005). After her suicide, Shin's parents sued the institution, MIT administrators, members of the mental health team, campus police, and the housemother. Shin's parents argued the administrators and staff failed to coordinate Shin's care and the mental health professionals did not take her suicide plan seriously enough (Dickerson, 2006). They also argued that they should have been made aware that their daughter had a deteriorating mental health condition (Jed Foundation, 2017). The case was eventually settled for an undisclosed amount in 2006 (Bombardieri, 2006).

In the wake of incidents such as those at Virginia Tech and MIT, universities have been more apt to involve family in cases of a student's concerning behavior. Along with legal liability considerations, this approach of including family is also taken to engage the student in support mechanisms that help maintain a safe and prosperous environment, for not only their student but the residential community as a whole.

The law does allow institutions to contact parents in the event there is a substance abuse concern, but again, many institutions do not use the ability to contact family unless their housing or schooling is at risk. However, the Family Policy Compliance Office of the U.S. Department of Education interprets FERPA to "permit schools to disclose information from education records to

✚ Additional Readings

With the increased awareness of mental health issues, particularly among college and university students, there has been an increase in available resources. These are valuable resources to consider for additional information.

Books

- *Beyond the Americans with Disabilities Act: Inclusive Policy and Practice for Higher Education*
  Mary Lee Vance, Neal E. Lipsitz, and Kaela Parks, NASPA (2014)

- *College of the Overwhelmed: The Campus Mental Health Crisis and What to Do About It*
  Richard Kadison and Theresa Foy DiGeronimo, Jossey-Bass (2005)

- *College Student Mental Health: Effective Services and Strategies Across Campus*
  Sherry A. Benton and Stephen L. Benton, NASPA (2006)

- *The Handbook for Campus Threat Assessment and Management Teams*
  Gene Deisinger, Marisa Randazzo, Daniel O'Neill, and Jenna Savage, Applied Risk Management, LLC (2008)

- *Helping College Students: Developing Essential Support Skills for Student Affairs Practice*
  Amy L. Reynolds, Jossey-Bass (2008)

- *Mental Health and Student Conduct Issues on the College Campus*
  Gerald Amada, Biographical Publishing Company (2015)

Professional Associations

- *American College Health Association - acha.org*

- *Association for University and College Counseling Center Directors - aucccd.org*

- *Center for Collegiate Mental Health - ccmh.psu.edu*

- *Higher Education Case Managers Association - hecma.org*

- *National Alliance on Mental Illness - nami.org*

- *Jed Foundation - jedfoundation.org*

parents if a health or safety emergency involves their son or daughter" (U.S. Department of Education).

Although FERPA allows a call to parents when a student is at risk of harming themselves or others, it may be worth reviewing a student's emergency contact information before calling parents. If parents are not the first or second contacts listed on the emergency contact list, be aware this could be an indication of uncomfortable family dynamics. This may be especially true when working with students who struggle with mental health issues. Whenever possible, professionals are urged to consult with the student before making a phone call to family and to have the student present when making that call. This will ensure the university is working within the expectations of the legislation while taking care and concern for the student into consideration.

CONCLUSION

It should be celebrated that colleges and universities are increasingly accessible to students with mental health issues. However, it is also true these mental issues have the potential to affect the student's behavior in the campus community and there are a variety of challenges in addressing student behavior in these regards. Residential life professionals and student conduct professionals must be knowledgeable about the disability laws and regulations with an impact on student conduct to avoid discriminatory practices. Administrators also must have policies and procedures in place that satisfy existing laws and address a student's behavior.

When addressing behavior that may be influenced by a student experiencing a mental health crisis, it is important to use resources in the campus community through collaborative and coordinated efforts by multiple campus administrators. Most campuses today have developed multiple systems to intervene with students who present a potential threat, to ensure all are safe within their community.

"Cases such as these have exploded in number and frequency on contemporary college campuses. They are complex and time intensive, and they typically draw in several campus systems" (Hollingsworth, Dunkle, & Douce, 2009, p. 38). An example of this collaborative nature can be used in the introductory anecdote for this chapter. In this situation, the residence life staff is fully aware of the student's pattern of behavior — knowledge crucial in determining a possible outcome to address this student's behavior. The systems used to address Jennifer's behavior may include the office of student conduct, a behavioral intervention team, case management or a case manager, the residence life staff, or the university counseling office. It is important to identify the factors that may influence which system will address the student's behavior. These factors include the student's history or pattern of behavior, how the student's behavior affects the campus community, or whether the student is a potential threat to self or others (Deisinger, et al., 2008; Jed Foundation, 2013).

The challenge to enforce conduct standards, maintain residence hall communities, and respect individual student rights simultaneously is only heightened when mental health issues also must be considered. Fortunately, it has been established there are successful strategies. Early connections between students with known mental health conditions and campus and community resources are valuable aids. Residence life staff should be trained in mental health conditions and how they may affect behavior so early intervention and support can take place. Faculty and staff should be encouraged to share information as FERPA allows. Support should be given to establishing partnerships and collaborations across campus to create a web of support for students. The community should understand barriers to help for all students, especially those from underrepresented populations. Campus administrators also must create clear student conduct policies and procedures (including those for voluntary and involuntary withdrawals) that address student behaviors and not their mental health. If these and related steps are taken, the staff members have not only strengthened the overall sense of community, but have supported the commendable goal of accessibility for all students.

REFERENCES

Amada, G. (2015). *Mental health and student conduct issues on the college campus.* Prospect, CT: The Higher Administration Series, Biographical Publishing Company.

American College Health Association (2017). National college health assessment II. Retrieved from http://www.acha-ncha.org/docs/ncha-ii_spring_2017_undergraduate_reference_group_executive_summary.pdf.

American Psychological Association College Mental Health. (n.d.). Retrieved March 3, 2018, from http://www.apa.org/advocacy/higher-education/mental-health/index.aspx.

Angermeyer, M. C., van der Auwera, S., Carta, M. G., & Schomerus, G. (2017). Public attitudes towards psychiatry and psychiatric treatment at the beginning of the 21st century: A systematic review and meta-analysis of population surveys. *World Psychiatry, 16*: 50–61. doi:10.1002/wps.20383.

Barger, T. S., (2016, July 1). ADA compliance across the campus: Providing accommodations to level the playing field for students with both visible and invisible disabilities. *University Business.* Retrieved from https://www.universitybusiness.com/article/ada-compliance-across-campus.

Bombardieri, M. (2006). Parents strike settlement with MIT in death of daughter. *Boston Globe.* Retrieved from http://archive.boston.com/news/education/higher/articles/2006/04/04/parents_strike_settlement_with_mit_in_death_of_daughter/.

Centers for Disease Control and Prevention. (2017). Retrieved from https://www.cdc.gov/mentalhealth/basics/mental-illness.htm.

Centers for Disease Control and Prevention. (2014). Suicide and self-inflicted injury. Retrieved from https://www.cdc.gov/nchs/fastats/suicide.htm.

Dannells, M. (1997). *From discipline to development: Rethinking student conduct in higher education.* In J. D. Fife (Ed). Washington, DC: George Washington University.

Deisinger, G., Randazzo, M., O'Neill, D., & Savage, J. (2008). *The handbook for campus threat assessment and management teams.* Stoneham, MA: Applied Risk Management.

Delworth, U. (1989/2009). The AISP model: Assessment-intervention of student problems. *New Directions for Student Services, 1989*(45), 3–14. doi:10.1002/ss.37119894503.

Dickerson, D. (2006). Legal issues for campus administrators, faculty, and staff. In Benton, S. A., & Benton, S. L. (Eds.), *College student mental health: Effective services and strategies across America* (35–119). Washington, DC: National Association of Student Personnel Administrators.

Dickstein, G. (2011). Student discipline intervention strategies: A case study of two institutions' processes utilized to resolve misconduct of students who concomitantly experience a mental health crisis. (Doctoral dissertation). Available from ProQuest database (3478432).

Dickstein, G., & Christensen, A. N. (2008). Addressing students' well-being and mental health. In J. Lancaster & D. Waryold (Eds.), *Student conduct practice: The complete guide for student affairs professionals* (216–240). Sterling, VA: Stylus Publishing.

Dunkle, J. H., Silverstein, Z. B., & Warner, S. L. (2008). Managing violent and other troubling students: The role of threat assessment teams on campus. *Journal of College and University Law, 34*(3), 585–636.

Gallagher, R. P. (2012). Thirty years of the national survey of counseling center directors: A personal account. *Journal of College Student Psychotherapy, 26*(172–184). doi:10.1080/87568225.2012.685852.

Gallagher, R. P. (2015). National survey of college counseling centers 2014. Retrieved from http://d-scholarship.pitt.edu/28178/.

Grace, T. (2014). Self-endangering Students: The Public Policy Conundrum. Retrieved from https://www.naspa.org/rpi/posts/self-endangering-students-the-public-policy-conundrum.

Gruttadaro, D., & Crudo, D. (2012). College students speak: A survey report on mental health. Retrieved from National Alliance on Mental Illness https://www.nami.org/collegesurvey.

Grace, T. (2014). Self-endangering students, the public policy conundrum. Retrieved from National Association of Student Affairs Administrators in Higher Education (NASPA) website: https://www.naspa.org/rpi/posts/self-endangering-students-the-public-policy-conundrum.

Hollingsworth, K. R., Dunkle, J. H., & Douce, L. (2009). The high risk (disturbed and disturbing) college student. *New Directions for Student Services*, 2009 (*128*), 37–54. doi:10.1002/ss.340.

Jed Foundation. (2017). Crisis on campus. Retrieved from https://www.jedfoundation.org/crisis-on-campus/.

Jed Foundation. (2017). Students with mental troubles on rise: Colleges add suicide response teams, counselors. Retrieved from https://www.jedfoundation.org/students-with-mental-troubles-on-rise/.

Jed Foundation. (2008). *Student mental health and the law: A resource for institutions of higher education*. New York, NY: Author.

Jed Foundation. (2013). *Balancing safety and support on campus: A guide to campus teams*. New York, NY: Author.

Judge David L. Bazelon Center for Mental Health Law. (2006). Hunter College settles lawsuit by student barred from dorm after treatment for depression. Retrieved from http://www.bazelon.org/newsroom/archive/2006/8-23-06 hunter-settlement.html.

Kitzrow, M. A. (2003). The mental health needs of today's college students: Challenges and recommendations. *NASPA Journal*, *41*(1), 167–181.

Lannon, P.G., Jr. (2014). Direct threat and caring for students at risk for self-harm: Where we stand now. *National Association of College and University Attorneys Notes*, *12*(8), par. 2).

McKendall, M. (2010, April 25). How to navigate the intersection of student disability and discipline issues. *Chronicle of Higher Education*.

National Alliance on Mental Illness. (2017). Retrieved from https://www.nami.org/Learn-More/Mental-Health-Conditions.

Osfield, K. J., & Junco, R. (2006). Support Services for Students with Mental Health Disabilities. In Benton, S. A., & Benton, S. L. (Eds.), *College student mental health: Effective services and strategies across America* (169–188). Washington, DC: National Association of Student Personnel Administrators.

Pena, M. F. (2008). *Reevaluating privacy and disability laws in the wake of the Virginia Tech tragedy: Considerations for administrators and lawmakers. North Carolina Law Review*, *87*, 1–69.

Ragle, J. D. and Paine, G. E. (2009). The disturbing student and the judicial process. *New Directions for Student Services*, 23–36. doi:10.1002/ss.339

University of Georgia. (2017). University of Georgia Housing Contract.

Retrieved from https://housing.uga.edu/uploads/documents/housing_con-tract_2017-18.pdf.

University of Houston. (2017). University of Houston Student Code of Conduct. Retrieved from http://www.uh.edu/dos/_files/student-code-of-conduct.pdf.

U.S. Department of Education. (2009). Americans with Disabilities Act of 1990, as amended. 42 U.S.C. 12111 (3) Retrieved from http://www.ada.gove/pubs/adastatute08mark.htm#12111.

U.S. Department of Education. (n.d.) Section 504 of the Rehabilitation Act of 1973. Retrieved from http://www.section508.gov/docs/sections504.pdf.

U.S. Department of Education. (n.d.). 20 U.S.C. § 1232g; 34 CFR Part 99 of the Family Education Rights and Privacy Act. Retrieved from https://www2.ed.gov/policy/gen/guid/fpco/ferpa/index.html.

U.S. Department of Justice. (2016). Nondiscrimination on the basis of disability in state and local government services. Americans with Disabilities Act Title II Regulations. Retrieved from https://www.ada.gov/regs2010/titleII_2010/titleII_2010_regulations.htm#a35139.

Virginia Tech Review Panel. (2007). Mass shootings at Virginia Tech. Retrieved from http://www.governor.virginia.gov/TempContent/techpanelreport.cfm.

Van Brunt, B., Reese, A., & Lewis, W. S. (2015). Who's on the team? Mission, membership and motivation. Retrieved from https://nabita.org/wordpress/wp-content/uploads/2015/07/2015-NaBITA-Whitepaper.pdf .

Von Bergen, C. W. (2015). Emotional Support Animals, Service Animals and Pets on Campus. *Administrative Issues Journal: Connecting Education, Practice and Research, 5*(1), 15–34.

Wei, M. (2008). University policy and procedural responses to students at risk of suicide. Retrieved from http://digitalcommons.law.yale.edu/.

1. How does your campus train hearing officers on the difference between addressing the behavior (conduct) as opposed to the illness (condition)?

2. What happens if a student discloses a mental health issue during a conduct meeting?

3. Does your institution address harm to self (suicide attempt or self-harm) through the conduct process? What are the pros and cons to this approach?

4. Other than during staff training, how often does your housing department review its crisis protocol? Do the live-in staff members understand what happens when residents are transported to a health facility for a mental health concern? Are staff expected to have a role in the follow-up with the resident?

5. What happens to a resident when they come back into the community after a mental health incident? What strategies can best help a resident reintegrate into the community?

6. Consider the pros and cons of administratively moving a resident after a mental health incident. How might this benefit the resident? How might this harm the resident? In this situation, who has the greater right; the resident or the roommate(s)?

7. What are ways community building and mental health outreach intersect?

8. How do you maximize campus and community partnerships in addressing mental health concerns?

DETERMINING SANCTIONS AND OUTCOMES

Lyndsay Anderson, Nicole Kogan, and Christina Liang

WHEN MOST people encounter the term *sanction*, they consider it strictly in its punitive sense: a punishment or penalty suffered as a result of an earlier violation. However, exploring the word's origins further reveals its primary definitions are, as a noun, "a formal decree" or, as a verb, "to make valid or binding[,] usually by a formal procedure" (Mish, 2014). In short, while a sanction may be a result of, or a reaction to, an event, that does not mean it is the end of a process. Rather, it is the beginning of a new one.

Sanctioning is the process of weighing mitigating and aggravating factors to determine what outcomes are appropriate to address the behavior, and these outcomes can serve various purposes (Olshak, 2008). As befitting common student affairs goals, these outcomes should focus on the student's education. As Zdziarski and Wood wrote, for sanctions "to be truly developmental and educative, it is also critical that the student understand how his or her behavior affects others and how engaging in that behavior may affect the student's behavior" (2008, p. 98).

This type of learning is a component of why conduct officers hold students accountable for their behaviors. Conduct officers' ultimate goal is for students to reflect on and understand what they did, recognize how their actions affect the rest of the community, and be prepared to make better choices in the future. While the conduct process typically focuses on an individual student, residence life staff who serve as conduct officers also have to recognize the need to protect the health, safety, and well-being of not only the campus community, but more specifically, the residential community.

PHILOSOPHICAL CONSIDERATIONS

Determining effective sanctions and outcomes after a student is found responsible for a violation is arguably one of the most important elements of the conduct process; at least, it is the part that garners the most interest and opinions. In many cases, the first question a conduct or a housing officer will hear from a student, resident assistant, parent, colleague, or supervisor after an incident is, "What's going to happen to them?" Or, perhaps, a report about a student's behavior is accompanied by a recommended sanction offered by a non-conduct professional. Other times, the students, campus partners, and stakeholders are not even interested in a specific learning process or outcome, but just want to know how the student will be punished. They are looking for assurance the student will be held accountable for their actions, even though accountability can mean various things to different people. It is difficult for residence life conduct officers to satisfy all parties and stakeholders with a sanctioning decision. However, various strategies and philosophies can increase the likelihood that decisions will be understood and supported.

Although residence life conduct systems are not intended to be criminal justice systems, some conduct sanctions are based on philosophies found in criminal justice theory. That makes it important for residence life professionals to consider the outcomes they are trying to achieve with their sanctions. Typical outcomes residence life professionals are looking to accomplish with their sanctions include deterring future wrongdoing, either by that specific student or others, and correcting or educating students by letting them learn how to change their behavior. Understanding the aims of punishment (Marsh, Cochrane, & Melville, 2014) as used in criminal justice can assist with shaping sanctioning practices within the conduct system and can be a valuable learning exercise.

In recent years, however, there has been a broader conversation in the student conduct field about providing educational sanctions versus punishments. This shift focuses on providing educational opportunities to help students see the impact of their choices on not only themselves, but also on others in their communities. It also aligns with the educational mission of most institutions. Residence life conduct officers are increasingly aware punitive or retributive sanctions may have the effect of "resentment and alienation in the offenders rather than making them thoughtful or regretful about the behavior and its impact" (Goldblum, 2009, p. 140). Educational sanctioning involves the use of projects, assignments, or tasks intended to educate the student on the residential rules and their purpose. This can include developing an understanding of the impact of the offending behaviors on individuals and the community.

Learning is the preeminent objective for students in any institution of higher education. Within the context of a conduct process, learning is centered on an individual student's decisions and their recognition of the impact of those decisions on themselves and others. These learning opportunities continue even after a student is found responsible for a violation. The learning potential of sanctions can provide students an opportunity to make different decisions in the future, ideally better ones, which ultimately reflects a reduction of recidivism in violations on-campus broadly and in residential communities specifically.

Institutions of higher education across the globe are built on a foundation that includes a mission, vision, values, and goals. Typically, behavior that violates a university code of conduct or a residential code is inconsistent with institutional goals. It is possible the students whom residence life staff meet with do not even know or realize this is the case. When residence life conduct officers meet with a student and hold them accountable for their behaviors, these staff members expose the student to a new path to discuss institutional and personal values, as well as ways to cease behavior not in alignment with institutional expectations. Conduct officers have the unique opportunity to assess what kind of educational interventions may help a student learn about their own choices and decisions, as well as be positioned to require the resulting tasks be completed.

Sanctioning processes and decisions should involve a number of other considerations, many of which are campus-specific, such as aligning residence life conduct sanctions with those of the larger campus conduct office (if applicable) and ensuring sanctions reflect the campus culture and institutional mission, values, and goals. It is essential to include possible sanctions in any student code of conduct or other conduct policy review, which may also be required by governing (state) laws or board of regents. Residence life conduct officers can also use professional resources regarding campus conduct systems to help guide sanctioning decisions.

SANCTIONS

Residence life conduct systems have a range of sanctions available. Common sanctions found on many campuses include:

- Verbal warning
- Written warning
- Fees or fines
- Monetary restitution
- Reflection papers
- Apology letters
- Community service
- Probation

- Relocation from on-campus housing (to a different residence hall)
- Non-renewal of housing contract
- Cancellation of housing contract
- Removal or eviction from on-campus housing
- Separation from the college or university (i.e., suspension, dismissal, or expulsion)

Regardless of what sanctions the program uses, they should be stated clearly in codes of conduct or housing contracts. It also is important to include an explanation of how sanctions are determined and by whom, since more-accessible and transparent policies help students and stakeholders understand sanctioning decisions better. It is vital to establish which staff members have the authority to assign varying level of sanctions. For example, can entry-level residence hall professionals cancel a student's housing contract? Can the director of residence life assign a reflection paper? These designations may have an impact on training, the appeals process, and the due process afforded to students.

There are numerous considerations a residence life professional will use to determine appropriate educational sanctions. While some institutions may require residence life professionals to assign particular sanctions to specific violations, other tools can support the sanction assignment process. Some mechanisms available to residence life professionals include referring to sanctioning guides, using established theories, considering a student's prior history, and the systematic approval and assessment of sanctions.

Some institutions use a sanctioning guide, otherwise known as a matrix or rubric, for obligatory or mandatory sanctioning (See supporting material 8.1). For example, an institution may prescribe that for every first-time alcohol violation of low severity, the student is assigned conduct probation for six months, has to attend an alcohol education workshop on-campus, and must complete a substantial reflection paper. On the other hand, a first-time fire safety policy violation (e.g., a candle found during health and safety inspections) may result only in a written warning and a shorter reflection paper.

When creating a matrix or rubric, the institution's prior history and context should be reviewed. Is the residence life professional in a position to formally adjust what has been the normal operating procedure, or are they just documenting current practice for the department when creating this matrix? Does the campus use what is sometimes referred to as a progressive discipline model (moving a student through a sequential series of punitive and educational sanctions) for repeat violations, or does a student get a clean slate every year? Residence life professionals also have to factor in departmental learning outcomes, mission, expectations, and residential curricula when determining how many, or the depth of, sanctions to assign students.

✚ Federal or State Regulations and Laws

The legal rights of a responsible student must be considered. It is important for residence life conduct officers to be aware of any legislation, legal regulations, or laws affecting sanctions. In the United States, one regulation whose impact on sanctioning has increased is the Fair Housing Act (FHA). In *U.S. v. University of Nebraska,* "The Court ruled that university housing is a dwelling within the meaning of the FHA" (2013). This means institutional housing operations need to approach their function and any sanctioning implications with a law like this one in mind.

Other laws for residence life professionals to consider when sanctioning a student through the conduct process include the Americans with Disabilities Act (ADA), Family Educational Rights and Privacy Act (FERPA), and Title IX of the Civil Rights Act of 1964. Understandably, laws like FHA, ADA, FERPA, and Title IX do not apply to non-American institutions, but it is important for institutions and housing professionals to understand what regulations and laws would affect sanctioning ability or carry addition stipulations. Review Chapter 3, "Understanding State and Federal Laws," for further guidance.

A matrix provides a base level of consistency for the department. This can be helpful when working with staff whose full-time jobs are not in conduct, and who may have limited experience or backgrounds with a conduct process. Matrices provide a starting point when professionals otherwise may not be sure of what to do. It also provides some level of equity in the residence life conduct system, so different students who may have similar policy violations receive equitable sanctions (e.g., two students found responsible for a first-time fire safety violation both receive written warnings and an educational activity, versus one student receiving a verbal warning and assigned three hours of community service, but the other student is placed on probation and assigned a reflection paper).

Theory-based questions are beneficial in cases where residence life conduct officers are determining what questions to ask students to receive the information necessary to determine appropriate sanctions. For example, even in cases where the institution does not use a restorative justice model, residence life professionals can still use the information obtained from asking restorative justice questions. What did the student say about the impact of their behavior, the harms that may have occurred, and ways they can go about rebuilding the trust and correcting the harms that occurred?

Residence life professionals can also give the student the opportunity to discuss how they want to make amends with those affected and what they would learn from participating in that redemptive behavior. Building the question into the conversation gives the student more of a voice and lets the residence life professional determine if the sanction is appropriate.

Using Lawrence Kohlberg's Stages of Moral Development (Kohlberg, 1973) can also provide a foundation for those unaccustomed to asking developmental questions. If a residence life professional can establish what stage a student is at from their responses, they can provide a sanction that can help them learn from their behavior and choices.

Another factor to consider when creating and assigning educational sanctions is to include a level of flexibility. As stated earlier, some institutions have obligatory or mandatory sanctions for certain behaviors, meaning professionals may be positioned to assign a sanction the student has already completed. If this occurs, can professionals adapt the sanction? For example, if a student found to have covered a smoke detector had previously written a reflection paper for another offense, could the student instead be required to research residence hall fires from the last decade and write about how they would feel if their behavior created a similar situation? Can a professional adapt a sanction to different learning styles, such as having students create a painting, record a song, or choreograph a dance routine rather than write a paper?

It is essential for a residence life conduct officer to determine first whether they have the authority to create and assign sanctions not already established at the institution. This may mean they have to seek approval from their supervisors before creating certain activities. For example, having students accompany professional or para-professional staff during their duty shifts is a common sanction. However, some residence life directors do not approve of having students who are not resident assistants participate in this manner. Housing professionals also must determine whether the sanctions they have created align with the institutional and departmental mission and any established learning outcomes. For example, if housing professionals work in a department with a residential curriculum, does the reflective activity they want to assign students connect back to the learning outcomes or competencies the curriculum outlines?

Residence life professionals also have to consider whether the department or institution has assessment strategies already in place for sanctions. If so, they must consider whether those assessments were taken into account when creating the activity. If not, a key question to reflect on is the kind of learning the student is receiving with this sanction and how that learning is assessed.

Educational Sanctions

In establishing the philosophical lens a department's sanctions are built upon, it is important to consider the vast array of learning opportunities conduct officers can expose students to through educational sanctioning. According to Baldizan (2008), "as professionals in a field devoted to student behavior and misbehavior within higher education, our goal and purpose is to facilitate the integration of student development with student accountability" (pp. 135–136).

While there is a time and place to use punitive sanctions, residence life conduct officers increasingly integrate student growth and accountability into the conduct sanction process. Since culture, policies, and procedures of every institution are different, it would not be feasible to offer a prescribed list of appropriate sanctions for all types of behavior. Instead, residence life professionals are encouraged to consider what opportunities they provide to students outside of the conduct meeting to facilitate student education, growth, and personal development in accordance with the institution's mission, vision, and values.

Some institutions also provide discretion to conduct officers to create alternative sanctions and activities to complement common or mandatory sanctions. It is helpful to consider what was learned about the student in the conduct meeting to design an appropriate sanction. It is important to think about ways to frame educational or alternative activities. For instance, what options are available to the residence life professional for a student who says they do not like writing papers, even for a class, and are working toward a fine arts degree? Instead of a reflection paper, could the student address the subject through two works of art; one to express what the student was experiencing before and during the incident, and the second to express what they have learned from the incident, the conduct process, and how they plan to do things differently in the future? The student may still be required to complete a short writing assignment to explain the two works of art, but what type of learning may happen when the student is provided an experience in a manner in which they learn best? It is possible the student could receive better insight into their decisions this way. Educational and alternative sanctions do not prevent residence life professionals from assigning punitive sanctions; yet, assigning an alternative educational activity may open a door for students to think about their behavior in a different way and to support them in learning to make better choices in their daily lives.

The following are educational sanctions commonly levied in residential communities. Individual housing and conduct offices should establish what they believe are appropriate standards for sanctions (e.g., word count, spelling and grammar expectations, and format for written responses; methods to confirm completion of sanction, etc.) to maintain consistency in enforcement. Note that some of these sanctions could apply to organizations as well as individual students.

Letter of apology. The student writes an apology to individuals affected by the conduct violation that includes reflections on how decisions may have affected them and how their behavior will be adjusted in the future. The apology is then delivered to the affected individuals.

Letter to future self. The student writes a letter addressed to their future self that reminds them of values, feelings, lessons learned, and hopes for future behavior spurred by the offending incident. It serves as a reminder of why the student is in college and what they have to lose from future violations. One way this process can be facilitated is by using the website Future Me (futureme.org).

Letters of gratitude. The student reads the first book of *Meditations* by Marcus Aurelius. They then write their own meditation, which will identify five people in their life to whom they are grateful, identifying the ethical and intellectual debts they owe to those people. The letters also should include details of the offending incident and how the behavior and decisions made are, or are not, in line with what the student has learned from them.

Research and reflection paper. The student researches a subject related to their violation (e.g., fire safety, issues of diversity, etc.) or read an article assigned by the conduct office (e.g., a newspaper story about a suspended fraternity), and then write a report about the material and include a reflection on lessons learned from the research as they apply to the incident, what they have learned from this experience, and how they could have acted differently.

Review of life goals. The student identifies three life goals, followed by four action steps they will take to achieve each goal. These goals should be real-world–based and have some relation to the student's academic career. They can also provide a reflection on how actions, and the influence of peer pressure, led to the incident and the impact it could have on life goals.

Attend university programs. The student attends three programs to learn about different campus organizations and events. Students can also be asked to bring others with them to events.

Community service. The student completes a set number of hours of community service work. The work may be related to the violating incident (e.g., a student who is found to have vandalized campus property could be required to assist with a public art project).

Bulletin board series. The student creates a bulletin board, often in the hall in which the violation occurred, that includes educational material (e.g., alcohol abuse, campus safety, issues of diversity, etc.) that informs the student and members of the community about the chosen topic.

Educational or social programming. The student works with appropriate professional staff to plan and facilitate a social program for the residence hall community.

Review of housing policies. The student reads the campus code of conduct and then reports on six policies of which the student was not previously aware, and includes a brief paragraph that reflects on how their future behavior will be different now that they know the policies.

Meet with housing staff. The student sets up an appointment with the hall or area coordinator involved in the violation to apologize, discuss policies, talk about community expectations, and other topics as needed. The student then submits a reflection paper about what this experience has taught them, how they felt about the conversation, and how they will adjust their behavior in the future.

Meet with campus office. The student meets with representatives of a campus office (e.g., career services, campus health, etc.) and writes a reflection paper about what they learned from this meeting and how they could apply those lessons.

Review meetings with hearing officer. The student attends one conduct review meeting to assist in living up to community standards and to talk about decisions made.

Restorative Justice and Sanctioning

Residence life communities offer students a place to form relationships, but these relationships can be damaged by adverse behaviors of community members. In approaches like restorative justice, community damage can be addressed as the violating student is held accountable; as those affected — victims or other affected parties — are given a voice in the process; and the sanction or outcome is determined by all involved.

Restorative justice is increasingly used in many on-campus residential communities and conduct systems. Although restorative justice takes an investment of time and resources, and sometimes a fundamental shift in how to approach the conduct process and sanctioning, using this approach may generate positive results for a residence life community.

Professional staff working in residence life conduct systems may have observed that punitive responses, while sometimes necessary, can result in the punished student feeling isolated or angry, and lacking remorse for their behavior. In such a case, no real learning occurs. In a residence life community, this reaction can result in further issues in the form of additional policy violations, severed relationships, distrust among students and staff, and safety concerns for the community. Restorative justice approaches allow for a focus on the community and those directly affected by the wrongdoing, which is critical in a residence life community where the responsible student and affected parties may share a dining hall, living space, or even a bathroom.

It is difficult to pin down restorative justice with a specific definition. Scholars of restorative justice worry about specifying a rigid meaning, and see it as a compass rather than a roadmap (Zehr, 2002). In *The Little Book of Restorative Justice*, Zehr suggests a working definition of restorative justice as "a process to involve, to the extent possible, those who have a stake in a specific offense and to collectively identify and address harms, needs, and obligations, in order to heal and put things as right as possible" (2002, p. 37). While punitive or developmental approaches to conduct focus on the responsible student and rules, restorative justice focuses on the victim, community, and relationships. In fact, "restorative justice is grounded in a commitment to understanding the fact of relationship and connection as central to the work of justice" (Llewellyn, 2014, p. 89).

For residence life professionals, this prioritization of relationship and connection should sound familiar. Housing professionals know on-campus residential living is more than just a roof over a student's head, and they work diligently to create a sense of community in those residences and a place where relationships and connections matter. Restorative approaches and practices can be used to help build and strengthen communities (Miller & Olstad, 2012), so when things go wrong, students and staff are naturally positioned to use a restorative approach, if not a full restorative justice system, to repair the harms.

Here, restorative justice is not just used in the sanctioning phase of a residence life conduct system, but is important throughout the accountability process. Certain sanctions may have restorative elements intended to repair harm and rebuild trust, such as restitution and community service. However, simply assigning this type of sanction without using any other restorative justice principles is not necessarily congruent with a full restorative justice process.

While restorative justice is most often known in the context of the criminal justice system, it originates from a diverse set of practices found in indigenous communities throughout North America and New Zealand, in addition to faith-based community practices. It can be valuable to acknowledge the indigenous origins of restorative justice when incorporated into modern systems such as residence conduct systems. For example, at the start of any restorative circle process or conference, during introductions, residence life professionals could mention the many historical uses of restorative justice and encourage participants to learn more about its background.

This history is illustrated through the use of the Restorative Justice Medicine Wheel (Figure 8.1). In *The Little Book of Restorative Justice for Colleges and Universities* (2013), David R. Karp encourages residence life professionals to use the symbolic medicine wheel, developed from indigenous traditions, to "discover how storytelling helps reveal the many layers of harm caused by student misconduct" (p. 34). According to Karp, "the medicine wheel is composed of four quadrants. The first highlights the importance of storytelling — allowing each participant to describe the incident and how it affected them. The other quadrants make distinctions between three types of harm: material/physical, emotional/spiritual, and relational/communal" (2013, p. 34).

The medicine wheel offers a model for residence life staff to ensure their restorative practice is effective in highlighting harms caused and identifying solutions to repair those harms. Karp notes that for some conduct staff, "consistency is important: similar violations should lead to similar sanctions" (2013, p. 38), calling attention to one of the significant challenges to the use of restorative justice: It allows for a recognition of the uniqueness of each incident based on the relationships involved and the specific harms caused. Sanctions can, therefore, be applied to recognize and address the needs of the affected parties, including the offender.

Consistency can be achieved not by having the same sanctions imposed in all cases of a specific offense, but by using a consistent approach, such as the medicine wheel, in all cases where a full restorative justice process is desired, even if the eventual outcome and sanction differ from case to case. It is critical to provide clear explanations in policy documents, digital spaces, handouts, or elsewhere about how restorative justice works in a conduct system and how students can be involved.

While there are resources that provide a step-by-step explanation of how to replicate a restorative justice process in residence life communities, it is not possible to prescribe a defined restorative justice model or program suitable for all institutions. Restorative justice has to be responsive to the residential environment and the people who make up the community.

Karp encourages professionals who are starting a program to ask, "What kind of restorative process resonates best with your campus culture or with the kinds of cases on which your program will focus?" (2013, p. 55). For example, many residence life conduct systems may offer restorative justice as a diversionary or alternative process from the traditional accountability approaches. However, there are recent examples of schools where the residence life conduct systems use restorative justice as the standard initial approach and only defer to punitive responses under particular conditions. Others still may not have incorporated restorative justice into their systems or processes in formal ways, but incorporate restorative practices and language, such as a staff member facilitating a discussion of who was affected and what harms have been caused (Goldblum, 2009).

No matter the model, it is important to let the values and principles of restorative justice guide a professional's work and reflect their specific residence environment for the approaches to be authentic and effective.

Residence professionals should include some important factors in any restorative justice model they might use (Goldblum, 2009), including:

- An admission of responsibility by the offender;
- involvement of the victim and other affected parties;
- the identification of harms;
- an agreement of how to repair harms;
- staff with skills to facilitate restorative processes; and
- staff with skills to identify and address power imbalances.

While not an exhaustive list, these factors may help in determining a model or approach of restorative justice for any residence life conduct system. Before implementing any restorative justice model, staff are strongly encouraged to familiarize themselves with current publications and attend training in facilitating restorative justice.

One successful example of this approach is the restorative justice program at Dalhousie University in Halifax, Nova Scotia, Canada. From 2012 until 2016, Dalhousie partnered with the provincial department of justice and local police to implement a restorative justice pilot program for students causing harm to the community through violations of the Liquor Control Act and criminal offenses. Students were referred by police or justice officials to make contact with the program manager at Dalhousie, where they would complete an intake meeting and participate in a restorative conference along with affected parties and other members of the university and the local community.

Many of the students in the restorative justice program lived in residence halls at the time of their offenses, and residence life staff were often invited to attend the conferences. The staff determined the processes used to address the harms in this program would be very useful in the residence life conduct system. The restorative justice program manager worked with residence life staff to implement restorative approaches in several operational areas, such as community-building, programming, and conduct.

One specific highlight of this work is for every violation of the residence code of conduct, the trained RAs follow up with the students involved in the incident, facilitating a restorative conversation about harms, allowing the student to tell

FIGURE 8.1 The Restorative Justice Medicine Wheel

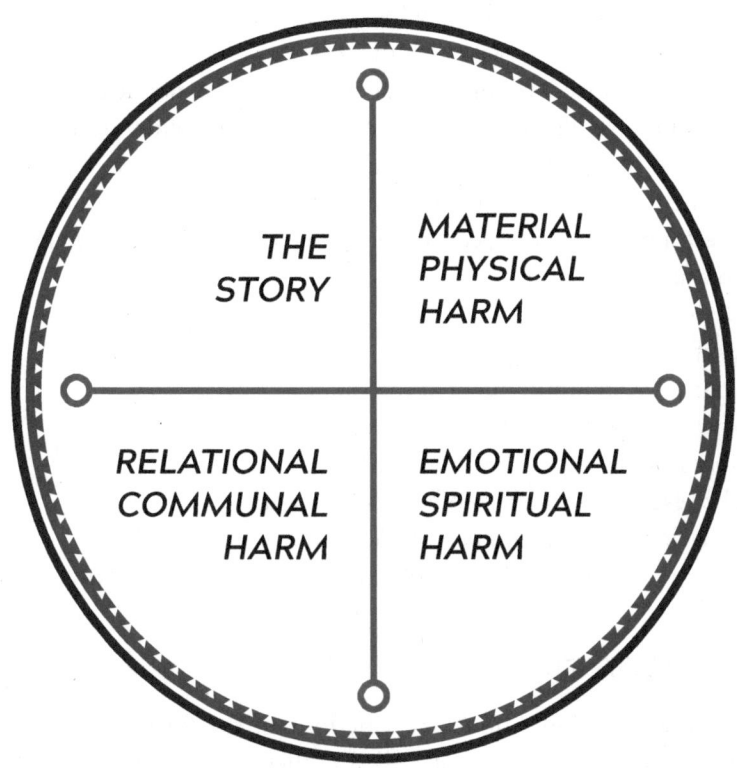

Source: The Little Book of Restorative Justice for Colleges or Universities *(Karp, 2013)*
Used with permission.

their story, and ensuring they feel heard. After this conversation, Dalhousie's residence conduct process follows. While the residence life conduct process that ensues is not a fully restorative one, the staff have introduced a dialogue based in restorative philosophy and allows for a growing capacity and understanding of restorative principles in the student body and staff.

In addition, restorative impact panels are a sanctioning option that uses restorative justice practices to engage students in a discussion with affected parties and stakeholders. Students found responsible for residence life conduct violations are required to attend the impact panel, sometimes scheduled at times of the year when multiple student conduct violations may occur, such as homecoming, Halloween, or major sporting events. Impact panels may include event organizers, RAs, students, facilities staff, campus police, or emergency services staff, and allow for each person on the panel to describe how the student's behavior affected them or the individuals and communities they represent. The responsible students have an opportunity to listen, reflect on the comments they hear, and explore how this information relates to and affects their behavior and decision-making. Students may be asked to make a commitment to future actions and the group can assist with the terms of that commitment.

Where a formalized restorative justice process is not feasible, questions can be incorporated during conduct meetings or in follow-up conversations with residence life staff or RAs to determine the harms and impacts. The assigned sanctions can be suited to address those harms. These questions from a formal restorative justice process can help determine harms from the allegedly responsible student's point of view:

- What happened?
- What were you thinking of at the time?
- What have you thought about since?
- What has the impact been on you?
- Who else has been affected by this incident?
- What do you think you need to do to make things right?
- Is there anything else you would like to say or ask at this time?

Monetary Sanctions

Some institutions include monetary sanctions in the form of fines, fees, and other related costs. It is important to define these terms when discussing how these play a role in a residential conduct setting. While often used interchangeably, understanding the differences between the terms can help fine-tune the goal to be accomplished. A "cost" is the amount or equivalent paid or charged for something; a "fee" is a sum paid or charged for a service; and a "fine" is a sum imposed as punishment for an offense (*Merriam-Webster Online*, n.d.). In a conduct setting, costs and fees are generally the monetary amounts used to cover the expense of a service in the educational conduct process. Fines are more likely to be punitive and intended to deter a particular behavior.

Before introducing any combination of fees, fines, or costs into the sanctioning process, residence life professionals should consider how such monetary sanctions are collected. For example, certain institutions may only accept money orders as a secure method of confirming funds are available. Others institutions can bill the amount directly to a student account by collaborating with their bursar or financial aid offices. The institution may limit which offices may accept any type of currency, or the ability for an office to have a discretionary account separate from payroll or operations.

If the conduct department establishes a new procedure of mandatory fines associated with a finding of responsibility, implementation should be transparent and include feedback from community partners. In executing the procedure, the change should be broadly advertised to help explain the rationale, promote transparency, and increase its operational effectiveness in reducing recidivism. Residence life conduct officers also should evaluate the campus cultural change once a responsibility fine is imposed.

For institutions where funds generated from a responsibility fee are reallocated to the residence life or conduct office, students may have a negative perception that conduct officers have an incentive to determine responsibility. Consequently, it is important to take campus culture into account to determine whether a responsibility fine is appropriate.

. Fees, fines, and related costs have long been used in the conduct setting, but the rationale for the imposition of fees and fines constantly evolves. Some common monetary conduct sanctions include restorative costs, educational sanction costs, responsibility fines, and administrative fees for non-compliance.

Restorative costs. When considering restorative costs, many institutions will use restitution to repair the harm caused. Examples of restitution include the responsible student paying for a phone they broke in a fight, a laptop sleeve they took from the campus store without paying, or a fire extinguisher they tampered with in a residence hall. When the student pays for these damages, it makes the affected individual or institution whole again.

Assigning restitution as a restorative cost is a more-direct form of repairing a harm that can still be used today. When using restorative costs, consider how the fair market value of the item lost is appropriately valued, how the payment should be dispensed, and whether to offer the responsible student a payment plan for monetary amounts above a certain amount.

Restitution can also be implemented through end-of-the-year damage billing for residence hall vandalism. Per the terms of a housing contract, damage billing (where institutions charge students for any damage to institutional property outside normal wear and tear) is another method of using restitution to make the institution whole. Examples of such charges may include the costs of repainting the room or replacing damaged furniture, bathroom tiles, and window blinds.

Educational sanction costs. Alcohol and other drug education courses or services are regularly used as sanctions. These options, though, are accompanied by an educational cost. While the cost affiliated with this type of sanction is not necessarily imposed or even set by the conduct office, it is one that must be upheld and enforced. As long as these costs are enforced consistently, and students receive prior notice of the fee, these fees generally do not create issues.

Some critics of educational sanction costs are concerned about possible inequities. The argument is that a student may incur the cost of an educational sanction as a result of an alcohol violation (a minor violation) juxtaposed with a student involved in a physical assault that did not involve alcohol (a more-serious violation) who would not incur educational sanction costs. To address these potential inequities, some institutions think creatively by inventing their own innovative educational seminars or workshops (which include a cost) that use personality assessment tools to encourage better decision-making, address the behaviors, and reduce recidivism. The costs associated with these seminars or workshops are for administering these personality assessment tools and can be a way to address the inequities mentioned before.

Responsibility fines. Fines accompanying any finding of responsibility in a conduct setting are commonplace. The responsibility fine often is used as a way to deter future misconduct. Certain institutions will increase a student's responsibility fine for subsequent violations, with the hope of reducing further recidivism.

Another reason the responsibility fine has been appealing is while (non-housing–affiliated) conduct traditionally is a non-revenue-generating office, funds generated from responsibility fines have been instrumental in covering administrative costs associated with managing the conduct process. These include hiring additional staff or summer interns, as well as purchasing educational tools to be used as sanctions. For housing-affiliated conduct offices, a responsibility fine can provide a financial cushion for an otherwise-tight programming budget.

While some institutions may observe a responsibility fine as effective in lowering repeat offender numbers, the imposition of responsibility fines is not without its consequences. Because responsibility fines must be administered consistently and allow very little discretion for waiving the fine, the cost of a conduct violation can become a financial burden on students of a lower socio-economic status. Add on any of the other costs and fees sanctioned, and the responsibility fine can be deemed disproportionate and extremely punitive for certain students. Conversely, for students of a higher socio-economic status, fines can be billed to a student's account and paid for by the student's parent or guardian, effectively removing the intended deterrent nature of the fine.

Administrative fees for non-compliance. While a responsibility fine registers some type of moral disapproval (i.e., a student did something inconsistent with policy), a fee implies no judgment and is imposed because of some administrative task a conduct office must now bear. An example of using administrative fees in a conduct setting is when a student has a disciplinary hold on their student account for either non-compliance with sanctions or lack of communication with the conduct office regarding a pending conduct violation. In this example, an administrative fee may be imposed for a temporary removal of a disciplinary hold so the student may have access to their student account and can register for classes and handle other campus business.

Fees for having the conduct office remove the disciplinary hold is another method used to deter future non-compliance and encourage communication between the student and the conduct office. While not all residence life conduct systems have authority to request or place conduct holds, it is important to provide context for how a financial sanction may affect a student.

Relocation or Removal from Housing

The most serious sanctions a housing operation can impose is either relocation or removal of a student from the residence halls, since these can have a significant, serious impact on the ability of the student to be academically successful, or in some cases, remain enrolled at the institution. When applying a sanction of relocation, reassignment, or housing suspension, is the housing department acting in a non-discriminatory manner equitable to all students who are sanctioned? Some questions to reflect upon include:

- What kind of violations are resulting in relocation or removal?
- Are only certain demographics of the student body being found in violation of those policies?
- What areas of campus are students relocated to, and are they comparable to the locations they were separated from?

For example, if a student is relocated due to behavioral concerns, is the student being assigned to a lower-quality residence hall rather than being allowed to relocate to a preferable residence hall with additional amenities? Why is the lower-quality residence hall chosen for relocating students who are responsible for infractions? If a student is relocated or removed from a university housing property, were the behavioral expectations clearly stated not only in the code, but in the housing contract? The Fair Housing Act does not say landlords — the university — cannot evict students, but asks whether due diligence was exercised in regard to providing a fair and equitable process (T. Reilly, personal communication, 2017).

APPELLATE AND GRIEVANCE PROCESSES

While residence life conduct officers do not often serve as an appellate officer in the conduct process, that does not mean residence life conduct officers are an idle entity in an appellate process. In fact, many appellate processes provide deference to a conduct officer's decision-making.

Conduct officers often use adjectives like *reasonable, proportionate,* and *educational* to determine appropriate sanctions. A conduct officer should, generally, not consider the appellate process when determining sanctions and instead focus on educating and addressing the behavior of the student. Furthermore, a conduct officer should have already imposed sanctions consistent with department philosophy and proportionate to the student's behavior.

If the conduct system includes an appellate process, any appeals of a conduct officer's decision should not be taken personally. Instead, conduct officers should embrace an appeal of their decision as an opportunity to use the appellate process as a check and balance tool to the conduct office's systems and practices.

An appellate officer's job is difficult. It requires a person to decide a matter investigated or adjudicated by another individual. An appellate officer often receives an appeal via writing, and seldom has the opportunity to discuss the matter with the conduct officer and the student before rendering a decision. When considering an appeal related to sanctions, some considerations to take into account include:

- Is there a sanctioning guide or philosophy to use as a resource? Is there a standard for reviewing the appeal?
- What are the grounds for the appeal? What is the student claiming?
- Does the original conduct officer have an opportunity to respond to the student's appeal? If so, what is the conduct officer's rationale for inposing the sanction?
- What circumstances warrant changing a sanction on appeal? Some accepted examples include:
  » New information found (the student recently completed the sanction or a very similar sanction)
  » Mitigating factors (the student has financial difficulty or is otherwise unable to complete the sanction due to something outside the student's control)
  » Aggravating factors (the student has not accepted responsibility, lied during the original investigation, or has prior conduct history)
- How will the rationale for the decision be articulated? What is the basis for changing a sanction?

If an appellate officer is to assign alternative sanctions to those imposed by the original conduct officer, they should consider the facts of the underlying matter, information missing from the investigation, facts or circumstances leading to the decision to modify the sanction, and whether the modification is consistent with similar cases; if not, what sets this case aside from others.

A grievance process also can be made available to any student who does not necessarily wish to appeal an outcome, but has concerns related to the student conduct process. For example, a student may express concerns about how they were treated by campus safety officers or a resident assistant during the initial documentation of the incident. A grievance process also may be relevant when a student believes a student conduct officer was rude or judgmental during the conduct meeting. The student may be independently satisfied with the outcome of the case, but wish to share concerns about individual components of the process.

Standard grievance procedures typically involve documenting the student's concerns and directing the student to request a meeting with the direct supervisor or next level in the reporting structure to discuss those concerns. These procedures are far more informal compared to an appellate process. An ombuds office or human resources office may also be an appropriate referral to a student who wishes to file a formal complaint.

CAMPUS COLLABORATION

There are instances where completing student sanctions requires collaboration with campus partners outside the housing or conduct offices. These may include law enforcement and campus security offices, the environmental or emergency health and safety professionals, other student affairs departments, and the departments that work with student organizations. Involving these partners in sanctions creates more meaningful opportunities for students to understand the impacts of their behavior.

Law Enforcement and Campus Security

Law enforcement and campus security agencies can be valuable partners in addressing student behavior through the sanctioning process. One common and effective example is for students who were unruly or disorderly, especially due to alcohol or drug intoxication, to ride with law enforcement on their rounds to better understand the role of law enforcement on a campus. This provides insight into how difficult law enforcement officers' job can be.

For some students, being able to visualize their conduct from security camera footage can be very effective, especially if the student was incapacitated due to intoxication during the conduct issue. If an institution uses security cameras, coordinating a viewing of the camera footage with law enforcement and campus security and the responsible student would serve to demonstrate the impact of their choices on the residential community or institution.

When considering working with law enforcement and campus security on sanctions, it is important to consider any potential previous experience students may have had with these types of agencies. Working with law enforcement and campus security's supervisory staff in setting expectations regarding the goals of any sanctions assigned in conjunction with these agencies is also highly encouraged. It is also recommended that the student complete a follow-up reflective exercise to gauge what the student believes they have learned from these experiences.

Environmental or Emergency Health and Safety Professionals

The welfare of the residential community as it relates to environmental or health safety has been heightened by numerous high-profile incidents, including the Boland Hall fire at Seton Hall University in 2000. These incidents have led to fire safety training sessions for residence life staff across the United States. Some institutions created sanctions of fire safety training for individual students who fail to comply with fire safety policies or otherwise put the residential facility and community at risk (i.e., tampering with fire safety equipment, propping fire doors open, failing to leave when the fire alarm sounds).

It is important to include proper debriefing and a one-on-one or small-group discussion that follows a large group discussion or demonstration to provide a more well-rounded educational experience from these issues. Using authorities such as a fire marshal, first responders, risk management employees, or even the residence hall director as the facilitator of the sanction can provide customized context specific to the institution. This sanction can also be used in a large-group setting where a student organization or a larger community is involved in the violation of policy.

Student Affairs Departments

Some sanctions allow for collaboration between residence life and other student affairs departments. Consider an instance where a student, during the conduct process, admits to abusing alcohol because they self-disclose they have not dealt successfully with the death of a loved one. Is the institution one whose campus partners agree to allow conduct staff to assign a student to complete a session with on-campus counselors? If not, even just mentioning the resource available to the student in the one-on-one meeting can provide a referral the student may not have otherwise received.

Another example is a student who is causing community disturbances in the early hours of the morning and admits they do not know what they want to do with their life or why they are in college. Perhaps a trip to the career development office for a one-on-one advising appointment could be beneficial. Once students have been connected to a resource on campus, they may choose to revise their decisions, which could lead to a positive impact on the residential community.

When sanctions must be levied against entire student organizations, they also can provide an opportunity for residence life professionals to collaborate with campus partners. At some institutions, code policies also apply to student organizations, and these student organizations may reside in on-campus housing or can reserve on-campus housing event spaces. When holding a student organization accountable, think about educational activities that can be created to support a stronger community. For example, a social fraternity can be paired with a residence hall association council to provide a risk management presentation for all residential students.

CONCLUSION

Conduct sanctions — whether they be punitive, educational, or monetary — provide learning opportunities to students. Clearly articulating the sanctioning goals and purposes to the campus's student body, faculty, and staff provides yet another opportunity to reinforce the department's commitment to the education and well-being of the campus community. Fortunately, residence life and conduct professionals who assign sanctions as a part of the conduct process have multiple, varied dynamics on which to deliberate.

As professionals consider possible sanctions, they draw from the philosophy behind why, when, and which educational, alternative, punitive, or monetary sanctions are assigned. They consider how, if at all, to use restorative justice in the sanctioning process. They understand how and when to engage campus colleagues, the applicable state and federal laws, and how to ensure the sanctions align with institutional and departmental goals. As they establish less-punitive and more-educational sanctions, they align these with the goals of an institution's residence life conduct system, as well as with larger institutional goals and values. Residence life and conduct professionals who keep these aspects in mind can do even more than meet short-term goals such as deterrence; they can start the process of creating a conduct system that maximizes student learning and greatly reduces recidivism.

REFERENCES

Bladizan, E. (2008). Ethics and Decision Making. In J. M. Lancaster & D. M. Warylord (Eds.), *Student Conduct Practice: The Complete Guide for Student Affairs Professionals* (135-151). Sterling, VA: Stylus.

___ Cost. [Def. 1]. (n.d.). In *Merriam-Webster Online.* In Merriam-Webster. Retrieved October 31, 2017, from http://www.merriam-webster.com/dictionary/cost.

Fair Housing Act of 1968. (n.d.) *West's Encyclopedia of American Law,* Edition 2. (2008). Retrieved October 20, 2017, from https://legal-dictionary.thefreedictionary.com/Fair+Housing+Act+of+1968.

___ Fee. [Def. 2.] (n.d.). In *Merriam-Webster Online.* In Merriam-Webster. Retrieved October 31, 2017, from http://www.merriam-webster.com/dictionary/fee.

___ Fine. [Def. 2]. (n.d.). In *Merriam-Webster Online.* In Merriam-Webster. Retrieved October 31, 2017, from http://www.merriam-webster.com/dictionary/fine.

Goldblum, A. (2009). Restorative Justice from Theory to Practice. In J. M. Schrage & N. G. Giacomini (Eds.), *Reframing Campus Conflict: Student Conduct Practice Through a Social Justice Lens* (pp. 141-154). Sterling: Stylus Publishing.

GoodReads (n.d.). Albert Einstein. Retrieved November 30, 2017, from https://www.goodreads.com/quotes/253933-i-never-teach-my-pupils-i-only-attempt-to-provide.

Grasgreen, A. (2012). *Conduct gets costly.* https://www.insidehighered.com/news/2012/02/24/university-student-codes-conduct-include-fines-violations.

Haas, J. M., & Street, Jr., J. L. (2008). Dealing with Student Group Misconduct. In J. M. Lancaster & D. M. Warylord (Eds.), *Student Conduct Practice; The Complete Guide for Student Affairs Professionals* (241–257). Sterling, VA: Stylus Publishing.

Karp, D. (2013). *The little book of restorative justice for colleges and universities: Repairing harm and rebuilding trust in response to student misconduct.* Intercourse, PA: Good Books.

Kohlberg, L. (1973). The claim to moral adequacy of a highest stage of moral judgment. *Journal of Philosophy, 70*(18), 630–646.

Llewellyn, J. (2014). Restorative Justice: Thinking Relationally about Justice. In J. Downie & J. Llewellyn (Eds.), *Being Relational: Reflections on Relational Theory and Health Law* (pp. 89–108). Vancouver: UBC Press.

Lowery, J. W. (2013). Competency One: The Code of Student Conduct-Policies and Processes. In D. Waryold, & D. Lancaster (Eds.). *The State of Student Conduct: Current Forces and Future Challenges: Revisited* (pp. 15-17). College Station, TX: Association for Student Conduct Administration.

Marsh, I., Cochrane, J., & Melville, G. (2004). *Criminal justice: An introduction to philosophies, theories and practice.* London: Routledge.

Miller, S., & Olstad, C. (2012, August 1). *The offspring of restorative justice: Understanding the power of restorative practices in residential communities* [eForum

Archive]. Retrieved from https://www.iirp.edu/eforum-archive/4466-the-off-spring-of-restorative-justice-understanding-the-power-of-restorative-practices-in-residential-communities.

Mish, F. C. (2014). *Merriam-Websters collegiate dictionary.* Springfield, MA: Merriam-Webster.

Olshak, R. (2008). *A guide for effective sanctioning: From theory to practice.* Retrieved from https://deanofstudents.illinoisstate.edu/downloads/2008 SanctionGuide.pdf.

U.S. v. University of Nebraska at Kearney. 4:11-CV-3209. (2013). Retrieved from http://www.uscourts.gov/cameras-courts/united-states-america-vs-university-nebraska-kearney-et-al.

Zdziarski, E. L., & Wood, N. L. (2008). Forums for Resolution. In J. M. Lancaster & D. M. Warylord (Eds.), *Student Conduct Practice; The Complete Guide for Student Affairs Professionals* (pp. 97–111). Sterling, VA: Stylus Publishing.

Zehr, H. (2002). *The Little Book of Restorative Justice.* Intercourse, PA: Good Books.

1. Does your institution have mandates from outside entities (e.g., state legislature, Board of Regents, university systems, etc.) that would have an impact on your sanctions, appeals, or other outcomes? How do those mandates affect your ability to establish and assess educational sanctions?

2. Does your department have programs funded by conduct fees or fines? How would establishing or canceling those monetary sanctions affect the ability to continue such educational programming? If other offices enact fees (e.g., alcohol workshop presented by health services), do you have the ability and relationship to ask to enact or cancel those fees?

3. What are you using to establish educational sanctions? Do you refer to earning outcomes, vision and mission of the office, as well as pre-established assessments?

4. How do you plan to assess the learning students experience from the educational sanctions you assign?

5. With which individuals, campus partners, and external agencies must your residence life conduct staff maintain partnerships to implement effective sanctions?

6. Would your institution sustain a full restorative model? If so which stakeholders should be part of that process? What steps would you take to get started?

9

FACILITATING CONFLICT RESOLUTION

Lauren Mauriello and Molly C. S. Pierson

> *Tori tentatively stepped into the lobby of her first-year residence hall with questions whirling in her head. A first-generation college student, she arrived on campus excited but also nervous about making her family proud. She felt welcomed when she visited during her search process (and the scholarships they offered certainly didn't hurt), but she also worried that feeling might go away. What would the next year have in store for her? How was she, a Black woman from the West Coast, going to fit in at this highly-selective, predominantly-White institution located in the heart of the Midwest? How was this campus eventually going to become a place she could call home?*

CAMPUS RESIDENTIAL communities are places where students live, learn, relax, study, question, and explore. They are laboratories for students to experiment as they question who they are and what they believe. As students continue along this path of self-discovery, conflict is inevitable. The conflict could be as simple as a disagreement between roommates over dirty laundry or music turned up too loud. It could be as serious as an act of bias, vandalized property, bullying, or an intoxicated neighbor out of control on a Friday night. Without proper support systems for students to navigate these disruptive conflicts, they could create chaos for the individual students and the community as a whole. However, with a developmental approach that incorporates conflict resolution, these conflicts can lead to personal and group growth, effective and inclusive decisions, and a better climate and health of a community (Wachtel & Wachtel, 2012). Campuses increasingly are turning to conflict resolution as a way to move beyond administrative processes and proactively support personal and community growth.

Living as part of a community plays a valuable role in the student learning experience. It is critical to student development and integral to the overall mission of higher education institutions. The combination of challenge and support residence life staff provide in managing conflict offers students a significant developmental opportunity to make meaning in the context of their own lived experience (Magolda, 2004). However, students overwhelmed by the process of self-discovery, personal growth, and working toward graduation may find it more comfortable in the short term to avoid facing conflict.

When conflict occurs, students may request administrators quickly move them to a new room, punish the other party, or fix the issue through a formal conduct process. In their role as educators, administrators can and should think critically about ways to resolve conflicts in a developmentally and culturally appropriate way.

Before developing ways of addressing conflict, it is essential first to understand how individuals interact with and enter difficult situations and conversations. Ting-Toomey, et al. (1991) assert it is not the conflict itself that leads to stress. Rather, stress and anxiety arise from the differences between individual conflict management styles. Key proactive steps in building community and in resolving a conflict include educating students about conflict styles or patterns, and providing training to notice the ways they experience and engage in conflict.

An individual's conflict style refers broadly to how they engage in resolving disagreements over goals, values, or other issues. Ting-Toomey (2000, p. 48) defines conflict styles as a "patterned response to conflict in a variety of situations." In other words, people develop habitual ways of responding to conflict. Because these patterns become habitual, an individual may not be aware of how the patterns are informing their conflict management style. In addition, stressors in the environment may prevent individuals from noticing how their patterns of engagement with a conflict issue affects the community. This can happen frequently in residential communities, where students experience many stressors, like rigorous academics, living away from home, societal events, and encountering new people and perspectives.

The Thomas-Kilmann Conflict Mode Instrument (also known as the TKI assessment) is one of several conflict typologies to assess how a person behaves in the face of conflict (Kilmann, 1974). The TKI assessment takes participants' answers and plots them along the dimensions of assertiveness and cooperativeness as they relate to concerns about personal goals and relationships (Kilmann, 1974). The results illustrate a participant's default conflict-management style. Thomas and Kilmann identified five styles: accommodating, avoiding, compromising, collaborating, and competing (Kilmann, 1974).

FIGURE 9.1 Thomas-Killman Conflict Mode Instrument

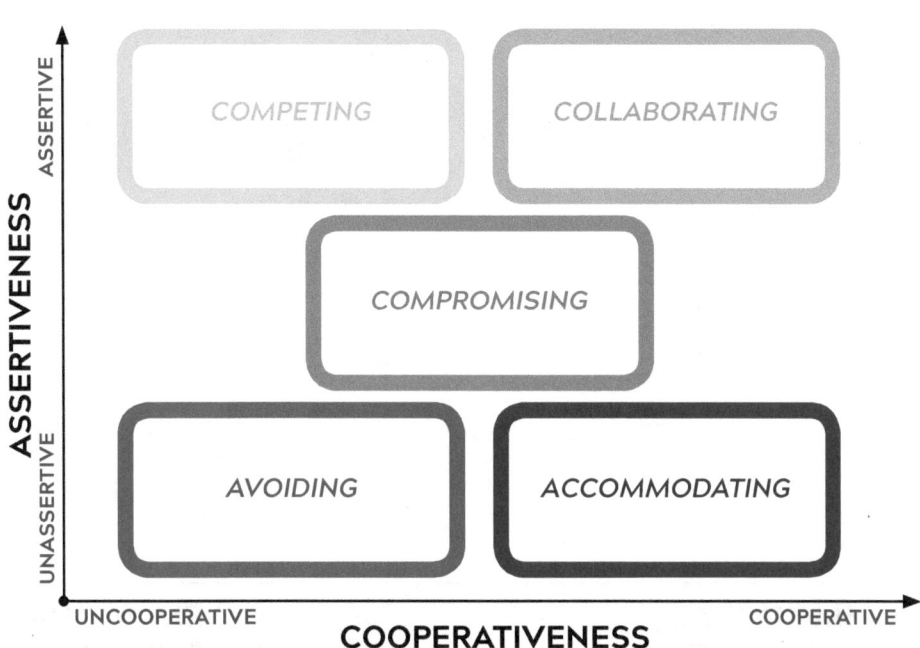

Source: Thomas and Killman, 2008

It is important to note the detailed explanations of these styles; all contain characteristics that could be described as positive or negative. For example, the definition of *accommodating* states it "might take form of selfless generosity or charity, obeying another person's order when you would prefer not to, or yielding to another's point of view," while *competing* "might mean standing up for your rights, defending a position you believe is correct, or simply trying to win" (Thomas, 2008, p. 3). It also is important to recognize these conflict-management styles are situation-based, meaning each approach can be appropriate depending on the goals of the involved parties and the context of the conflict. In addition, it is valuable to remember while each person has a default conflict-management style, anyone can use any of the styles as needs dictate.

Students' beliefs, values, and cultural patterns also influence their responses to conflict situations. The Intercultural Conflict Style Inventory (ICS) developed by Mitch Hammer is a conflict-style typology that addresses conflict through an intercultural lens (Hammer, 2009). The basic premise of the model is individuals adapt their behaviors based on their expectations about the issues at hand; what Hammer calls a *frame* (Hammer, 2009). In other words, the way a person

FIGURE 9.2 Intercultural Conflict Styles Inventory

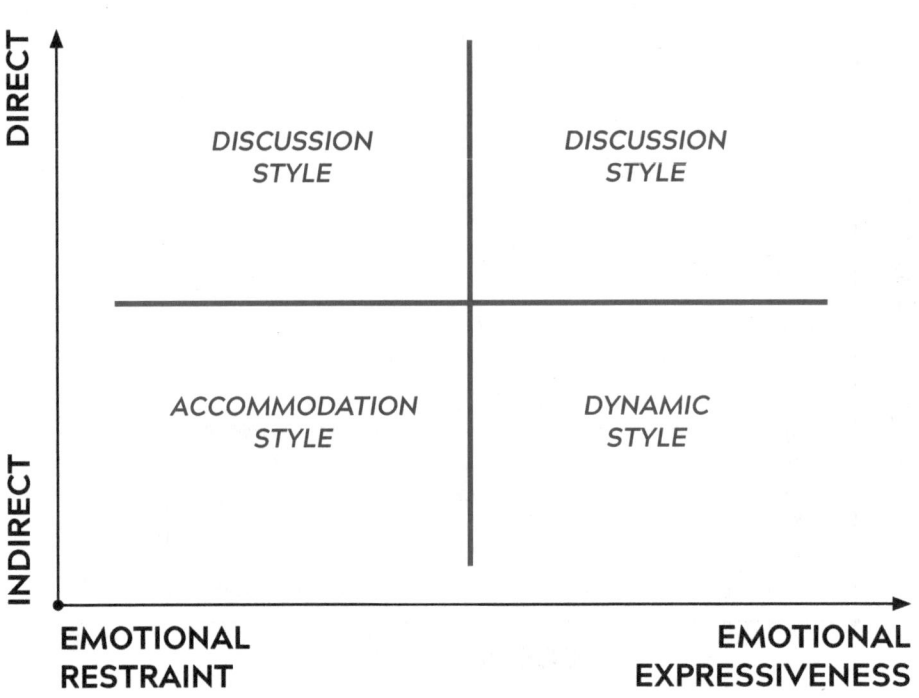

Source: Hammer, 2009.

perceives (or frames) a situation informs the way they respond to it. Thus, "frames serve as the lens through which an individual perceives and behaves in relation to a particular issue, problem or concern" (Hammer, 2009, p. 224). After completing the ICS, students can identify how they solve problems and resolve conflicts along two dimensions: direct versus indirect, and emotionally expressive versus emotionally restrained (Hammer, 2009).

The habits and cultural patterns identified by the TKI and ICS are not intended to stereotype groups or individuals. Rather, they are designed to build self-awareness and an understanding of the various lenses through which people engage in conflict (Hammer, 2009). These instruments and inventories can be included in staff training, introduced through programming, or administered as part of a conflict resolution process (such as before a group mediation or during conflict coaching). Professionals should consider coaching students to recognize how their current placement on either of the matrices affects their response to conflict. Students could also benefit from studying their concern for personal goals, as well as their interest in maintaining relationships if faced with a conflict. This type of coaching will improve students' future abilities to resolve or respond to conflict.

CONFLICT RESOLUTION FRAMEWORKS

By the second week of classes, the honeymoon period for Tori and her roommate had begun to fade. While they got on fine most of the time and often ate dinner together, Tori felt Kerry, a White woman whose parents were paying her tuition and did not need financial assistance, was starting to dominate their shared space with her belongings and visitors. Every time Tori tried to broach the subject with her, Kerry simply would shut down and avoid Tori for a few hours, only to return later and act as if nothing had happened. Later, Tori heard from other floormates that Kerry referred to her as being "aggressive." What cultural or racial dynamics could be at play in this roommate conflict? How could their individual conflict styles be playing a part in how it unfolds?

As residence life professionals approach their work, they are informed by a number of community and student development models. Fortunately, they also can draw from, and build upon, established conflict resolution frameworks. These frameworks empower staff to create strategies that enable conflict resolution to happen, supplement formal conduct approaches, or, in some cases, even replace a more-formalized conduct process. These frameworks use a pragmatic focus (e.g., risk management) as well as more-general applications common in student affairs (such as student development, social justice, and restorative practices).

The Model Student Code, developed by Stoner and Lowery (2004), allows the use of dispute resolution methods before engaging in the conduct process. After becoming aware of a student conduct situation and reviewing the facts of the case, student affairs professionals may "dispose of the matter administratively by the mutual consent of the parties involved on a basis acceptable to the Student Conduct Administrator" (Stoner & Lowery, 2004).

Stoner conceptualized this administrative opportunity as an acknowledgment that not only is there a role for conflict resolution, but non-adversarial resolution could be the path practitioners first choose when a student is in conflict with another community member, or their behavior is in conflict with the community standards. Later, Thompson and Schrage formalized the opportunity identified by Stoner and Lowery for conflict resolution in their Spectrum of Resolution Options Model (2008).

In addition to developing multiple resolution options, expanding conflict resolution strategies beyond administrative processes like room changes or conduct hearings forces residence life professionals to also consider proactive steps that can be taken to implement practices that support healthy conflict resolution before conflict occurs. These proactive community-building practices educate students about community expectations and give them a voice in how they want to coexist within a community. Together, these responsive and proactive practices create a new model for addressing conflict in residential communities.

In their book *Reframing Campus Conflict*, Schrage and Giacomini (2009) envision conflict and conduct resolution processes that balance the needs of the individual, community, and institutional responsibilities of managing risk. This approach is a conceptual shift away from a legalistic or liability perspective toward one of individual rights, justice, and fairness. In 1993, the Association for Student Conduct Administration (ASCA) and the National Association of Student Personnel Administration (NASPA) supported this type of balance, stating student affairs professionals have a responsibility to consider social and restorative justice in their work, and the individual needs of students (Ethical Principles and Standards of Conduct, 1993).

This philosophical shift also manifests itself through real-world applications where the conduct professional service model has shifted from formal adjudication to less-formal resolution processes. In 2013, Jay Wilgus and Jennifer Schrage surveyed ASCA members to assess the use of conflict resolution services outlined in the Spectrum of Resolution Options model (Schrage & Thompson, 2008). Of the 94 institutions they surveyed, 82% used at least one of these conflict resolution practices (Schrage, 2014).

A later study by Katz and Kovak (2016) attempted to understand further how prevalent the shift was. Their efforts found 100 universities in the U.S. that employed a range of the methods outlined in the Spectrum of Resolution Options model, with peer mediation being the method used most often (Katz & Kovak, 2016). Highlighting several universities' application of this model, Katz and Kovak illustrated how universities adapt the Spectrum of Resolution Options model creatively by modifying their methods, findings, staff structures, and where the related programs and services are placed within the university's administrative structure. All this was done while maintaining the fundamental concepts of student-centered practice that promotes social justice, inclusion, and fairness.

While the application, staffing, funding, and organization of the conflict and conduct resolution offerings in the 100 universities sampled varied widely, Katz and Kovak found the number of universities using conflict resolution methods serves as practical evidence to support a shift away from legalistic disciplinary procedures and toward using conflict resolution methods. In 2017, Peter F. Lake, a law professor and director of the Center for Higher Education Law and Policy at Stetson University College of Law, encouraged the continuation of the shift in a column in the *Chronicle of Higher Education* (2017). Noting that heavy reliance on legalistic discipline or honor codes is unsustainable, and citing successful examples of conflict resolution programs across the county, Lake encouraged universities to continue to consider the types of educational experiences in which future students will want to invest.

As more institutions use these methods, they must develop a framework for providing educational experiences through conflict resolution. This framework should provide the scaffolding upon which the institution can interpret conflict resolution in the context of residential education. In most cases, these frameworks are adapted from established research and best practices in conflict resolution in higher education. At their core, they support the educational value of living in a community, provide methods based on the needs of the individual student as well as the community, and are developmentally and culturally responsive. Finally, they include implementation of relationship- and community-building options that ensure healthy, constructive management of conflict.

Risk Management

To protect the institution from liability, conflict resolution, like all campus processes, must be performed in a way that adheres to existing law and internal policies. To that end, residence life professionals and conduct officers must identify ways to provide students with fundamental fairness and meet the unique developmental needs of each student in a way that honors their identities while considering the health and safety risks their actions pose to the university. As Taylor and Varner (2009) state in *Reframing Campus Conflict*, this obligation can sometimes be interpreted as treating every case the same way (p. 33). However, fairness does not mean sameness.

A fair and educationally driven conflict resolution pathway can achieve the same level of compliance as an adjudicative process if the conflict resolution processes are voluntary and transparent, and the staff who manage or facilitate them are trained and capable (Schrage & Giacomini, 2009). It is also important to recognize the limits of conflict resolution pathways when power dynamics are at play, and inequality or safety are threatened.

Student Development and Learning

John Paul Lederach, known for his scholarly and practical work in peacebuilding and conflict transformation, asserts conflict can transform people and relationships positively when managed in a way that restores people and communities. This means the individuals experience a fundamental change in attitude, behavior, or both (Lederach, 1996). Residence life professionals can use conflict resolution methods to create space for these transformative experiences (big and small) by using student development theory to guide their practice. The key is that efforts are not limited to solving the specifics of the conflict at hand, but instead, the resolution can alter the way in which those involved view themselves (consciousness of self), their community (citizenship), and how they interact with others in the long term.

In addition to transformative educational experiences in college, student affairs professionals strive to create opportunities for students to define and evolve their understanding of who they are and want to be. Baxter Magolda defines self-authorship as "the internal capacity to define one's beliefs, identity, and social relations" and answers the questions of How do I know? Who am I? and How do I want to construct relationships with others? (Evans, et al., 2010, p. 184; Magolda, 1998, 2004). To create these opportunities, students must question how they have come to know things, what this means for them personally, and how it relates to their relationship with others as a part of the learning experience. Self-authorship integrates the epistemological, intrapersonal, and interpersonal elements of a student's experience toward the development of cognitive maturity, integrated identity, and mature relationships, which come together to create citizenship (Magolda, 2004).

Thoughtfully implemented, conflict resolution methods create opportunities for students to engage in personal development and transformative educational experiences. Conflict coaching assists students in reflecting on who they are and how their actions align with who they want to be. Setting community standards and negotiating living agreements is a way to ask students how they want to present themselves to their community. Responsive community and restorative justice circles facilitate learning in students' personal lives. Where there is the most dissonance, professional staff can help students see themselves as capable of creating their own knowledge and developing deeper emotional intelligence.

Social Justice and Inclusion

A campus community includes an untold number of individuals and identities. Within those identities, there are levels of privilege and power that affect virtually everything that occurs, including community building, conduct, and conflict resolution. Creating diverse, just, and inclusive communities where individuals of all identities feel at home and can express themselves in ways that are authentic and sincere is essential to the residence life mission and purpose.

Engaging in dialogue where students are not only able to tell their stories but listen with open minds to others' voices is where conflict resolution tools and skills truly support learning, relationship-building, and citizenship. Implemented properly, these empower students to be part of their own relationship-building and solution-making process, instead of a system dictating what should matter to them and how they should be held accountable. This is consistent with the fundamental premise of social justice that "involves social actors who have a sense of their own agency as well as a sense of social responsibility toward and with others, their society, and the broader world in which they live" (Bell, p. 2).

Restorative Justice and Restorative Practice

Conflict resolution methods benefit from being rooted in restorative justice. Restorative justice is a philosophy that focuses on relationships, obligations that exist because of those relationships, and the need for involvement by all to address needs that arise from harm (Zehr, 2015). It is a philosophy based on community building, where all members matter and there is a collective desire to make the community more whole. The values of restorative justice — the interconnectedness of community, equity, and respect — ensure restorative conflict resolution practices are socially just (Zehr, 2015).

As described by Zehr (2015, p. 49), restorative justice-based methods should ask the questions:

- Who has been harmed?
- What are their needs?
- Whose obligations are these?
- Who has a stake in the situation?
- What are the causes?
- What is the appropriate process to involve stakeholders in an effort to put things right and address underlying causes?

When community members engage in a restorative manner as they form relationships, they are more likely to choose to engage in a restorative way when conflict occurs. A restorative orientation allows residence life professionals to use community-building and conflict resolution tools as they build healthy communities, increase social capital, decrease misconduct and antisocial behavior, repair harm, and restore relationships (Wachtel & Wachtel, 2012).

The philosophy of applying restorative values to community building is known as restorative practice. Ted Wachtel, the founder of the International Institute for Restorative Practices (IIRP), identifies the most important elements of restorative practices as exercising inclusive decision-making (or fair process); doing things with, rather than to or for community members; and maximizing opportunities for expression of emotion (or positive affect) (Wachtel & Wachtel, 2012). Using these elements can transform a group of residents who are simply living in the same building into a community with a common purpose and commitment to one another.

Spectrum of Resolution Options Model

The Spectrum of Resolution Options Model (Schrage & Thompson, 2008), often referred to as the Spectrum Model, is recognized as a best practice in conflict resolution in higher education (Katz & Kovak, 2016). The model, formulated in 2008 by Jennifer Meyer Schrage in collaboration with Monita C. Thompson, draws from a variety of established frameworks. It was envisioned as a more socially just and inclusive approach that leverages the education-rich opportunities that exist before adjudicating cases of misconduct (what Schrage and Thompson labeled the "magic real estate") while honoring all the needs of a diverse campus population (Schrage & Thompson, 2008).

The Spectrum Model advocates institutions move away from a one-size-fits-all approach and provide educators the ability to address incidents using a continuum of methods (Schrage & Giacomini, 2009). These methods exist on a spectrum ranging from the most informal practices (i.e., dialogue, conflict coaching, and mediation) to more-formal processes (i.e., shuttle diplomacy and adjudication). These steps include:

- **No conflict management.** The institution does not become involved in the students' conflict.

- **Dialogue, debate, or discussion.** Students engage in conversation to resolve the conflict without institutional participation.

- **Conflict coaching.** Students, individually or collectively, receive guidance from institutional representatives to help resolve the conflict.

- **Facilitated dialogue.** Institutional representatives facilitate a dialogue between the conflicted parties to manage the process better, while the students maintain ownership of the conflict resolution.

- **Mediation.** Institutional representatives coordinate a formal, structured process to resolve the conflict and determine next steps while tending to both results and relationships.

- **Restorative justice practice.** Institutional representatives oversee the process to determine steps necessary to repair community damage; the process includes the offending and affected parties. This may be done in the place of, or as a part of, the adjudication process for someone found responsible for harmful behavior.

- **Shuttle diplomacy.** A multi-partial institutional representative negotiates an agreement between parties who do not wish to meet directly with each other.

- **Informal adjudication.** The institutional administration follows an established process (i.e., conduct policy, housing contract, etc.) to meet with the offending student and resolve the conduct violation. Resolution is considered to be achieved when the student accepts responsibility and agrees to sanctions.

- **Formal adjudication.** The institutional administration follows an established process, including a hearing, where an impartial third-party determines whether a violation has occurred. If one has, sanctions are issued against the offending student (Schrage & Thompson, 2009).

There is an important intentionality and analysis to maintain in the shift from formal to informal. The Spectrum Model provides the flexibility to keep student needs at the center. It allows residence life staff to ensure residential communities are not places protected from outside influences or potentially damaging events, but are environments where students can make sense of the world around them, even in the face of different viewpoints.

FIGURE 9.3 Spectrum of Resolution Options Model. Developed by Jennifer Meyer Schrage and Monita C. Thompson.

Source: Schrage and Thompson, 2008. Used with permission.

For example, the transformative and developmental nature of conflict resolution allows for students to develop the capacity to live together in inclusive communities where they feel capable of resolving and managing conflicts in a way that invites all voices into a dialogue. Giacomini and Schrage refer to the informal side of the spectrum as the ideal state of community, where students have learned to discuss and manage conflict without the intervention of administrators. At the same time, though, they warn "when we deformalize, we risk oppressing, informally" (Giacomini & Schrage, personal communication, April 20, 2018).

Ensuring practices are fair and student-centered means methods to resolve conflict are selected thoughtfully and staff and students facilitating those processes are properly trained. To appropriately and ethically use the conflict resolution methods to support the educational experience, student affairs practitioners must keep inclusion at the heart of their efforts by examining their thinking and practice. In turn, this means institutions must keep social justice competencies and a commitment to inclusive excellence at the core of their professional development and practice to better prepare institutions to shift from formal to informal conflict resolution practices in a socially just way.

Finally, restorative justice practices, including circles, are process options as well as foundational values of the model. Informal processes may suffice for issues such as roommate conflicts, but the more-formal methods may be needed to address incidents of misconduct. While each of the conflict resolution practices along the spectrum is unique, each involves a process of helping parties define the problem, searching for alternative ways to understand another perspective, and plotting a way forward (Schrage & Giacomini, 2009).

Residential Education Conflict Resolution Model

Just as the Spectrum Model built upon existing frameworks, it also is possible to expand upon Schrage and Thompson's work to create a model that includes proactive community-building methods. While conflict resolution methods in residential communities are valuable in helping students explore more about themselves, learn how to engage with others in difficult conversation, and consider their role as community members, strategies remain that could lessen the need for institutional intervention, or even avoid unnecessary conflict. These proactive community-building methods draw from the competencies and responsibilities of most housing and residence life professionals and, in addition, acknowledge the ways in which these residence life practitioners are positioned perfectly to capitalize on the magic real estate concept (Giacomini & Schrage, personal communication, April 20, 2018; Schrage & Thompson, 2008).

The authors of this chapter call this the Residential Education Conflict Resolution Model. This model gives residence life practitioners a variety of practices

FIGURE 9.4 Residential Education Conflict Resolution Model

PROACTIVE COMMUNITY-BUILDING PRACTICES	RESPONSIVE COMMUNITY-BUILDING PRACTICES
Community Standards	Conflict Coaching
Living Agreements	Facilitated Dialogues (mediations)
Community-building Circles	Responsive Community Circles
Socials and Gatherings	Restorative Justice-based Conduct Meetings
One-on-One Conversations	Restorative Circles

INCLUSIVE COMMUNITY

SOCIAL AND RESTORATIVE JUSTICE FOUNDATION

Source: Mauriello and Pierson, 2018.

to cultivate student learning, nurture a sense of community, and act in a just manner while keeping inclusion at the center. The model demonstrates proactive and responsive community-building practices build on and interact with one another and they are in motion continuously as they are applied to living, breathing communities. Finally, the Residential Education Conflict Resolution Model, like the Spectrum Model, uses restorative justice and social justice as its foundation.

PROACTIVE COMMUNITY-BUILDING PRACTICES

Frances was the RA who lived just a few doors down from Tori and Kerry. Even as an experienced senior, Frances still felt uncomfortable when she found herself in the middle of roommate conflicts but recognized it came with the territory.

Today, she would host her first community meeting of the semester, something she truly enjoyed. After welcoming everyone, Frances asked all of the residents to sit in a circle and share the one thing they valued most in a community. When it came to her turn, Tori said her value was honesty and it was something her mom taught her from a young age. Later, as Frances helped Tori and Kerry draft a living agreement, she noted how Tori again brought up how much she valued honesty.

As the semester progressed, there were the usual issues, but Frances could see the residents on her floor begin to make connections. They participated in the programs she put on. One group bonded over a shared love of action movies. Frances also found herself having regular conversations with Tori. During these one-on-one meetings, they could share some common experiences, since she also was a first-generation college student. She also heard stories about the friction Tori and Kerry were experiencing.

What impact did it have for Tori to be able to speak to her whole floor community about her values? What are some ways Frances could help ensure Tori and her roommate could live out Tori's value of honesty?

Community building may be the most-significant responsibility for those who work in a campus housing organization, particularly RAs and hall directors, who have the most direct contact with residential students. They accomplish this through educational and social programming, as well as additional exercises to draw residents out of their rooms and help them form interpersonal relationships with their neighbors. The success of these efforts often is noted through retention rates and student learning and satisfaction surveys. What can be overlooked, though, is the role of community building in reducing incidents of conflict.

From a restorative paradigm, the community is the owner of the conflict rather than the institution (McCold, 1995). Understanding this concept increases the importance of nurturing the community and providing opportunities for relationships to grow, empowering community members to resolve conflicts more effectively and to avoid unnecessary, destructive conflicts altogether. This means the common understanding of community-building efforts in a residence hall should expand to include work such as defining community through inclusive decision making; expectation setting; and commitments to the community (living agreements and community standards setting) and relationship building (impromptu gatherings, community circles).

Community Standards and Living Agreements

Establishing living agreements and community standards through dialogue are important first steps in community building. Community standards are a set of expectations groups set for living together. These often include community values that revolve around respect for others, space, and self. Living agreements are used among residents who live in shared rooms, suites, or apartments. These agreements focus on day-to-day functioning, such as sleep schedules and space use.

Essentially, community standards and living agreements serve as a map to answering the question of how groups of residents — be they a pair of room-mates, dozens of residents on the same floor, or hundreds in the same residence hall — will live together in a shared space for an academic year. The standards establish purpose and expectations, as well as how the community will uphold expectations of one another and hold others accountable if those expectations are not met.

Setting community standards is a theoretical model that uses dialogue to create mutually agreed-upon community expectations (Wachtel & Wachtel, 2012). These processes, at their best, are collaborative and rely on inclusive decision-making or consensus-building processes that acknowledge the interdependence of residential community members. Referring back to the foundational elements of restorative practices, these agreements are a means of creating peer-to-peer accountability through boundary- and expectation-setting, as well as providing high-level support in the form of peer commitments to each other (Wachtel & Wachtel, 2012). The peer engagement element of community standards-setting is developmentally important, since, according to Astin (1993), peer interactions are the most-influential source of development in college students.

The process of establishing agreements about how students expect to live together as community members and roommates centers their residential experience as a relational one. From an educational perspective, the process of community standards-setting forces students to recognize the tension between individual autonomy and the best interests of the community. Peer accountability, and the realization residents live alongside other people, and will continue to live alongside them when disputes occur, motivates negotiation, collaboration, and frequent revisiting when expectations change or a violation of the agreement occurs.

Community-building Circles

Community standards and living agreements can be set in various ways. One strong practice is the use of community-building circles to guide the conversation. The circle is a powerful symbol. Facilitators often draw attention to its meaning and introduce practices or rituals that maintain the egalitarian nature of the circle and create an environment conducive to addressing complex conflicts in groups (Pranis, 2015). Much of restorative practice work is done in circles, which invites all participants to participate in community building within it. The circle represents connection, continuity, and equity. It requires consensus-based decision making where all participants have an equal say. Author Stacey Miller refers to circles as a "powerful mechanism to help students get to know one another and begin the process of openly discussing their needs and wants, consistent with the community standards process" (Wachtel & Wachtel, 2012, p. 6).

One example of a common practice used in circles is the use of a talking piece. The talking piece can be any object "passed around the circle creating a unique rhythm of dialogue" (Karp, 2015, p. 28). Whoever holds the talking piece is the only one who is allowed to speak. The piece is then passed around the circle, providing all participants a chance to speak and reinforcing the idea that as one person speaks, everyone else listens.

A good practice for using circle-style processes to develop community standards based in restorative philosophy is to begin as soon as residential students arrive on campus to live in a community for the first time. These conversations can be peer-led by RAs who start a round of conversation by posing a question or prompt and asking everyone around the circle to respond. The RA facilitator can then focus on hearing, contributing to, and putting into writing what everyone has to offer. Sample questions to help first-year students begin to think about what it means to live in community include:

- What are your hopes for this year?
- What are your concerns?
- What behaviors might lead to achieving an ideal community?
- What behaviors might interfere with achieving our ideal community?
- What can we do as individuals and as a group to overcome those obstacles to achieve an ideal community? (Wachtel & Wachtel, 2012)

When community standards are set using restorative tools and a restorative framework, the community is more likely to accept and support them. This accountability manifests because restorative framework allows for rejecting an unacceptable act or behavior because it fails to meet community norms or standards while continuing to welcome and accept the person responsible. A restorative justice framework requires these standards be available to community members, be adaptable to meet the changing needs of the community, and have a process of accountability.

Social Gatherings and Conversations

Proactive community-building practices are foundational to the residence life experience because they demonstrate to students they matter and give them opportunities to interact with other residents. RAs have the responsibility to host regularly scheduled floor gatherings to encourage engagement in their communities. These gatherings can be both educational and social. The relationships developed through these activities are important because they help build care and rapport among residents. They help students develop a sense of accountability to one another. These sorts of gatherings can lead to community ownership and give students a reason to care to engage in conflict resolution when it happens.

Along with these gatherings, it is important RAs develop an individual rapport with residents. This is often done through intentional one-on-one meetings where RAs ask specific questions about a student's experience to better learn who they are and provide advice where applicable. Building individual relationships with residents gives RAs an opportunity to know who their residents are when entering a conflict or difficult situation.

RESPONSIVE COMMUNITY-BUILDING PRACTICES

When Frances answered the knock on her door, she was not surprised to see Kerry standing in the hallway, looking upset. "I want Tori to move out" were the first words out of Kerry's mouth. Frances invited her inside, closed the door, and offered her a seat.

"I want Tori to move out," Kerry repeated. "She has been changing the thermostat without my permission and it is in our roommate agreement that we leave the temperature at 70 degrees."

"It sounds like you are unhappy that Tori is not communicating with you before she changes the temperature," Frances responded, keeping her voice calm.

"Right. I want her to move out since she is violating our contract."

"It is important to you that your roommate follows the agreement. Have you talked with her about this?"

"No. I don't want to escalate things more than they already are."

Frances nodded to herself as she remembered having almost the exact same conversation with Tori three days earlier. It seemed as though a facilitated conversation for the two of them was on the horizon. In what ways could Frances help the roommates explore their feelings about the conflict, specifically as it relates to the dynamics at play? How can she help the roommates explore more about their own involvement in the conflict?

The debate over a thermostat setting would seem minor in comparison by the next semester. Over the course of several weeks, there were a variety of racial bias incidents directed at Black students through social media. Tori began to question whether she felt at home and safe in this campus community. She was pleased to see an email from Frances inviting her and the rest of their residence hall to a community circle to discuss the incidents and how they affected the residential community.

While Tori attended the meeting and listened to her hallmates share their thoughts, she felt a mixture of emotions. On the one hand, she was frustrated by the varying levels of connection to the issue and was particularly upset when a White resident said she didn't even know these incidents had occurred. On the other hand, Tori felt strengthened and appreciative as she heard from other residents who shared many of her concerns.

What questions could Frances and the other RAs have asked to encourage all the residents to consider how they were connected to the issue? How could the RAs have set the ground rules to encourage everyone to participate in the discussion? What kind of training and support from a professional staff member might have been needed for the RA to be ready to facilitate this dialogue?

When conflict does arise, whether it is between two individuals or large groups of people, the responsive community-building methods provide tools for constructive resolution and management of conflict. For example, conflict coaching methods facilitate skill building and equip students with the self-knowledge and skills to address conflict on their own. Methods such as facilitated dialogue and mediation can be used to address incidents while providing the opportunity for those affected by a serious incident in their community to have a voice. Meanwhile, more-formalized procedures are available for situations where more serious offenses have occurred or resolution could not be reached among the affected parties.

Conflict Coaching

Conflict coaching occurs in a meeting or series of sessions between a coach and a person who is experiencing conflict. This coaching equips a person with the skills to address the conflict effectively and leads them to a better understanding of the conflicts they are experiencing (Jones & Ross, 2008). Compared to other methods, this coaching is considered to be relatively informal (Schrage & Giacomini, 2009). Generally, in residence life contexts, conflict coaching occurs when a student brings a concern to a staff member because they are either unsure about how to address it, or unwilling to participate in a facilitated dialogue. Conflict coaching can often serve as preparation work done as a pre-meeting held before facilitated dialogues and restorative circles.

When acting as a conflict coach, residence life professional staff should build rapport, model behaviors such as active listening and using "I" statements, and use additional tools like problem-solving skills, cross-cultural communication skills, and knowledge of conflict styles (Schrage & Giacomini, 2012). In addition to tips for building rapport, three important strategies for conflict coaching include building consciousness of self, examining the conflict from a needs — rather than positions — perspective, and role-playing communication strategies.

Rapport. Rapport building is appropriate for any responsive conflict-resolution methodology. In conflict coaching, it is particularly important for building trust and can assist with determining areas of focus for the coaching session. Using reflective listening strategies during a conversation can help the coach better understand the student's point of view and often aid students in their own self-work to communicate their personal experiences better. To help students explore their feelings more deeply, staff can use comments such as:

- "I am hearing you say you felt this way. Is that accurate?"
- "Can you share a little more about why you felt this way and how you feel now?"
- "I heard you say you need this. How would you feel if those things were addressed?"

Consciousness of self. The use of conflict typologies or instruments to stimulate self-awareness is an effective conflict coaching strategy. Residence life professionals should recall conflict styles can reflect cultural patterns and can be adapted depending on context (Ting-Toomey, 2000; Kilmann, 1974). Residence life professionals can also use tools like the ICS and TKI to stimulate thinking and discussion of implicit assumptions. They also create development opportunities in leadership skills such as managing controversy with care and thoughtfulness. Using these instruments can also help the coach diagnose areas to focus on when role-playing communication strategies.

Positions and interests. An effective strategy in conflict coaching is to distinguish between a person's position and their interests. Fisher and Ury are credited with developing the idea of moving parties engaged in a conflict from focusing on positions to focusing on interests as an effective way to resolve underlying issues. They define *interests* as an individual's needs or underlying issues and *positions* as their desired outcomes (2011). To better understand the value of moving a person from thinking about their position(s) to reflecting upon their interests, consider the case of a simmering roommate conflict.

Often, by the time students engage residence life staff to help resolve a matter, the students have entrenched their positions (i.e., wanting a room change). The more a student is asked to answer why they want a room change, the more they become attached to that idea. On the other hand, reframing the student's position as an interest (i.e., needing a roommate to stop having overnight guests) can open up opportunities for collaboration or compromise and a revisiting of living agreements (Warters, 2000).

TABLE 9.1 Residential Education Restorative Justice-based Conflict Resolution Methods

	Evidence-based Guideline	Practice Strategy	Topics for Consideration
Proactive Community-Building Practices	**Community Standards:** Community expectations based on shared needs	A public display of community expectations (RAs, community members)	Establishing quiet hours, guest expectations, use of common space, noise levels, shared social norms, expectations for addressing conflict
	Living Agreements: Living space expectations based on individual needs	Written agreement available to reference and revise as needed (RA, roommates, suitemates)	Individual sleep schedules, use of shared space, study habits, cleaning schedule, guest expectations
	Community Building Circles: Community based dialogues focused on relationship building	Participants sit in circle formation, answer questions, and engage in dialogue (RAs, community members)	Personal stories, interests, connection to the community
	Gatherings/Socials: Programs fostering a shared experience for students	Planned and spontaneous group activities (RAs, community members, live-in staff and faculty)	Educational programs, floor meetings, activities, projects
	One-on-One Meetings: Peer-to-peer meeting focused on fostering individual relationship and developing trust	Planned and spontaneous private meetings (RAs, community members, live-in staff and faculty)	Discuss individual background, campus involvement, relationships, academics, personal needs

TABLE 9.1 (continued)

	Evidence-based Guideline	Practice Strategy	Topics for Consideration
Responsive Community-Building Practices	**Conflict Coaching:** To guide or coach an individual on how to address conflict on their own	Private coaching conversation with students experiencing conflict. (RA and student who has the concern)	Roommate and suitemate concerns, community conflicts, student disagreements with family
	Facilitated Dialogues (mediations): A conversation focused on resolving a conflict between individuals and guided by a multi-partial facilitator	Participants sit in a small circle in a neutral location and engage in a guided conversation (RA with involved parties)	Roommate and suitemate conflict where a formal agreement is needed
	Responsive Community Circles: A public dialogue that focuses on issues affecting the community, resulting in a shared plan of action	Open forum with guiding questions that encourages all voices to be heard. (RAs, community members, live-in staff and faculty)	Community-wide issues, bias incident with no identified person, party culture, vandalism by an unknown person, campus-wide incident, current issues
	Restorative Justice-based Conduct Meetings: Conduct meeting where restorative justice questions and obligations are used	Presents behavior of concern, discussing responsibility, and developing obligations to address harm when necessary (Live-in staff and responsible student)	Drinking incident with low community impact, drug use, noise violation
	Restorative Circles: A facilitated dialogue regarding a specific student conduct-related incident between an identified responsible party and those directly affected, resulting in documented obligations	Participants sit in a circle in a private setting and are guided through a series of steps by a multi-partial facilitator; results in a community agreement (Facilitators, RAs, live-in staff, affected parties, responsible parties, affected community members)	Student conduct-related behavior with high community impact, bias incident, vandalism, community disruption, drunk and disorderly conduct, physical or verbal altercation, disruptive parties

Adapted from the Washington University in St. Louis Restorative Justice Ambassador Guidebook.

Motivational interviewing. Developed by Miller and Rollnick, this technique is "a counseling method that helps people resolve ambivalent feelings and insecurities to find the internal motivation they need to change their behavior. It is a practical, empathetic, and short-term process that takes into consideration how difficult it is to make life changes" (1991).

Originally created to elicit behavior change in addicts, motivational interviewing strategies have also been used in settings such as public health and social work, as well as for conduct meetings and conflict resolution (Miller & Rollnick, 1991; Prochaska, Norcross, & DiClemente, 1995; Taylor, et al., 2012; Wachtel, 2016). In conflict settings, combining motivational interviewing with restorative questions is an effective way to motivate those experiencing conflict to examine their behavior, determine how that behavior affects themselves and others, and decide whether they need to make a change to reach their future goals (Wachtel, 2016). Another benefit of this strategy is it supports the student's development by centering the conflict in their own experience (Magolda, 2004). Finally, this strategy also allows the facilitator to work with community members' values, making it conducive to honoring and understanding cultural differences.

Motivational interviewing techniques encourage the student to develop a plan, anticipate barriers to change, and identify support systems (Miller & Rollnick, 1991). This is accomplished by having practitioners be engaging, focusing, evoking, and planning. These strategies, along with asking open-ended questions, offering affirmations, and being reflective, express empathy, develop discrepancy, roll with resistance, and support self-efficacy (Miller & Rollnick, 2002). Examples of using motivational interviewing techniques with a restorative justice lens, include:

- **Engaging.** How have you been affected? What were you thinking about then and what are you thinking about now?

- **Focusing.** What has been the most difficult part for you? If you could communicate one thing to the other individuals involved, what would it be?

- **Evoking.** What have you done since the incident? What do you need moving forward? What can you contribute?

- **Planning.** What specific areas would you like to address or need to be addressed, and what does that timeline look like? (Miller & Rollnick, 2002; Washington University of St. Louis Residence Life, 2018).

Finally, as a conflict coaching technique, motivational interviewing can be used by coaches to help students center their own stories and experiences instead of focusing on others. This prepares them to speak to this when in dialogue with others and commit to one of the most-important ground rules of any facilitated dialogue: Speak from the "I" perspective. Students often want to hide in the "we" or speak for their peers. The use of "I" statements keeps students from doing so and requires them to own their own stories.

Facilitated Dialogue

In residence life settings, the practice of facilitated dialogue (sometimes referred to as "small-m mediation") creates opportunities for peace and relationship building (Wilgus & Holmes, 2009). Facilitated dialogues act as a broad brush that can be used in problem-solving, reaching agreements, or simply reaching understanding (Wilgus & Holmes, 2009, p. 114). The term *mediation* is often used in residence life programs to define any efforts to address roommate or other interpersonal conflicts. These efforts, however, are more closely aligned with the concept of facilitated dialogue.

While the elements of a facilitated dialogue align with the goals of mediations, it is important to know the difference and the more-universal understanding of the word mediation. To be a trained mediator in the world of conflict resolution requires specific training, and a formal mediation includes elements that are often not included in residence life mediations (Warters, 2000).

In a residence life context, facilitated dialogues address conflicts of attitude, behavior, or perspective, where the process of coming to understand is just as important as (if not more than) the outcome. More important than just moving the parties involved toward an agreement on a particular issue — consider Tori, Kerry, and their thermostat — is the fact the process of discussing the issue will move the involved parties to a better understanding of each other as individuals.

Facilitated dialogue is often the first formal opportunity for a facilitator to become involved in a conflict (Wilgus & Holmes, 2009). The role of a third-party facilitator is to open communication and foster mutual understanding and trust. The goal is to assist the parties in overcoming communication barriers so they can engage in productive conversation. These meetings may be one-off conversations or require multiple sessions. A facilitator must be multi-partial, meaning they are able to understand and be attentive to the varying needs and experiences of all participants in the context of the conflict. This moves beyond the concept of being neutral and requires the facilitator to be active in listening, digesting, and making sense of all the stories being shared.

To prepare for a facilitated dialogue in a social justice and restorative context, the facilitators should meet with both parties individually to build rapport and understand each individual side of the conflict. This also gives the facilitator an opportunity to explore with both parties individually what they are willing to compromise on and what matters most to them.

The next step is finding a location that is private, comfortable for all participants, and lets the parties to look at one another when they speak. The facilitator then leads the conversation based on what the intentions of the facilitated conversation are set out to be.

Educational resources to improve facilitation skills include the chapter "Facilitated Dialogue: An Overview and Introduction for Student Conduct Professionals" by Holmes and Wilgus in Schrage and Giacomini's *Reframing Campus Conflict* (2009). These guidelines are provided to RAs at Washington University in St. Louis, Missouri, to assist them as they facilitate a conversation between two residents in conflict.

- **Welcome.** Introduce all participants. Explain the role of the mediator, the meeting process, and conflict of interest.

- **Set ground rules.** Establish a time for mediation, the standards of respect, and additional ground rules as needed.

- **Share stories.** Each party is given a chance to tell their side of the story. Remind participants to speak from their own perspective using "I" statements.

- **Address the conflict.** Each party identifies their role in the conflict and how the actions of others make them feel.

- **Consider needs-based resolution.** Once each party has discussed their personal responsibility, ask for ideas on how to resolve the conflict and how best to meet individual needs.

- **Create agreement.** Write an agreement and have it signed by all parties (including the mediator).

- **Follow up.** Touch base with residents periodically about the agreement and encourage positive engagement.

Responsive Community Circle

Community dialogues or responsive circles represent another area where Schrage and Thompson's (2008) model expands for residential education contexts. Circles are "simple, structured, and provide equal status for all participants" (Wachtel, Wachtel, and Miller, 2012). They are intended to create an opportunity for meaningful dialogue where all parties have an opportunity to speak and all must engage in active listening. Facilitators or community members convene circles when a group dialogue is needed about a particular topic.

Returning to the developmental importance of peer interaction (Astin,

1993), one of the fundamental elements of a community dialogue is the engagement of the group through open-ended questions intended to elicit or explore the reason for convening. As a responsive practice, a community dialogue can take the form of a responsive circle when harm has occurred in the community. Responsive circles can be used when the identity of the person who caused harm is unknown, or a community issue has to be addressed (Wachtel & Wachtel, 2012; Karp, 2015). Erhart and Meyer (2012) recommend considering the following when deciding whether a responsive community circle is appropriate:

- Are there many issues or concerns involved in the conflict?
- Is there a clear harm?
- Are there unanswered questions on the part of one or more of the parties?
- Does one of the parties wish to share their story?
- Is there an ongoing relationship?

When the choice is made to proceed with a responsive community circle, it is important to approach the process in a thoughtful and purposeful manner. The community dialogue facilitator checklist created by Darling, Karp, and Pierson (2013) includes steps considered to be a best practice for the profession. In their model, facilitators will:

- Read and explain the ground rules, and ask for questions. Invite participants to add other ground rules they think are necessary to create a safe space. Ground rules may include inclusion, no interruptions, one speaker at a time, active listening, confidentiality, voluntary participation, no cellphones, etc.
- Read an opening inspiration together (optional).
- Explain the purpose of the circle and that each participant may share as much or as little as they desire, but must be mindful of others' time to speak. Involvement is voluntary.
- Take a moment for everyone to focus quietly on the task at hand.
- Pose the first question and then, as the facilitator, answer the question, to give participants time to think and as an example.
- After everyone has answered the first question, ask if anyone would like to comment about what has been said.
- Take a moment to briefly summarize points made, then pose the second question, following the same procedure.
- At the conclusion of all the questions, hold another moment of silent reflection and conclude with a summary (optional).

Restorative Justice-based Conduct Meetings

Both conduct meetings and circle processes in this model are based on the theory of restorative justice. The distinction is one is partly restorative while the other is fully restorative. Restorative conduct meetings apply the restorative justice theoretical framework to conduct meetings, through the use of restorative questions, restorative outcomes, and sanctions or obligations. By using restorative questions in conduct meetings, residence life professionals can help responsible parties learn the impact their behavior has on themselves and their community, and help them get back to what matters most. For many, that is being a successful student.

Restorative Circle

Restorative circles bring stakeholders together to address a harm caused by a responsible party with the intention for resolution (Zehr, 2015). The most-important distinction between a restorative-based conduct meeting and a restorative circle is the restorative circle is more connected to restorative justice theory because it includes the community members who are affected by the harm. As described by practitioners at James Madison University, in restorative circles:

> The parties with a stake in a particular offense (the victim, the offender, and community members) are supported and voluntarily participate, with the assistance of a facilitator, in a discussion of the circumstances surrounding the harm. The purpose is to understand its underlying causes [and] the effects on those who have been harmed, and to address the parties' needs for healing and reparation. Restorative justice provides opportunities to ask and answer questions, share stories, express feelings, and hopefully develop a better understanding of the other. (Restorative Justice, n.d., para. 1)

Before a circle can take place, an intake process must occur. The intake process includes the meetings and work done before bringing interested parties together for dialogue and, in many ways, resembles conflict coaching conversations. It requires a multi-partial facilitator to take the lead in assessing who has been affected, sharing what the process is like for participants, and meeting with each individual to ensure they feel equipped to participate fully. Creating a space that eliminates power differences as much as possible and where all participants can feel fully heard requires rapport building and preparation. Key questions asked in any intake process include:

- How have you been affected?
- What has been the hardest thing for you?
- What do you need moving forward? (Karp, 2015).

These intake meetings help the facilitator better understand the emotions involved and can help determine who should be part of the conversation and what role they will play. Likely stakeholders include:

Responsible party or person. The individual identified as responsible for the behavior in question. In some campus conduct processes, they may be referred to as the offender or the accused student. However, conflict resolution-focused language does not label individuals, but instead describes their involvement as it relates to the purpose of the process.

Affected party or person. The individual who has been affected directly by an incident and has needs because of it. Some conduct processes use the terms "charging party" or "complainant" to describe this person.

Multi-partial facilitator. The individual responsible for overseeing and maintaining the integrity of the process and helping participants reach a resolution. This person often has no previous relationship with any of the participants and is chosen to demonstrate no favoritism to either party. Important aspects to consider when choosing a facilitator are the perceived visible identities and the identity power dynamics of a situation.

Invested community members. The individuals who were not directly harmed by an action or affected directly, but have a vested interest in the situation's outcome and moving the community forward. These individuals are often leaders in the community, such as RAs or live-in professional staff. They can often be helpful when creating ways to move forward and think about issues beyond the specific incident.

Support people. The individuals invited to support either the affected or responsible party during the process. This role is valuable since issues addressed in the process can be deeply personal. Individuals may feel challenged by the difficult dialogue, so having an individual present who knows them personally can be supportive.

During the circle, basic restorative questions are used to guide the conversation toward resolution. These questions demonstrate a genuine desire for understanding and focus on who has been harmed, what harm was done, and what has to be done to make things right (Karp, 2015). Circles are often facilitated by two people to let one facilitator focus on asking questions and guiding the conversation, and the other write down what is shared. All participants sit in a circle to encourage eye contact and direct engagement.

In general, the process will include a similar series of steps. The process begins with helping the group get to know one another better and progresses through hearing everyone's stories to the final stage of developing obligations to repair the harm and move forward. For example:

- **Find common ground.** Humanize all participants, and share individual connections to the circle.

- **Identify harms.** Give participants the opportunity to tell their stories.

- **List harms.** Facilitators write down stated harms and ensure all effects and harms have been heard and are considered in the stage of addressing harms.

- **Check on progress.** Take a small break in the proceedings as needed and give everyone a chance to reflect on what has been written.

- **Address harms.** Create a written agreement that outlines what has to be addressed for restoration and a deadline for completion. Use it to ensure all obligations are completed; only after that is the matter considered resolved.

- **Close the circle.** Can be as simple as having participants do a one-word check-in on how they feel at the conclusion of the dialogue.

FACILITATOR SKILLS

As the year progressed, Tori and Kerry grew considerably more friendly. However, a week before final exams, Kerry went out with a group of friends to hit the town and blow off some steam. Late that night, when she returned to the room obviously intoxicated, she threw up in the hallway, banged loudly on the door because she couldn't find her key, and then passed out on the restroom floor. When Tori was not able to wake her up, she called emergency services, who transported Kerry to the hospital.

A few days later, even though Kerry was safe, Tori still was upset by the incident and went to her RA for advice. She told Frances she wanted to talk to Kerry about the night but didn't know how. Frances responded she would take those concerns to her supervisor and get back to Tori.

Later that week, Tori heard from the residential community director, inviting her to participate in a restorative circle regarding her roommate's behavior. Tori was nervous about having such a challenging conversation, but also intrigued by the prospect of sharing with Kerry how her actions that night had made Tori feel.

What aspects of this situation made it a good case for a restorative circle? Who else could be invited as affected parties? How might the circle and the circle outcome be transformative for Tori and her relationship with her roommate? How might the circle and the circle outcome be transformative for the community?

Taking conflict resolution methods and practices from good to great does not necessarily require more resources, but instead a deepening of interpersonal skills, translating them into practice, and gaining experience through practice. Providing staff with opportunities to fine-tune their skills in the areas of active listening and use of inclusive language can make a difference in a department's ability to apply conflict resolution methods and develop staff into stronger facilitators.

Familiarity with facilitator skills is a valuable asset for housing professionals because these skills can be applied in a variety of settings, including small-group and one-on-one interactions. Pairing well-trained facilitators with established practices such as responsive community circles, restorative circles, conflict coaching, and other techniques provides students with the most-optimal learning experiences.

In all these situations, it is important the facilitator be a part of the circle or dialogue, not to dominate it (Wachtel & Wachtel, 2012). The facilitator is present simply to guide the conversation, maintain an inclusive environment, and help voices be heard. By using open-ended questions and other strategies to form connections, the process removes the adversarial aspects, fosters an atmosphere of understanding, and strives to repair harm and restore trust in a way that satisfies the community.

Active Listening

It is important to remember listening means more than just paying attention to what is said. Even if the method of resolution calls for facilitators to remain multi-partial and allow participants to own the process of resolution, facilitators should remain attentive and committed to actively engaging in the process through listening. When the facilitator is challenged, practicing active listening can require a great deal of energy since the facilitator must be able to hold two competing thoughts in their head at the same time.

Active listening is a key skill for facilitators of community-building and conflict resolution methods. Research indicates combining active listening skills with empathy is the most effective way to listen, especially in challenging facilitation situations (Comer & Drollinger, 1999). Several models of active listening are particularly useful for facilitators of conflict resolution: nonviolent communication (Rosenberg, 2015); compassionate listening (Hoffman et al., 2003); communication across divides (Herzig, 2006); and the L.A.R.A. Process (Tinker, 2004).

In the L.A.R.A. Process, for example, participants should:

- "Listen behind the words until you can hear how a person of principle could possibly hold the view being expressed. Listen until your heart understands how what they are saying connects to something you believe to be true. Don't say anything until you have heard this."
- "Affirm, with the first words out of your mouth, that you share some principle or value with this person. Don't talk about the shared belief, but demonstrate it by using an 'I' statement."
- "Respond with a direct answer to the concern expressed. By not dodging the question or issue, you show that you respect the other person, and you show that you are not afraid of their opinion."
- "Add some new fact, or better yet, something from your personal experience that gives some new information, or a different point of view." (Tinker, 2004).

Creating Ground Rules

Creating common ground before any conflict resolution process is a key step to creating an environment where all individuals feel supported in being able to share their stories in the most authentic way possible. Ground rules serve as an opportunity to guide the process of engagement, create collective ownership, and provide a starting place to refer back to if the conversation goes off track. Providing some basic ground rules and inviting participants to offer others to add is a great way to start. Basic ground rules to start a dialogue include:

- Use "I" statements
- Ask clarifying questions
- Trust intent
- Own intent
- Listen to understand and not to respond

Follow up and Agreements

Preparation for and follow up to conflict resolution practices are integral to addressing the issues discussed and can help eliminate future conflict arising from the same incident. Three categories to help facilitators establish what obligations can arise out of the conflict resolution process are: (a) apologies to address harm to relationships and emotional needs, (b) restitution to address physical harms, and (c) community engagement and service to address community harms (Darling, Karp, & Pierson, 2013).

Helping participants frame what they need in moving onward within these categories, along with tangible, reasonable deadlines, is a key component to participants achieving a sense of resolution at the end of the conversation and empowerment to take the steps needed to move forward. Creating an agreement in writing accessible to all participants and followed up by the facilitator is critical to ensuring the harm is addressed and behaviors do not regress back to before the process.

CONCLUSION

Before she knew it, the time had come for Tori to pack up her belongings and prepare for her trip back home. Her first year had been an eventful one. Despite the issues she and her roommate had over the past months, Tori could still say she was happy to have become friends with someone new. Moreover, as scary as Kerry's trip to the hospital had been, she was strangely-relieved to learn how concerned Tori had been for her well-being.

Tori was already looking forward to her sophomore year. Plans were set for her to live with some of her first-year floormates in a four-person suite and continue their tradition of screening action movies once a week. Drawing on her lessons learned, Tori knows that when they sit down to craft their roommate agreement, she will better understand what she values and be better prepared to communicate what she needs and expects from a roommate. She is not so naïve to think there won't be any disagreements, but she also knows that if they do occur, she will be equipped to address them in an honest and productive manner.

As for Frances, she was preparing for a few weeks of vacation before she moved off to graduate school and took her next step on the road to becoming a student affairs professional. She has discovered she has a knack for building and maintaining community, even in the face of conflict.

For many residence life professionals, day-to-day practice can often seem consumed by conflict resolution. By expanding the menu of resolution options available to students, these professionals are afforded more possibilities and a greater opportunity to act in a way that meets the needs of the individuals and the community as a whole. By leveraging the benefits of conflict resolution, residence life staff can create pathways to (a) reduce the adversarial nature of traditional adjudication methods, (b) preserve the values at the heart of a residential community that can be lost or misunderstood when disputes enter the conduct system, (c) intervene and educate students about conflict informally or at the lowest possible level of adjudication, and (d) live into multicultural competence and institutionalized equity where the community can notice and account for the real and perceived impact of structural inequality based on identities often found in traditional punitive models of justice (adapted from Schrage & Giacomini, 2009).

This movement is done with an understanding that legal implications and institutional standards remain that must be accounted for in terms of the conflict resolution methods. Often, these factors overlap with due process concerns or established expectations for student records and confidentiality. Including conflict resolution in a code of conduct is a means of institutionalizing the process and providing clear guidelines to students about what expectations exist when it comes to student behavior. Conflict resolution methods, most often restorative circles, can take the place of more-formal adjudication. At some universities, participation in these processes can result in the incident not being a part of students' formal conduct record.

Since conflict resolution methods are voluntary processes where individuals involved choose how they want to engage and what they want to share, it is important to maintain and respect privacy. By opting into the process, individuals know there will be an element of sharing about the personal connection to an incident and vulnerability is encouraged to develop the best resolution method. Similarly, in mediations and restorative processes, the mediator or facilitator often requests all parties agree to keep the content of their discussion confidential, sometimes even securing written confidentiality agreement. It is also a common ground rule established to encourage vulnerability and authenticity.

It also is important to remember that, as stated in connection with the Model Code (Stoner and Lowery, 2004), once a case has been reviewed, colleagues consulted, and institutional norms and possible legal issues are taken into account, professional judgment is the best measure for whether actions meet the needs of the student responsible. As Stoner states, "courts do respect and honor the judgment of college administrators — when that judgment is to pick approaches that thoughtfully address the students and institutions they serve" (as cited in Schrage & Giacomini, 2009, p. XVI). It is important to think deeply about how the process of resolution, rather than the outcome, may transform perspectives, relationships, and community.

Conflict resolution is more than just a practice. It can and should be something institutionalized in residence life departments. It is at the core of what housing professionals commit their work to: to cultivate communities of learning and growth. If done well, conflict resolution is not only a part of the cultural norm of residential communities, but embedded in the established

✚ Additional Resources

As college and university campuses increasingly use conflict resolution and restorative justice techniques, the number of available resources increases as well. These titles are just some of the publications that can enhance the reader's understanding of these subjects and go into greater detail than is possible here.

- *Building Campus Community, Restorative Practices in Residence Life*
  Joshua Wachtel and Ted Wachtel
  International Institute for Restorative Practices (2002)

- *Reframing Campus Conflict: Student Conduct Process through a Social Justice Lens*
  Jennifer Meyer Schrage and Nancy Geist Giacomini
  Stylus Publishing (2009)

- *The Little Book of Circle Processes*
  Kay Pranis
  Good Books (2005)

- *The Little Book of Restorative Justice*
  Howard Zehr
  Good Books (2002)

- *The Little Book of Restorative Justice for Colleges and Universities*
  David R. Karp
  Good Books (2013)

- *Peacemaking Circles*
  Kay Pranis, Barry Stuart, and Mark Wedge
  Living Justice Press (2003)

- *Restorative Justice Dialogues: An Essential Guide for Research and Practice*
  Mark S. Umbreit and Marilyn Peterson Armour
  Springer (2010)

- *Restorative Justice: How it Works*
  Marian Liebmann
  Jessica Kingsley Publishers. (2007)

programming or curriculum model. It is a part of both professional training and student leadership training. Internal teams can focus on implementation and yearly training. Professional development efforts can focus on helping staff develop skill sets that not only benefit the students, but help staff model what it means to be a restoratively minded community member. Residence life departments should be seen as the experts in community building and, thus, as experts in helping students engage in difficult conversation and be in community with others who are different than themselves.

In the end, for all of its processes and theory, the value of conflict resolution can be summed up by the words of Jordan Peters, a residential community director at Washington University in St. Louis:

> When first learning about restorative justice as an RA, my interest [in] — and eventually investment and commitment — this concept was almost immediate. I have always been one who was unsettled with quick or superficial fixes to problems involving how we as humans relate, communicate, and often harm one another. What I did not know at the conclusion of my undergraduate career is that restorative justice would, in fact, become a lifestyle and how I would infuse it into my passion for mentorship and coaching of other individuals. This newfound level of understanding and passion eventually led me to the realization that I wanted to be a student affairs professional to continue to equip students with these life skills and to be better engaged in all of their varying communities. (J. Peters, personal communication, January 14, 2018)

REFERENCES

Adams, M., Bell, L. A., & Griffin, P. (2016). *Teaching for diversity and social justice* (2nd ed.). New York: Routledge.

Astin, A. W. (2010) *What matters in college? Four critical years revisited.* San Francisco: Jossey-Bass.

Association of Student Conduct Administration. (1993). *Ethical principles and standards of conduct* [PDF]. Retrieved from: http://www.theasca.org/files/Governing%20Documents/Ethical%20Principles%20and%20Standards%20of%20Conduct.pdf.

Comer, L. B., & Drollinger, T. (1999). Active empathetic listening and selling success: A conceptual framework. *Journal of Personal Selling and Sales Management, 19*(1), 15–29.

Darling, J., Karp D., & Pierson, M. (2013, March). Restorative justice practices in student conduct administration. Presented at Student Affairs Administrators in Higher Education (NASPA) 2013 Annual Conference. Orlando, FL.

Ehrhart, C., & Meyer, G., (2012, March). Applying restorative justice in a higher education setting. Presented at the Fifth International Conference on Conflict Resolution Education. Cleveland, OH.

Evans, N. J., Forney, D. S., Guido, F., Patton, L. D., & Renn, K. A. (2010). *Student development in college: Theory, research, and practice* (2nd ed.). San Francisco: Jossey-Bass.

Fisher, R. C., Ury, W., & Patton, B. (2011). *Getting to yes: Negotiating agreement without giving in.* New York: Penguin.

Giacomini, N. G. (2009), The Art of Conflict Coaching. In J.M. Schrage and N.G. Giacomini (Eds.) *Reframing campus conflict: Student conduct practice through a social justice lens* (pp. 100–111). Sterling, VA: Stylus Publishing.

Hammer, M.R. (2009). Solving Problems and Resolving Conflict Using the Intercultural Conflict Style Model and Inventory. In M.A. Moodian (Ed.), *Contemporary leadership and intercultural competence: Exploring the cross-cultural dynamics within organizations.* (pp. 219–232). Thousand Oaks, CA: Sage Publications.

Hammer, M. R. (2003). *The Intercultural Conflict Style Inventory: Interpretive guide.* Berlin, MD: Hammer Consulting Group.

Hammer, M. R. (2003). *The Intercultural Conflict Style Inventory: Facilitator's manual.* Berlin, MD: Hammer Consulting Group.

Hammer, M. R. (2005). The Intercultural Conflict Style Inventory: A conceptual framework and measure of intercultural conflict resolution approaches. *International Journal of Intercultural Relations, 29*(6), 675-695. doi:10.1016/j.ijintrel.2005.08.010.

Herzig, M., & Chasin, L. (2006). *Fostering dialogue across divides: A nuts and bolts guide from the Public Conversations Project.* Watertown, MA: Public Conversations Project.

Hoffman, G. K., Monroe, C., Green, L., & Rivers, D. (2003). *Compassionate listening. An exploratory sourcebook about conflict transformation.* NewConversations.net.

Jones, T. S., & Brinkert, R. (2008). *Conflict coaching: Conflict management strategies and skills for the individual.* Los Angeles: Sage Publications.

Katz, N. H., & Kovack, L. N. (2016, August 21). Higher Education's Current State of Alternative Dispute Resolution Services for Students. Retrieved from https://ssrn.com/abstract=2822846.

Karp, D. R. (2015). *The little book of restorative justice for colleges and universities: Repairing harm and rebuilding trust in response to student misconduct.* New York: Skyhorse Publishing.

Lake, P. F. (2017, November 26). From Discipline Codes to Contractual Respect. *Chronicle of Higher Education.* Retrieved from: https://www.chronicle.com/

article/From-Discipline-Codes-to/241865.

Lederach, J. P. (1996). *Preparing for peace: Conflict transformation across cultures*. Syracuse, NY: Syracuse University Press.

Magolda, B. (1998). Developing self-authorship in young adult life. *Journal of College Student Development, 39*(2), 143–56.

Magolda, B. (2004). Self-authorship as the common goal. *Learning partnerships: Theory and models of practice to educate for self-authorship*, 1–35. Sterling, VA: Stylus Publishing.

McCold, P. (1995, March). Restorative justice: The role of the community. Paper presented at the Academy of Criminal Justice Sciences Annual Conference. Boston, MA.

Miller, S. (2012). Foreword in J. Wachtel and T. Wachtel *Building campus community: Restorative practices in residence life*. Bethlehem, PA: International Institute for Restorative Practices.

Miller, W. R., and Rollnick, S. (1991). *Motivational interviewing: Preparing people to change addictive behavior*. New York: Guilford Press.

Miller, W. R., & Rollnick, S. (2002). *Motivational interviewing: Preparing people to change addictive behavior* (2nd ed.). New York: Guilford Press.

Prochaska, J. O., DiClemente, C. C., & Norcross, J. C. (2002). *Changing for good: A revolutionary six-stage program for overcoming bad habits and moving your life positively forward*. New York: Avon Books.

Pranis, K. (2015). *Little book of circle processes: A new/old approach to peacemaking*. New York: Skyhorse Publishing, Inc.

Restorative Justice. (2018, January 16). Retrieved April 10, 2018, from: https://www.jmu.edu/osarp/restorative/restorative-justice.shtml.

Rosenberg, M., & Chopra, D. (2015). *Nonviolent Communication: A Language of Life: Life-Changing Tools for Healthy Relationships*. Encinitas, CA: Puddle Dancer Press.

Schrage, J. M. (2014). A Sea Change on the Horizon: Transforming Our Students and Campuses through Innovative Conflict Management. *About Campus, 19*(3), 17–25. doi:10.1002/abc.21158.

Schrage J. M. & Giacomini, N. G. (2018, April 20). Telephone interview.

Schrage, J. M., & Giacomini, N. G. (2009). *Reframing campus conflict: student conduct practice through a social justice lens*. Sterling, VA: Stylus Publishing.

Schrage, J.M. and Thompson, M.C. (2009). Providing a spectrum of resolution options. In J.M. Schrage and N. G. Giacomini (Eds.), *Reframing campus conflict: Student conduct practice through a social justice lens* (pp. 65–84). Sterling, VA: Stylus Publishing.

Schrage, J. M., & Thompson, M. C. (2008, June). *Using a social justice model for conflict resolution to ensure access for all students*. Paper presented at the

Donald D. Gehring Academy for Student Conduct Administration. Salt Lake City, UT.

Stoner, E., Lowery, J. (2004). Navigating past the "spirit of insubordination": A twenty-first century model student conduct code with a model hearing script. *Journal of College and University Law, 31*, 1–77.

Taylor, S.H., & Varner, D.T. (2009). When student learning and law merge to create educational student conflict resolution and effective conduct management programs. In J.M. Schrage and N. G. Giacomini (Eds.), *Reframing campus conflict: Student conduct practice through a social justice lens* (pp. 22–49). Sterling, VA: Stylus Publishing, LLC.

Thomas, K. W., & Kilmann, R. H. (1974, 2007). Sample Thomas-Kilmann Conflict Mode Instrument: Profile and Interpretive Report. Mountain View, CA: CPP, Inc. Retrieved from: https://www.cpp.com/en-US/Products-and-Services/Sample-Reports#tki.

Tinker, B. (2004). *L.A.R.A.: Engaging Controversy with a Non-violent, Transformative Response.* Workshop handout; available by request from info@LMFamily.org.

Ting-Toomey, S., Yee-Jung, K. K., Shapiro, R. B., Garcia, W., Wright, R.J., & Oetzel, J. G. (2004). Translating conflict face negotiation theory into practice. *International Journal of Intercultural Relations, 24*, 47–82.

Ting-Toomey, S., Yee-Jung, K. K., Shapiro, R. B., Garcia, W., Wright, T. J., & Oetzel, J. G. (2000). Ethnic/cultural identity salience and conflict styles in four US ethnic groups. *International Journal of Intercultural Relations, 24*(1), 47–81. doi:10.1016/s0147-1767(99)00023-1.

Ting-Toomey, S., Gao, G., Trubisky, P., Yang, Z., Kim, H. S., Lin, S., & Nishida, T. (1991). Culture, Face Maintenance, and Styles of Handling Interpersonal Conflict: A Study in Five Cultures. *International Journal of Conflict Management, 2*(4), 275-296. doi:10.1108/eb022702.

Thomas, K. W., & Kilmann, R. H. (1974). Conflict Mode Instrument. New York: Tuxedo.

Wachtel, T. (2003). Restorative justice in everyday life: Beyond the formal ritual. *Reclaiming Children and Youth, 12*(2), 83–87.

Wachtel, J., Wachtel, T. (2012). *Building campus community: Restorative practices in residence life.* Bethlehem, PA: International Institute for Restorative Practices.

Wachtel, J. (2016). Helping people help themselves with Motivational Interviewing. Retrieved from: https://www.iirp.edu/news-from-iirp/helping-people-help-themselves-with-motivational-interviewing.

Warters, W. C. (2000). *Mediation in the campus community: Designing and managing effective programs.* San Francisco: Jossey-Bass.

Wilgus, J. K., & Holmes, R. C. (2009). Facilitated dialogue: An overview and introduction for student conduct professionals. In J. M. Schrage & N. G. Giacomini (Eds.), *Reframing campus conflict: Student conduct practice through a social justice lens* (pp.112-125). Sterling, VA: Stylus Publishing.

Zehr, H. (2016). *The little book of restorative justice.* Vancouver, BC: Langara College.

DISCUSSION QUESTIONS

1. How does the mission of your university and department affect your response to incidents of conflict? Is there a relevant campus history or culture that you need to consider?

2. What resources are available to you (on and off campus) that you could use to strengthen the conflict resolution options you can offer students?

3. What have you found to be the most-important conflict resolution methods to train your professional staff on and your student staff on?

4. What are some of the most-useful facilitation skills or techniques you use when conducting conflict resolution?

5. Are there methods that you prefer to have professional staff facilitate rather than student staff? Are training level/competency, restorative concepts (e.g., community affiliation and fair process), and student development theory (e.g., self-authorship, peer learning, and identity) considerations included in your decision making?

6. Given the community standards and norms that already exist at your institution and in your community, how can you involve members of the community in the dialogue process before, during, and after conflicts occur?

7. How might you work with students to develop awareness of alternative conflict resolution methods on your campus?

8. If conflict resolution methods are to be viewed as a legitimate resolution pathway, taking the place of the tradition conduct process in some instances, what are the appropriate instances?

9. What are the institutional procedural or legal concerns that supervisors, general counsel, or others might express when conflict resolution is suggested instead of or before a formal conduct process?

10. How does conflict resolution fit into your overall residence life daily operations and residential education approach?

10

ASSESSING CONDUCT AND STUDENT BEHAVIOR

Ciji A. Heiser, Amy P. Gauthier, Kathryn A. DiCato, and Kathryn M. Bartholomew

HOUSING AND residential education programs are ripe with opportunities to measure student learning, program effectiveness, and the impact living on campus has on student academic success, retention, and graduation. Similar opportunities exist to weave assessment practices into the student conduct process, measure outcomes, and demonstrate the impact: How effective are the hearing officers? How effective is the training for hearing officers? What database and tracking systems are used? What are the appeal numbers? Do hearing officers give consistent sanctions for similar offenses? Are the sanctions effective? How effective is the partnership with other offices on campus that may be involved in students' cases?

Despite this potential, there is a gap in the literature in assessing the impact of the housing conduct process on students living in campus residential facilities (Janosik & Stimpson, 2017; King, 2012). We must introduce practitioners to the core concepts of using conduct philosophy to inform the assessment process. They must learn to determine factors and outcomes to assess; operationalize best practices in data collection, methodology, and ethics; and share assessment results, as well as use assessment to improve their practice and create a more-proactive conduct process.

The student conduct process is a valuable opportunity to help students understand core principles of ethical behavior, the impact of their actions on others, giving back to the community, and learning from their mistakes to improve decision-making. Assessment is a process that, when appropriately employed, enables administrators to make data-informed decisions to improve services and demonstrate student learning. Assessing the impact of the student conduct process on student learning and success empowers conduct administrators to understand the role their interventions play in helping students stay on the path toward academic success. Assessing student conduct, particularly in the residential context, is still an emerging practice and is evolving quickly.

Results of outcomes-based assessment practices can be used to demonstrate student learning and improve student and institutional performance (National Institute for Learning Outcomes Assessment [NILOA], 2016). Culp (2012) notes "the role of assessment is to help student affairs professionals determine whether they are doing their best work and whether that work is having a positive effect on students and the institution" (p. 9).

In considering the intersections of conduct and assessment work, it is clear data can be used to inform the conduct process in a variety of ways. Data collected in the conduct process can also be used to work collaboratively with other offices to identify trends in at-risk behaviors for individual students, as well as the broader student population. The data can also show which sanctions are most effective, reduce repeat offenders, improve the turnaround time between incident reports and hearing outcomes, and coach emerging practitioners in developing their skills as conduct hearing officers.

Historically, assessment in higher education has focused on tracking student progress toward attaining a degree, which is motivated by external accountability and, more recently, the desire of administrators to understand the impact of their work on student success (Keeling, Wall, Underhile, & Dungy, 2008; Kuh, Jankowski, Ikenberry, & Kinzie, 2014). Keeling, et al. (2008), broadly define assessment as "the formal or informal process of observing and assigning value or worth to an event or activity" (p. 10). Incorporating assessment measures into the conduct process gives administrators the opportunity to develop meaningful encounters and for students to reflect appropriately on their behavior and decision-making.

The assessment process is cyclical and, when conducted appropriately, allows time and space for appropriate reflection and program recalibration. As administrators improve their understanding of the broad concept of assessment, it becomes increasingly important to think about how to incorporate the process of assessment into the daily work of conduct administration.

In addition to the mission of the organization and issues integral to students and staff engaged in conduct, each of the grounding philosophies of conduct work provides guidance when determining what factors and outcomes should be established and then assessed meaningfully. Although there are multiple dimensions to consider in determining outcomes and factors to measure, sage advice remains: "In determining the priorities for assessment, keep in mind the words often attributed to Albert Einstein: 'Not everything that counts can be counted,

FIGURE 10.1 The Double-Loop Assessment Model

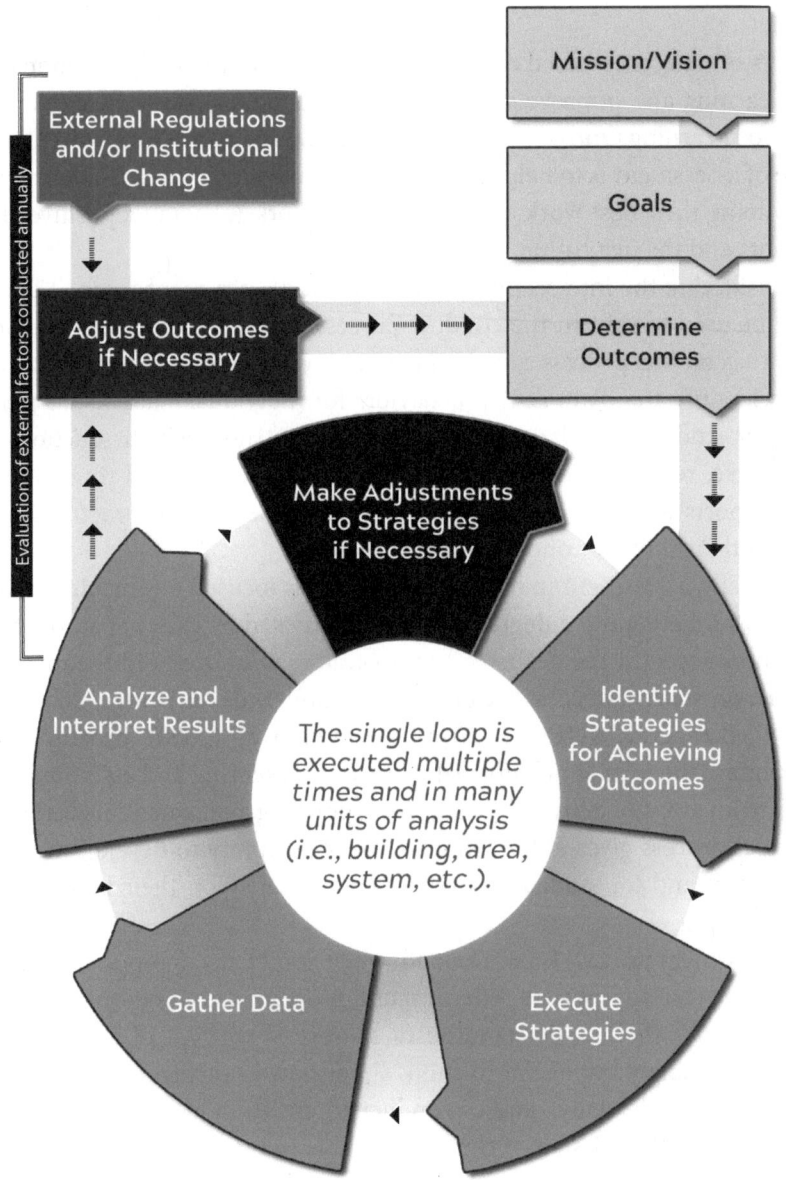

The Double Loop Assessment model introduced by Kirsten Kennedy, stresses the value of practitioners to continually assess and link results back to desired outcomes. (Kennedy, 2016)

and not everything that can be counted counts'" (Busby & Robinson, 2012, p. 42).

Since time, energy, and resources are usually limited, it is important to give careful consideration to where to start and what is meaningful. Consider the following questions before assessing a conduct process or system.

- What type of system does the campus use?
- What core components of this system should be assessed?
- In addition to federal or state statutes, are there other regulations, stipulations, or guidelines that shape conduct work?
- When it comes to student interactions, is the campus or department interested in assessing student learning, needs, or satisfaction, or something else?
- Is the campus or department interested in assessing the protocols, policies, or other administrative items in the system?
- Would other pieces of assessment data help influence the evaluation of the overarching conduct system?

The process of assessment, also described as the assessment cycle (Maki, 2010), is centered on the mission and educational objectives of the context measured. The cycle includes identifying learning and operational outcomes, gathering evidence, interpreting evidence, and making data-informed changes to improve processes and student learning. The mission or educational purpose of the organization or program informs and drives each component of the assessment process.

While Maki (2010) laid a foundation for the assessment loop, Kennedy (2016) expanded on this notion and introduced the double-loop assessment model. The double-loop assessment model calls for practitioners to continually examine assessment results and link them back to stated student learning outcomes, adjust for any institutional or departmental changes, and keep abreast of emerging trends or best practices in the field. In the context of student conduct in student affairs within higher education, the philosophy that guides the conduct process will also guide the assessment process.

CONNECTING ASSESSMENT AND CONDUCT PHILOSOPHY

To assess program effectiveness and student learning in the conduct process, practitioners must start with the result in mind by identifying what kind of information or data would be valuable and informative. Data collected must serve a purpose and inform decisions regarding housing conduct. In 1992, the American Association of Higher Education (AAHE) established nine principles of good practice for assessing student learning. These principles of good practice, while applied broadly, also can be used to guide housing conduct practitioners in their work. Assessment of student learning:

- Begins with educational values.
- Is most effective when it reflects an understanding of learning as multidimensional, integrated, and revealed in performance over time.
- Works best when the programs it seeks to improve have clear, explicitly stated purposes.
- Requires attending to outcomes, but also and equally to the experiences that lead to those outcomes.
- Yields the best results when it is ongoing, not episodic.
- Fosters wider improvement when it involves representatives from throughout the educational community.
- Makes a difference when it begins with issues of use and illuminates questions that people care about.
- Is most likely to lead to improvement when it is part of a larger set of conditions that promote change.
- Enables educators to meet their responsibilities to students and the public.

Based on these recommendations for good assessment practice, assessing the housing conduct process should be driven by the vision, mission, and values of the organization; grounding philosophy and purpose of the conduct process; and integral issues facing students and staff engaged in conduct work.

The vision, mission, and values of an organization serve as a framework through which to determine the ideas that matter most and should be assessed. When identifying learning outcomes and goals for a housing conduct process, it is important to recall the mission and vision, as stated by the department, to ensure reflecting those outcomes and goals. The underlying theoretical framework that guides the conduct process informs the development of learning and operational outcomes to be measured. Keeling, et al. (2008), note, "the effective use of theory to guide comprehensive assessment planning includes consideration of staff capacity, cultural 'fit' between any given theoretical approach and institutional expectations, and the ability of a candidate theory to support the achievement of desired student learning outcomes" (p. 15).

Issues facing students and staff provide additional information about the factors and outcomes that should be assessed. If student staff and students living in the residence halls are reporting challenges with quiet hours enforcement and noise levels in the halls, for instance, additional information should be collected to enable data-informed decisions about changes for improvement.

A connection between the assessment process with the type of housing conduct system used on campus becomes critical to effectively measure the impact of the housing conduct process on students, staff, and the community. Assessment is contextual, so it becomes meaningless when operationalized in isolation. Determining learning and operational outcomes, assessment measures, and data analysis, and then using data to inform decisions, are all shaped by the type of conduct and housing system employed. To best showcase examples of how to connect assessment practice with the philosophy guiding housing conduct practitioners, consider the three most-predominant housing conduct philosophies.

Traditional or Administrative

Major components of a traditional conduct system include a staff person responsible for coordinating the system (sometimes with several other staff members to help), as well as campus administrators, who hear cases, assign sanctions, and handle appeals. It also includes the use of student, faculty, and staff conduct boards and the supervision of residence hall conduct processes, as well as mediation and other forms of conflict resolution. Although careful not to describe their outline as a model system, the American College Personnel Association (ACPA-College Student Educators International) *Student Conduct Board Manual and Reference* (2010) outlines what many schools would consider a traditional conduct system.

Restorative Justice

Restorative justice can be broadly defined as "a process to involve, to the extent possible, those who have a stake in a specific offense and to collectively identify and address harms, needs, and obligations ... to heal and put things as right as possible" (Zehr, 2002, p. 37). Based on this broad definition, Karp (2015) outlines four main tenets of restorative practices: inclusive decision-making, active accountability, repairing harm, and rebuilding trust. Dahl, Meagher, and Vander Velde (2014) outline important factors to consider in a restorative justice program, including the respondent's feelings about meeting with the affected party, likelihood of committing another offense, and attitude toward the harmed party.

A number of institutions use restorative practices in their conduct process, including the University of Kentucky (n.d.), which operates under the following definition.

Restorative justice, at its most basic level, is a way for an individual to take responsibility for any harm they may have caused to another individual or the community. This process allows for all parties affected (victim, offender, and community) to process how the harm can be restored for the individuals involved. On a college campus[,] often students, staff, faculty, and other on- and off-campus community members may find that they have been affected directly or indirectly by an individual or group's behavior. Restorative justice practices can provide the space for profound learning moments and reparation. (http://www.uky.edu/studentconduct/restorative-justice)

Honor Code

Schools with honor codes focus heavily on the role of faculty, students, and staff in promoting integrity and reducing dishonest behavior in the community (McCabe, Butterfield, & Treviño, 2012). In an honor code, unlike the traditional model, students are expected or required to be active participants, not bystanders, in the conduct system. Many honor code systems engage students in student-organized honor boards or other phases of the conduct process that provide additional opportunities for student learning. An honor code environment typically includes these four components.

- A written pledge in which students affirm they have not cheated on a particular exam or assignment.
- A judicial or hearing body in which students play a major role (e.g., student serves as chairperson, students constitute a majority of the panel, or student consent is needed to change the constitution of this body).
- Un-proctored exams.
- An expectation that students should report any violations of the code they may observe (McCabe, Butterfield, & Treviño, 2012).

DETERMINING FACTORS AND OUTCOMES TO ASSESS

Weaving together established best practices in assessment of student learning and institutional conduct philosophies allows practitioners to focus on the factors and outcomes that should be assessed. As Schuh, Upcraft, and Associates (2001) point out, assessing conduct satisfaction is unique as students aim to *decrease* interactions with the office. Therefore, it is difficult to assess a change in student behavior beyond examining the recidivism rate. Many students report they do not change behaviors, but simply are more cautious and do not get caught (Gehring, Lowery, & Palmer, 2012; Howell, 2005).

This condition is unique to conduct, as opposed to other contexts such as student leadership positions or offices of student engagement, where repeated interactions are connected to student learning, satisfaction, retention, and graduation. Even the ubiquitous notion of measuring student satisfaction is framed differently in the context of conduct.

In conduct, satisfaction is tied to notions of fairness and justness in the conduct process, rather than the outcome of a hearing (Janosik & Stimpson, 2017; King, 2012). The mission statement, conduct grounding philosophy, and issues facing students shape the questions developed for the conduct process. With these guides in mind, there are numerous questions to consider. What must be known about the conduct process? How will the answers shape, inform, or improve the work? How will data be collected?

Learning and Operational Outcomes

Establishing learning outcomes, operational outcomes related to effectiveness, and key performance indicators are foundational starting places in determining what to measure in a conduct process. Howell (2005) provides additional guidance in suggesting there are three broad categories of outcomes for a conduct process: "administrative adherence to procedures and guidelines, reduction of negative behaviors that affect the campus community, and the promotion of education and development among those students who become involved in the judicial process, either by way of violation or implementation" (p. 377).

Context also influences the design of the learning outcomes of the housing conduct process. Learning interventions resulting from a conduct violation are typically one-time and short-term. Identifying learning outcomes to measure begins with defining and establishing these terms. Keeling, et al. (2008), define student learning outcomes as "the goals of learning experiences; they specify what a student should be able to know, do, or value after participating in those activities" (p. 13). Learning outcomes in the student conduct process should focus on student's understanding and knowing the community standards, as well as the consequences for violating established standards (Stimpson & Janosik, 2011).

Ample literature provides coaching for learning outcome development (Bresciani, Zelna, & Anderson, 2004; Heinich, Molenda, Russell, & Smaldino, 2002). This set of core principles, derived from this literature, is worth following when writing learning outcomes for the student housing conduct process.

- Learning outcomes should be manageable, meaningful, and measurable (Bresciani, Zelna, & Anderson, 2004). Because most colleges and universities have limited time, resources, and staff, the outcomes established must be meaningful to stakeholders in the organization and the staff administering the process. That means establishing a list of 20 outcomes to be measured each year by one conduct administrator is probably unrealistic. It is also difficult to measure broad concepts like "learn" or "understand." The outcomes have to be measurable.

- Follow a formula for writing learnings outcomes across the organization. A commonly used method is the A (audience), B (behavior), C (condition), D (depth) model (Heinich, Molenda, Russell, & Smaldino, 2002). The audience is the person or group the learning opportunity is designed to affect — typically students. The behavior is the knowledge, skills, or awareness the audience should demonstrate after engaging in the learning opportunity. Learning taxonomies such as Bloom's Taxonomy (Bloom, Englehart, Furst, Hill, & Krathwohl, 1956) often serve as a compelling reference point when articulating behavior. The condition is the specification of the learning opportunity. The depth represents the minimum expectation that serves as a demonstration of the learning outcome behavior. Bloom's Taxonomy (Bloom, et al., 1956) organizes learning from remembering and retaining knowledge toward the more rigorous creation or production of original work. The levels of the taxonomy graduate from the lowest level of learning — described as "remembering" — to "understanding," "application," "analysis," "evaluation," and "creation."

- How the learning outcome is written will drive how the outcome is measured. An example of student learning outcomes in a housing conduct process would be to ask students, after participating in the housing conduct process, to describe their rights as they pertain to the housing conduct process, reflect on how their values and principles affect decision-making, or articulate the effect of their behavior on others in the residential community (UNC-Chapel Hill Department of Housing, 2017).

To illustrate the third point, consider the first learning outcome. To ask a student in the conduct process to describe their rights would fall into the "understanding" category of Bloom's Taxonomy (Bloom, et al., 1956). The tool used to measure the learning outcome should match the depth of the learning demonstrated. For example, a survey, minute paper, pre- and post-test, or retrospective pre- and post-test could all be used to assess whether a student can accurately describe their rights in the housing conduct process.

Reflection could represent a higher order of thinking in the taxonomy. Students could demonstrate this reflection in a variety of ways. One would be to have the student write a one-page, single-spaced reflection paper that is evaluated by the conduct hearing officer, using a rubric.

Operational or program outcomes articulate and measure what the housing conduct process should accomplish, the desired impact of the process, the aggregated effect of the process, and what an effective process should look like in the context of the division and institution (Culp & Dungy, 2012).

It is crucial to assess the effectiveness of the conduct process in addition to the learning outcomes. Metrics often serve as informative data points that can be shared with internal and external audiences as indicators of the effectiveness of the conduct process. A conduct process naturally collects quantitative data. Some examples of operational outcomes for conduct in housing could be that the case turnaround time from incident to case decision will be 10 days or fewer, overall recidivism rates will be less than 10%, or quiet hours violations will decrease by 5%.

Key Performance Indicators

In addition to student learning and operational outcomes, key performance indicators (KPIs) help to communicate to internal and external audiences the core numbers that tell the story of the housing conduct operation. Variables such as "timeliness of adjudication, clarity of communications with students, perceived procedural fairness, [and] sufficiency of information given to students about processes" (Janosik & Stimpson, 2015, slide 12) contribute to evaluating the housing conduct process, or "system efficacy" (Stimpson & Janosik, 2015, p. 63). These tangible and measurable data points can point toward satisfaction with a conduct process, timeliness, workload for professional staff, and trends in violations.

When examining system efficacy, a housing conduct practitioner might focus on these KPIs (CampusLabs, n.d.):

- Number of incidents by category and overall number
- Knowledge of code of conduct
- Perception/reporting of the process (e.g., fairness, understanding)
- Recidivism rates
- Average rubric dimensions on reflection papers
- Number of sanctions by type and overall
- Grade point averages

In addition to assessing student satisfaction with the housing conduct process, professionals can also examine sanction efficacy. For example, a study conducted by Gehring, Lowery, and Palmer (2012) asked students who had violated the university's alcohol policy to reflect on how the assigned sanctions affected their future behavior and what they had learned. While 57% of students were assigned an educational alcohol program, they said the most-effective deterrent to repeating their behavior would be parental notification.

In the conduct process, the perception of fairness is essential to student learning (Janosik & Stimpson, 2011; Stimpson & Janosik, 2015). "The more students perceive the conduct hearing process to be fair, timely, and consistent, the more students report learning" (Janosik & Stimpson, 2017, p. 39). A conduct process should be rooted in consistency and fairness in policies and procedures (ACPA, 2010).

A post-process assessment can evaluate feedback from students regarding their satisfaction with the housing conduct process. For example, to assess the pre-hearing component of the conduct process for system efficacy, one could ask if the student received sufficient information and clear communication. For the hearing component, one could examine whether the student was treated respectfully and if the hearing officer heard the student's side. To examine the post-hearing component, one would try to determine whether the outcome was consistent and the student was treated fairly (Janosik & Stimpson, 2011, Appendix A, p. 11)

Once outcomes and key performance indicators have been established, a tool must be implemented or developed to measure whether the outcomes have been reached. When collecting evidence, it is important to keep in mind the audience that will receive the evidence. What information does your culture value? Are senior-level staff or other stakeholders drawn to numbers (quantitative data) or narrative (qualitative data), or both? What information will be considered trustworthy and credible by stakeholders?

Again, as with determining what to measure, starting with the end in mind is a crucial part of measuring outcomes and KPIs. Any question asked in an assessment should add value for the administrator or student experience and provide information about the completion of outcomes or drive improvement.

COLLECTING AND ANALYZING DATA

Much of the information collected from and during the housing conduct process can be analyzed and treated as data. In other words, data are everywhere. Collected data are quantitative, qualitative, or mixed (qualitative and quantitative) in nature. Quantitative data can be collected via surveys when asking students to respond to Likert-style questions or in rating their learning or experience. Topics such as whether a student understood the process, perceived it to be fair and equitable, and felt heard (Schuh, Upcraft, & Associates, 2001) could easily be measured by a survey.

Information collected about the number and type of cases and sanctions also provides a wealth of information. What are the most-assigned sanctions? Are the students who engaged in those sanctions more or less likely to have repeat violations than students who do not use those sanctions? Are students of color sanctioned at the same frequency and severity as other students? All of these can be explored with day-to-day administrative data collected on the process.

Qualitative data can also be collected, particularly when stakeholders are interested in how students feel about something. As a part of a sanction, students can be asked to reflect on what they learned. This reflection can later be evaluated with a rubric informed by the learning and operational outcomes, or the reflection can be coded for themes and aggregated with the themes from other reflections to develop a higher level of understanding about the impact of the program on all students, as well as the individual. This reflection could also be accomplished using a rubric and aggregating the results across students.

When collecting data, it is important to consider the outcomes and the stakeholder with which the information is shared. It is also important to consider how student respondents can best spend their time, and how much time the practitioner will have to spend on analyzing, interpreting (making meaning), and sharing the findings. For example, if students are asked who their hearing officer was in an open-ended question, there could be a multitude of responses and spellings for a single person, making data difficult to collect and time-consuming to clean (Goldstein & Sukys, 2016). An alternative to this would be to create a drop-down menu from which students simply can select their hearing officer's name. This creates less work for both the student and the practitioner in reporting the data and provides better-quality information.

Popular conduct database systems store information securely regarding the conduct process. These systems are used to assess system efficacy and recidivism rates. A conduct practitioner may look at a database and infer that low recidivism rates indicate student learning has occurred. However, these databases do not collect qualitative data about student learning. Assessment software can assess student learning as a result of the conduct process. For those institutions where conduct processes have fewer violations of policy, even a homegrown survey tool or spreadsheet can be useful.

When collecting and analyzing data, it is often beneficial to have data from more than one source for triangulation (Bresciani, et al., 2009). The combination, or triangulation, of data from multiple sources strengthens the credibility of the findings and frames a more well-rounded picture of the conduct process. The most commonly used instruments in higher education are national student surveys and rubrics (Kuh, Jankowski, Ikenberry, & Kinzie, 2014). However, the context of the housing conduct process provides unique considerations.

For example, asking students who go through the housing conduct process to take a survey reflecting on a set of outcomes core to the process could also be combined with a reflection paper or brief minute paper that reflects their learning in the process, as well as with data collected from the conduct tracking software or spreadsheet. Depending on the situation, it may not be appropriate to have a focus group of students who have had a violation (Schuh, Upcraft, & Associates, 2001).

Regardless of the methods used, privacy standards and FERPA guidelines are primary concerns when collecting data regarding students. In the context of the conduct process, however, multiple assessment tools are available for measuring effectiveness and student learning. Each tool has benefits and drawbacks worth considering.

Surveys

Many conduct processes use surveys to assess student learning since these are one of the best ways to measure a change in knowledge, skills, attitudes, or beliefs (Palomba & Banta, 1999). Surveys can be implemented after a student engages in the housing conduct process or as a pre- or post-hearing to measure a change in knowledge, skills, attitudes, or beliefs. Surveys can use various rating scales (i.e., Likert, Ecosystem) or a short text response, which allow students to reflect and self-report. According to Suskie (2009), some benefits to using a survey include capturing experiences for a large number of responses, allowing for quick participation, and being conducted online, in-person, by mail, or on the phone. Failure to keep a survey non-intrusive and brief can lower response rates.

Give careful thought to how students should respond to the survey and spend their time, and what information will lead to informed decisions about the established outcomes. For example, it will not be necessary to solicit demographic data collected by the university from students each time they are surveyed, as long as it can be cross-referenced. Unfortunately, a major drawback to using a survey is low response rate due to a lack of motivation to complete.

When developing a survey, the following key considerations would ensure developing a strong instrument.

- Limit the survey to questions that will inform the practice or provide evidence of student learning.
- Start with questions that may be easier for students to answer and then progress to more-difficult questions — the order of the questions matters.
- Make sure the response options (or the response scale) make sense with the question. For example, if asking students to respond to the statement "I feel I was treated fairly by my hearing officer," use an "agreeance" scale such as strongly agree, agree, neither agree nor disagree, disagree, strongly disagree.
- Use short-answer response options as an opportunity to collect both quantitative and qualitative data.

- Share the questions with students in advance to receive feedback and ensure students read and understand questions as intended.

Self-reflection Assignments

"First and foremost, student conduct is an educational process," according to the Association for Student Conduct Administration (ASCA; 2014, p. 5). For that reason, the conduct process uses measures of accountability (sanctions), including reflection assignments. This educational exercise encourages student learning and behavior change, which have been found to lower recidivism rates compared to those who are assigned passive sanctions (Kompalla & McCarthy, 2001).

Student self-reflections provide a wealth of information related to the student learning experience. Conduct officers can read and code simple, one-page, single-spaced reflection like open-ended data to identify themes in an individual student response and then throughout many student responses. This has worked at Truman State University, where first-time violators of the alcohol policy were asked to complete a short reflection essay (Banta, Jones, & Black, 2009). The assessment measured satisfaction with the sanction and indicators of student learning ("taking responsibility … gaining useful knowledge … and indicating a desire to change behavior based on the incident" (Banta, Jones, & Black, 2009, p. 215).

A rubric focused on student learning outcomes could also be used to evaluate the self-reflection. The rubric data from student reflections could then be aggregated across rubrics and serve as concrete, direct evidence of student learning in the housing conduct process.

Self-reflection assignments provide staff the opportunity to craft prompts that align with desired learning outcomes. Consider a case where the learning outcome would be to have the student reflect on the impact of their values and principles on decision-making. The conduct officer could ask the student to write a one-page, single-spaced paper responding to the prompt, "Reflect on how your personal values and principles affected your decision-making leading up to the incident and how it will affect your decisions in the future. What did you learn about your personal values and principles as a result of the housing conduct process?"

A second example self-reflection assignment where the learning outcome is to articulate the effect of the student's behavior on others in the residential community would be to provide a prompt that asks the student to "Reflect on how your actions and behaviors impacted other members of your floor and residence hall. What did you learn about the impact of your actions as a result of the housing conduct process?"

Pre-test, Post-test, and Retrospective Pre- and Post-test

Pre- and post-tests or retrospective pre- and post-tests are efficient tools for learning about students' knowledge and perspectives before and after their interactions with the housing conduct process (Starcke & DeLoach, 2012). Students could respond to a pre-test that asks questions about their rights and responsibilities, which policy they believe they violated, etc. After the hearing, as part of their exit process, students could respond to the same set of questions as a post-test. A similar process — a retrospective pre- and post-test — is where students receive both sets of questions at the end of their hearing and are asked to provide feedback on their experience.

It is worth considering that students are not required to participate in assessment instruments. It should be clear to students that, as a part of their rights, they are not mandated to participate and that their participation — or decision not to participate — will not affect the outcome of their hearing. If students believe their participation in an assessment will affect their outcome, either positively or negatively, it creates bias. Both approaches yield data with which administrators can demonstrate student learning. The retrospective pre- and post-test has the added benefit of only asking students to respond to one instrument and thus provides a better chance for higher response rates.

Minute Papers

Educational sanctions in the form of a workshop or educational seminar are prime opportunities for a minute paper. Minute papers are brief responses on quarter- or half-sheets of paper that pose one to two questions about the student experience, named as such because it should not take students more than a minute or two to respond to the prompt. Typically, minute papers are open-ended questions that ask broader, more-general questions. Minute paper questions could ask for details about a key take-away from the experience, what ideas or topics remain unclear, and what the student learned from engaging in this workshop.

Minute papers, surveys, and self-reflections are only a small set of tools at a residence life professional's disposal when measuring the housing conduct process and student experience. Whether measuring the effectiveness of the process, relationships with campus partners, student learning, staff conduct hearing competency, honor board training, or residence hall climate, it is important to ask the right questions and pick the right tool for answering the questions.

A focus group might be a good avenue for seeking feedback from students, faculty, and staff on their training as conduct hearing panelists, because focus groups are designed for exploring perspectives and opinions. To measure the impact of a hearing on a student's perception of their rights and responsibilities at the institution, a survey with a brief series of questions might be the best option.

Additional advice from Wall (2012) suggests that, "while an assessment process might not be able to answer the questions and honor the divergent perspectives of all stakeholders, it is the responsibility of those conducting assessments to explicitly consider stakeholder needs as they select and implement their data[-]gathering approach" (p. 90). In other words, when considering an assessment tool for measuring outcomes and effectiveness, residence life professionals should consider what kind of information will resonate with the audience and take into account the time and resources available for analyzing the results of the data.

ANALYZING AND INTERPRETING DATA

Once what is important to measure has been established, the right questions asked, an assessment tool implemented, and data collected, it then is time to make meaning out of the information. To collect data and leave them unanalyzed is a waste of student and administrator time, and could be considered data negligence.

The type of information collected directly influences how a residence life professional analyzes the data. A full description of data analysis for quantitative and qualitative data is beyond the scope of this chapter, but because this is a critical component of the assessment process and what leads to data-driven decisions, there are some core elements to know about such analysis. In this context, the primary purpose of data analysis is to transform raw data and student feedback into usable information that resonates with stakeholders and empowers them to make well-informed decisions.

Some general tips to consider when interpreting data include start big and then go small, prioritizing which questions should be answered first. Large sets of data about a functional area such as student learning or effectiveness can serve as a starting point. Data that are being collected for the second time can be compared to the data collected in previous iterations to identify trends. Data also should be triangulated to other sources whenever possible.

Beyond those suggestions, it is valuable in assessment to set targets before analyzing quantitative or qualitative data. Targets establish what the team is aiming for; setting targets gives staff something to aim for and helps determine whether any changes made have an impact over time. When thinking in terms of the data collected from the Skyfactor Residence Life Survey, for example, a reasonable target could be to see the students' average satisfaction with noise levels in the residence halls at a 5.5 out of 7. Another way to establish a target would be to say 85% of students will agree or strongly agree they are satisfied with the noise levels in the residence halls.

Establishing targets before data analysis provides an anchor for the analysis and prevents the creation of a moving target (e.g., 75% satisfaction was reasonable for quiet hours violations, but not for dissatisfaction with roommates) when discussing the data with others. The target also provides another useful function: It provides context for analyzing and interpreting data. If 76% of students report that they agree or strongly agree they are satisfied with the level of quiet hours, then the survey did not meet the target, so this is a focus area that requires developing and implementing action items. Another take on the same example is if the average student response to their satisfaction with quiet hours was a 4.9, this again fell below the 5.5 target.

With quantitative, or numbers-driven, data, a helpful first step is to determine where the data fell above target and below the target for each question asked. Frequencies and percentages are meaningful on their own and can be used to describe the number of people or percentage of people responding to specific categories for each assessment question. For example, regarding the quiet hours question, 70% reported they were very satisfied or satisfied, 10% were neither satisfied nor dissatisfied, and 20% were dissatisfied or very dissatisfied. To provide additional context for frequencies (1 out of 10 respondents) or percentages (10% of respondents), always provide a summary overview of how many people responded to the assessment tool used.

Another common approach to summarizing quantitative data is to talk about the mean, or the average response, of the group or of the entire responding population. At other times, disaggregating the data might be a more-useful approach. Disaggregating the data allows practitioners to obtain information about specific populations and identify whether they are serving the population equitably. When asking for a survey of whether students feel safe, for instance, it might be important to identify whether the predefined target includes students identifying as male, female, gender non-conforming, or transgender.

Another example of disaggregating data may come when examining the distribution of sanctions. In this case, questions may focus on whether students from different groups are receiving the same amount of severe sanctions or if appeals are overturned equitably. It is worth noting that our institutions of higher education operate within our societal structures and norms, so trends likely to be found at the national level might be evident in the societal microcosm of a college campus. What matters is how practitioners approach these possible findings.

Conversations with practitioners typically unveil the common misconception that working with qualitative data is easier than working with quantitative data. What is often not considered is that analyzing qualitative data is a time-intensive process that demands nuance and skill. As with interpreting quantitative data, analyzing qualitative data varies dramatically based on the method used. The basic premise behind interpreting qualitative data is the art of using themes and codes to identify trends or patterns in the material. Through this coding process, information emerges that can be useful to practitioners. Examples of ways qualitative data are collected include minute papers, reflection papers, open-ended questions, and focus groups.

A common conduct sanction is the reflection paper. Conduct officers interested in assessing the type of learning that occurred with students who went through a conduct process using restorative practices could review these reflection papers for themes that include the concept of community, repairing harm, and rebuilding trust. If students are able to articulate some of the major principles of restorative practices through their reflections, they might be demonstrating a strong understanding of the process and learning outcomes established for restorative justice.

SHARING ASSESSMENT RESULTS

Just as the failure of acting upon assessment results is a missed opportunity, so is the failure to share assessment results effectively in a way that educates, inspires, or motivates different audiences. The double-loop assessment model created by Kennedy (2016) stresses the importance of closing the assessment loop by sharing results, both positive and negative, with key stakeholders.

The concept of developing a strong culture of assessment is woven throughout the research and literature on the topic of assessment. According to Schuh (2013), "in a culture of assessment, staff members recognize that they must collect evidence systematically to demonstrate accountability to their stakeholders and that they must use that evidence to improve" (p. 89). This basic premise, connected with the work of Suskie (2009), sets a foundation for student affairs practitioners to begin to cultivate an environment where assessment is not considered an afterthought, but rather, a priority in the development of intentional opportunities for learning and engagement.

Using assessment data will help conduct officers make informed decisions about how to improve their practices. Professionals in departments with a strong culture of assessment are poised and ready to engage with assessment results to improve practice and can expect to receive assessment results on an ongoing basis.

It is also important to remember that information has to be shared even if it is negative. Assessments are conducted to help facilitate student learning, and this means often reflecting on the results, even if results are not positive. Be prepared to change a practice or procedure until demonstrated learning takes place.

Assessment tools will help identify areas of strength and weakness, and then make changes accordingly. Anderson-Isaacson and Anderson (2016) discuss the need for integrity when interpreting and reporting on the data. Such honesty will give stakeholders the opportunity to interpret the data fairly and accurately on their own, and then chart a course of action.

It can be argued that if assessment results are not disseminated widely and often, then not only has the assessment loop not been closed, but time and energy have been wasted. It is important to remember that the goal of assessing student conduct practices is to determine whether students are learning from the process (Kennedy, 2016).

Failure to share results removes the opportunity for practitioners to reflect on their practices and amend their processes as necessary, so this critical step of the assessment loop should not be taken lightly. On the other hand, the process of sharing assessment results is not a simple task — it requires a great deal of intentional thought and political astuteness. If the purpose of assessment is to improve opportunities for student learning, sharing results with key stakeholders will allow for a deep look at what programs or services are working well, and where there is room for improvement.

The assessment process generates an array of results to be studied and shared with stakeholders. Anderson-Isaacson and Anderson (2016) and Suskie (2009) provide some guidance on items to consider when determining sharing results, including the audience, stakeholders, delivery methods, and presenting results.

Audience

When sharing assessment results, the audience must be considered for practitioners to communicate in a meaningful way. Suskie (2009, p. 275) poses four critical questions that can help practitioners better understand the audience:

- Who are your audiences?
- What are their perspectives, needs, and priorities?
- What decisions do they need to make?
- What information do they need from your assessment to make those decisions?

Making assessment data accessible to all stakeholders is a complex task, but using these questions as a guide will aid in the process. The complexity is heightened because an audience is made up of different types of stakeholders, each with a different level of investment in the results. Understanding who the target audience is will help guide how to share the information. Suskie (pp. 278–279) also provides pointers on items to consider when sharing data with an audience.

- Discuss the study with stakeholders who may feel defensive about the results.
- Balance negatives with positives.
- Be gentle and sensitive.
- Provide corroborating information.
- Document the quality of the assessment strategy.
- Acknowledge possible flaws in your assessment strategy.
- Help audiences identify possible solutions.

Stakeholders

Due to the nature of the work associated with a residence life program, particularly in the area of student conduct, a wide variety of stakeholders is invested in the type of learning environment created in university housing programs.

Key stakeholders to be considered include students, student staff, departmental professional staff, campus partners (i.e., university conduct officers, Title IX staff, the ombuds office, the dean of students office, etc.), faculty, and executive administrators. Each of these groups is probably looking for different information from the conduct process. Stakeholders could have questions about the housing conduct process in regard to student learning, the residence hall environment, the development of resident advisor (RA) and hearing officers' skills, and the climate of the overall campus community. Often, different data may be accessed to answer questions posed by these different stakeholders.

It is important to refer back to the guidance provided by Suskie (2009) when determining the type of information to be shared with particular audiences. For instance, the information shared with RA staff members is likely to be different from the information shared with someone at a director-level position. This traces back to the idea of the scope of the position and its sphere of influence. The RA focuses on the beginning stages of the conduct process: explaining community living standards, undertaking a behavioral intervention, and following up with the resident. On the other hand, a director may ask questions about how and if demographic information plays a role in the conduct process. For example, are male-identified or female-identified individuals navigating the process at different rates or levels? Is there a difference in the population when examining sanctioning? When stakeholders have appropriate information for their particular spheres of influence, they can make data-informed decisions that help the organization move forward.

Delivery Methods

After carefully considering the nature and scope of the audience, the next step is to determine the appropriate delivery method for the results. For departmental or divisional leadership teams, brief executive summaries and dashboard reports may be the best avenue for conveying the most mission-critical information. Information about campus safety, assaults, and drugs and alcohol often rises to this level.

Major concerns or successes (such as a decrease in recidivism) may also be shared in this venue. On the other hand, an executive summary may not be the most appropriate way to deliver assessment results to students or student staff members. Students may appreciate a more-dynamic and engaging presentation style, such as a PowerPoint presentation or other types of technology. In essence, if assessment results are not heard, considered, and discussed, the assessment process may be considered a waste of time. Consider the audience and stakeholders, and then prepare the information accordingly.

The format and delivery of assessment results are just as critical as with whom the information is shared. Anderson-Isaacson and Anderson (2016) and Suskie (2009) provide insight into how results should be disseminated. It is important to remember that an assessment report is not the same as a research paper. Research papers are often read once and then cast aside because they tend to be dense and overwhelming. For this reason, it is important to report assessment results in a way that appeals to the audience.

Regardless of reporting mechanisms (presentations, posters, flyers, reports, executive summaries, postcards, infographics, etc.), the type of assessment used, the reason for the assessment, key findings, and action items related to those findings should be conveyed. The audience should walk away with a clear understanding of how the assessment was conducted, an unbiased report of the results, and a desire to develop solutions to strengthen or change programs to maximize student learning.

Written reports. Suskie (2009) spends a significant amount of time on discussing what to include in a written report and what should be excluded. First and foremost, the document should be easy to read and the information easy to digest. Suskie (2009) says that graphs and pictures are easier to digest than text-dense documents. While this seems intuitive, it is important to remember when building a culture of assessment that it is critical to ensure that stakeholders are not intimidated or overwhelmed by the material. Providing a succinct, easy-to-understand written document makes it much less daunting to assess and integrate assessment results into decision-making.

Presentations. When determining how the assessment data should be presented, it is important to consider the audience and how best to communicate in a meaningful way. The information should provide highlights and snapshots, and be presented in a way that engages the audience and inspires them to take action.

Is the presentation for a group of resident advisors or the director of housing? When to the audience will be a group of students, spend some time on thinking about how to present the material engagingly. Presenting material to senior administrators may not require the same level of enthusiasm, but will have to focus on content and action steps.

Flyers and posters. Thinking about what an audience needs or wants to know is important when developing an effective avenue for sharing material through flyers and posters. Focusing on a key piece of information instead of the entire assessment report might help students remain engaged.

One effective way to share results with students is to create a branding campaign based on the assessment results. As an example, the Housing and Residential Education department at the University of North Carolina-Chapel Hill, developed an assessment branding campaign called Tar Heels Talk Back.

The philosophy behind this branding campaign was two-fold. First, the goal was to share one data point that would resonate with the students living in the residence halls as well as their families or visitors. This demonstrated that the student data were not sitting on a shelf, unused, but rather, someone saw the information. The second goal was to share an action item related to the data point. This showed that not only had the student feedback been heard, but something was happening because of their feedback.

OVERCOMING ASSESSMENT CHALLENGES

No matter how much thought and effort go into conduct assessment efforts, there are inherent challenges to be faced. As Schuh, Upcraft, and Associates (2001) explain, "the major problem associated with assessing an [office of student conduct] is that it can be very difficult to secure the cooperation of those involved in cases heard by the office to cooperate in an assessment project" (p. 426). They also point out how challenging it can be to work with those affected by negative behaviors or violations, since incidents may have been serious.

An important consideration throughout the process is determining when to distribute the assessment. Some institutions send a survey link in a decision or outcome letter after the process concludes. Others send a link as a separate email message after the outcome letter has been transmitted. Response rates may vary based on amount of time lapsed; however, long-term student learning may be measured more effectively after time has passed. King (2012) found that "individuals adjudicated within the five months prior to the study portrayed their disciplinary experience as fairer and more educational" (p. 576), illustrating that student learning may not be as long-lasting as administrators of the process hope.

There are limitations to sending out an assessment link to students. In the conduct process, there are more male violators, but more women participated in post-process assessment than men (Nelson, 2017). This can be a limitation because it may skew and bias the responses. Another limitation is low response rates, especially through electronic surveying (King, 2012; Nelson, 2017) — students say they are over-surveyed (Porter, Whitcomb, & Weitzer, 2004; Tschepikow, 2012).

Another consideration and potential barrier when assessing the conduct proces is confidentiality versus anonymity. A measure that is anonymous has no data that would trace a response to the student, while a confidential measure may have student ID numbers as a unique identifier. Some electronic measures require validation to enter into the assessment. This may create the perception a response will be attached to an individual student, which may affect response rates and, at worst, create a climate of intimidation for students if it is not clear their responses are in no way connected to the outcome of their hearings.

MAKING DATA-INFORMED DECISIONS

Sharing data with key stakeholders is often when the theoretical becomes the real. This is when when the raw data, now transformed into meaningful information driven by the purpose of the housing conduct process, conduct philosophy, and mission and values of the organization, turn into dialogue. Sharing the data with others opens the door to engage in dialogue about what areas of the data should be celebrated and which data require additional action planning to make changes or improve processes and the student experience.

Sharing the data with stakeholders is also an opportunity to solicit diverse opinions about what the data could mean and what questions should be examined further. The housing conduct process influences individual student learning, the residence hall environment, and the campus community, as shown in these examples. In addition, housing conduct is a process, so an example of measuring the effectiveness and efficiency or system efficacy of this process should be helpful.

Student Learning

The learning outcomes listed earlier in the chapter are the basis of an example related to student learning. The learning outcomes state that after engaging in the housing conduct process, students will articulate the effect of their behavior on others in the residential community, and reflect on how their personal values and principles affect decision-making. One way this information could be measured is through a post-adjudication survey.

Students could be asked to rate their level of agreement in regard to these two outcomes. A possible response may indicate that 74% agree or strongly agree that, in their hearing, they discussed how their personal values and principles affected their decision-making, while 61% agreed or strongly agreed they recognized the effect of their behavior on others in the residential community. This is a good example of how a survey can be used to capture data at a snapshot in time.

For a more in-depth understanding of these two outcomes, tools such as reflecion papers or service-learning projects could be implemented, followed with self-reflections.

Residence Hall Environment

When participating in the Skyfactor Resident Assessment survey, students at UNC-Chapel Hill shared they were dissatisfied with the noise levels on the floors in the residence halls. Through incident report and conduct tracking software, staff members were able to identify the number of warning and violations relating to quiet hours. Digging more deeply, the staff examined open-ended responses to the questions like "What do you like least about living on campus?" "What would you change about living on campus?" and "What do you like most about living on campus?" with specific attention to comments about noise. A critical question in practice was whether students were responding to their communities being disruptively loud or to overly strict enforcement of quiet hours. In other words, what did dissatisfaction with the noise levels mean in this context?

Using the multiple data sources discussed, it was clear that students wanted stronger enforcement of quiet hours. When considering the implications of this change for staff and the residence hall culture, the staff drew a correlation between the noise level of on the residence hall floors and other factors considered to be important, such as the ability to sleep or study on the residence hall floor. The combination of these data and subsequent statistical analysis allowed conduct administrators to present this detailed information to student staff and mandate stronger enforcement of quiet hours.

Instead of hall staff giving warnings for quiet hours infractions, all interactions were to be documented. Warning letters for first-time quiet hours infractions were given and documented in the conduct management database. The result was an increase in quiet hours warning letters, from 19% to 35%, in all conduct cases. The next year's Skyfactor data showed a statistically sig-

FIGURE 10.2 Data-informed Decisions

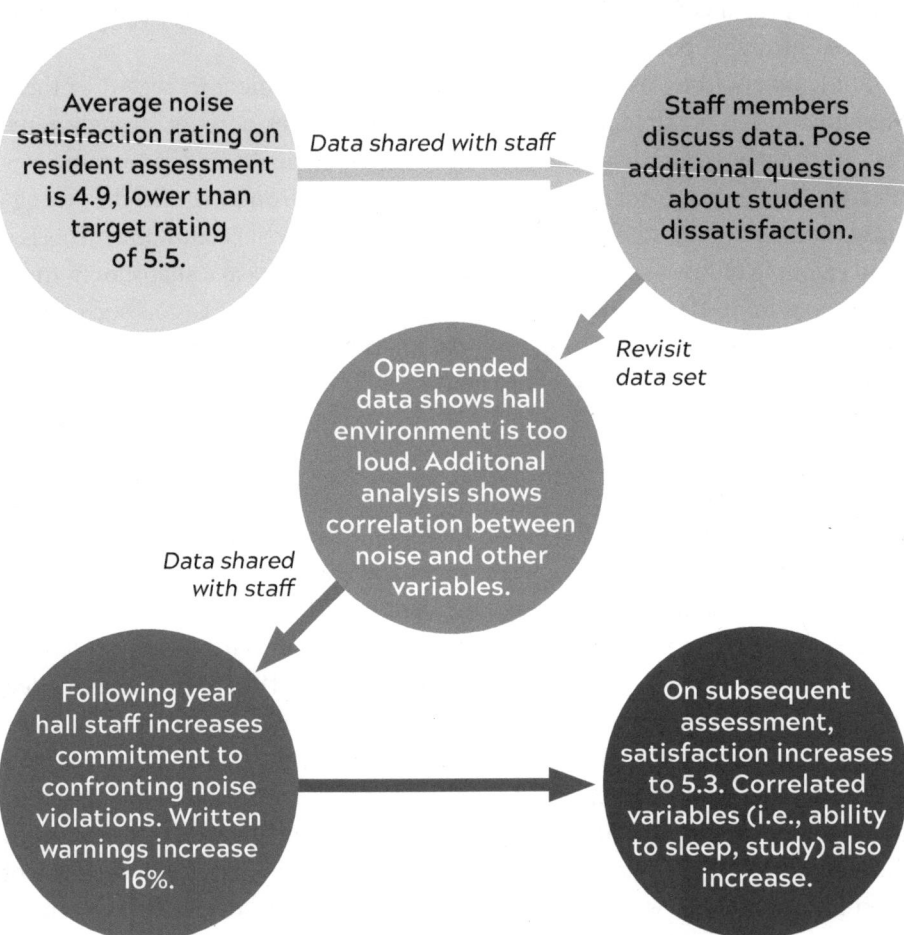

An example of how a housing office uses assessment results to make data-informed decisions.

nificant increase in the average satisfaction, with the noise levels moving from 5.19 to 5.30. Correlated variables of ability to sleep and study on the residence hall floors were also positively influenced and showed an increase in average satisfaction.

Campus Community

Several years ago, the Department of Housing and Residential Education at UNC-Chapel Hill began to examine alcohol incidents that involved a student requiring medical attention. Nationwide, students report they fear getting in trouble as a barrier to calling for help (Lewis & Marchell, 2006). It was noted that students who were transported to the hospital for overconsumption were treated through the conduct system in ways similar to those who had a few servings of alcoholic beverages. After examining best practices and engaging in benchmarking, the department adopted a medical amnesty policy.

At the same time, many things at the university triggered the examination of this policy. Student Wellness was doing a great deal of research and encouraging a public health approach to working with substance use among college students, and the university was working on a new campus alcohol policy.

In the fall of 2016, the new campus alcohol policy launched at UNC-Chapel Hill, which included a clause for medical amnesty. Students were still held accountable for violating the policy, but the conduct system the worked to educate students about making healthy choices for themselves and the greater community. After the launch of a university-wide policy, the housing department saw the number of medical amnesty cases double. This may be due in part to more calls for assistance or to an increase in high-risk drinking behaviors. Future assessment data should provide more clarity about the reason(s) behind the increase.

CONCLUSION

The housing conduct process is well-positioned to affect student learning, improve the residence hall environment, and help create a healthy and safe university. In addition, the housing conduct process operates with its own measures of effectiveness and operational outcomes. The residential student population is an important part of a thriving college or university system. Therefore, the art of guiding and nurturing students through the process of good decision-making is a critical component of any housing conduct system.

Housing conduct practitioners use assessment to report on the impact their work has on the residential experience through student learning. Conduct officers use assessment to make sure the students who engage in the conduct process learn from that process. In addition, a strong assessment process will allow conduct officers to improve their practice and skills when adjudicating conduct hearings.

Professionals must recognize this final step as they close the assessment loop. After data are collected and analyzed, and the assessment results are shared with appropriate stakeholders, housing and conduct professionals must use this knowledge to determine appropriate action. There are times when programs or services need to be altered to meet student needs better. There also are times

➕ Recommended Readings

As recognition of the importance of assessment in higher education and student affairs continues to grow, an increasing number of related resources is available. While the goal of this chapter was to provide a broad overview of the assessment process, it was beyond its scope to walk a practitioner through each step of the assessment process. The following resources, many of which are cited in this chapter, are recommended to develop a greater understanding of the assessment process.

• *Assessing for Learning: Building a Sustainable Commitment Across the Institution, 2nd edition*
Peggy L. Maki (2010)

• *Assessment Practice in Student Affairs: A Guide for Practitioners*
M. Lee Upcraft and John H. Schuh (1996)

• *Assessing Student Learning: A Common Sense Guide, 2nd edition*
Linda Suskie (2009)

• *Assessing Student Learning and Development: A Handbook for Practitioners*
Marilee J. Bresciani, Carrie L. Zelna, and James A. Anderson (2004)

• *Building a Culture of Evidence in Student Affairs: A Guide for Leaders and Practitioners*
Marguerite McGann Culp and Gwendolyn Jordan Dungy (2012)

• *Learning is Not a Sprint: Assessing and Documenting Student Leader Learning in Co-Curricular Involvement*
Darby M. Roberts and D. Stanley Carpenter (2012)

• *Making a Difference: Improving Residence Life Assessment Practices*
Kirsten Kennedy (2016)

---

when information highlights what it is hoped students learn — and what they actually learn.

Assessing learning in the student conduct process has often been treated as an afterthought or a practice that emerges only when there has been time and space for that piece of the process. However, as illustrated, collecting data can happen in many different forms — and the results can be powerful. While much progress has been made in assessing housing conduct, work remains, especially as it relates to "communication of desired learning outcomes with students and diversity of assessment methods" (Goldstein & Stimpson, 2013, p. 44).

As the campus culture shifts and becomes increasingly reliant on technology, assessment methods and practices must adjust to meet such innovation. As Goldstein and Stimpson (2013) explain, the data about conduct assessment are quite limited, despite the ongoing work in which institutions are engaged. Residence life and conduct professionals must continue to examine and assess their practice, and work toward improving processes as well as student learning and behavior change.

REFERENCES

American College Personnel Association (2010). Student conduct board manual and reference. Washington, DC.

Association for Student Conduct Administration (2014). *Student conduct administration & title IX: Gold standard practices for resolution of allegations of sexual misconduct on college campuses.* Retrieved January 9, 2018, from https://www.myacpa.org/sites/default/files/ASCA%202014%20Gold%20 Standard%20Report.pdf.

Anderson-Isaacson, H., & Anderson, S. (2016). Sharing assessment results. In K. Kennedy (Ed.), *Making a difference*: *Improving residence life assessment practices* (101–131). Columbus, OH: Association of College & University Housing Officers-International.

Banta, T. W., & Blaich, C. (2011). Closing the assessment loop. *Change: The magazine of higher learning. 43*(1), 22–27.

Banta, T. W., Jones, E. A., & Black, K. E. (2009). *Designing effective assessment: Principles and profiles of good practice.* Hoboken, NJ: John Wiley & Sons.

Bloom, B. S., Englehart, M. D., Furst, E. J., Hill, W. H., & Krathwohl, D. R. (1956). *The Taxonomy of educational objectives, handbook I: The Cognitive domain.* New York: David McKay Co., Inc.

Bresciani, M. J., Gardner, M. M., & Hickmott, J. (2009). *Demonstrating student success: A practical guide to outcomes-based assessment of learning and development in student affairs.* Sterling, VA: Stylus Publishing.

Bresciani, M. J., Zelna, C. L., & Anderson, J. A. (2004). *Assessing student learning and development: A handbook for practitioners.* Washington, DC: NASPA-Student Affairs Administrators in Higher Education.

Busby, K., & Robinson B. G. (2012). Starting the Culture of Evidence Journey. In M.M. Culp and G.J. Dungy (Eds.), *Building a culture of evidence in student affairs: A guide for leaders and practitioners.* Washington, DC: NASPA: Student Affairs Administrators in Higher Education.

CampusLabs (n.d.). *Departmental Key Performance Indicators.* Retrieved from https://baselinesupport.campuslabs.com/hc/en-us/articles/204304915-Key-Performance-Indicators-KPIs-.

Collins, K. M., & Roberts, D. M. (2012). *Learning is not a sprint.* Washington, DC: National Association of Student Personnel Administrators.

Culp, M. M. (2012). Starting the Culture of Evidence Journey. In M.M. Culp and G.J. Dungy (Eds.), *Building a culture of evidence in student affairs: A guide for leaders and practitioners.* Washington, DC: NASPA: Student Affairs Administrators in Higher Education.

Gallagher Dahl, M., Meagher, P., & Vander Velde, S. (2014). Motivation and outcomes for university students in a restorative justice program. *Journal of Student Affairs Research and Practice, 51*(4), 364–379.

Gehring, D. D., Lowery, J. W., & Palmer, C. J. (2012). Students' views of effective alcohol sanctions on college campuses: A national study. Washington, DC: Century Council.

Goldstein, A., & Stimpson, M. (2013). Competency nine: assessment. In D. M. Waryold & J. M. Lancaster (Eds.), *The state of student conduct* (pp. 42–44). Association for Student Conduct Administration.

Goldstein, R., & Sukys, S. (2016). Data Collection Systems. In K. Kennedy (Ed.), *Making a difference: Improving residence life assessment practices* (55–76). Columbus, OH: Association of College & University Housing Officers-International.

Heinich, R., Molenda, M., Russell, J., & Smaldino, S. (2002). *Instructional media and technologies for learning* (7th ed.). Boston: Merrill Prentice Hall.

Howell, M. T. (2005). Students' perceived learning and anticipated future behaviors as a result of participation in the student judicial process. *Journal of College Student Development, 46*(4), 374–392.

Janosik, S. M., & Stimpson, M. T. (2015). *The NASCAP project: Transforming student conduct administration practice through outcomes assessment* [PowerPoint slides]. Retrieved from http://eduoutcomes.com/wp-content/uploads/2015/04/NASCAP.pdf.

Janosik, S. M., & Stimpson, M. T. (2017). The influence of the conduct system and campus environments on student learning. *Journal of Student Affairs Research and Practice, 54*(1), 28–41.

Janosik, S. M., & Stimpson, R. L. (2011). Outcomes assessment of the student conduct administration process: University of Florida 2010–2011 SCAPQ report. *NASCAP Project.* Blacksburg, VA: NASCAP.

Karp, D. R. (2015). Restorative justice for colleges and universities. New York, NY: Good Books.

Keeling, R. P., Wall, A. F., Underhile, R., & Dungy, G. J. (2008). *Assessment reconsidered: Institutional effectiveness for student success.* United States: ICSSIA.

Kennedy, K. (2016). The double-loop assessment model. In K. Kennedy (Ed.), *Making a difference: Improving residence life assessment practices* (13–25). Columbus, OH: Association of College & University Housing Officers-International.

King, R. H. (2012). Student conduct administration: How students perceive the educational value and procedural fairness of their disciplinary experiences. *Journal of College Student Development, 54*(4), 563–580.

Kompalla, S. L., & McCarthy, M. C. (2001). The effect of judicial sanctions on recidivism and retention. *College Student Journal, 35*(2), 223.

Kuh, G. D., Jankowski, N., Ikenberry, S. O., & Kinzie, J. (2014). Knowing What Students Know and Can Do: The Current State of Student Learning Outcomes Assessment in US College and Universities. Urbana, IL: University of Illinois and Indiana University, National Institute for Learning Outcomes Assessment (NILOA).

Lewis, D. K., & Marchell, T. C. (2006). Safety first: A medical amnesty approach to alcohol poisoning at a U.S. university. *The International Journal of Drug Policy, 17,* 329–338.

Maki, P. M. (2004). *Assessing for learning: Building a sustainable commitment across the institution.* Sterling, VA: Stylus Publishing.

Maki, P. M. (2010). *Assessing for learning: Building a sustainable commitment across the institution* (2nd ed.). Sterling, VA: Stylus Publishing.

McCabe, D. L., Butterfield, K. D., & Treviño, L. K. (2012). *Cheating in college: Why students do it and what educators can do about it.* Retrieved from https://ebookcentral-proquest.com.libproxy.lib.unc.edu.

Nelson, A. R. (2017). Measure of development for student conduct administration. *Journal of College Student Development, 58*(8), 1274–1280.

National Institute for Learning Outcomes Assessment (2016). *Higher education quality: Why documenting learning matters.* Champaign, IL: National Institute for Learning Outcomes Assessment.

Palomba, C. A., & Banta, T. W. (1999). *Assessment essentials: Planning, implementing, and improving assessment in higher education* (1st ed.). San Francisco, CA: Jossey-Bass.

Porter, S. R., Whitcomb, M. E., & Weitzer, W. H. (2004). Multiple surveys of students and survey fatigue. *New Directions for Institutional Research, 2004*(121), 63–73.

Schuh, J. H. (2013). Developing a Culture of Assessment in Student Affairs. *New Directions for Student Services, 2013*(142), 89–98.

Schuh, J. H., Upcraft, M. L., & Associates. (2001). *Assessment practice in student affairs: An applications manual.* San Francisco, CA: Jossey-Bass.

Starcke, M., & DeLoach, A. (2012). Assessing and documenting student learning. In K. M. Collins & D. M. Roberts (Eds.), *Learning is not a sprint* (73–101).

Washington, DC: National Association of Student Personnel Administrators.

Stimpson, M. T., & Janosik, S. M. (2015). The conduct system and its influence on student learning. *Journal of College Student Development, 56,* 61–66.

Stimpson, M. T., & Janosik, S. M. (2011). Variability in reported student learning as a result of participating in a student conduct system. *College Student Affairs Journal, 30*(1), 19–30.

Suskie, L. (2009). *Assessing student learning: A common sense guide* (2nd ed.). San Francisco, CA: Jossey-Bass.

Tschepikow, W. K. (2012) Why don't our students respond? Understanding declining participation in survey research among college students. *Journal of Student Affairs Research and Practice, 49*(4), 447–462. doi: 10.1515/jsarp-2012-6333.

University of Kentucky, Office of Student Conduct (n.d.). Retrieved from http://www.uky.edu/studentconduct/restorative-justice.

University of North Carolina at Chapel Hill (2017). *Community living standards & housing conduct process.* Retrieved from https://housing.unc.edu/about-us/policies/community-living-standards.

Upcraft, M. L., & Schuh, J. H. (1996). *Assessment in student affairs: A guide for practitioners.* San Francisco, CA: Jossey-Bass.

Wall, A.F. (2012). Applying various assessment approaches to gather credible, usable data. In M. M. Culp and G. J. Dungy (Eds.), *Building a culture of evidence in student affairs: A guide for leaders and practitioners.* Washington, DC: NASPA: Student Affairs Administrators in Higher Education.

Zehr, H. (2002). *The little book of restorative justice.* Intercourse, PA: Good Books.

1. Where do you already have information available that you could use to inform your practice (number and type of violation, turnaround time on cases, number of cases heard by each hearing officer, etc.)?

2. What information would help you to have a better understanding of your practice and your impact on students? What opportunities do you have to start collecting this information?

3. After interacting with the conduct system, what are the most-important things for students to have learned?

4. When assessing your current housing conduct process, what is its greatest strength? Greatest opportunity for change? What systems are available to collect data and information?

5. When collecting data, what kind of information will be well-received by key stakeholders and audiences with whom you will share data? Will they be more interested in qualitative data, quantitative data, or both?

6. Before asking students questions about their experiences, identify what you will do with the data once collected. How will you analyze the data? What do you hope to see? What is your target? How will you report on and share this information? With whom?

7. When it comes to student interactions, are you interested in assessing student learning, needs, or satisfaction, or something else?

8. What methods do you use to collect data from students in the housing conduct process? Are there any drawbacks to consider with these methods?

9. When sharing your assessment results, what challenges or roadblocks do you foresee? How might you navigate sharing results that are not positive? How might sharing results look different depending on your audience (stakeholders as opposed to supervisors or supervisees)?

10. What is your conduct system trying to accomplish? Is it meeting your goals?

Conclusion

LESSONS LEARNED

Ryan C. Holmes, Alan Acosta, and JoCynda Hudson

COMMUNITY IS a basic foundation of interpersonal interaction, but that does not mean it is something that occurs naturally. At higher education institutions, residence life staff purposely create environments that serve as labs where students learn the life skills that create community. The on-campus communities expose students to new ideas and experiences in a supportive environment while also posing challenges to students' values and beliefs. Students learn that there are expectations to respond to and roles to play as a community member. According to Lockean philosophy, students even may need to relinquish some individual rights to gain the benefits of living on campus. This balance of individual and collective rights and responsibilities is at the heart of our concept of conduct and community.

The authors of this book have leveraged their research, their experience, and their expertise to provide thoughtful discussion of what constitutes the foundation of residence life student conduct practice. It was an intentional choice that the authors would represent various institutional types to showcase the intersectionality of conduct and residence life staff. From this combination, the result is a book robust in contributions from practitioners representing both ACUHO-I and the Association of Student Conduct Administration (ASCA). While theory is addressed throughout the book, the focus is on the practical application of theory and best practice. This has created a handbook that can be used for training, professional development, and informed practice for both conduct and housing staff.

The common themes of the book chapters all connect back to the idea of community. We expect that each reader, as they approach this book, is likely to have specific scenes from their campus community in mind. Our communities are unique in their own ways, and that diversity should be viewed as our greatest strength, even though it sometimes is regarded as a hindrance. Inclusion is also critical to our campuses and should be infused into the desired community, rather than achieved as a by-product of it.

While receiving an academic degree is most often the culminating event for students, the challenges of the environment with the necessary support are also key to a holistic education. Paulo Freire, in his book *Pedagogy of the Oppressed* (1970), discussed dueling educational philosophies he called banking and problem-posing.

Simply stated, banking education is a system in which the instructor possesses all knowledge and authority. The students are unknowing vessels who are to be sponges that simply restate the given information for credit and accept their station as less than that of the instructor. Such an approach hardly sounds like a recipe for a thriving community. Rather, almost everything that could be said about contemporary college students points to their being practitioners of problem-posing education. This is the belief that both the instructors and the students have parts of the answers and, through discussion and challenges, the community's truth will emerge (Freire, 1970). The same can be applied to residential communities when considering the concepts of learning, authority, and community. Students falter in a "do as I say" community presented without reasons or partnership. In the problem-posing mode of education, many aspects of the living community (e.g., power, privilege, oppressions, rights, responsibilities, conflict management, etc.) can be experienced in ways that further their education. Through the ebb and flow of strength, strain, and recovery, students — through community — transform into better versions of themselves while contributing to the larger community needs.

Within these pages, the authors explain how a campus' institutional mission serves as the core of any conduct philosophy. Because divisional and departmental philosophies can never be completely separate from the overall mission, it follows that the operations at the departmental level, and even the workings of the staff, are connected as well. Connectivity speaks volumes to the culture of an institution. Culture sustains itself through buy-in and collaboration between campus partners and others who are essential parts of the institution's fabric. While the overall essence may be altered by external stimuli (e.g., laws, mandates, societal changes), it is the interpretation of such changes under the scope of the mission that allows a conduct philosophy to evolve as needed to maintain relevance. This has been seen many times in the national and educational landscapes, as illustrated throughout this book.

If change has been necessary for higher education to remain relevant all these years, it should not be a surprise that change may continue to occur in the coming years as the interim guidance on Title IX solidifies, philosophies that affect transgender populations and services due to them materialize into mandates, and free speech laws and practices transform. Surely, as the landscape changes, so will conduct philosophies. The same may especially be true in housing populations, where students spend an immense amount of time with each other and must navigate these philosophies.

Laws will continue to guide college and university operations. While in the United States, public institutions are always required to abide by constitutional law and private institutions are required to do so when acting under the color of the law, it is important for all personnel to understand the laws that affect their areas. It is just as important for students to understand the laws since, in many ways, their understanding of such laws guides their behaviors. Further, since institutional policies are crafted under the laws, and because students are expected to abide by institutional policies, the underlying laws must be understood to inspire appropriate behavior and to ensure policies do not infringe upon understood freedoms. When all institutional community members have an understanding of the expectations, less dissonance occurs, especially among those acting in good faith.

At this point in higher education history, there is no shortage of educational opportunities, information, and trainings by which conduct and housing professionals can be prepared. However, even with the abundance of trainings, professionals have to be built to function in service to the community they have chosen and that has chosen them. When problems surface in conduct and housing, rarely have the policies, regulations, and rules caused the concerns. The same cannot be stated about the personnel charged with delivering what the handbooks and manuals demand. For this reason, it is imperative, as the authors note, to devote time and resources to training professional and student employees. The people in the relevant positions, far more than the guiding documents, have an affect on the feel of the campus and the flow of the community. Their behavior develops precedence and expectations, and gives students the institutional story through actions. With successful training and practice, conduct and housing staff are prepared to forge a sense of belonging for all students, faculty, and staff.

In addition to fostering a sense of belonging, professionals also have the duty to influence community standards and accountability. In many ways, these two aspects go hand-in-hand; they are shaped in policy through original crafting and revisions to shape the development of our students. While laws, policies, and professionals all have influence on the standards, associations and councils such as ACUHO-I, ASCA, and the Council for the Advancement of Standards in Higher Education (CAS) are valuable resources that help institutions shape standards for uniformity, as well as provide the flexibility to meet the needs of individual campuses.

The authors have shown the best foundational information is needed to craft the original conduct codes used by institutions. Yet, since the only constant over time is change, revisions to codes and community standards must be ongoing as well. For instance, 10 years ago, there were no discussions about the difference between a service animal and an emotional support animal, or debates over whether using a vape pen was considered smoking. However, each time a new societal component enters the community, revisions will not be far behind. Again, since students will always move more quickly than the systems in which we function, operating in partnership with students is imperative.

As campus communities become more diverse, both in surface diversity and increasing expressions of difference, it is important all students feel valued. More so, it is important students know equitable access to opportunities, programs, and resources is standard across each institution. In living spaces and in conduct processes, it is paramount students feel they have been heard; continue to be a part of all important conversations; and understand that who they are is affirmed, valued, welcomed, and included. Students should have the comfort of knowing that, unless their behaviors violate laws or policies, they will be accepted in the campus environment where the recruitment process told them they would be valued.

Students have to feel this sense of safety and comfort to perform at their optimum levels in and outside the classroom Social justice philosophy, as interwoven into the institutional fabric, allows student growth and development to occur. Nonetheless, it also is important to avoid painting a utopian picture for students. Life is real and the time may come when students are confronted with varying levels of bigotry, ignorance, or hatred. When this occurs, they will need to know how to address these situations for themselves and possibly advocate for others. An environment embedded in social justice philosophy can assist with these lessons.

Finding strength in one's identity and value in others is helpful as well. Much of the strength necessary to challenge biased and oppressive systems comes from seeing good systems function, and students should be able to find these examples in our housing structures, conduct systems, and interactions with professionals. While housing professionals may find themselves in more positions to drive conversations and programs of social justice forward, and while conduct professionals may not be able to move openly in the promotion of social justice depending on the situation, all professionals should seek ways to strengthen the culture of equity and inclusion within the framework of the institution. Many institutions were founded on oppressive practices, power differences, and bias. As this is understood better, residence life and conduct professionals are confronted with the need and opportunity to do better. Students, faculty, staff, and the public at large demand it.

It is equally important for readers of this book to remember students, once admitted to an institution, continue to be students regardless of the struggles they may have. For instance, many higher education professionals do not expect the number of students with mental health concerns to decrease. Therefore, it is the responsibility of conduct and housing professionals to be aware of the behaviors of all students; intervene when behaviors cause (or threaten to cause) danger, disruption, or harm to other members of the community; offer assistance to students who exhibit unusual behaviors if they are receptive to help; and provide resources for any student in need.

Because of recent instances where the mental health of students has come into question, many institutions have established teams and structures to assist students. Even so, more can always be done, especially when considering the many identities students possess and how those identities can be affected by the style of assistance offered. Assistance, regardless of how needed it is, should never be perceived as coming at the expense of a student's dignity or privacy. Keeping this in mind reduces any chilling effect that can surface. Students are always watching the experiences of their peers.

Throughout the conduct process, even with the determination of sanctions and outcomes, the effect of an incident on community is integral. For years, there has been movement to clearly show the student conduct process and the criminal system are not the same and should not be treated as such. While both are designed, in theory, to uphold the values of their communities, the criminal system focuses on punishment for broken laws while the conduct system is designed to educate policy violators about the institution's values, restore the community, and deliver punitive outcomes, where necessary. Each of these aspects, ideally, leads to a positive change in student behaviors. However, unless a student's status is altered through suspension or expulsion, the offending party probably will remain part of the community. In other words, those who break the rules are still our students, and the community should be restored to maintain its balance with members potentially living in close proximity of each other.

Generally speaking, when any student enters a campus, it has been changed forever. It has been transformed into an organism that did not exist before. When the community is affected in a negative fashion, it is further transformed. The space may never regain the makeup that existed previously; however, it does not have to, as long as it continues through a progression with the current students, while being in line with the institution's mission and values. Viewed this way, the key is restoration rather than maintenance of the status quo. Higher education professionals encourage students to take risks and grow; institutions and institutional leaders need permission to do the same.

A familiar saying proposes, "if all you have is a hammer, everything looks like a nail." This has been true in the case of institutions that, for generations, may have believed adjudication was the only way to solve student concerns and policy violations. However, recent developments have shown the ability of conduct and housing to explore a growing number of options and be less hammer-like. As a result, students and professionals alike can use alternative methods to knowingly address concerns before conduct issues grow large and unmanageable. With a spectrum of resolution options that include conflict coaching (which allows parties to maintain the process and content at the lowest levels) and adjudication (which totally maintains the process and allows regimented input), students now have the possibility of more options while determining when and how they want professionals to assist.

When students are told to take ownership of interpersonal situations, they require encouragement, guidance, and the proper tools to be successful. Is there an opportunity for additional conflict resolution methods to be added to the process? If so, what avenues exist to move forward? If not, are there ways to infuse conflict resolution methods without disturbing current processes? When these are provided, the housing community grows stronger because of new methods to aid in education while providing avenues for advocates and bystanders to come forward. In additional, when conflicts can be identified and addressed sooner, conduct staff can be supported through the potential decrease in cases they must hear. This reduction may allow more time to be dedicated to students and situations who truly need professional intervention in heightened ways. Also, as professionals gather skills and knowledge of self through training, self-reflection, and purposeful growth, the community has no choice but to get better.

This book provides great insight, philosophies, scenarios, and tools with which professionals can become better so students and institutions become better. However, professionals increasingly are asked to demonstrate this improvement through assessment. Assessment brings the services to light that separate on-campus housing operations from off-campus accommodations and showcases the added value of the on-campus experience.

It is valuable to remember efforts to meet the needs of students and their community can always be improved, especially since today's students may be the most consumer-based ones in higher education history. They do not hesitate to tell professionals what works well, and also what can be improved. Likewise, various populations within the community also interact with students and want to know about the conduct process and any changes or trends in student behavior. Assessment is a great way to craft the story. In the absence of information, stories can be crafted for the storyteller.

There may be something inherent in the conduct and residence life realms that shines a spotlight on the differences between generations. Perhaps this is why professionals are often reminded to "meet students where they are." This is something professionals should not lose sight of when students' methods do not add up to their expectations: when students choose to argue through texting rather than have a conversation; discuss their conflicts with the world on social media rather than address the other party involved; or when they struggle to find the necessary words to get to the core of their dilemma. Professionals must do better than listening to that voice in the back of their mind that says, "Back when I was in school ..."

Certainly the professional may have found personal comfort through different means. Maybe one found comfort in meeting new people when they arrived in a new place. Maybe current students have maintained that, or maybe students find comfort in using their phones to maintain contact with friends from home. Parental involvement is said to have changed over time as well. It could be true that today's parents stifle student development by being too involved at crucial junctures. It could also be true that parents know the best ways to support their students based on past experiences.

There also is the growing concern of student expectations of campus comforts. As long as students (and families) see themselves as customers and the educational experience as a commodity, higher education will continue to be an environment that stresses the importance of customer service. As many institutional missions concentrate on service to the community, families have a right to expect high levels of service. Education professionals have the task of showing that service to the community is expected of everyone through actions and the educational methods they employ. These types of considerations are necessary to understand relational points of entry with students, better educate them on expectations, and keep them safe while on campus.

By reading this book, professionals recognize continued education is important. This book was written to provide information without knowing the individual reader's strengths and weaknesses. However, since it covers many areas, professionals can strengthen themselves in the areas they believe may cause concerns for their community while realizing the areas of strength so they can offer leadership when an opportunity arises. In many ways, this book may be a checklist of competency areas into which professionals can take a deep dive. They may choose to focus their energies on understanding guidance and laws at the federal level; deciphering the nuances of case law; understanding statutes and the operations of education boards at state levels; or focusing on components of the institution, guided by the many manuals and documents connected to the conduct and housing areas.

Since this book concentrates on the importance of community, professionals ideally will reexamine their own networks to determine if their communities are as strong as they need to be and whether they consult its resources enough. As critical thoughts come to mind, professionals should take a moment to record them for further analysis. Professionals may even decide to focus their energies on re-examining and rebuilding self. In what ways are they affecting the community positively or negatively? What biases have surfaced as a result of interacting with the information in this book? What opportunities, under their direct control, could professionals advance to display a culture of equity?

Since communities are composed of people, it is important for each person to be as whole as they can be while supporting others and themselves. It is the hope of the editors and authors that this book will help all higher education professionals find renewed energy and focus to continue to build themselves for the benefit of their community.

Supporting Resources

AS BEFITTING its name, this book was created with the practitioner in mind. While there has been a great deal of insightful research done regarding both conduct and community, there remained a need to connect that theory to practice. The following pages — along with the discussion questions at the end of each chapter — are designed to do just that. These curated materials are numbered to correspond with the earlier chapters* and are divided into four categories: resources, insights, exercises, and case studies.

The material in the Resources category can be considered more grist for the mill; information that may have not fit conveniently in one of the preceding chapters, but still delivers great value to housing and conduct professionals. These could serve as materials for supervisors to share with staff to spur conversation during training.

Insights are similar in that while they may not have been completely appropriate to include in a chapter, the material does provide additional value. They deliver more of a deep-dive into a particular topic, often accompanied by the authors' first-person experiences. In many cases, these articles illustrate ways in which a professional (or team of professionals) have internalized the lessons they have learned and directed that knowledge to enhance their day-to-day work.

The Exercises are just as they say; training materials to be integrated easily into most any staff or student-staff preparation. Practitioners understand knowledge of theory is useful, but like any muscle it must be flexed. Exercises such as the popular Behind Closed Doors or others included here let individuals come face-to-face with real-world versions of concepts such as conflict resolution, privilege, and identity.

Finally, the Case Studies provide hypothetical scenarios (and maybe some that aren't so hypothetical) common to the contemporary college and university campus. Considering such scenarios before they occur, and considering the spectrum of possible responses, is an invaluable, proactive approach particularly in the area of conduct.

While some of these supplemental resources were created by the chapter authors, much of it was contributed by additional housing and conduct professionals who drew on their own experiences and expertise. Those individuals, as well as the institutions that provided permission to use the material, are credited in each entry. The editors, as well as ACUHO-I and ASCA, thank them for their willingness to share their work and for doing their part to strengthen our own community of professionals.

Editors' Note: There are no supplemental materials for chapter 5, "Crafting and Revising Conduct Processes." As the premise of the chapter is that institutions must consider their unique institutional culture, mission, and mores in crafting policies and practices — as well as remain nimble to accommodate changes — the decision was made it would not be responsible to attempt to provide models or best practices. One size cannot fit all in this instance.

 **1.1** | CASE STUDY

EMPOWERMENT

It may seem like hardly a week goes by without a sexual assault incident on a college campus being highlighted in the news. Institutions around the world are striving for ways to educate male students more effectively about the importance of healthy relationships and sexual assault prevention while developing leadership skills. The United States Department of Civil Rights has championed the effort to decrease sexual assaults on college campuses.

Jennifer Forry, dean of student affairs at Newbury College in Brookline, Massachusetts, identified the need to develop a program that would assist male students with developing a campus mentoring relationship. This relationship would enable them to learn how they can influence others, teach self-advocacy skills, work collaboratively to develop more male leaders on campus, and instill proactive bystander skills. This program was named empowerMENt.

The program brought together faculty- and staff-nominated male students to attend a one-day retreat and biweekly one-on-one meetings with a faculty or staff mentor to prepare them to act as empowerMENt campus leaders on campus. The NASPA Foundation funded it through an inaugural Innovation Grant. Newbury College was one of four institutions nationwide to receive grant funding. The pilot program launched in September 2017 and had 50 participants. The research and design of this program came from Forry's doctoral research focusing on Title IX Investigations and male students accused of sexual misconduct.

OBJECTIVES

The empowerMENt project goals were to develop more male student leaders on campus, influence men to be part of the solution for sexual assault on campus, and develop a campus culture of respect. The learning outcomes were that participants would be able to:

- Influence change on campus by using their voices and their action(s).
- Develop effective bystander and advocacy skills that they can apply to prevent or respond to sexual assault incidents.
- Hold themselves and others accountable for respectable standards of personal behavior.
- Propose solutions for incidents of sexual assault and personal behavior.

Retreat Design

The empowerMENt retreat was an interactive, day-long, male-based program that focused on male leadership, sexual assault bystander skill development, sexual assault prevention, and male-to-male mentoring. The program featured cross-campus collaboration and met the needs of a specific population at Newbury College, featuring 60% students of color and first-generation college students.

- All participants completed the Gallup Strength Finders 2.0 Assessment before the retreat. The results of this assessment were used during the retreat.
- Each participant was paired with a male faculty or staff member during the retreat.
- Participants and mentors were led through a series of icebreakers and team-building challenges.
- The morning speaker was from a local (Boston-area) institution who reviewed the Strength Finder results with the group and how the results play into male-identified/male masculinities.
- The afternoon speaker was from a Worcester-area institution and serves as the NASPA Region I Men & Masculinities chair. This content focused on men and sexual assault, and influencing culture change by teaching men how to be proactive bystanders.
- After each speaker session, all participants engaged in a thought-provoking discussion with their mentors.

Post-Retreat Assessment

At the conclusion of the event, participants were surveyed on their thoughts regarding the program. Among the findings, participants reported that they:

- Would recommend empowerment to others — 100%.
- Learned something new — 100%.
- Had talked/spent time with someone they had never met before — 92.9%
- Know how to make a difference in sexual assault prevention — 85.7%
- They know how to influence change on campus — 78.6%
- Developed a relationship with their mentor/mentee — 78.6%
- Stepped out of their comfort zones — 71.4%

Information provided by Jennifer Forry, dean of student affairs at Newbury College. For more information about this program, contact her at jennifer.forry@newbury. edu.

CASE STUDY

IMPLEMENTING CULTURE CHANGE

Shana Warkentine Meyer and Lyn Reddington

Tanya Massey, an assistant director at Oklahoma State University, has more than 15 years of professional residence life experience and was first introduced to the concept of culture change as a live-on professional at Kansas State University. The approach has benefited her when addressing communities with a low level of involvement or buy-in by students and staff, as well as with communities where there are a large number of conduct incidents. Her experience has shown ongoing patterns can be addressed and changed through intentional, time-intensive programming and a community-building model.

Although the set-the-tone approach works particularly well in first-year communities, staff can begin to change a culture by presenting community-building initiatives as "this is how things are in ABC Hall" rather than "This is how we want them to be." Will all of these efforts change everything immediately? Of course not. Visualize trying to turn a massive ship; enormous, heavy pistons slowing to a stop and then revving up again. It will take awhile. It will take a lot of energy. There will be failures and successes. But eventually, the boat will turn.

The following are simple community-building initiatives that proved successful for Massey and Oklahoma State University.

1. Turn the name of the residence hall into an acrostic where each letter stands for a value. At least one of the values should relate to conduct and behavior. Students will appreciate the openness and also see staff as serious about addressing conduct issues, while recognizing the other elements (i.e., diversity, academics) that make up the community. For example, at the University of Northern Iowa, Dancer Hall stands for:

   - **D**iversity
   - **A**cademics
   - **N**ew Friends
   - **C**onduct yourself responsibly
   - **E**xperiences
   - **R**espect

2. During the check-in process, provide students and families with items such as pens or keychains that have the acronym printed on them. These small items promote the idea that living in the community is something special.

3. Create a common hall-wide theme and display it through high-quality bulletin boards, door decorations, and other common area décor. Decorate and maintain common spaces, and post eye-catching fliers with the acronym in common spaces as well.

4. To advertise welcome week programs, have the RAs and hall leaders promote them aggressively through word of mouth. This approach sets the tone for future programs.

5. RAs should run the opening meeting, but the professional or graduate staff should also be present to introduce themselves, encourage involvement, and address policies and conduct philosophy. Again, be honest and upfront about any rumors and stereotypes, and then spend time on all of the other, equally valid and valuable, components of your community.

6. Student staff need to know their community and know it well. Beyond knowing the residents' names (although this is crucial) and running programs, consider student development. Throughout the first six weeks prepare RAs to answer questions such as:
   a. What does their community look like?
   b. What does it sound like?
   c. How can they tell things are going well?
   d. What can they tell their supervisor about the students who are involved the most, and the least?
   e. What trends do they see?

7. Assign collateral assignments that are not frivolous to student staff and encourage the RAs to take them seriously. Some examples include helping with student government, serving on departmental committees, and working with recognition. Here again, staff should be committed to representing the hall and representing it well so they are not only known for living in a hall with a poor reputation.

8. Train RAs thoroughly in confrontation procedures. Communicate to residents it is important for them to feel respected during a conduct interaction, and to be respectful to staff as well. Be sure to ask in each hearing whether the staff behaved respectfully as well as whether the offending student was respectful toward the staff.

9. Collaborate with facilities and custodial crews, other student employees and leaders, and professional staff across campus (e.g., counseling, multicultural affairs, academic success, etc.). Bring these leaders in and ask them for advice about addressing issues in the community.

10. If staff demonstrates care about the physical space, the students will begin to do the same. Staff should walk with custodians in the morning

and look at damaged or vandalized items in communities. Staff also can model positive behaviors such as not walking past a piece of trash but, instead, picking it up and throwing it away. Students will notice if the staff advocates for better or updated furniture in their common spaces. They will appreciate the staff pushing for permission to paint common areas. (Make sure artwork, wall quotes, etc., are representative and inclusive of the community's population.)

11. Communicate with colleagues and supervisors about these initiatives. Reach out to admissions, orientation, and other staff who communicate with incoming students. Set the expectation to speak positively about all communities on campus and not perpetuate negative stereotypes about any community.

Case study prepared by Shana Warkentine Meyer and Lyn Reddington with input from Tanya Massey, assistant director at Oklahoma State University. Used with permission.

INSIGHTS

STUDENT CONDUCT PHILOSOPHY FOR A GLOBAL CONTEXT

Jill L. Creighton

Author's note: This section focuses on developing a global student conduct philosophy from a primarily United States lens, but many of the action items can prove transferable within multiple global contexts in student conduct.

According to the Institute of International Education's Open Doors report, United States institutions of higher education hosted more than 1 million international students from dozens of countries on all six habitable continents during the 2016–2017 academic year. With international student enrollment increasing each year, both residence life and student conduct professionals must work to become more aware of how student conduct processes can best serve international students.

If those efforts are done well, the student conduct officer can make a meaningful connection and open one's own worldview while simultaneously providing a fundamentally fair process and becoming an institutional resource for the student. If done poorly, the international student can be affected disproportionately by a United States-centric student conduct system. Disproportionate impact can occur when a student may not be equipped to navigate or understand the U.S. student conduct process because they have grown up in a different cultural context. This may lead to a misunderstanding of how their voice may be heard in a student conduct process or a fear that providing a dissenting opinion in a student conduct meeting may result in more-significant sanctions.

The student conduct officer must consider when a sanction may result in hidden consequences beyond the intention of the sanction. For example, a sanction such as a probationary status lets domestic students know that their violative behavior warrants a more-critical examination of future behavior. However, that same probationary status for an international student may affect them in a number of ways, including potential loss of their sponsorships, scholarships, and visa eligibility status. Should an international student lose their housing as a result of an incident, that can affect whether the student can retain their visa to study in the United States.

Parent notification policies tend to come from cultural assumptions that the parents are partners for student success, which may not hold true in other cultural contexts. The same sanction for the domestic and international student may be identical, consistent, or both, but still may result in an inequitable outcome. Aligned with other elements of the student conduct process, student conduct officers must engage in critical thinking and use good judgment to avoid such unintended impacts.

Much like domestic students, international students may misconstrue television and pop culture shows about courts of law as the model for student conduct systems. When working with international students, and in aiming for a more fundamentally fair processes, it can be helpful for a student conduct officer to begin by discussing the linear steps in the student conduct process, followed by sharing the institution's philosophy of student conduct. Conduct officers should ask themselves, "What do international students expect from the conduct process as a result of their cultural lenses?"

In some countries, colleges and universities do not address student misconduct and instead either encourage self-agency of students to work out challenges among themselves or guide students toward formal reporting to law enforcement agencies. In other countries, conflict resolution methods rule the student conduct process. Some countries also root their discipline processes in a lens of shame. International students' worldviews have been shaped by their experiences with discipline and their expectations of discipline. Therefore, housing and conduct professionals can better prepare for their meetings by asking themselves what the student expects.

Creating a more fundamentally fair process for international students requires student conduct officers to focus on their own cultural humility and personal processes in becoming a global citizen. True cultural competency in each of the world's cultures and sub-cultures, and the nuances of these cultures is simply not attainable for any individual. However, conduct officers can take active strides to change individual worldviews and make the student experience better by increasing their knowledge of the world.

Before meeting with an international student, the conduct officer should perform a self-check for knowledge and a basic understanding of the student's cultural context. A student conduct officer should avoid making assumptions about a student's culture based on pop-culture knowledge, superficial understanding of a culture, or inherent bias about a culture. For example, in the United States, privilege often is assigned to Westernized values and English-speaking countries. The privilege of status and intelligence can be assigned to certain speaking accents while others are marginalized societally. In addition to the general social justice work, student conduct officers should ask themselves how they perceive a speaking accent and check in with themselves to work toward eliminating the impact of that inherent bias against the student.

A self-check should also include basic information, such as whether the professional can identify the student's hometown on a map of the world. Unfortunately, most Americans have been educated in such an ethnocentric way that basic geography is lacking. It can be a humbling experience to realize that one's formal education has not prioritized the larger global context.

After performing this self-check to illustrate where cultural humility begins, it begs further reflective questions: How can housing and conduct professionals serve the international student population if they are unable to identify countries and cities on a map, let alone begin to identify cultural frameworks? What does this say about existing values as individual administrators and as institutional representatives?

These questions led to my development of the following paradigm for working with international students:

- If you don't know where my home is on a map, you don't know where I'm from.
- If you don't know where I'm from, you won't know my culture.
- If you don't know my culture, you can't know me.
- If you can't know me, you can't assess my behavior or understand my needs.
- If you can't understand my needs, you can't value me.
- If you can't value me, I can't trust you.

This framework provides linkages and reminders that while geography can seem like basic knowledge and perhaps even unimportant, it serves as the basis for internalizing the importance of beginning to know a student. Globalization of student conduct processes requires much more time and attention than is achievable in this abbreviated section, but this paradigm provides a place to begin the process.

As practitioners strive to become more globally-inclusive professionals, these questions can guide the reflexive learning process.

- How do international students know what to expect from your campus' student conduct process?
- If you can't answer this question, what work will you do next?
- How do you create inclusion for those who are not familiar with U.S. or Western culture?
- Do your materials use plain language with no idioms, colloquialisms, or clichés in your writing?
- Do your materials clearly delineate your process?
- Might you be able to represent your process visually to create easier access and understanding?

- What assumptions do you make about your students' cultural understandings?
- Does your staff adequately represent your student body?

Once professionals have considered these questions, they can take concrete actions to further efforts to serve the international student population. Among these steps:

- Review student conduct policies, procedures, websites, publications, letter templates, and other communications to identify and replace idioms and clichés.
- Consider specific orientation sessions for international students.
- Perform a self-check before each meeting with an international student. Can you point to that student's home on a map? What can you learn about how discipline functions in that country or culture?

As students increasingly cross international borders in pursuit of their education, all institutions must revisit their policies and practices to ensure they meet the needs of all students.

Jill L. Creighton serves as the assistant dean of students for conduct and operations at the University of Oregon and was president of the Association for Student Conduct Administration from 2017-2018.

INSIGHTS

DISABILITY AND STUDENT CONDUCT SYSTEMS

Joseph T. DiMaria

Many student housing and conduct administrators struggle with whether to consider student disability during the conduct process and, if it is considered, exactly how it should factor into student accountability. Given that a number of social and emotional disabilities are associated with specific negative behavioral patterns, students with these specific disabilities may be at higher risk of violating codes of student conduct. Therefore, it is important to understand how to balance student rights, accountability, and expectations for disabled students.

K–12 STUDENT CONDUCT PROCESSES

Perhaps the best place to begin understanding student expectations about the role of disability in addressing student conduct is to look at the current systems in place throughout K–12 education. Because this is the system that the vast majority of students are familiar with before enrolling at a higher education institution, it is fair to recognize that it shapes their understanding of their rights and the obligations of the institution.

The major piece of legislation that protects students with disabilities is the Individuals with Disabilities in Education Act (IDEA). Through this law, the United States Congress developed the procedural safeguard of a "manifestation determination" to ensure that a student was not punished for behavior that is a direct result of their disability. Under current provisions of IDEA, any student with a disability who is subject to student conduct action that may result in a "change in placement" (i.e., removal from school for longer than 10 days) is entitled to a "manifestation determination."

A manifestation determination is a meeting held outside the student conduct process to determine whether the behavior for which the student is being disciplined is a direct result of the student's specific disability. The process includes a review of the student's record, as well as input from special education practitioners, the classroom teacher, and parents. If the behavior is determined to be a manifestation of the student's disability, the school cannot change the student's educational placement, although the student can be required to follow a behavioral plan or be subject to certain restrictions on privileges. If the behavior is not found to be a manifestation of the student's specific disability, they can be held accountable to the same extent as any other student who engages in the same behavior.

There are two important exceptions to the manifestation determination requirement: the "10-day rule" and situations involving "inherent and immediate danger," specifically in incidents related to weapons, controlled substances, or serious bodily injury. The first exception bypasses the requirement for a manifestation determination in situations where the student would be removed from school for fewer than 10 days because such a removal would not constitute a "change of placement" under IDEA.

The second exception allows administrators to act quickly to protect the health and safety of all students, teachers, and other personnel. However, in situations where safety is a factor, the school is still required to conduct a manifestation determination to prescribe outcomes and sanctions to the same extent as for any other student (for example, by expulsion).

Although this is not the appropriate venue for a full discussion of the entire manifestation determination process and its potential outcomes, it is critical to summarize it to understand that this is the backdrop against which students with disabilities have existed in relation to addressing their behavior at school. It has informed their understanding of their rights, as well as created their expectations about the concepts of due process and fairness. While institutions of higher education are not subject to IDEA, knowing and understanding students' K–12 background is beneficial to student conduct practitioners.

HIGHER EDUCATION STUDENT CONDUCT PROCESSES

No current federal statutes or regulations guide institutions of higher education about the accommodation of students with disabilities in student conduct processes. In the absence of such legislative action, institutions draw guidance from two key pieces of legislation: Section 504 of the Rehabilitation Act of 1973 (Section 504) and the Americans with Disabilities Act (ADA). Unlike K–12 education, there is no duty for colleges and universities to identify students with disabilities. Rather, it is the responsibility of the student to notify the institution of their disability if they need accommodation. Therefore, students who do not need accommodations may keep their disability status private if they choose to do so.

In contrast to K–12 education, disability status is not considered in higher education student conduct processes. Students with disabilities are not shielded from student conduct outcomes because they can demonstrate that the behavior was related to their disability. Therefore, students with disabilities in higher education may be subject to the same sanctions as any other students, up to and including dismissal, regardless of whether the behavior was connected to their disability.

Current practice in higher education conduct systems holds all students to the same standard of behavior, regardless of disability status. While in compliance with the requirements of the ADA and Section 504, this approach may put a student whose behavior is a direct result of their disability at risk of an adverse student conduct outcome, regardless of whether they were fully in control of their actions or entirely cognizant or conscious of the potential results of their actions. For this reason, institutions may consider employing additional safeguards to protect the educational rights of students with documented disabilities.

ACTION STEPS FOR INSTITUTIONS

As a result of the role disability may play in a student's behavior, institutions may consider adopting any of the following practices.

Statement of non-discrimination. The ADA and Section 504 prohibit discrimination on the basis of disability in all aspects of an educational program or activity, including the student conduct process. Therefore, student conduct policies should be developed to include language that gives the institution the flexibility to work with the student outside the typical student conduct process to address behavior when the situation involves issues relating to disability. Including this language in institutional policies allows administrators to deviate from written processes and procedures without being seen as giving favorable or preferential treatment to students with disabilities.

Accommodations in the student conduct process. While it is not advisable to accommodate inappropriate student behavior, institutions should certainly offer accommodations in the student conduct process to ensure students with disabilities receive full procedural due process. Notice of available accommodations could be accomplished simply by including language in charge letters that alert students to the availability of accommodations in partnership with campus disability services. For example: "Students with disabilities who would like to request an accommodation in the student conduct process should contact disability services."

Upon receiving a request for accommodation, disability services should work directly with the student conduct administrator to determine what accommodations, if any, are appropriate for the student. As for other campus accommodation, the student should be required to supply supporting documentation from qualified professionals.

Inclusion of disability services in CARE and behavioral intervention teams. One way to share information about conduct issues broadly with professionals in disability services is to include these individuals in student concern team meetings. This facilitates broader information-sharing on a need-to-know basis that bypasses any concerns an institution may have about conflicts with FERPA. Disability services professionals also would be able to follow up individually with students about whom concerns were raised in the meetings, potentially avoiding future student conduct situations.

Manifestation determinations. Institutions could, if they choose, adopt a process that mirrors the manifestation determination under IDEA. In such cases, the manifestation determination should only be triggered in situations similar to those where it is used in K–12 education: The student (1) is identified particularly as having a disability and registered for an accommodation with the intuition; (2) has allegedly violated the code of conduct in such a manner that could result in separation from the institution (suspension or expulsion); and (3) committed an offense that did not involve carrying or possessing a weapon, knowingly using or possessing illegal drugs, selling or soliciting the sale of a controlled substance, or inflicting serious bodily injury upon another person. If the student did not meet all three criteria, there would be no need to conduct a manifestation determination.

During the manifestation determination process, the student conduct officer, disability services representative, and student would review all relevant information about the alleged conduct and the student's disability with the goal of answering these questions: (1) Did the behavior have a direct and substantial relationship to the student's disability? and (2) Was the behavior a direct result of the institution's failure to accommodate the student?

The answer to either question would be "yes" if the consensus among the conduct officer, disability services representative, and the student is that either could be answered in the affirmative. There would not have to be full consensus, but a general understanding should be reached as to whether or not the behavior was a manifestation of the student's disability. Appeals would be heard by the designated appellate officer and any interim measures would remain in place until the appeal is complete.

If the conduct is determined to be a manifestation of the student's disability, the judicial officer, disability services representative, and student would confer about the student's behavior and implement a behavioral management plan. Such a plan might involve a temporary suspension, a temporary or permanent change of housing assignment, no-contact orders, restrictions on campus access or activities, or other similar sanctions. The plan should consider all appropriate social, affective, and environmental factors to best address the student's behavior. Once the behavioral management plan is developed and implemented, the student should be allowed to return to classes. If the conduct was a result of the institution's failure to accommodate the student, immediate steps should be taken to rectify the situation.

If it is determined that the conduct was not a manifestation of the student's disability, the student conduct officer should apply the relevant sanctions in the same manner and to the same extent as would be applied to any other student.

In drafting such a policy, there would be no need to include a provision for "reopening" a manifestation determination where a student seeks accommodation for a documented disability after a student conduct proceeding has taken place. However, if a student discloses a pending evaluation during the student conduct process, the results of that evaluation should be considered in whether to grant a manifestation determination. In addition, the institutional policy should address whether the student is entitled to a manifestation determination if the institution had constructive knowledge of the disability.

Joseph T. DiMaria is the director of student rights and responsibilities at Massasoit Community College in Brockton, Massachusetts. Elements of the action steps were created and expanded from a format used by the University of Kansas and are cited with permission.

 INSIGHTS

A FREE SPEECH TO-DO LIST FOR COLLEGE ADMINISTRATORS

Erwin Cherminsky and Howard Gillman

During the past year, appearances by controversial speakers on college campuses have led to a string of tense, sometimes violent, incidents. As students return to school, administrators will again face the challenge of protecting freedom of speech while ensuring safety for their students, staff, and faculty. We offer this checklist to prepare for the difficult issues that are sure to arise.

❑ **Disseminate a clear statement of free-speech values and create opportunities to teach the campus community about free speech.** Senior administrators at colleges and universities need to communicate with their communities about the vital importance for higher education of freedom of expression and academic freedom. At a minimum, they must state that all ideas and views can be expressed, no matter how controversial or offensive, and must explain why a university can't fulfill its core purpose without this freedom.

Campus officials can no longer assume this is obvious and therefore unnecessary. Our experience is that too many students, faculty, and administrators lack familiarity with basic principles of free expression and academic freedom. Because protection of offensive speech comes naturally to few, campuses should supplement strong free-speech statements with online resources and educational programming that allow all members of the community to develop a better understanding of the issues. For example, schools can include a discussion of free-speech issues at their freshman orientation programs.

But freedom of expression is never absolute. Some speech — such as true threats and harassment and interfering with the speech of others — is not protected. Campuses can enact regulations that ensure ample opportunities for communication while preventing interference with the teaching and research of faculty and students.

❑ **Publish a clear statement supporting the presence of controversial speakers before particular incidents occur.** Speakers should never be excluded because of their views, but campus officials also have to explain that it is completely appropriate, and indeed desirable, for students and faculty to express disagreement with speakers they find objectionable. There can be non-disruptive protests at events, statements of objection through the media (including student outlets), and counter-events that highlight different messages. As the old saying goes, the answer to speech we don't like is more speech.

❏ **Devise and publicize transparent and neutral procedures for approving events.** Campuses typically require advance permission for the use of their facilities. There is no free-speech right for groups to demand unconditional access to limited campus venues at a time of their choosing. The procedures and the criteria for receiving such approval must be clear, stated in advance, and applicable to all so such fair limitations are not abused.

❏ **Ensure everyone's safety.** Campuses must prepare security assessments that ensure adequate protection for controversial speakers and their audiences. A campus might insist on venues that make it easier to prevent protesters from blocking access to the event, and might require tickets or university identification to minimize the chances of disruption. Speakers in uncontrolled venues in campus public spaces have no right to speak without interruption or rebuttal from a gathering audience, but they do have a right to be protected from violence or threats of violence.

❏ **Put rules in place that prohibit disrupting the speech of others during authorized campus events – with disciplinary measures when appropriate.** Campuses undermine free speech by not responding adequately to those who disrupt others when they are exercising their First Amendment rights. Administrators must defend against the heckler's veto, where the reaction of the audience can silence the speaker. This does not mean that every minor disruption be treated with severe sanctions — that would also chill speech — but severe or persistent efforts by students to prevent the expression of certain views should be treated as a serious violation of codes of student conduct.

In our roles as university officials, we are aware of the difficulty many campuses face regarding free speech. Careful messaging and planning before crises develop can make a huge difference.

Erwin Cherminsky is dean of the University of California, Berkeley School of Law, and Howard Gillman is chancellor of the University of California, Irvine. This article originally appeared in the Wall Street Journal *on September 4, 2017. It is reprinted with permission from the authors. Minor edits have been made.*

3.3 | CASE STUDY

FREE SPEECH ON CAMPUS

Lori Berry

Free speech issues policies on college campus are seeing increasing scrutiny by students, faculty, press, and the government. By examining a common scenario, administrators can take a deeper dive into how the presence of a controversial speaker on a college or university campus can affect a community. This case study is designed to help administrators review policies that address free speech issues on their respective campuses.

THREE EVENTS IN OCTOBER

You work at Midwest State University, a large public university in the center of the United States. You have been approached by College Students for Free Speech to have a series of speakers on campus. The group wants to bring at least three controversial speakers to your campus to demonstrate how the institution embraces all types of free speech. While the student group has a distinct leaning toward the conservative side of the political spectrum, it wants to try to have a variety of speakers be a part of its Free Speech Series.

The initial proposal was for three speakers in October from the following: Laura Kipnis, James Comey, Ann Coulter, Milo Yiannopoulos, or Chelsea Manning. After looking into the contracts and fees for the speakers, the group decided it would have enough sponsorship for two speakers. The speakers chosen are Ann Coulter and James Comey.

Another group of students, from the Young Democrats organization, also wants to have a speaker come to campus, also in October to discuss the presidential election from a more-liberal point of view. They initially wanted to invite Chelsea Clinton or Huma Abedin, but found their fees to be more than they could afford. They were able to secure Robby Mook, who served as Hillary Clinton's 2016 campaign manager.

Your charge is to work with the administration to help get the community ready for these three speakers to appear within two weeks of each other. Both student groups want to advertise to the public and expect large crowds. Based on the campus climate and the interest in bringing speakers to campus who can be polarizing to certain groups, you believe preparations must be made beyond venue and program logistics — you anticipate there could be protests as well.

The largest indoor venue on your campus is the basketball arena. It can accommodate 7,500 people. The football stadium can accommodate about 22,000. With the weather being unpredictable in October, it is recommended all three speakers use the basketball arena. There is ample parking via the parking garage and two surface lots adjacent to the arena.

QUESTIONS FOR CONSIDERATION

- How would you and the vice president for student affairs help Midwest State University prepare for these speakers?
  - Which administrators and managers would you include on your team?
  - What role would each team member assume?
- What state and federal laws apply to these types of events on campus?
- What policies does your campus have in place that will frame your response?
  - Do any areas of the policies and procedures address large-scale programs like the ones these organizations are proposing?
  - Would you have to expand any aspects of those policies and procedures to handle the capacity and anticipated counter-responses?
- What has to be considered to help get the campus community ready to receive these types of events?
  - How would you describe your campus community's understanding of free speech issues on campus?
  - Are there differences in how faculty and staff perceive the university's stance?
  - How do the students view free speech?
  - How can faculty and staff talk with students about issues of free speech and civility?
  - Are civil discourse and free speech addressed in your orientation program or classes?
- How would you organize the response on the ground the day of these events?
  - What is your reporting structure?
  - Who is ultimately in charge?
  - How will issues be communicated and responded to?
- What follow up will be done at the conclusion of the event to help prepare for the next event?
- How would a smaller event be handled on your campus? What differences are there, if any?

Lori Berry is the assistant dean of students at the University of Southern Indiana.

 RESOURCE

ACUHO-I CORE COMPETENCIES FOR STUDENT BEHAVIOR

The ACUHO-I Core Competencies identify what campus housing professionals need to be able to do (function competencies) and what they must know (knowledge needed) to further their departmental and institutional missions: to provide a place for students to live, learn, and grow. To address the complex nature of campus housing, 12 knowledge domains, many of which are further delineated by sub-domains, were identified. The domains are: (a) Ancillary Partnerships, (b) Conference Services, (c) Crisis Management, (d) Dining, (e) Evaluation and Planning, (f) Facilities, (g) Fiscal Resources and Control, (h) Human Resources, (i) Information Technology, (j) Occupancy, (k) Residence Education, and (l) Student Behavior.

The individual domains and sub-domains were divided further into three separate service functions. These divisions identify how an individual may be involved with one or several knowledge domains throughout a career and how their functions within that domain may change. More specifically, it shows how someone begins with more operational responsibilities as an advancing-level employee, eventually transitioning into a supervisory or management role while continuing to build upon existing knowledge. These three levels are:

- **Direct Service Function:** Provide support and/or service directly to campus housing customers or other housing personnel.

- **Management Function:** Oversee the performance and/or operation of campus housing activities and/or personnel.

- **Strategy and Policy Function:** Establish and/or approve the plans to achieve the departmental goals or the organizational mission.

It is important to note while these knowledge domains and service functions may align with different positions in the housing organization, they are not selected nor organized in an effort to represent the housing program organizationally. Housing operations vary in responsibilities and in the staffing arrangements used to accomplish those responsibilities.

The following competencies address the responsibilities most pertinent to this publication: student conduct, conflict resolution, and community development.

STUDENT BEHAVIOR COMPETENCIES: STUDENT CONDUCT

Direct Service Function: Competencies

- Identify potential violations of codes, policies, and regulations.
- Document potential violations.
- Educate constituents about behavioral codes, policies, and regulations.
- Explain student conduct processes to constituents.
- Administer student conduct hearings when appropriate.
- Apply appropriate sanctions to those found in violation.
- Administer processes in a way that preserves individual dignity, protects individual and community rights, and fosters learning and development.
- Uphold governmental requirements and institutional policies regarding student conduct records protected by laws/regulations controlling access to information.
- Communicate outcome of student conduct process as required by institutional practices or legal requirements.
- Provide opportunities for student leadership and representation in student conduct processes when appropriate.

Direct Service Function: Knowledge Needed

- Departmental procedures for documenting constituent behavior or events
- Departmental community standards
- Institutional code of conduct, policies, and regulations
- Restorative justice/other methods of resolution
- Student development theory
- Sanctioning practices and options appropriate for various violations
- Cultural constructs in authority and dispute resolution

Management Function: Competencies

- Develop protocols for managing student conduct processes in the department that are consistent with institutional practices and legal requirements.
- Ensure student conduct processes abide by the established protocol.
- Communicate with experts outside residence life office when appropriate.
- Provide reports as required by departmental practice or when requested by others.
- Recognize when a conduct case should be referred to another professional outside the department.
- Assess the effectiveness of student conduct processes and policies in the department.

- Train staff on policies, regulations, and protocols related to student conduct administration.
- Create sanctions that are consistent with all laws and eviction policies.
- Educate student leader representatives about student conduct processes, departmental policies, ethical decision-making, legal issues, diversity, and cross-cultural communication approaches.
- Establish responsibilities of each staff role in enforcement and reporting.

Management Function: Knowledge Needed

- All items under "Direct Service"
- Departmental policies and regulations
- Governmental laws affecting residential community standards
- Industry best practices for addressing student behavior of concern
- Industry best practices for educating constituents about ethical decision-making, legal issues, diversity, and cross-cultural communication approaches
- Current trends and research in student behavior

Strategy and Policy Function: Competencies

- Formulate codes, policies, and regulations to ensure a safe and effective living and learning environment for occupants.
- Determine when codes, policies, and regulations should be developed or changed to address emerging issues.
- Ensure codes, policies, and regulations are consistent with institutional practices and legal requirements.
- Develop partnerships with offices/agencies outside of department when additional expertise is needed.
- Provide continued professional development with respect to awareness and education of best practices and legal requirements in the administration of student conduct processes.
- Ensure records retention and mandated reporting processes are in place and effective.
- Develop a marketing plan to communicate behavioral expectations, policies, codes, and regulations via the departmental website and social media platforms.
- Develop an appropriate appeals/grievance process.

Strategy and Policy Function: Knowledge Needed

- All items under "Management"

- Institutional code of conduct, policies, and regulations
- Legal requirements for student conduct processes
- External resources pertinent to student conduct
- Fair housing laws and evictions

STUDENT BEHAVIOR COMPETENCIES: CONFLICT RESOLUTION

Direct Service Function: Competencies

- Describe to constituents various approaches to conflict resolution.
- Mediate or facilitate conversations between conflicting parties in a way that preserves individual dignity, protects individual and community rights, and fosters learning and development.
- Document outcome of conflict resolution effort as required by institutional practices or legal requirements.
- Educate about sources, strategies, and resolution options for those who are in conflict.

Direct Service Function: Knowledge Needed

- Conflict resolution methods and approaches
- Facilitation and mediation processes
- Cross-cultural communication approaches
- Cultural constructs around authority and dispute resolution
- Provide reports as required by departmental practices or when requested by others
- Assess the effectiveness of conflict resolution processes and policies in the department
- Train staff on conflict resolution approaches and protocol

Management Function: Competencies

- Develop protocol(s) for managing conflict resolution processes in the department that are consistent with institutional practices and legal requirements.
- Ensure conflict resolution efforts abide by the established protocol.
- Determine when conflict resolution approaches should be used instead of traditional student conduct processes.
- Communicate with experts outside the department when appropriate.

Management Function: Knowledge Needed

- All items under "Direct Service"
- Institutional and legal requirements pertaining to conflict resolution practices
- Assessment methods
- Industry best practices for conflict resolution
- Current trends and research in conflict resolution
- Industry best practices for cross-cultural communication approaches

Strategy and Policy Function: Competencies

- Ensure conflict resolution practices are consistent with institutional practices and legal requirements.
- Develop partnerships with offices/agencies outside department when additional expertise is needed.
- Provide continued professional development with respect to awareness and education in conflict resolution practices.
- Engage in mediations and facilitations to stay current in skill development.
- Educate constituents on effective cross-cultural communication approaches.
- Communicate expected standards of behavior for those engaged in dispute resolution.

Strategy and Policy Function: Knowledge Needed

- All items under "Management"
- External resources pertinent to student conduct resolution
- Institutional code of conduct, policies, and regulations
- Legal requirements for conflict resolution processes
- Unique characteristics of specialized populations that may affect resolution efforts

---

RESIDENT EDUCATIONAL SERVICES: COMMUNITY DEVELOPMENT

Direct Service Function: Competencies

- Create environments for constituents that support community development goals.
- Promote the value of community development to constituents.
- Develop and implement programs for constituents which support educational goals.

- Provide a variety of small and large group social, educational, leadership, and involvement activities.
- Create environments which support student leadership and employment opportunities.
- Promote the values of social justice to constituents.

Direct Service Function: Knowledge Needed

- Departmental philosophy regarding community living and student engagement
- Benefits of community development
- Role of community development in student learning
- Campus culture pertaining to community development
- Basic tenets of counseling, advising, and community development

Management Function: Competencies

- Develop positional responsibilities that oversee goals of programming and community development.
- Train staff in how to create and promote activities that enhance the residential community.
- Assess the effectiveness of community development programs.
- Train staff on social justice principles.

Management Function: Knowledge Needed

- All items under "Direct Service"
- Student development theories and models, including those pertaining to underrepresented groups
- Social justice theories and models
- Assessment methodologies
- Training/facilitation methods

Strategy and Policy Function: Competencies

- Define overall goals of community development.
- Oversee and assess the philosophy, means, and rationale for campus and residential programming.
- Design or redesign community spaces.

Strategy and Policy Function: Knowledge Needed

- All items under "Management"
- Current research and trends affecting community development
- Institutional building/renovation policies and procedures

Adopted from ACUHO-I Core Competencies: The Body of Knowledge for Campus Housing Professionals *(2012), edited by Tony W. Cawthon, Pamela J. Schreiber, and associates. Used with permission.*

PREPARING STAFF FOR INTERNATIONAL·STUDENTS

Bob Alston

As increasing numbers of students travel abroad to pursue their degrees, campus housing and conduct departments must be prepared to meet their specific needs. Professionals should explore a variety of strategies to meet this goal, including simplifying policies, processes, and conversations for cases in which they interact with students who may not be cultural natives to the institution.

When international students arrive on U.S. campuses, American culture can be a new language all of its own, even if the student has had the opportunity to understand the spoken language. Certainly, many institutions have international student orientation programs to introduce the institution and assist in the transition to American college life. Some schools provide elective courses and even year-long extracurricular programs (Geary, 2016). Others may incorporate international students into broader new-student orientation programs.

In any case, students arrive, potentially without language alignment, and assuredly without cultural alignment. An international student arriving for their first semester is not only transitioning as a new college student, but also experiencing that adjustment in the larger transition to the new cultural setting.

Conduct officers and residential life staff can help international students adjust to the U.S. college experience in four primary ways: (1) establishing and maintaining a positive relationship with the international student support office, (2) translating ideas and language, (3) focusing on cultivating sense of place, and (4) keeping things simple.

International Student Support Offices

Building campus partnerships is an expected responsibility for any student affairs professional. Often, residential living staff members are practiced in this area since they are expected to create well-rounded experiences for their residents. Although student conduct professionals may connect with campus partners in different ways , they are also adept at creating and maintaining relationships to benefit the success of the student with whom they work.

To support international students' success, start with the experts: the international student support (ISS) office. The staff in ISS offices will know the most about the institution's students, and will most likely have resources to add to staff knowledge.

As with most campus partners, it is best to establish and maintain a relationship before needing to leverage that relationship. Doing so gives the conduct officer, or residence life staff member the opportunity to better connect with the main support for international students on campus, which can lead to proactive education opportunities for both. Of course, reaction to incidents can always be informed through these relationships as well. Specifically, if an international student is involved in a conduct situation, international student support staff will be able to provide context to the student's situation for consideration if you should have to levy sanctions.

If a student faces housing separation, for instance, and has an F1 visa, their visa status could be affected. In a similar vein, cultural norms may affect seemingly routine sanctions when they are assigned to international students. Sanctions like parental notifications may carry more or less impact when dealing with cultures that process and feel familial shame in different ways from modern American families. That means housing and conduct staff should consider sanctions carefully when working with international students, since some sanctions could be seen as more punitive than educational, and could have a disparate impact on an international student.

ISS staff also may have connections to students who have already become more adjusted to your institution. These more-experienced international students can be invaluable in facilitating peer-to-peer conversations, or when working to translate ideas and language.

Language and Ideas

According to Danielle Geary in her manuscript "How Do We Get People to Interact? International Students and the American Experience" that appeared in the *Journal of International Students,* "even if a student has a high level of classroom-based English skill, for example, it does not normally translate into language proficiency when immersed in an environment of regional linguistic expressions, colloquialisms, cultural jargon, and accents." One of the key ways to connect international students with the residence community, as well as the conduct process, is through translating policy language and American ideas.

One potential barrier that can be removed easily is that of the English language. Generally, an institution might expect to have varying levels of English proficiency within its international student population. Some schools may have intensive English programs, others may have developmental options, but in any case, international students' first challenge is using another language. Most residence life policies, or institutional codes of conduct, are dense collections of verbiage. Even American students can be challenged to understand the ins and outs of institutional policies. These comprehension challenges can be compounded for international students.

One example to consider is using relationships with the ISS to find people on campus who will help translate policies into languages most commonly understood by the institution's international student population. The student bill of rights or a similar statement could be a good place to start. The entire policy may not have to be translated, but key pieces could be to ensure the students' understanding of policies.

Another way to facilitate the translation of the student conduct process is to use infographics, flowcharts, and other visual aids to help explain particular concepts in a conduct meeting. Creating a diagram to show the spectrum of information and identifying points on the spectrum (i.e., reasonable suspicion, preponderance, clear and convincing, beyond a reasonable doubt, etc.) can help students see the different thresholds of proof. A visual representation of the student's process options can also help show students how the institution upholds their rights and provide the occasion to discuss those rights with a student who may be less-familiar with concepts like due process, as described in the U.S. Constitution.

One effective example of translation when working with international students is to collaborate with campus partners to translate the language, ideas, and concepts into a student's preferred language. At one institution, the staff members were fortunate to have a consistent group of international students from a particular country come through its intensive English program (IEP) and then move into its other academic offerings. Based on the relationships with the campus' ISS office, and on the strategic goals of the student conduct staff, a presentation was created about institutional rules, with a specific focus on consent education, for students about to graduate from the IEP program. Every incoming student at that institution was required to complete an online consent education module. The desire was to enhance that experience with an in-person session.

The institution was lucky to have its ISS office recommend a student who was older and well-respected in this cultural group, to be available to translate the complex language and ideas involved in explaining potential Title IX violations.

Cultivating Sense of Place

One element of acculturation for international students is redefining meanings of place after a geographical relocation. Fortunately for residence life professionals, helping students connect to their new community is already a goal. For some specific international students, researchers Elizabeth Terrazas-Carrillo, Ji Hong, and Terry Pace identified in a 2014 issue of *Journal of College Student Development* ("Adjusting to New Places: International Student Adjustment and Place Attachment"), three places that fostered the development of bonds to their new country: "places that facilitated social interaction, places experienced in congruence with the self, and places that allowed expression of individual emotional experiences."

While these places may intersect in the residential community, they are not always the first learning outcomes for a conduct process. Thus, when working with international student conduct, hearing officers should be mindful of how the process can affect students, especially by ostracizing or stigmatizing a student's behavior. While it is a fine line to walk, and identifying policy violations as part of the American college experience is problematic, the hearing officer should be careful not to make value judgments about the student's actions. Such value judgments can set barriers and boundaries between students and the community, instead of helping them navigate the issue as a way to get the student integrated more closely into the community.

Reframing an investigation conversation as an adjustment, instead of a correction, can support any student's desire to connect with the community more closely. While facilitating social interaction, self-discovery, and self-expression can help bond an international student to the residential community and the campus community at large, the conduct officer should be careful to approach international student conversations in a way that preserves their place in the community.

Keeping Things Simple

At Massasoit Community College in Brockton, Massachusetts, the student conduct staff was able to present to a group of incoming international students through a relationship cultivated with the international programs office. The new students arrived from many different countries, social structures, and cultures, and were arguably more overwhelmed than an American student coming through a first-year orientation program.

For the available hour, the choice was made to keep things simple. The staff prepared by identifying the top issues for which students were charged. Unsurprisingly, these issues were underage alcohol violations, controlled substance violations (including misuse of prescriptions), and residential policy violations. Based on this information, the group chose to focus the presentation on examples of alcohol consumption that would violate the code, examples of controlled substances and how they can be misused, and how to connect with residential living staff (or off-campus apartment staff) about community expectations.

When completing (or developing) training sessions like this example, it benefits student comprehension to build scaffolding for complex ideas. As an example, when explaining the concept of consent to a student, it's best to start small. Although staff members may want to explain that they are completing a demonstration first, they can start cementing the foundations with this exercise.

1. Ask any student in the room for a piece of paper, a pen, or bottle of water.

2. When you receive an item, ask the participants if they gave consent for you to have that item.

3. Next, take an item from a student in the room without permission.

4. Ask whether you had consent to have that item.

Most students can understand the concepts of possession and permission, so when teaching consent, that foundation is beneficial. Then, once those concepts are established, staff can share some of the more-nuanced elements of consent using a handshake exercise. (Check with the students in the room before completing this exercise, since cultural norms may dictate comfort levels with shaking hands.)

1. Ask the group if you can shake someone's hand.

2. When someone offers, shake hands as you normally would.

3. Check with the group to see if consent was given and received.

4. Next, attempt to shake the same person's hand again without asking.

5. Ask the group if consent was given or received, and explain that consent is required every time.

6. Next, ask someone in the room to shake hands. When you are about to connect, stop.

7. Ask the group about consent in that situation, and explain how it displays that consent can be revoked at any time.

Other variations could continue to further translation of the concept, but the core device remains the same: Build complex concept education from simpler parts to enhance understanding. Roommate mediations over shampoo use, community standard violations related to noise, and other code violations can also be translated by building from simple ideas.

Through examples like these and direct support of future relationship-building with institutional staff, the students left feeling more informed. While each of these presentations results in at least one "why is 21 the legal age of consumption?" conversation, colleagues in the international student support office say that the students claim to know more about the expectations of their new community as a result of such events.

By keeping things simple, cultivating a sense of place, translating ideas and language, and establishing and maintaining a positive relationship with the international student support office, residence life staff and conduct officers can support the success of international students in the community. Through supporting these needs in our communities, housing and conduct professionals can respect these students' layers of transition into institutions, be aware of the barriers that can leave them feeling ostracized, and build their understanding of how community members are valued at the institution.

Bob Alston is the assistant dean of students at Northern Kentucky University.

 **4.3** | EXERCISES

BEHIND CLOSED DOORS

*Patience Bryant, D. Matthew Gregory, and
Virginia Albanesco Koch*

The Behind Closed Doors (BCD) exercise provides resident assistants (RAs) with practical, hands-on experiential learning. In this exercise, actors portray familiar campus scenes, usually based on some conflict. RAs then negotiate the situation, drawing on campus policies and practices, as well as techniques they have been taught in previous sessions. On many campuses, the RAs describe BCD as one of the most-effective learning experiences of their training.

Much of the value of BCD comes from its mixture of foundational knowledge with its practical application. The scenarios are realistic and require students to use their RA knowledge and skills wisely and demonstrate sound judgment to resolve the scenarios successfully. Through direct participation and indirect, or vicarious, peer observation, new RAs rehearse and practice their knowledge and skills in a safe and nurturing learning environment.

The value is illustrated by the established learning outcomes of BCD drawn from Fink's taxonomy.

- **Foundational knowledge**
  - Know the responsibilities of the RA position.
  - Remember campus resources and be able to refer people appropriately.
  - Respond to a variety of crisis and emergency situations appropriately.
  - Identify a variety of safety and security concerns and address in a manner appropriate to the circumstances.
- **Application**
  - Hold oneself and others accountable for their own actions.
  - Respond effectively to unexpected experiences.
  - Analyze the needs of community members.
  - Identify inappropriate behaviors and respond accordingly.
  - Adapt one's behaviors, including verbal and non-verbal communication, appropriately to interact with diverse community members.
- **Integration**
  - Make decisions that are congruent with one's personal values and beliefs while considering the perspectives of others.
- **Human dimension**
  - Influence others in making positive and healthy choices.

- Interact respectfully and compassionately with others.
- Become more comfortable with the ambiguity of the RA role.
- **Caring**
  - Value and demonstrate care and concern for others.
  - Listen to others with respect.
- **Learning how to learn**
  - Exhibit self-reliant behavior, resilience, and persistence.
  - Learn from one's mistakes and experiences.

LOGISTICS

A number of resources focus on the logistics of the BCD exercise, and many campuses have modified them to fit their particular needs, staff size, available space, and other factors. However, each campus should try to integrate some basic elements to maximize the training process.

- Exercises often are done in actual residence hall rooms. Rooms should be spaced sufficiently so different groups do not distract each other.
- Professional and graduate staff should facilitate the exercise. They are responsible for managing time, as well as facilitating discussion, and will have received scripts for different scenarios in advance.
- Use returning RAs as actors in the scenarios. Having experienced this exercise before helps them create a safe and supportive learning environment for new staff. When volunteering for scenarios, RAs are encouraged to consider their comfort levels with the topics and their personal experiences in relation to a scenario.
- It is the actor's responsibility to make the scenarios as realistic as possible. The goal is to provide the appropriate levels of challenge and support to incoming RAs and build their confidence without intimidating them. A facilitator who believes that an actor is overacting or stretching the limits of the scenario should ask the actor to revise the performance. Remember, no hazing!
- Campus partners (e.g., campus police, counseling center, women's center, and health promotion and wellness staff, etc.) are often present during parts or all of the BCD activity. Actors are to defer to campus partner staff when questions arise related to policy and procedures.
- The scenario scripts include a list of characters, props that might be needed, and a short description of the scene and issue to be addressed. Facilitators and actors receive these in advance so they can prepare.
- When providing prior information for the RAs in the exercise, facilitators should only read the *underlined* portion of the script. The other details are to be used by the actors as they prepare their scene.
- Each scenario should allow for three to five minutes for the scenario followed by 10 to 11 minutes of discussion and one minute of feedback.

DISCUSSION AND DEBRIEFING PROCESS

At the conclusion of each scenario, the facilitator will lead a debriefing process. In this process, they should ask the RAs who interacted in the scenario to describe what occurred in the scenario, as well as what worked well and what did not. They also should ask the actors for feedback about what the RAs did well and what could they take away from the experience. Additional debriefing questions could include:

- What happened in this scenario?
- What strategies worked well? What didn't?
- What policy violations (if any) occurred in this scenario?
- What advice returners and other observers have for the RAs?

Ask the RA observers and campus partner representatives for their FIDeLity feedback: Frequent, Immediate, and Discriminating (that is, based on clear criteria and standards), and delivered Lovingly (or supportively). By using the FIDeLity feedback method during Behind Closed Doors, students and supervisors can practice giving feedback in a highly discriminating manner that is both immediate and frequent.

Many housing and residence life staff members will be called on to use this approach throughout their careers. The expectation that feedback is provided in a supportive or loving manner cannot be overstated. "When there is empathy, personal understanding, and love, students are more likely to open up and internalize the multiple meanings of feedback in a fuller way" (Fink, 2013, p. 106). Since BCD occurs over multiple days, there will be time to see new RAs strengthen their abilities. Encourage student growth through appropriate levels of challenge and support. Fink adds, "when other students, the teacher, or external assessors compliment learners on their success in learning, they provide a powerful incentive to continue learning and to continue improving (p. 108)."

BCD SCENARIOS: EMOTIONAL AND MENTAL HEALTH

Roommate Problem

Characters: 2 students
Props: None

You are conducting duty rounds and hear two roommates arguing loudly. These roommates are both first-year students and until now, seemed to be getting along. When you arrive at the room, you find one roommate accusing the other of stealing some personal belonging. The roommates are of different ethnic backgrounds and there is much tension between them at the moment.

Severely Depressed Resident

Characters: 2 students
Props: None

You just received a text message from a resident's parent saying they got a desperate text from your resident, but did not see it until now (4 hours later) and are very concerned. From conversations in the past, you know that the resident has their heart set on going to medical school. When you go to the resident's room, you find their roommate outside the locked door, trying to get in. The roommate said they have been talking to the resident through the door for about 15 minutes, but the resident won't let the roommate get in the room. The resident, who is usually social, has become withdrawn and quiet lately. The roommate said that this morning, the resident seemed to take a turn for the worse. You learn that the apparently depressed resident has just learned about failing an exam.

Resident With an Eating Disorder

Characters: 2 residents
Props: None

A resident comes to you, concerned about a neighbor who is a first-year student. The resident doesn't know the student very well, but has seen this person in the bathroom vomiting after meals. The resident is a member of a sports team and seems obsessive about exercise and diet.

Disappointed by Sorority Recruitment Outcome

Characters: 1 resident
Props: None

It is sorority bid day — the day your residents learn which Panhellenic sororities have chosen them. You are walking down the hall, and you hear one of your residents crying. She has learned that she did not get into the sorority of her choice and is devastated. She has been talking about joining this organization since she moved in and was certain she would get a bid.

Relationship Violence

Characters: 2 same-gender residents who have been dating, 1 concerned neighbor
Props: None

Two residents in your building have been dating since freshman year. Both are sophomores. They have what some students who know them call a tumultuous relationship. There is a rumored history of abuse against one another, and the relationship seems to have been escalating negatively lately as academic and personal pressures pile on them.

Resident Attempts Suicide

Characters: 2 residents
Props: Several empty pill bottles

You are in your room when a resident knocks on your door and says that her room-mate has locked her out of the room and is not responding to their knocking. The resident is certain that the roommate is still in the room and is worried because they have been depressed lately but didn't want the roommate to say anything to anyone. The RA enters the room to find the student is unresponsive but breathing. An empty pill bottle is on the student's desk.

Failing an Exam

Characters: 1 resident
Props: None

You are walking to your room after class when you see one of your residents crying in the lounge. They have just failed an exam that will severely affect their grade in the class. This class is a prerequisite for their major. The resident is a first-generation student and is struggling to adjust to college.

Relationship Break-up

Characters: 2 residents
Props: None

You are on rounds when you hear yelling coming from a student room. You knock on the door to make sure everything is okay. Two residents who have been dating for several months are fighting. When you knock, one of the residents storms out of the room and yells, "It is over!" The couple has just broken up, and the resident is upset.

BCD SCENARIOS: ALCOHOL AND OTHER DRUG MEDICAL EMERGENCY

Smoking Marijuana in Student Room

Characters: 3–4 students in a room (two people smoking, the others not)
Props: Rolled paper to look like joints, a rolled-up towel near the door

It is 10:30 on a Friday night and you are completing rounds on your floor when you smell what you suspect to be marijuana coming from a room. You knock on the door of the room you believe is the source of the smell. Smoking marijuana is not legal where your institution is located. As the door opens, you see what appears to be the objects used for smoking marijuana, in addition to the room being full of smoke. Only two of the students in the room are smoking marijuana.

Snapchat Party

Characters: 2 resident students
Props: Alcohol bottles

You see a SnapChat message about two residents having lots of alcohol and an invitation for everyone to come to their room. You are stunned — you would not expect these two residents to do such a thing. They must have forgotten that you follow them on SnapChat. You go to their room to see what's up.

Intoxicated Resident

Characters: Several students trying to carry a resident up the stairs to her room
Props: None

You are on rounds and see a group of students walking down the hallway. They are carrying a resident who is unable to walk without assistance. The resident has vomit on their shirt and their speech is slurred.

Emergency Medical Situation

Characters: 2 students
Props: Something red to simulate blood

You are walking down the hall when a resident runs up to you and asks you to come to their room quickly. Their roommate is on the floor of the room having a seizure of unknown cause. There is blood coming from a deep cut on the roomate's head.

Loud Party With Alcohol

Characters: Several partying students and an RA who is present at the party
Props: Beer cans, cups, boom box

As you are making rounds of the building, you hear loud music and laughter coming from a room at the end of the hall. The door is open as you approach the room and you notice that people inside appear intoxicated. One student is hostile and does not comply with your requests to keep quiet, get rid of the alcohol, etc. One of the students openly complains that there is "nothing to do but drink around here."

Prescription Drug Misuse

Characters: 2 students studying in the lounge
Props: Books, laptops, prescription pill bottle

You walk by two students studying and overhear one offer to give the other a couple of Adderall to help them study for a test. You do not see any pills exchange hands.

Beer Pong (With all Residents Over 21)

Characters: 3–4 students in the room, all older than 21
Props: Makeshift beer pong table with cups

You hear loud sounds of cheering and laughter coming from a room early one evening. You knock on the door and hear "Shhhh" and sounds of scuffling inside. When the door opens, you see the cups of beer and the beer pong drinking game set up.

Resident's 21st-birthday Celebration

Characters: 3 students doing shots to celebrate the birthday of a student. One student is 21 years old, the other is 20, and the third is celebrating their 21st birthday.
Props: Shot glasses, bottle

It's 11:55 p.m. You are walking down the hall and hear loud music and cheering coming from the room next to yours. You know it is your resident's birthday and you are curious to see what the students in the room are up to.

BCD SCENARIOS: COMMUNITY

Theft

Characters: Resident and 2 friends
Props: Cellphone and an earring box

You are on rounds when approached in the hall by a frantic resident. Her two friends are with her and she is talking with her mom on the phone. The resident claims that her roommate stole her earrings. The resident has no proof, other than generalizations about her roommate's upbringing. On the phone, the resident's mother makes remarks like, "You have no idea what a person like that will do when they see a pair of $1,000 diamond earrings." The resident demands that the RA search the room and call the police. The resident also belittles the RA for their lack of ability to do anything that can help them. The resident says that her mother wants to talk with the RA immediately.

Harassed Student

Characters: 2 residents
Props: Homophobic and threatening graffiti on the door of a resident's room (use signs taped to the door)

A resident comes to you saying that their next door neighbor came home to find graffiti on their door. The resident privately disclosed to you that they are gay, but have not come out to anyone yet. The resident is now in their room crying and won't let anyone in.

Noisy Neighbors (No Alcohol Involved)

Characters: 2 residents
Props: Music speakers and signs to note a damaged chair and that screen is out of the window

You are on duty and as you walk onto the fourth floor, you hear music and loud laughter. Before you even reach the door, you know from which room the noise is coming. Many of your fellow RAs have had problems with this room for noise, as well as putting trash in the hallways. As the door opens, you notice a window screen has been removed, and there is obvious damage to one of the university chairs.

Hall Sports (No Alcohol Involved)

Characters: 3 residents
Props: Water guns

You are walking through your floor after quiet hours have started. Someone sprays you with water — three students are having a water-gun fight in the hallway after quiet hours. They are loud and rowdy, and appear to be having a great time.

Active Shooter

Characters: 3–4 residents
Props: Cellphone

There is an active shooter on campus. The entire campus is on lockdown. You are walking around the second floor of your residence hall and you find panicked residents in the lounge. Another resident wants to climb out a window onto the roof to get a better look at what is happening. During the scenario, a third resident receives some text messages from a friend who is at the location where the shooting is taking place. (Actor's note: This scenario can get chaotic; do not overact.)

Staff Member Integrity Issue

Characters: 1 RA
Props: None

Last night, when you returned from studying, you notice that your duty signs from the previous night are still up. You attempted to contact the RA on duty and they answered. This morning, you talk to the RA who was supposed to be on duty the previous night about what happened.

Room Change

Characters: 1 resident
Props: None

While on duty, you receive a call on the duty phone from a student who is upset. The student claims that a mistake has been made because they can't get into their room. You have limited information about why the student does not have their room key. It turns out that the student is displeased with their housing assignment from the waitlist and has moved their belongings to an empty double room on the floor without permission and demands the keys to it. The student is hostile as the confrontation escalates, insisting that as a junior, they should be able to have the open double room as a single.

Person Behaving Suspiciously

Characters: 3–4 residents
Props: None

Residents have begun to prop doors open to each floor to encourage community. They often let non-residents follow them onto the floor to visit friends. The RA has talked to residents on several occasions about the safety issue of propping open hallway doors. A resident comes to the RA saying that an unknown male entered her room but left immediately when she woke up. In addition, other unknown males have been seen in the female restrooms.

RESOURCE

CONDUCT AND COMMUNITY COMPETENCIES FOR RESIDENT ASSISTANTS

In his book, *Student Learning in College Residence Halls: What Works, What Doesn't, and Why* (Jossey-Bass, 2015), Gregory Blimling identifies 11 skill-based educational competencies that resident assistants should possess. Here are brief descriptions of each skill, as well as a listing of select knowledge and abilities specifically related to the housing conduct process.

1. **Helping.** Recognize students in need of assistance and connect them to professionals who can assist further. Provide emotional support to students with less-severe emotional challenges and those struggling with the routine stresses of college life.

2. **Crisis management.** Have knowledge and training to respond appropriately when a student is in crisis or there is a threat to student safety.

3. **Conflict resolution.** Resolve as much conflict between students as possible, recognizing that some conflicts will require the intervention of professional staff with more training and skills.

4. **Multicultural.** Treat all students fairly and show every student the same courtesy and friendship while addressing the disrespectful behavior of others.

5. **Administrative.** Manage the administrative tasks necessary to operate a residence hall.

6. **Resource.** Help students navigate institutional offices, policies, and procedures.

7. **Problem-solving.** Use knowledge of institutional resources and systematic analysis to provide perspective and help students resolve personal, financial, academic, or family problems.

8. **Leadership.** Inspire students and put the interests of residents and the housing and residence life program ahead of self-interests.

9. **Educational.** Lead programs, organize group activities, develop community, connect students with educational resources, stimulate discus-

sions, and create opportunities for students to interact and learn from one another.

10. **Relationship.** Enjoy personal interaction and convey a sense of warmth and approachability.

11. **Technology.** Communicate using contemporary electronic communication and be knowledgeable enough to provide basic help to students.

Material adopted by Patience Bryant, D. Matthew Gregory, and Virginia Albaneso Koch from Student Learning in College Residence Halls: What Works, What Doesn't, and Why *(Jossey-Bass, 2015) by Gregory Blimling (p. 169–176).*

6.1 | EXERCISE

PRACTICAL APPLICATIONS OF SOCIAL JUSTICE PRINCIPLES

Jill L. Creighton and Kateeka Harris

The following examples serve as a facilitator's guide to three practical exercises a student conduct team or residence life team can apply in a staff training. We present these through a lens of cultural humility — a concept that goes one step further than cultural competency. No one can become culturally competent in a lifetime; there simply are too many cultures and too many components to understand fully, and there is an accompanying risk of cultural appropriation in the process. Cultural humility is a framework with which to approach intentional inclusion.

As Melanie Tervalon and Jean Murray-Garcia wrote in the *Journal of Health Care for the Poor and Underserved,* "cultural humility incorporates a lifelong commitment to self-evaluation and self-critique, to redressing the power imbalances." Essentially, cultural humility asks the individual to focus on their own internalized identities and biases. Through that awareness, professionals can begin to address inequities in their work and their systems.

This collection is not intended to be a complete guide to intentional inclusion. Rather, it is only a starting point. These exercises encourage both self-reflection and introspection, as well as provide a framework to initiate dialogue among staff teams. Through these exploratory activities, program managers can begin conversations and work to examine systems in holistic contexts.

These exercises should not serve as the only resources or readings on social justice, cultural humility, diversity, and intentional inclusion. Professionals should be encouraged to dive deeper into the available literature on this topic.

DROP THE CARD

This exercise encourages participants to consider the intersectionality of identity as it relates to a person's overall identity. It aims to illustrate the complexity and harm of being asked to identify as only one component of ourselves. The exercise should take 30–45 minutes to complete, depending on group size.

Supplies

- One package of 3" x 5" index cards
- One pen or pencil per participant

Instructions

STEP 1. Provide each participant with five index cards. Instruct the participants to think about five salient characteristics that describe their identity. For example, gender, racial, ethnic, familial, ability status, etc. Allow participants at least five to seven minutes to reflect and write one identity on each index card.

STEP 2. Once the participants have documented their identity characteristics, invite them to share their five characteristics with the group and why they chose them. (Depending on the size of the group, allow at least three to five people to share.)

STEP 3. Once participants have shared their responses, ask each participant to select one card to drop, thereby sacrificing that salient identity. Ask some participants which card they chose to drop and why. Continue until each participant has one last card. The facilitator may notice throughout this process that "dropping" an identity becomes more difficult and may result in participants experiencing difficult emotions around having to choose between identities.

STEP 4. When the last card is reached, or throughout the exercise, use these questions to prompt reflection and dialogue in the group.
- Which card did you hold onto and why?
- What did it feel like to have let go of all but one of your cards?
- Was it difficult to choose which card to keep?

STEP 5. Use these questions to debrief participants in the exercise.
- What would it be like to have to move through life limited to only one of the five identity characteristics you wrote down?
  - o What would that feel like?
  - o What are some of the challenges you can anticipate?
- How does this exercise apply to work with students?
- How do our systems in higher education force students to choose just one identity?
  - o How can we change those systems?
- What action steps can be taken in work to embrace and celebrate intersectional identity?

STEP 6. Conclude the discussion by reminding participants what it felt like to have to let go of aspects of their identity. Remind participants authenticity requires including one's full self.

PRIVILEGE BEADS

This exercise explores ways in which different social identity groups in the United States enjoy privileges. This exercise is not meant to make participants feel guilty or ashamed of their/zir privilege or lack of privilege related to any social identity categories. Rather, the exercise seeks to highlight the fact everyone has *some* privilege, even as some people have more privilege than others. By illuminating various privileges as individuals, participants can recognize ways that privileges can be used individually and collectively to work for equity and social justice.

These lists are not meant to be exhaustive or comprehensive. Participants may think of other items that might be appropriate to include. However, the purpose of the exercise is to offer and discuss possible points of privilege that arise from being a member of certain social identity groups in the United States and to invite participants to reflect on the concept of privilege and ways privileges overlap.

Materials

- Privilege lists (see below)
- Small beads of assorted colors
- Small bowls or cups to hold beads
- A 3 oz. disposable cup for each participant
- Cord or twine for stringing beads (optional)

Setup

1. Create seven bead stations around the room, spacing them out so multiple participants can stand around each station.

2. Place one or two bowls of multicolored beads at each station.

3. Post two or three copies of each privilege list at each station so multiple participants can read them. This is to make it possible to move participants through all stations quickly and easily. Adjust as needed to your room's layout.

4. Explain the purpose of the exercise. Suggested talking points:
    a. We're going to explore our privilege as related to various social identities. Privilege refers to ways individuals or groups can enjoy advantages based on their real or perceived membership in identity categories (e.g., gender, race, sexuality, nationality, religion, etc.).
    b. This exercise is not meant to make anyone feel guilty or ashamed of having or not having particular privileges, but rather to explore how we all have some privilege, and therefore explore how to engage that aspect of our life.

     c.   We believe it is critical for everyone to reflect on privilege in this way to use our individual and collective privilege for equity and social justice.

     d.   Focus only on your own experience.

5. Provide each participant with a cup in which they will place their beads.

Instructions

1. Ask participants not to talk during this phase of the exercise.

2. Identify the stations around the room and provide instructions.

     a.   Each station has a list of seven statements related to a specific social identity.

     b.   Each statement describes one possible example of privilege related to that category's system of oppression and privilege; that is, the likelihood an individual might experience an advantage or a disadvantage.

     c.   Note that neither the stations nor the statements are meant to be exhaustive or comprehensive. They are meant to be a sampling and a starting point for discussion given a limited time.

     d.   Note participants may think of other categories to include or may contest some of the items. They should not over-analyze the statements since the goal is to begin reflection and discussion.

3. Participants visit each station and read every item on each list. For every answer on the list to which the participant can answer yes, they take one bead. If their answer is no, they do not take a bead. When finished with every list, participants will have a set of beads representing their composite of privileges.

     a.   Note each list is meant to focus on participants' current life status. This may mean the participants haven't always enjoyed the privileges they can identify currently, or that they may have less privilege in a category than they once did.

     b.   The facilitator should do a demonstration with one full list. It is recommended to do so with a list for which they will answer yes to most, if not all, of the options.

4. As participants finish collecting beads, provide them with a length of string and invite them to make some jewelry or accessory for themselves with their beads. However, let them know this is optional; they do not have to use all of their beads if they decide to make an accessory. They can continue crafting once discussion begins, as long as they engage in the discussion as well.

Discussion Suggestions

Before starting the group discussion, note the bead selection was based on our current experience here (in the United States, in college, etc.) and now, as opposed to where participants, their families, or others of their identity group have been before. Some identities and privileges can and do change over time, for better or worse. Also, note if the conversation about any question must be cut off due to time constraints, emphasize the activity is meant to begin larger conversations.

1. Invite participants to reflect about what it was like to focus on privilege and advantage, rather than on oppression or disadvantage as is often done in diversity activities. Was it a new experience? Was it comfortable? Was it enlightening? How did it feel?

2. Why is it important to be aware of privilege as an aspect of identity and experience? Why don't we (have to) attend to it on a regular basis?

3. What does it mean to have multiple, intersecting identities, where we experience some privileges (through some identities) as well as some oppression (through others)? What insight can this give us in connecting with others — being patient and generous with them and ourselves? holding ourselves and others responsible for our actions? being allies or advocates?

4. What identities (systems of privilege) are not represented here today? If they had been, how would that affect the bead collection?

5. We asked you to turn your beads into something wearable. What would it mean for you to wear this noticeably for the rest of the day? What messages could others take from your set of beads? How noticeable, to us and others, are our privileges on a daily basis? Can we — and how do we — hide (deny, justify, or ignore) our privilege on a daily basis?

6. What does the collective privilege here mean for us as individual leaders? What does it mean for collaboration in our workplaces, campuses, or communities?

7. Consider concluding by asking participants to commit to acting on what they have experienced. Ask for volunteers to state their commitment and consider offering something that you will do. Suggestions include:
   a. Continue to learn about privilege and power.
   b. Hold yourself accountable (in a loving way).
   c. Create opportunities for dialogue.
   d. Request or provide training/professional development.
   e. Educate others in your sphere of influence.
   f. Strive for equitable structural change.
   g. Speak up about (but not for) people who might be disadvantaged.
   h. Share (with interested others) your experiences regarding privilege and disadvantage.

Privilege Checklists

For this exercise, the facilitator will create individual checklists that include the privilege and multiple examples of how that privilege can manifest itself as listed. The lists can be revised as needed to tailor them to a particular event. The facilitator may laminate the sheets.

- Sexuality Privilege

  - I have formalized or could formalize my love relationship legally through marriage.
  - I can move about in public without fear of being harassed or physically attacked because of my sexual identity.
  - I do not have to fear negative consequences if my co-workers find out about my sexual identity.
  - If I want to, I can easily find a religious community that welcomes people of my sexual identity.
  - No one questions the "normality" of my sexuality.
  - People don't ask me why I "chose" my sexual identity.
  - I easily can find sex education literature about my sexual identity.

- Ability Privilege

  - I can assume that I will easily have physical access to any building.
  - I have never been taunted, teased, or ostracized due to a disability.
  - I can do well in a challenging situation without being told I am an inspiration because of my ability status.
  - I can go shopping alone and expect to find appropriate accommodations to make the experience hassle-free.
  - I do not have to request accommodations due to my ability status.
  - If I am not hired for a job, I do not question whether it was due to my physical or mental ability.
  - Other people do not think that my mental ability is limited because of my physical ability.

- Gender/Sex Privilege

  - If I have children and a successful career, few people will ask me how I balance work and home.
  - I do not have to think about the message my wardrobe sends about my sexual availability.
  - I never worry about being recognized as the sex/gender with which I identify.
  - A decision to hire me will never be based on assumptions about whether I might plan to have a family soon.

- I am less likely to be sexually harassed at work than people of other gender identities.
- In general, I am not under much pressure to be thin or to worry about how people will respond to me if I'm overweight.
- Major religions in the world are led mainly by people of my sex.

- Race Privilege

  - Mainstream media routinely depict people of my race/ethnicity in a wide range of roles.
  - Children in my racial/ethnic group do not have to be educated about systemic racism for their daily physical safety.
  - I can be sure that if I need legal or medical help, my race/ethnicity will not work against me.
  - I can take a job without people thinking I was hired only because of my race/ethnicity.
  - I can do well in a challenging situation without being called a credit to my race/ethnicity.
  - I am never asked to speak for all the people of my racial/ethnic group.
  - I can go shopping without concern that store employees will monitor me because of my race/ethnicity.

- Religious Privilege

  - I can assume that I will not have to work or go to school on my religious holidays.
  - I can be sure that mainstream media will celebrate the holidays of my religion.
  - My religious views are reflected by the majority of government officials and political candidates.
  - Food that honors my religious practices can be easily found in any restaurant or grocery store.
  - Places to worship or practice my religion are numerous in my community.
  - Most people do not consider my religious practices to be "weird."
  - I do not need to worry about negative consequences of disclosing my religious identity to others.

- Class Privilege

  - I can be sure that my social class will be an advantage when I seek medical or legal help.
  - I am fairly certain that I will not have to skip meals because I cannot afford to eat.

- I have a savings account with at least a month's expenses in case of emergency.
- In case of a medical emergency, I won't have to decide against visiting a doctor or a hospital due to economic reasons.
- I don't have to rely on public transportation; I can afford my own vehicle.
- My neighborhood is relatively free of obvious drug use, prostitution, and violent crime.
- Most experts appearing in mass media seem to be from my social class.

- Nationality/Citizenship Privilege (U.S.)

  - If I apply for a job, my legal right to work in this country probably will not be questioned.
  - I will never be denied housing in the United States due to my citizenship.
  - I can go into any bank and establish a checking account without fear of discrimination because of my nationality/citizenship.
  - I can be reasonably sure that if I need legal or medical assistance, my citizenship status will not matter.
  - I do not fear that my employer will threaten me with deportation.
  - If I wanted to, I could travel freely to almost any country and be admitted back into the United States.
  - If I were a victim of a crime, I wouldn't think twice about seeking police assistance due to my citizenship status.

EXPLORING LANGUAGE

For this exercise, participants are asked to find definitions for the words "prejudice," "discrimination," "racism," "sexism," and "homophobia." Definitions for each word should come from two sources: the person's existing understanding and a scholarly source.

Divide the participants into groups of six to 10 people to ensure everyone will have ample chance to participate. Each group's facilitator will begin the session by having each participant share their definition of prejudice. The group will proceed with the rest of the definitions attempting, if possible, to reach a consensus on one definition for each word. (Rarely will the group agree on one definition.) All definitions should be discussed. When small groups are finished, bring everyone back together for a final discussion.

The objectives are:

- To help participants understand these five words and explore the intricacies and implications of different definitions for each word.

- To help participants learn to appreciate the importance of language in discussing multicultural and social justice issues, and how the process of discussing the definitions adds to understanding the terms.

Facilitator Notes

1. Use these definitions
   a. Prejudice: an attitude about another person or group of people based on stereotypes.
   b. Discrimination: an action or behavior based on prejudice.
   c. Racism: the systemic conditions that give some people more-consistent and easier access to opportunities based on (perceived) race or ethnicity.
   d. Sexism: the systemic conditions that give some people more-consistent and easier access to opportunities based on (perceived) sex, gender, or gender expression.
   e. Homophobia: the systemic conditions that provide some people more consistent and easier access to opportunities based on (perceived) sexual orientation.

2. An issue that arises regularly is prejudice and discrimination can be positive. ("I am prejudiced toward my children; I am a discriminating eater.") It is important to note when these issues are discussed in the context of social justice, a prejudice toward somebody is matched by an equal prejudice against somebody else.

According to these definitions, anyone can be racist or sexist. It is vital to bring the issue of power into the discussion. For example, a definition of racism might be "prejudice or discrimination based on race, plus the power to enforce it." In that case, in the U.S., only men can be sexist and only white people can be racist. This perspective has a major impact on people, and some respond by insisting that the "other" group can be as racist as her or his group. This response provides an important opportunity to differentiate between an individual-focused basis of racism (which gives privilege to the current power structure by ignoring systemic conditions) and an institutional-focused basis.

1. Some people might not be familiar with the term "heterosexism." Ask students to consider the "phobia" framing of the more common term, "homophobia." This can lead to other strands of discussion, such as who has power over language, the evolution of language, and so on.

2. Spend a lot of time on power. Many participants will have a hard time understanding it. Talk about individual acts of racism, which may be done by anyone, as opposed to institutional acts of racism, which involve economic, class, and social factors that all add up to power. Some groups

in the U.S. do not have the political, economic, or social power to be racist on an institutional level. It is important to acknowledge we all have personal power and how we exercise it is very important. Do we stand up for the right things? Who gets to make the rules and whom do those rules benefit (this is a question of institutional power)?

3. The major point of this activity is to get people talking about these terms and realizing different people mean different things even though they are using the same words. How does the way we are socialized to relate to these terms inform the ways we imagine they might be made more clear?

4. Mention how we go to the dictionary when we don't know the meaning of a word and accept its definition as truth. Challenge people to look up definitions for "black" and "white" and notice the connotations.

References

Tervalon, M., & Murray-García, J. (1998). Cultural humility versus cultural competence: a critical distinction in defining physician training outcomes in multicultural education. *Journal of Health Care for the Poor and Underserved, 9*(20), 117–125.

Drop the Card exercise adapted and provided with permission from Aura Consulting Agency (2015). Privilege Bead exercise lightly modified by Brenda J. Allen and Thomas Walker and provided with permission. Exploring Language exercise created by Paul C. Gorski for the Equity Literacy Institute and EdChange (educhange.org.), and used with permission.

6.2 | INSIGHTS

PROMISING PRACTICES FOR SOCIAL JUSTICE

Mallory Martin-Ferguson, Delmy M. Lendof, and Denise Balfour Simpson

The following examples demonstrate a sample of socially-just student conduct policies, practices, programs, and services. While this is far from an exhaustive list, these colleges and universities are examples of how institutions can make a conscious step toward serving the inclusive needs of their campus communities. This section is meant to initiate and continue dialogue about models and practices from across the country to further develop inclusive student conduct models on college campuses across the country. While no campus is perfect, and no two campuses will develop policies, practices, programs, and services in the same way, the hope is to move all student conduct practice one step further in developing socially just campuses for all.

University of Michigan Spectrum Model

The University of Michigan is a large public research school that is home to more than 44,000 students. Its Office for Student Conflict Resolution (OSCR) oversees a Statement of Student Rights and Responsibilities and uses a spectrum model that makes multiple methods of conflict resolution available to students, based on behavioral concerns, complexity, and the unique needs of the student. That gives the school a process that best suits a student's needs. This adaptable approach to conflict resolution is a key component of OSCR's mission to "Build trust, promote justice, and teach peace." OSCR uses a team of student staff to facilitate intake meetings and other processes with their peers.

University housing also uses the Community Living at Michigan expectations with the 11,000 residential students on campus (graduate and undergraduate), and focuses on a restorative approach to student conduct meetings. Housing also has a Community Circle program that brings together students who have been involved in or affected by an incident in a group setting to share what happened and determine together what can be done to make things right. OSCR and Housing have worked to create a Commitment to Collaborate document that describes the shared values of restorative justice, social justice, and community to adhere to in case management and follow up, as evidenced in this excerpt.

> We share a commitment to exercising our responsibilities through a social justice lens. We make conscious efforts to be aware of how social

identities and other social justice issues may surface during our respective processes. We see our work as directly advancing a social justice agenda.

We voice a preference for the use of adaptable conflict resolution processes to be used to resolve conflicts peacefully wherever possible while acknowledging the desirability and the need for formal conflict resolution should the circumstances or the parties require it.

We are committed to the philosophy and practice of restorative justice and to using restorative justice principles in our work. We intentionally and consciously employ restorative justice, particularly when partnering with respondents (accused students) to help them understand both the harm their actions caused and the opportunity to repair that harm. We acknowledge a role for individual community members who were adversely impacted.

More information about OSCR and Housing can be found at *https://oscr.umich. edu/article/adaptable-conflict-resolution-acr and http://housing.umich.edu/*.

Skidmore College Campus Restorative Justice

Restorative justice practices inform most of the student conduct practices at Skidmore College, a private liberal arts college that serves approximately 2,600 students. Harmed parties, students who have accepted responsibility for violating the Code of Conduct, and others wanting to hold students accountable engage in a collaborative decision-making process that aims to resolve the harm and repair the community. Students, faculty, and staff are trained in Skidmore's restorative practices. Details about Skidmore College's restorative justice program can be found at *http://www.skidmore.edu/student_handbook/social-conduct. php#code*.

University of Kentucky Code of Student Conduct and Citizens Police Academy

The University of Kentucky is a four-year public institution that serves almost 10,000 residential students. The Office of Student Conduct administers the Code of Student Conduct and works collaboratively with the Office of Residential Life and faculty, staff, and students to facilitate the student conduct process.

Through the recommendations of a university alcohol and other drug task force, the Division of Student Affairs was challenged to look for new ways to develop and improve campus community partnerships, and educate students about civility, interpersonal relationships, and healthy alcohol and drug use. This led to a revision of the Code of Student Conduct to reflect new ways to partner with students to address policy violations and alternatives to traditional student conduct processes. The revised code now includes a procedural resolution option of alternative conflict resolution processes (e.g., mediation, restorative conferences, restorative justice circles) and an all-student hearing board to resolve incidents involving any registered student organization.

From this, the Office of Student Conduct unveiled a series of trainings for hearing boards, offering conflict coaching skills for advising students through resolving conflict on their own; restorative justice circles to resolve harms to the community collaboratively; and facilitator training to provide support on, resolve, and debrief conflicts outside the student conduct process. The goal of the updated code is to continue to move the campus toward a healthier climate of accountability and conflict resolution in inclusive ways.

The UKPD Citizens Police Academy is designed to foster a more-inclusive relationship between law enforcement and the campus community. Participants become more familiar with police practices, and the academy is used as an opportunity to break down barriers, build trust, and discuss topics related to protecting student safety and providing student care. UKPD officers also collaborate with the Office of Student Conduct and Office of Residential Life on programming and outreach to students related to social justice topics.

Details regarding the Code of Student Conduct at the University of Kentucky can be found at *http://www.uky.edu/studentconduct/*. Information about the UKPD Citizens Police Academy can be obtained at *http://www.uky.edu/Police/citizensacademy.html*.

University of Alberta Residence Community Standards

The University of Alberta is a public research university in Edmonton, Alberta, Canada, that serves more than 30,000 students. Residence Services "values dignity, respect, safety, equity, learning, and community" in the residence halls (University of Alberta, 2018). When misconduct occurs in the residential community, Residence Services provides three processes to address this behavior: the residence community standards, residence agreement, and code of student conduct.

The residence community standards are rooted in restorative justice principles with the goal of residents working together to improve their residential community and hold each other accountable. When harms occur in the community, students are brought together to participate in either community resolution or a restorative meeting, both of which involve resident assistants serving as coaches to assist students in resolving their own conflicts or facilitating dialogue between parties to address and repair the harm. Professional staff members are only involved if the incident involves a pattern of behavior or a breach of the residence contract or Code of Student Behavior.

Information about the Office of Residence Services and the Residence Community Standards can be found at *https://www.residence.ualberta.ca/current-residents/community-standards*.

Colorado State University Restorative Justice Program

Colorado State University is a public institution in Fort Collins, Colorado, that serves more than 30,000 students. The Student Resolution Center "encourages students to gain awareness, knowledge, skills, and opportunities as they navigate challenges and make informed decisions." The office "promote(s) safe, respectful, and inclusive communities by valuing integrity, perspective-taking, and personal responsibility."

Specifically, CSU has a restorative justice program that allows students to seek out a process to resolve conflict that also allows other campus community members to serve as active participants in the process. Materials about the restorative justice program at Colorado State University can be found at *https://resolutioncenter.colostate.edu/conduct-services/*.

Rutgers University Negotiation and Conflict Resolution Services

Within a large public research university in the state of New Jersey that serves more than 65,000 students, the Center for Negotiation and Conflict Resolution offers a spectrum of resolution options. The university also provides legal resources for students through Student Legal Services (RUSLS), facilitates a University Police Department Community Officer program, and has an Office of Off-Campus Living and Community Partnerships. These units build and maintain active partnerships among students, staff, faculty, and community members and provide support to students whenever alleged misconduct arises.

Rutgers' negotiation and conflict resolution practices include conflict negotiation/resolution, mediation, facilitated dialogue, justice circles/conferences, and impact panels. Student Legal Services (RUSLS) also provides students with professional legal advice and assistance at no cost from attorneys licensed to practice in New Jersey. RUSLS's services include legal consultation, pre-litigation services, attorney referral, community outreach and education, and pre-law advising.

More information about the negotiation and conflict resolution process at Rutgers University can be found at *http://cncr.rutgers.edu/. Student Legal Services information can be found at http://rusls.rutgers.edu.*

University of San Diego Restorative Justice Opportunities

Restorative justice is a key component of resolving harms hin the residential community at the University of San Diego, a private, Roman Catholic university that serves approximately 6,000 students. Residential life staff members are trained as restorative justice facilitators and work with the Office of Ethical Development and Restorative Practices to provide safe environments for dialoguing circles and restorative conferences. Faculty, staff, and students can use any of the restorative justice opportunities whenever conflict arises.

Details regarding restorative justice at the University of San Diego can be obtained from *https://www.sandiego.edu/conduct/restorative-justice/*.

6.3 | CASE STUDY

CONDUCT OR EDUCATIONAL CONVERSATION?

Mallory Martin-Ferguson, Delmy M. Lendof, and Denise Balfour Simpson

In connecting student conduct to social justice concepts and community-building, housing and residence life conduct officers are encouraged to consider how something that may appear to be a conduct matter could also be an educational conversation with no formal action. This is not an easy task and often entails consulting with colleagues across multiple departments. This example highlights this idea.

In this scenario, some residents are entertaining themselves in their residence hall lounge by playing video games and studying for a group project meeting scheduled to occur the next day. The following morning, one of the students emails their resident director to express concern over a text message received by another student from the previous evening and wants the resident director to act. The text message exchange includes reference to a third student in a highly derogatory way, a joke about the third student's identity, and language suggestive of a sexual advance toward the student who reported this to you. The reporting student now feels unsafe around the sender of the text message and wants that student to be moved to a different building.

Questions for Consideration

- What levels of accountability should occur in these types of situations? What actions should occur next?
- What concerns, if any, exist about the use of offensive language, language that jokes about a student's identity, and language of a sexually suggestive nature?
- If there is no previous history of interactions or concern regarding the student who sent the message, should this influence the response?
- If the resident director is unaware of how the students identify themselves, should knowing the identity of the students involved make a difference in the response?
- Considering the recipient of the text message reports feeling "unsafe" because of the text message, what impact should reading the word "unsafe" have in the response?
- The recipient of text message demands the student who sent the text message be moved from the residence hall. Should moving the student be considered as part of the response?

- What campus partners, if any, might the resident director use in forming a response to this incident?

Moving Forward

Housing and residence life conduct officers will come across many incidents that include offensive language, concerns regarding freedom of speech and civility, and behaviors that potentially threaten the health and safety of our students. Colleges and universities generally have policies that speak to such topics, but this is not always the case, nor are the policies always clear or easy to interpret. There are also incidents that go against a campus' or department commitment to social justice and inclusion, but such behaviors are not always a violation of policy.

While not every behavior rises to the level of a policy violation, the conduct process, particularly within the residential environment, can serve as a platform for conversations that inform and educate. Such conversations can become teaching and learning tools in making our campus communities more inclusive for all students.

In this scenario, the authors recommend weighing the feasibility of facilitating an educational conversation versus initiating the student conduct process. To determine the best response to the described behaviors, the resident director should consult with campus partners, such as their direct supervisor, campus conduct office, and potentially the Title IX compliance coordinator. Consulting with multiple parties is time-consuming, challenging, and stressful since it involves talking with one or more students. There also is the potential involvement of campus and external partners such as parents, attorneys, and the media. However, this is a case that calls for a social justice look at what could be perceived as a conduct incident.

In this example, the Title IX coordinator at the university was consulted and it was determined this incident was not a Title IX violation. Subsequently, the Office of Student Conduct determined that, at a maximum, the sanction would be a warning.

A conduct officer met with both students individually. The student who sent the text message was remorseful and wanted to apologize to the other student. The conduct officer offered to facilitate a meeting between the two students, but the student who received the text message declined the offer. That student met with at least five mid- to senior-level officials at the university, including the Title IX coordinator, to discuss concerns about allowing the student who sent the text message to continue living in the same residence hall. In every interaction, the student threatened to file legal action against the university.

The student who sent the text message later decided to move to another residence hall for an unrelated reason. The student who received the text message may have assumed the sending student moved because of the many meetings with high-level administrators and may never know the student moved out on their own accord.

6.4 | EXERCISE

SOCIAL IDENTITY SNAPSHOT

Mallory Martin-Ferguson, Delmy M. Lendof, and Denise Balfour Simpson

The manifestation of oppression, social identities, and privilege have evolved and differ in various countries. This worksheet is designed to be a resource for both professional and student staff who are exploring their social identities and group memberships. It provides a general overview of social categories, their location in a system of privilege, and the social identities connected to the categories. It includes forms of oppression in the United States based on contemporary and historical evidence and observations.

As participants review the material and self-identify the social identities to which they connect, facilitating its completion requires awareness of the included terms, as well as understanding the nuances of power, privilege, and oppression. Participants should recognize individuals belong to many social categories and may have multiple identities within each social category, creating unique experiences for the individual. Some identities connect to privileged groups, others to marginalized or less-privileged groups.

Social Identity	Common Form of Oppression	Privileged Groups	Less-privileged Groups / Underrepresented Groups	Membership
Age	Ageism	25–49 years old	Older than 50 or younger than 24	
Socio-economic Class	Classism	*Upper, middle,* and *ruling* class; wealthy in critical finances; education, training; resources, benefits, access, and opportunities. Social, political, safety, and financial capital	*Under, middle,* and *lower class;* poor; without critical access to resources, benefits, education, training, and opportunities in their daily networks. Lack of social, safety, political, and financial capital.	

Social Identity	Common Form of Oppression	Privileged Groups	Less-privileged Groups / Underrepresented Groups	Membership
National Origin	Xenophobia, global racism, ethnocide, and genocide	U.S.-born, naturalized citizen, documented American	Most immigrants, Native Americans, undocumented individuals	
Religion/ Spirituality/ Faith Meaning	Anti-Semitism, Islamophobia, religious bias	Christian	Atheist, agnostic, Jewish, Muslim, Hindu, Buddhist, pagan, and many other spiritual identities	
Ethnicity	Ethnic prejudice and discrimination; often racism; ethnocide and genocide	European; North American (U.S. and Canada)	Descendants of the people from Africa, Asia, Latin America, South America, Caribbean, Middle East, etc.	
Race	Racism, colorism	White American; very fair, light-skinned	People of color; medium-dark to dark-skinned	
Romantic and/or Sexual orientation/ Sexuality/ Attractionality	Homophobia, heterosexism, biphobia	Heterosexuals; straight individuals	Bisexual; gay; lesbian; queer; asexual; pansexual, etc.; those who are attracted to the same gender or spectrum of gender	
Abilities and accessibility/ Emotional, physical, mental, and learning	Ableism	Individuals with no or minimal disabilities	People with emotional, mental, learning, and/or physical disabilities	
Sex	Sexism; misogyny	Male	Females; intersex	

Social Identity	Common Form of Oppression	Privileged Groups	Less-privileged Groups / Underrepresented Groups	Membership
Gender identity	Genderphobia; misogyny; transphobia	Binary gender identified; cisgender; women and men	Non-binary, gender non-conforming; gender queer; transgender individuals	
Gender expression	Genderphobia, transphobia	Gender expressions of binary genders; linear characteristics of feminine and masculine	Recognized spectrum of fluidity of feminine and masculine characteristics Gender non-conforming	
Size	Sizeism, weight discrimination	People who fit narrow definition of weight, height, and size	People considered "fat," overweight, obese, morbidly obese; also underweight, "too skinny" or thin: too tall or short	

Matrix adapted by the University of Michigan Program on Intergroup Relations from the work of Fluerette King and her Diverse Democracy Snapshot Worksheet (2017). King is the assistant vice president for equity and inclusion and chief diversity officer at the University of Northern Colorado.

STUDENTS AND AUTISM SPECTRUM DISORDER

D. Matthew Gregory

Research on university students with Autism Spectrum Disorder (ASD) and the experiences or needs of ASD students is limited (Cai & Richdale, 2016). Even less research addresses common behavioral challenges associated with university students who may have ASD and how university practitioners may be able to assist these students better. Ru Ying Cai and Amanda L. Richdale use the American Psychiatric Association definition of ASD to begin to understand the challenges and limitations students with ASD may experience while in college: "A lifelong developmental disorder whose primary features are social-communication deficits, and restricted, repetitive and stereotyped patterns of activities, interests, and sensory sensitivities" (2016).

According to Cai and Richdale, few students with ASD enroll in college and many require support from their respective family units into adulthood (2016). When it comes to higher education, Cai and Richdale found that of 22 students identified to have or possibly have ASD, 63.6% felt their educational or academic needs were being met, while 27.3% of students felt their social needs were not met (2016). It is not unusual for ASD students to feel they are challenged socially, although social connections and relationships are often what they desire most while in college.

Challenges with social cues and social-oriented communication often lead to misunderstanding and misinterpretation for students with ASD (2016). As a result, while ASD students desire a social outlet, their attempts to connect socially with others may be received as odd or unwanted communication by peers. What is needed is staff engagement and guidance, often by setting specific expectations coupled with clear boundaries.

Meeting Anthony

Anthony arrived on campus during freshman move-in day just like any student. Within a few minutes of arriving on his floor, he was introducing himself to Mark, the resident assistant. Anthony was a tall, older-looking fellow with what appeared to be at least two days' worth of beard growth and hair cut short to hide what appeared to be natural curls. He wore a superhero T-shirt and retro gym shorts, both of which were too small for his frame.

Anthony extended his hand, eager to shake hands with his RA. Anthony's hand was sweaty and he had a very firm grasp. He shook hands with vigor and an obvious desire to meet new people and to make friends. He spoke with excitement about being on the floor and said he could not wait to meet the other students and make some new friends.

Mark felt Anthony was a bit odd and found talking with him to be awkward. Anthony stood close to Mark and seemed to have no self-awareness of body proximity or personal space. He had a deep voice with thick-tongue-like speech inflection. He spoke slowly and appeared to be self-conscious of how he spoke. Mark asked Anthony what he was going to study and Anthony gleefully said, "Computer coding and math." Knowing other students were waiting to check in, Mark told Anthony he needed to get back to work and would visit with Anthony later. Anthony said, "I don't have anything to do, I can hang out here in your room and help you." Mark thanked Anthony for the offer and said he needed to meet with residents alone because they would discuss private, personal information.

Mark again told Anthony he would see him later. As Anthony left the room, he waved enthusiastically at Mark and excitedly said, "I'll see you later, Mark."

About one week passed and orientation was about to close. Mark was conducting a nightly set of rounds on the floor. As Mark entered the hallway that housed Anthony's private room, he noticed a pile of items in front of Anthony's door. Upon closer inspection, Mark saw several bars of soap stacked in front of the room and shaving cream sprayed in thick circles on the door. Someone had written "Take a shower, retard!" on Anthony's marker board, Mark picked up the bars of soap, wiped up the shaving cream, cleaned off the marker board, and submitted an incident report on the incident.

The next day, Mark followed up with Anthony to ask if everything was okay, Anthony said he did not know why other residents on the floor hated him, were being mean to him, and were playing pranks on him. At the same time, Anthony would not tell Mark who was being mean and said he did not know who was behind the pranks. Anthony said he had always been different and was bullied in junior high and high school. He said that he takes medicine for his condition, makes straight As (especially in math and sciences), and has helped other students who struggle in those subjects.

After further discussion, Anthony revealed that he was diagnosed with autism and his condition complicated his ability to make friends.

Note: A summary of the actual events that followed the incident is included after the case study discussion questions. Readers should process the questions before proceeding to the epilogue.

Discussion Questions

- What themes or concerns are present in this scenario?
- How would you approach the concerning conduct of other residents directed at Anthony?

- Does the concerning behavior violate your campus policy?
- What environmental or community issues may have to be addressed? How would you address them?
- What campus stakeholders might you involve or consult with to address the concerns?
- What action steps might you take to begin to address the situation on the floor?

Epilogue

During the discussion where Anthony disclosed his autism diagnosis, Mark asked if he wanted to pursue student conduct options related to the vandalism to his room door. Without hesitation and with confidence, Anthony replied that he did not wish to pursue any student conduct action. Instead, Anthony offered to present a program for the floor about students with autism. Anthony felt that if students on the floor knew him better and knew more about autism, there would be less concern and fewer incidents.

At first, Mark was unsure how good an idea such a program would be, so he conferred with his hall director, Mo. He, however, was excited about the prospect and strongly felt Mark should give it a try.

One week later, Mark and Anthony hosted a floor program about students with autism. Mark was pleasantly surprised to see 30 out of 45 of the floor residents attend, including some individuals who were suspected to be involved in the original incident. Anthony wowed the other residents by demonstrating his ability to memorize an entire deck of playing cards in sequence, as well as the T section of the campus phone directory. As other students called out a name from the directory, Anthony instantly told them the resident's campus address and phone number. Anthony spoke with pride about autism and his experiences while openly explaining the challenges that students like him experience in college and how he copes. The students were respectful and hung on every word Anthony said.

After the program, Mark received positive feedback with not one negative comment or evaluation. A few days later, when Mark again was conducting his nightly rounds, he saw Anthony sitting in the floor lounge and doing homework with two other residents. As Mark approached, he was told that Anthony had helped them understand their calculus assignment. For the remainder of the year, there were no more incidents directed at Anthony. Mark is unsure what Anthony is doing today, but has no doubt he is wowing whoever is around him.

References

Cai, R. Y., & Richdale, A. L. (2015). Educational Experiences and Needs of Higher Education Students with Autism Spectrum Disorder. *Journal of Autism and Developmental Disorders,46*(1), 31–41.

D. Matthew Gregory is the dean of students at Texas Tech University.

INSIGHTS

STUDENT RISK AND MENTAL HEALTH

Bob Alston

When working with a student who may be a threat to the community, professionals can make a recommendation that is easy to share on paper but can be challenging to implement during a conversation with a student. In those cases, professionals must compartmentalize what they think about the student's threatening behavior and keep it separate from how they see the student as a person. Certainly, the student's behavior can be a threat to staff members, other students in the community, or even themselves. In these cases, a staff member's care, especially in a moment when they feel they might face separation from the institution, can calm a threatening student.

To be clear, it is encouraged to focus on the behavior first, then extend care and consideration. By focusing on the behavior first, staff can act more consistently than if each community standards issue is reported or not reported based on an individual student's context.

As an example, I worked with a student once who was accused of stalking another resident. While I personally didn't feel threatened by the student said to be a stalker, a member of the community felt very unsafe by their continued presence on campus. The accused student chose to have their mother present as an advisor in the conduct process, and the mother told me that the student had a long-standing mental health diagnosis. During the meeting, when this student heard the word "stalking," they tensed up and responded in an agitated way. When we were not discussing policy language, everyone in the room was calmer. Even so, I knew I would be asking tough questions of the student, that suspension was a possibility (if the student was found responsible), and that having a parent in the room often gave students pause about answering questions honestly.

After identifying these challenges, my strategy was to focus on asking the student questions that got the information needed to make the best decisions possible without implying any value judgment. This meant remaining information-based and focusing on the behavior of the student, without referring to policy or using blaming words or language.

Generally, the student did not understand that their actions amounted to stalking, so it was my opportunity to help them understand this while showing care for them as a person. The student's mother was interested in what was best for her student, and she turned out to be an asset during the conversation. When I shared the accusatory information, and how the pattern of behavior had escalated to make the other party feel unsafe, the student could begin to see the impact of the behaviors.

During the conversation, even while the student's mother was helping to translate the impact of the student's behavior, I consistently asked how the student was doing. We took several breaks for personal comfort, and for the student and mother to speak in private. When the student did not understand something, I worked to present the same concept differently. This consistent reframing allowed the student to understand the situation from someone else's perspective.

The meeting took a bit longer than normal, but through the focus on the specific behaviors and the attention shown toward the individual needs of the student, the student (and the mother) came to understand that what had happened was disrupting the community and had made the affected student feel unsafe.

Student conduct hearing officers are practiced in having challenging conversations, but ensuring that a student understands why they are being held accountable is key. That is why I encourage focusing on a threatening student's behavior first and then showing care for the student's situation or needs. When approached with care and respect, though, threatening students can feel more satisfied with the outcomes of their interactions with a hearing officer. This is especially true when the hearing officer supports any decisions they make after having focused on the student's behavior and the facts presented by the student's situation.

SAMPLE RISK LEVEL ASSESSMENT

Mild Risk

No intimidation or threat made or present. Concerning symptoms or behavior are mild.

Mild risk signs and symptoms.

- Disruptive behavior.
- Changes in pattern of interaction and/or less participation the community.
- Increased irritability when talking and/or confrontational behavior.
- Changes in physical appearance such as deterioration of personal hygiene or major clothing style change.
- Repeated requests for special consideration.
- Problems focusing, remembering things, or making decisions.

Mild risk recommended actions.

- Meet with student and address observations.
- Provide student with campus resources (i.e., counseling services, disability services, campus food bank, other resources as appropriate).

- Complete referral to academic support office if appropriate.
- Consult with a supervisor.

Moderate Risk

Intimidation or threats are vague, indirect, and implausible. Concerning symptoms or behavior are moderate.

Moderate risk signs and symptoms.

- Persistence and/or escalation of mild risk behaviors listed above.
- Unusual or exaggerated emotional responses:
  - o Outbursts of anger and/or persistent sadness or unexplained crying.
  - o High level or consistent irritability or inappropriate excitement.

Moderate risk recommended actions. May include "mild risk" actions from above.

- Refer to students of concern committee or similar campus group.
- Escort student to health, counseling, and student wellness office if the student is willing.

Elevated Risk

Threats made or present. Concerning symptoms or behaviors are highly intensified.

Elevated risk signs and symptoms.

- Any expressions related to death.
- Irrational conversation or speech.
- Suspiciousness, irrational feelings of persecution, mistreatment, or harassment.
- Loss of contact with reality (i.e., seeing or hearing things that aren't perceived by others).
- Disruptive behavior beyond the scope of community management.
  - o Blocks/interferes with access to a facility of the university.
  - o Conducts self in a manner that adversely affects own safety or safety of others.
  - o Participates in or incites others to violent behavior such as assault/physical abuse or threatens physical abuse.
  - o Steals or knowingly is in possession of stolen property belonging to the university, other students, university employees, or guests.
  - o Loud, vulgar, or abusive language or any form of behavior acted out to incite others to disruptive behavior.
  - o Behavior that is destructive of property.
  - o Highly agitated, loud, or showing symptoms of abusing drugs, alcohol, or both.

Moderate risk recommended actions. May include "mild or medium risk" actions from above.

- Immediately notify local emergency services or campus emergency personnel if it is felt it is necessary.
- Immediately contact 'students of concern' committee.
- If threatening behaviors or actions have occurred, or if others' feel unsafe, contact campus 'threat assessment team' after evaluating the need for emergency personnel.

Bob Alston is the assistant dean of students at Northern Kentucky University. Sample threat assessment actions adapted from the Northern Kentucky University Student Risk Level Reference Sheet developed by the NKU Health, Counseling, and Student Wellness office directed by Ben Anderson. Used with permission.

 | CASE STUDY

RESIDENCE BOUNCE BACK

Jordan McLinden

The Residence Bounce Back initiative is a mentorship program for students living on campus who have multiple violations for drugs, alcohol, or both. Used at the University of Carleton in Ottawa, Ontario, its purpose is to reduce the occurrences of high-risk behaviors and provide behaviorally at-risk students with transitional, peer-based support. The peer-to-peer approach enables a student who wants to contribute positively to the residence community or may have been behaviorally at-risk in the past with an opportunity to help the students enrolled in the program improve their student experience and foster a positive sense of belonging in the residence community.

In the program, the Residence Bounce Back facilitator (the mentor) is tasked to build a meaningful coaching relationship with the enrolled student and address the negative behavior from a harm-reduction perspective. Together, they set positive goals, identify alternative coping strategies, as well as, outline the various supports and resources available to them to assist in their behavior change. This mutual and supportive relationship creates a non-judgmental space where students can honestly discuss their concerns and challenges, which results in an open line of communication where the student is willing to be vulnerable. This transparency and vulnerability often help the mentor better understand the student's various stressors and the underlying reason behind the negative behavior, which in turns helps them better support the student in their transformation journey.

The conduct officer administers the program, but it is implemented by the student facilitators, in teams of four, each with one senior facilitator who has previous experience as a program mentor. The senior facilitators are responsible for coordinating bi-weekly team meetings to share information and provide an opportunity for peer support. All facilitators also meet with the conduct officer bi-weekly to troubleshoot concerns and report progress, and are responsible for meeting with their mentee on a weekly basis for an hour. For the majority of the students involved, the duration of the program is six weeks, which has proven to be enough time for the student to identify areas for improvement and make changes. On some occasions, a student will persist in the program for longer, as they require more time to improve their behavior or continue to need the support of their mentor.

The program's approach to student development is grounded in the Stages of Change Model created by James Prochaska and Carlo Diclemente to assist those trying to stop smoking. Their model posits there are five stages of change: pre-contemplation, contemplation, preparation, action, and maintenance. The facilitators are trained in how to identify which level the student they are working with is at, which is a key step in the program because it helps the peers come to a common understanding about their direction moving forward and an idea of what success could look like. Depending on the identified stage, the pair may work toward harm-reduction strategies (i.e., reducing alcohol or drug consumption, spacing out usage, etc.) before discussing more-drastic strategies (i.e., moderation, abstention, etc.). Motivational interviewing is also a key training component for the mentors, since a large portion of their overall Residence Bounce Back training is spent learning motivational interviewing techniques and practicing facilitating conversations with peers.

Effective training is important to the success of this program, since the mentors need to be able to identify and explore a student's ambivalence about their behaviors. By spending time with the student exploring this area and amplifying the student's ambivalence, the facilitator can help influence the student's motivation for change in the future. The conversations focus on the student's negative behavior and work toward setting goals with the student for positive change. Furthermore, through intentional conversation, motivational interviewing, and understanding the student's situation, the pair can work together to define what success will look like for them, specific to the student's individualized needs, and set specific, measurable, attainable, realistic, and time-bound (SMART) goals for change.

As the peers start to develop goals and identify strategies for success, much emphasis is placed on utilizing resources on and off campus. This step is important because the facilitator should not be the sole support for the student in the future. The mentor offers a variety of resources to help students identify additional supports possibilities. Such resources may include counseling, substance use specialists, educational workshops, and academic supports. The pairs also make use of several other tools beyond SMART goals, which may include Brief Alcohol Screening and Intervention for College Students (BASICS) and the Marijuana Intervention Program (MIP), as well as audits through the eChug and eToke programs. These tools, along with many other academic recourses related to alcohol and drug use, support an effective peer-to-peer mentoring experience for both the mentor and the student.

All the students involved with the program participate in the assessment, including the facilitators. The students are given a self-confidence survey after the completion of the program, providing them with the opportunity to provide feedback as well as demonstrate the growth they have experienced as a result of the program. The facilitators are also responsible for demonstrating their learning through a capstone project, which encourages them to reflect on their own learning experience with the program. They are specifically asked to compile their thoughts and feelings about the program, noting while maintaining confidentiality, how they saw the students' move through the stages of change and which strategies and goals were most effective in their students' development. The Residence Bounce Back program is then reviewed and refined based on the assessment and evaluation results to continue to improve the experience for both the mentors and the students. Since its launch in 2014, more than 50 students have enrolled in the Residence Bounce Back program, and more than 95% have changed their behavior positively as a result.

Jordon McLinden is a residence student conduct coordinator at Carleton University in Ottawa, Ontario, Canada. More information about the program is available by contacting the author at jordon.mclinden@carleton.ca.

SANCTIONS MATRIX

Lyndsay Anderson, Nicole Kogan, and Christina Liang

While campuses move away from an one-size-fits-all approach to conduct and sanctions, it remains important to have established guidelines from which to work. The following matrix is a guide of suggested sanctions to assist housing and residence life conduct officers determine appropriate sanctions for violations. **Required sanctions are presented in bold text within the matrix while discretionary ones are in plain text.**

The educational activities listed typically are reflective in nature, asking the student found responsible to perform a task such as writing a research or reflection paper, drafting an apology letter, designing a bulletin board, hosting or attending a program, or other projects deemed to be appropriate. In the case of community service hours, the specified number of volunteer service hours should be served with a reputable off-campus organization or an on-campus department or organization. These can include activities to complete within a residence hall such as program assistance, cleaning, working with a logistics crew, or others. Finally, restrictions may include the student no longer being allowed to host guests or to visit certain areas within the residence halls. In more-severe cases, the student may face no-contact directives.

Policy Category	First Offense *Required / Discretionary Sanctions*	Second Offense *Required / Discretionary Sanctions*
Alcohol	• **Probation (1 semester)** • **Alcohol and other drugs workshop** • **Educational activity** • Community service (5-10 hours) • Parental notification (if student is younger than 21)	• **Probation (1 academic year)** • **Substance abuse screening** • Educational activity • Community service (5-20 hours based on the nature of the violation) • Alcohol consumption restriction
Drugs	• **Probation (1 semester)** • **Alcohol and other Drug Workshop** • **Educational Activity** • Community service (5-10 hours) • Parental notification (if student is younger than 21) • If severe enough drug testing is available	• Case referred to office of community standards or student conduct
Fire and other emergencies	• **Written warning (possible probation if violation is severe)** • Educational activity • Community service (5-10 hours)	• Case referred to office of community standards or student conduct
Theft	• **Written warning (possible probation if violation is severe)** • Educational activity • Community service (5-10 hours)	• Case referred to office of community standards or student conduct
Damage / destruction	• **Written warning (possible probation if violation is severe)** • Educational activity • Community service (5-10 hours) • Restitution if personal or institutional property needs to be replaced	• **Probation (1 academic year)** • Community service • Restitution
Deception	• **Written warning (possible probation if violation is severe)** • Educational activity • Apology	• **Probation (1 academic year)** • Educational activity (apology to person or group affected) • Community service (5-10 hours)

Policy Category	First Offense Required / Discretionary Sanctions	Second Offense Required / Discretionary Sanctions
Identification card or key misuse	• **Written warning** • Educational activity	• **Probation (1 academic year)** • Educational activity • Community service (5-10 hours)
Smoking	• **Written warning** • Educational activity	• **Probation (1 academic year)** • Educational activity • Community service (5-10 hours)
Animals and pets	• **Written warning** • Educational activity	• **Probation (1 academic year)** • Educational activity • Community service (5-10 hours)
Solicitation	• **Written warning** • Educational activity	• **Probation (1 academic year)** • Educational activity • Community service (5-10 hours)
Other published university regulations	• **Written warning** • Educational activity	• **Probation (1 academic year)** • Educational activity • Community service (5-10 hours)
Being in the presence of violations	• **Written warning** • Educational activity	• **Probation (1 academic year)** • Educational activity • Community service (5-10 hours)
Bullying	• **Probation (1 semester)** • Educational activity • No-contact directive	• **Probation (1 academic year) or removal from housing** • Educational activity • Community service (5-10 hours)

9.1 CASE STUDY

FACILIITATING CONFLICT RESOLUTION

Erik Wessel

You are a new professional live-in staff member. It is early in the academic year and a resident assistant (RA) on your team alerts you to the fact that several students on the floor were talking about an Instagram post circulating among residents on the floor and in the building. The RA described the Instagram post as "racist, but not specifically directed at any one individual or group."

What information would be helpful to explore further? Whom might you talk to and engage with? Who needs to know about this situation?

You have done a good job thus far in building relationships in your residential community. As a result, a few students are comfortable enough to stop you in the hall and confide that they have seen the social media post and have experienced harm as a result. They don't know the sender of the social media post, but describe feeling "unsafe." They also share with you that "someone needs to hold this person accountable" and that the person should be "punished."

Later in the day, another student stops you to express that they share several dominant identities with the original sender of the Instagram message, they find it objectionable, and they would like to help but don't know how to engage in a way that would be helpful.

Of course, you have shared information about this incident with your supervisor to put in motion all possible pathways for responding appropriately, but you are left wondering what role the community might have in using this as a transformative moment.

What needs might you expect to be expressed as a result of this situation? What support structures might you have access to for these students? How might you start thinking about and preparing for a process that allows for inclusive community decision-making?

Early the next morning, the sender of the Instagram message knocks on your door. You answer the door to find someone who is visibly upset. You invite them in and they tell you that they did indeed send the Instagram message. They originally thought it was "funny," but now "realize it was a mistake." Through the conversation, you are left with the impression that the sender of the Instagram message is genuine in recognizing a mistake, but lacks clarity on the harm done and doesn't fully comprehend why others feel so harmed by it.

What does accountability look like in this situation? How might you start helping this student toward a position of active accountability? What support might be helpful for this student? What options might be available to your community to repair the harm most effectively?

You recognize that although you have some ideas, your experience in responding to these kinds of situations is still limited. As such, after consulting with your supervisor, you identify and reach out to a staff member and a faculty member at your institution whom you know have some experience with facilitating restorative justice circles. You are intrigued by the idea and wonder whether this might be a useful technique to provide an opportunity for the community to engage in the peacebuilding process, repair harm, and rebuild trust.

Upon meeting with the seasoned staff and faculty member, you recognize that a circle process can be used for community-building, problem-solving, seeking understanding, resolving conflict, working toward healing, reintegrating members back into the community, and several other community-focused goals. You also learn that there is a considerable amount of preparation work to do. You determine that a circle process might provide a multi-partial facilitator for all parties to have their needs met and take action. With guidance from your faculty and staff mentors, you begin to meet individually with the parties (those harmed and those creating harm) to hear and understand their stories, perspectives, positions, and interests.

What basic learning and competency-building might you need to develop before engaging in a process such as a restorative justice circle?

By now, you have recognized that a restorative process takes effort and is not necessarily the easy way forward. However, you are fully committed to achieving the best outcomes possible and meeting needs as completely as possible. With that in mind, you have recruited the faculty member mentor to assist you as a co-facilitator.

As you strategize with your co-facilitator, you explore points of competency, self-awareness, and professional learning. Your co-facilitator walks you through the CLARA model of active listening (Calm and center, Listen, Affirm experience, Respond to the issue, and Add context and insight). Next, you discuss universal human needs (i.e., autonomy, honesty, empathy, transcendence/purpose, community, safety, and competency). You begin to think about this situation and the diversity of needs that might be expressed throughout the community. With the guidance of your co-facilitator, you talk through non-violent communication techniques, including the use of "I" statements (e.g., "I noticed . . . ," "I feel . . . ," "I need . . . ," and "Can we . . . ?"). Together, you and your co-facilitator begin the preparation work in anticipation of a community circle process.

Who should you meet with in preparation for a circle process? What has to be drawn out ahead of time to ensure parties are prepared? How might you begin to plan and prepare ahead of time for a future circle?

You begin to feel both excited (and a little nervous) as you embark on this new professional experience. Your first two action items are to meet individually with the student who posted the Instagram message and the two students who stopped you in the hall originally. You decide that sequence might be important and thus choose to reach out to the students who stopped you in the hall first. One student indicates that they would very much appreciate an opportunity to discuss their experience and the other politely declines. You decide to respect the boundaries of both decisions.

When you meet with the student who accepted your outreach, they can express articulately how the social media post was harmful to them because of their own multiple intersecting identities. They also say that they didn't want to speak for anyone else and that the thought of educating students holding dominant identities who express these sentiments is "exhausting." Through the conversation, it also becomes apparent that it will be important to elicit multiple voices and perspectives in the community. You share with this student your hope to have a restorative circle process and ask if this student would help you bring more students into the conversation who were affected by the behavior. This resulted in creating a community needs circle in preparation for what you hope will be a subsequent restorative community circle.

What kind of support might you be able to offer to students who choose to attend the needs circle?

You co-facilitator approves of doing preparation work through a community needs circle. You recognize that this provides the opportunity for marginalized voices to express harm, fear, and perhaps hope for a better possible future. The student you met with earlier reached out to their network of peers and an additional three students responded with interest in participating in the needs circle. You now have a commitment from several students who have expressed interest in exploring a restorative process.

In preparation for the next steps, your co-facilitator helps you think through values, any questions you might pose to the group for reflection, and an overview of (or script for) the circle process. You also discuss how the layout of the room and seating might be important to outcomes, given the unique circumstances of this situation.

On the day of the circle, the students all arrived early but were unsure of what to expect. However, their uneasiness was alleviated in part by your forethought on hospitality; the choice of a bright, comfortable, neutral meeting location and the snacks your supervisor provided for the meeting. You and your co-facilitator start by talking briefly about the intent and purpose of the circle, extending a warm welcome to those present, and inviting them to engage in a mindfulness moment with a brief breathing exercise. You then introduce the concept of a talking piece (to ensure equity in the opportunity to participate fully) and model the first round of the circle through introductions.

After introductions, you follow with a second round to express values and expectations that are important to the group. A third round offers participants an opportunity to share stories that speak to their personal experiences of harm. A fourth round explores issues, concerns, impact, and need. A fifth round determines what is needed to move forward. The sixth round asks for ideas about how to move forward in a positive direction and what commitments can be made. A seventh round works toward a shared approach or agreement, and the final round offers the opportunity for closing thoughts.

After spending time with students and actively listening to their experiences of harm, themes emerge from the group that speak to the need for justice. There is recognition that this is just one example of harm among many. There is a desire for the student creating the harm to learn from this moment and a feeling of exhaustion from those harmed as they are asked to educate the other. After assuring the students that their engagement was indeed voluntary, you affirm your deep appreciation for their willingness to voice their experience, thoughts, and perspectives with a shared goal of improving the community.

After the needs circle, three of the four students indicated an interest and willingness in exploring a subsequent restorative process with the student who created the harm.

Now that you have a better understanding of experience and have built trust in the community and secured commitment to move forward, what considerations might you think through before bringing the parties together?

You recognized early on that preparation work would have to be done with the student who sent the racist social media post; however, you are thankful that the student seemed willing to engage and perhaps even open to learning along the way. You scheduled an opportunity to meet with the student shortly after the community needs circle. In this meeting, you work with the student to clarify the issue, help prepare them for future engagement in the community, talk about the goals of a community circle process, and help the student understand their own multiple identities. Further, you start to help the student come up with their own ideas to repair the harm.

It did not surprise you to learn that the student had already been spending some time thinking about possible approaches to repair the harm and therefore, you spend the next hour helping them refine their approach and proposal. Before leaving, you take some time with the student to do some skill-building regarding conflict, including encouragement to be open and specific about feelings (i.e., afraid, confused, etc.). You provide communication tools such as "I" statements and share a strategy to listen well with the CLARA method.

After your meeting with the student, they voluntarily commit to engage in a community restoration circle where the student will have the opportunity to hear how their choices affected others, share their own thoughts and feelings, present their own ideas for repairing harm, and commit to working toward rebuilding trust in the community.

What final steps might be useful to seek a productive restorative process for the community?

Before your community restoration circle, you meet with your co-facilitator to talk through the process. You agree that you will serve as the circle keeper who will facilitate the process and your co-facilitator will keep time, take notes, and support the process. Similar to the last community needs circle, you have set up a comfortable space, some light refreshments, and arranged the room in a circle ahead of time. You are also mindful of when people arrive, how they are greeted and invited into the space, and where they sit. Strategically, you have already decided that you and your co-facilitator will place yourselves in different places in the circle. As the student participants settle in, you invite the group to enter into the circle, describe the structure of the circle, introduce the talking piece, and begin round one with introductions.

Since it is nearing a stressful point in the term, you ask the group to also reflect on the question, "Recognizing this is a challenging time in the semester, what might you need to set aside today to be fully present and engaged in the circle?" Round two generates, explores, and sets shared values and expectations. Round three allows for the sharing of personal stories (i.e., "What challenges have you experienced as a member of this community?" "… as a member of many intersecting identities and communities?").

Round four allows each person to speak about their primary concerns, specific impact, and current feelings. Round five allows for an assumption of responsibility and an exploration of what would be needed to move forward. In this stage of the process, the student who sent the social media messages was invited to express and explore with others their proposals for repairing the harm and rebuilding trust. Round six allows for further dialogue to refine the approach and work toward mutual understanding and a commitment to take action to repair harm and rebuild trust.

In this process, you find that your voice, as the keeper of the circle, is best reserved to summarize, clarify, and hold those participating to the values established in the early rounds of the process. As the circle keeper, it is important to respect the time that has been allotted. You close with one final round that asks two questions: "What are you taking from this circle that supports your healing?" and "Where do you see yourself as you continue to move forward?"

How might you continue to follow up to ensure the highest level of both support and accountability?

In the days after the restorative circle, you re-engage with the student who originally sent the racist social media post. In this meeting, you allow time for them to unpack their experience in the circle further. You further explore their learning and establish some clear shared understanding and expectation for actions steps they agreed to take. Wisely, you share with them that you have learned that conflict in a community is an opportunity for creating constructive change and thank them for their willingness to consider changing themself first.

You also take the time to regularly re-connect and keep up the relationship with the students who participated in the community needs circle and find these students have begun to think about community harm and conflict as an opportunity to take a restorative road that builds trust, promotes justice, and teaches peace.

Case study created by Erik Wessel, director of the Office of Student Conflict Resolution at the University of Michigan. Used with permission.

9.2 RESOURCES

RESTORATIVE PRACTICE FACILITATION

The International Institute for Restorative Practices, founded by Ted and Susan Wachtel, provides a variety of educational resources and programs that promote restorative practices as they are applied in higher education as well as elementary and secondary education, community health, organizational leadership, criminal justice, and counseling and social work. Among its work are training programs that prepare individuals to facilitate restorative practices in a variety of scenarios. The following sample scripts are useful in two different scenarios.

GENERAL CONFLICT: FACILITATOR'S SCRIPT

This script is to be used as a guide for incidents where there is no clear victim or offender. The focus of the restorative practice is to identify and help repair damage done to a community as a whole.

» STEP 1. *Welcome and introduction*

"Hello. As you know, my name is _____ and I have been asked to facilitate this meeting. (Introduce participants, if necessary.) I have spoken to all of you about the incident(s), and it is clear that what has happened has affected/ hurt/harmed everyone involved. This is an opportunity to talk about what has happened and how each of you has been affected/hurt. To help us all work together again, we need to discuss ways of stopping any further hurt/harm so we can improve relationships."

Say to everyone: *"Do you understand?"*

» STEP 2. *Address the person who has been most affected*

- *"I would like to start by asking (person's name) to talk about how he(s)he became involved and what happened?"*
- *"At the time, what were you thinking about?"*
- *"What have you thought since?"*
- *"How has this affected/hurt you and others?"*
- *"What has been the hardest thing for you?"*

» STEP 3. *Address all participants*

- Ask each participant, in turn, the questions in step 2.

» STEP 4. *Address all participants*

"Now that we have heard how all of you have been affected/hurt in some way by what has happened, is there anything anyone would like to say at this point?"

» STEP 5. *Invitation to all participants*

"What suggestions do you have that will stop any further hurt/harm?"
"What will help all of us work together again, without further conflict?"

» STEP 6. *Ask each participant*

"What would you like to see come out of today's meeting?"

» STEP 7. *Invitation to all participants (document responses if required)*

"What will each of you now do to help improve your relationships with one another?"

» STEP 8. *Final invitation to participants*

"What have you found useful from today's meeting?"

» STEP 9. *Close the meeting*

"Thank you for being involved. It has allowed us to share and understand what happened and, importantly, provided the opportunity to find positive ways of building better relationships with one another."

CONFERENCE FACILITATOR'S SCRIPT

This script is to be used as a guide for incidents where one or more individuals have been identified as responsible for an incident. The focus of the restorative practice is not to establish responsibility for an incident, but to assist individuals who were involved to repair the damage done and move beyond the incident.

» STEP 1. *Preamble*

"Welcome. As you know, my name is _____ and I will be facilitating this conference."

Introduce each conference participant and state his/her relationship to the offender(s) or victim(s). *"Thank you all for attending. I know that this is difficult for all of you, but your presence will help us deal with the matter that has brought us together. This is an opportunity for all of you to be involved in repairing the harm that has been done."*

"This conference will focus on an incident which happened (state the date, place, and nature of offense without elaborating). It is important to understand that we will focus on what (offender name(s)) did and how that unacceptable behavior has affected others. We are not here to decide whether (offender name(s)) is/are good or bad. We want to explore in what way people have been affected and hopefully work toward repairing the harm that has resulted. Does everyone understand this?"

"(Offender names) has/have admitted his/her/their part in the incident."

Say to offender(s): *"I must tell you that you do not have to participate in this conference and are free to leave at any time, as is anyone else. If you do leave, the matter may be referred to court/handled by the school disciplinary policy/ handled in another way. This matter, however, may be finalized if you participate in a positive manner and comply with the conference agreement. Do you understand?"*

» STEP 2. *Offender(s)*

"We'll start with (one of offenders' names)." If there is more than one offender, have each respond to all of the following questions.
- *"What happened?"*
- *"What were you thinking about at the time?"*
- *"What have you thought about since the incident?"*
- *"Who do you think has been affected by your actions?"*
- *"How have they been affected?"*

» STEP 3. *Victim(s)*

If there is more than one victim, have each respond to all of the following questions.
- *"What was your reaction at the time of the incident?"*
- *"How do you feel about what happened?"*
- *"What has been the hardest thing for you?"*
- *"How did your family and friends react when they heard about the incident?"*

» STEP 4. *Victim supporters*

Have each respond to all of the following questions.
- *"What did you think when you heard about the incident?"*
- *"How do you feel about what happened?"*
- *"What has been the hardest thing for you?"*
- *"What do you think are the main issues?"*

» STEP 5. *Offender supporters*

To friend/supporter of the offender ask: *"This has been difficult for you, hasn't it? Would you like to tell us about it?"*

Have each respond to all of the following questions.

- *"What did you think when you heard about the incident?"*
- *"How do you feel about what happened?"*
- *"What has been the hardest thing for you?"*
- *"What do you think are the main issues?"*

» STEP 6. Offender(s)

Ask the offender(s): "Is there anything you want to say at this time?"

» STEP 7. Reaching an agreement

Ask the victim(s): *"What would you like from today's conference?"* Ask the offender(s) to respond to the victim(s) response. At this point, the participants discuss what should be in the final agreement. Solicit comments from participants.

It is important to ask the offender(s) to respond to each suggestion before the group moves to the next suggestion, asking *"What do you think about that?"* Then determine that the offender(s) agree(s) before moving on. Allow for negotiation. As the agreement develops, clarify each item and make the written document as specific as possible, including details, deadlines, and follow-up arrangements.

As you sense that the agreement discussion is drawing to a close, say to the participants: *"Before I prepare the written agreement, I'd like to make sure that I have accurately recorded what has been decided."*

Read the items in the agreement aloud and look to the participants for acknowledgment. Make any necessary corrections.

» STEP 8. Closing the conference

"Before I formally close this conference, I would like to provide everyone with a final opportunity to speak. Is there anything anyone wants to say?" Allow time for participants to respond. When they are done, say: *"Thank you for your contributions in dealing with this difficult matter. Congratulations on the way you have worked through the issues. Please help yourselves to some refreshments while I prepare the agreement."*

Allow participants ample time to have refreshments and interact. The informal period after the formal conference is very important.

Adopted from The Conferencing Handbook: New Real Justice Training Manual *(1999, The Piper's Press) by Terry O'Connell, Ben Wachtel, and Ted Wachtel. Used with permission. To learn more about the International Institute of Restorative Practice visit iirp.edu.*

10.1 | CASE STUDY

ACTING ON ASSESSMENT

Ciji A. Heiser, Amy P. Gauthier, Kathryn A. DiCato, and Kathryn M. Bartholomew

At a large public institution, conduct and housing staff were reviewing incident reports when an interesting statistic jumped out at them. The previous academic year, the two days with the largest number of incident reports filed by student and professional staff were Halloween night and the last day of class of the spring semester. Intrigued, they reviewed reports from previous years and found similar results.

By using assessment practices to track incident data and student patterns of behavior, the staff measured the volume of student conduct incidents on both nights, with the incident volume rising significantly from a typical weekend night. In response to these data, and considering the department's KPI, the staff adjusted the coming year's duty coverage plan to address student safety.

	Typical Academic Year Night	Halloween and Last Day of Class
Resident Advisor Duty Coverage	2–3 RAs per community	Double coverage or half staff
Professional Staff Duty Coverage	Two professional staff for the campus	17 professional staff for the campus, plus student affairs campus partner support
Time	Structured start and end time	Duty starts early and extends late
Presence on campus	Staff can request a night away from campus	Staff must be present on campus
Programming	No set expectations for programming	Programming occurs in communities

QUESTIONS

- What other changes could the housing department make, based on these data?
- What other assumptions do you have about student conduct that could be proven or disproved by further assessment? What data would you use for that insight?
- When working with stakeholders and partners, it is important to be on the same page with data collection, understanding your institutional culture and what student support looks like. Based on this, how might you work together to address staffing needs?
- Many housing departments have multiple software systems that capture data and student trends. Although you are examining conduct data, are there other systems that could inform decisions you need to make, such as programming or students of concern? What stakeholders have data that would be helpful? What are other aspects that the housing department may consider changing?
- Who are the stakeholders that might have data to assist the housing department in gaining a more-holistic view of high-risk or high-volume days?
- Looking at data from three- to five-year trends, what active or passive programs or initiatives are there that you could implement to educate students?

About the Editors

DR. JOCYNDA HUDSON

Dr. JoCynda Hudson is associate director of housing for residence life and education at the University of Florida (UF). She supervises the office of conduct and community standards, conflict resolution, and the crisis intervention consultant program for the Department of Housing and Residence Education. Her approach to student conduct is focused on putting students back on the right track for success with less emphasis solely on accountability. She also serves on the UF campus threat assessment team and teaches higher education law as an adjunct faculty member in the College of Education. Hudson has presented on topics such as legislative issues, mental health concerns, conflict coaching, conflict resolution, and training housing conduct officers.

Hudson received her doctorate degree in higher education administration from UF and her master's degree from Texas A & M University. She has worked in housing as an assistant director of residence life at Vanderbilt University and a residence director at Northern Arizona University. Before her professional housing experience, she worked at Ivy Tech State College, Columbus (Indiana) as coordinator of admissions and served as the pre-nursing academic advisor as well as the primary recruiter and admissions counselor. While at Ivy Tech, she learned that success looks different for everyone and education — no matter its form — can help a person meet their goals.

Hudson is active in both ASCA and ACUHO-I. In 2015 and 2016, she served on the faculty of the ASCA Gehring Academy and coordinated its housing and residence life track. She is a past chair of the ASCA Membership Committee and served two years as the Conflict Resolution Committee chair. From 2013–2015, she had the honor to serve on the ACUHO-I STARS College faculty. She contributed a chapter to the Campus Housing Management book series published by ACUHO-I in 2013.

When not working with students, Hudson can be found reading a novel or streaming the latest sci-fi series. Fiction in all forms (books, movies, television, art, etc.) is her passion. With her dissertation defense complete, she hopes to again take up watercolor painting.

DR. ALAN ACOSTA

Dr. Alan Acosta is one of the associate deans of students in the Dean of Students Department at Florida State University (FSU), supervising the Office of New Student and Family Programs, Office of Student Rights and Responsibilities, and Office of Withdrawal Services. His work includes managing campus and student crises; interacting with campus partners; chairing the FSU Public Safety Committee; and helping create a safe, welcoming campus community. He believes in the necessity of growing college students into ethical global leaders for the future, and he thrives on weaving diversity and inclusion into his work.

Before becoming an associate dean, Acosta worked for university housing at FSU as a residence coordinator and assistant director for Residence Life, focusing on student conduct, student staff recruitment, selection, and training, and co-supervising the professional staff advisor to the FSU Inter-Residence Hall Council and the Garnet and Gold Chapter of the National Residence Hall Honorary.

He earned his bachelor of science in business and master of education from the University of Florida (UF) in 2004 and 2006, respectively, and his doctorate of philosophy in higher education administration from FSU in 2017.

Acosta has been actively involved in ACPA – College Student Educators International for more than 11 years. He is the chair of ACPA's Commission for Student Conduct and Legal Issues, and an ACPA Foundation Board trustee. He also has been actively involved in the Association for Student Conduct Administration, serving as the Educational Initiatives chair for the association's 2016 Annual Conference. He is also a past member of the Association for College and University Housing Officers – International.

Acosta enjoys spending time with his partner, Danielle, and their two cats, Ninja and Buster. He loves watching professional wrestling, cheering for his favorite sports teams, reading, and watching movies. Follow him on Twitter and Instagram at @alanacosta81.

DR. RYAN C. HOLMES

Dr. Ryan C. Holmes is associate vice president for student affairs and dean of students at the University of Miami (Florida). He has oversight of student conduct, Honor Council, Greek life, student crisis response, student assessment committee, alcohol and other drug education, veterans' services, and the chaplain's association. His work focuses on balancing students' rights, responsibilities, and access to resources while fostering campus-wide partnerships toward sustaining a culture of care.

Before his work at the U, Holmes was assistant vice president for student support at the University of Texas at El Paso, where he was the principal investigator for the Academic Institutions for Military Students Network and supervised the Center for Accommodations and Support Services, Military Student Success Center, Office of Student Conduct and Conflict Resolution, and University Counseling Center. Holmes also chaired the behavioral assessment team; was deputy Title IX coordinator, responsible for supervision of investigations regarding student concerns; and was the university lead for bystander intervention efforts regarding campus violence, including sexual assault, sexual harassment, and stalking.

Holmes has given talks and presentations in the areas of social justice, bias (as it relates to race, gender, and other unchangeable traits), conflict resolution, and entitlement, and also contributed to *Reframing Campus Conflict: Student Conduct Practice Through a Social Justice Lens*; *More Stories of Inspiration: 51 Uplifting Tales of Courage, Humor, Healing, and Learning in Student Affairs*; and *The State of Student Conduct: Current Forces & Future Challenges: Revisited*, among other publications.

Holmes served on the American College Personnel Association's Ethics Consortium Committee from 2013–2015, was vice chair for outreach of ACPA's Commission for Social Justice Educators, is a past president of the Association for Student Conduct Administration, and is past chair of the Raymond H. Goldstone ASCA Foundation Board.

Holmes earned a bachelor's of music education degree from Loyola University in New Orleans, completed a master's of arts degree in counseling and personnel services from the University of Maryland-College Park in 2004, was awarded a second master's degree in bilingual/bicultural studies from La Salle University in 2008, and completed his doctorate (Ed.D.) in educational leadership and administration at the University of Texas at El Paso in 2014.

Holmes enjoys experiencing life with his partner, Maria, and two children, Remaliah and Raziel. He also enjoys listening to and analyzing music, watching sports, continuing his self-guided research on oppression, and learning how to be a better father through activities with his children.

About the Authors

CHAPTER 1

DR. LEAH BARRETT is the vice president for student affairs at the Northern Wyoming Community College District, providing leadership to enrollment management and student affairs functions for two campuses: Gillette College and Sheridan College. Barrett has worked at several four-year institutions in the United States, providing administrative support to nearly every aspect of student affairs and enrollment management. Her dissertation, *The College Union and a Sense of Community for Students in Public Higher Education: Is there a Relationship?*, was a quantitative study on the impacts of physical space on students' sense of community. She has written several publications, and presented the results in conference workshops and poster sessions at ACUI, NASPA, and within higher education academic programs.

DR. DENISE BAUMANN is the associate director of residence life, housing, and dining services at Missouri State University. She was promoted to this role in 2004 was after serving as assistant director of education and development. Baumann oversees all staffing, training, and conduct processes in the residence halls. She previously held housing positions at the University of Nebraska at Kearney and the University of Northern Iowa. Baumann has been a faculty member at the Regional Entry Level Institute at the University of Northern Iowa on two occasions. She has received the Outstanding Exempt Staff Member Award in the Division of Student Affairs, SUCCESSability Award (for assisting students with disabilities), and Outstanding Affiliated Faculty Member Award in the Student Affairs in Higher Education Program.

DR. DONNA L. HIGHT is chief student life and enrollment services officer at the Ohio State University at Mansfield, where she has worked since 2005. She has led seven areas, including student engagement, athletics, and recreation; disability and student support services; diversity and inclusion; academic success services; career development and internships; admissions and financial aid; and registrar. She previously served as the associate director of pre-professional advising at the University of South Carolina and has held housing positions at UNC Wilmington and UNC Charlotte. Hight received the Distinguished Staff Service at award at The Ohio State University, Gerald L. Saddlemire Leadership Award from Ohio College Student Personnel Administrators, and Distinguished Service Award from the Association of Student Conduct Administration.

AMANDA MESIROW serves as the coordinator, code of conduct and as a Title IX Investigator at Moraine Valley Community College in Palos Hills, Illinois. She earned her MS in counseling and educational psychology from Kansas State University and worked in residence life for more than 10 years. Mesirow has presented and published professionally numerous times, most often on topics of social justice, sexual assault, leadership development, individual and organizational trauma response, and campus threat assessment and safety. She has worked at large public, small private, and religiously affiliated campuses. She is co-chair of the ASCA Membership Committee, has presented to international audiences at ASCA and on Academic Impressions webcasts, and has been invited to speak at several colleges through AJM Keynotes & Workshops. Mesirow is pursuing her PhD in higher education.

CHAPTER 2

SHANA WARKENTINE MEYER is vice president for student affairs at Missouri Western State University. She has more than 20 years of experience in higher education, including positions in student conduct, student organizations and activities, residence life, academic affairs, college advancement, and student life. She earned her bachelor's degree in English/journalism and her master's degree in counselor education/student personnel from Emporia State University. She has completed her coursework toward a doctorate degree in student affairs in higher education from Kansas State University and is working on her dissertation.

DR. LYN REDINGTON'S passion is supporting student success, both in and out of the classroom. She has worked in housing and residence life, student conduct, student care and assistance, student unions, and auxiliary services. She has also served as an adjunct assistant professor while teaching undergraduate and graduate courses in student affairs. Redington earned her BS, MS, and PhD from Iowa State University. She has worked at the University of Wisconsin-Whitewater, Indiana University, University of Arizona, University of Northern Iowa, and University of Iowa. Redington currently is a member of the team supporting student success at Idaho State University as vice president for student affairs. In this role, she oversees the Career Center, Student Life, Veteran Student Services, Counseling and Testing, Disability Services, University Housing, Pond Student Union and Involvement, Orientation and New Student Programs, and Student Affairs Business Office.

Redington has been active in ACUHO-I programs, serving as a faculty member for the STARS College, James C. Grimm National Housing Training Institute, Student Housing Training Institute in South Africa, and Senior Housing Officer Institute. She also is a member of the review team for the *Journal of College and University Student Housing* and served on ACUHO-I's Credentialing Task Force.

CHAPTER 3

ERIC NESTOR is associate director of the Office of Student Rights and Responsibilities at Syracuse University, where he has worked since 1998. He assumed his current position in 2013 after holding numerous roles during 15 years in the Office of Residence Life. As associate director, Nestor oversees the daily operations of the office, serves as a case manager, and advises conduct and appeals boards. He has published multiple articles and a book chapter on topics such as assessment, training, and staff recruitment and retention. He also has presented nationally on the topics of student conduct processes, student conduct software, social media, supervision, diversity, staff recruitment and retention, and assessment at ASCA, MaxFest, NASPA, and ACPA. Additionally, Nestor was a member of the ACUHO-I grant-funded research team on the recruitment and retention of entry-level housing professionals.

DR. JOHN WESLEY LOWERY is department chair and professor in the Student Affairs in Higher Education Department at Indiana University of Pennsylvania. He previously served on the faculty and coordinated graduate preparation programs at Oklahoma State University and the University of South Carolina. He earned his doctorate at Bowling Green State University (Ohio) in higher education administration. Before beginning his doctoral work, he was director of residence life at Adrian College in Michigan and university judicial administrator at Washington University in St. Louis. Lowery holds a master's degree in student personnel services from the University of South Carolina and an undergraduate degree in religious studies from the University of Virginia.

CHAPTER 4

DR. PATIENCE D. BRYANT is director for student conduct and ethical development at California State University at Long Beach, where she is overseeing the creation and implementation of the university's first restorative justice program: Welcoming Accountable Voices & Education (W.A.V.E.). Bryant holds a doctoral degree in conflict analysis and resolution from Nova Southeastern University. She formerly served as associate director for campus life & student development at Texas A&M University-Commerce and the first student conduct coordinator for the Department of Student Housing at the University of Mississippi, where she also implemented restorative justice in student conduct programs. Bryant was named a faculty fellow of the 2015 Donald D. Gehring Academy by the Association for Student Conduct Administrators (ASCA) and served as a faculty member for the restorative justice track of the academy by ASCA in 2016 and faculty/track coordinator for Conflict Resolution with a Focus on Bias Response for the 2017 Gehring Academy.

DR. D. MATTHEW GREGORY is dean of students and deputy Title IX administrator for students at Texas Tech University, where his supervision portfolio has consisted of the Center for Campus Life, Office for Student Conduct, Risk Intervention Safety Education Office, Student Concern and Behavior Intervention Team, Student Counseling Center, and Title IX Investigations. Previously, Gregory was associate dean of students and director of student advocacy and accountability and deputy Title IX coordinator at Louisiana State University in Baton Rouge. He has served as president of the ASCA board of directors.

Gregory has a doctor of philosophy degree in educational administration from Southern Illinois University, a master of education in counseling and student affairs from Western Kentucky University, and a bachelor of arts in biological sciences from Southern Illinois University. His research has focused on male advocacy against sexual violence, campus law enforcement, higher education law, and legislation affecting higher education. From 2015–2016, he served the Southeastern Conference (SEC) as a member of a working group tasked by the SEC commissioner to explore student-athlete conduct and student-athlete transfer policies at SEC institutions.

DR. VIRGINIA ALBANESO KOCH is director of residence life at Auburn University in Alabama, where she has worked since 2013. She previously served as assistant director of undergraduate residential life, senior assistant director of university residential life, and associate director of residential services at Northwestern University during her 20-year tenure there. She began her career at SUNY Fredonia as a residence hall director. Since completing her PhD in higher education at Loyola University Chicago, she has published several articles and led webinars related to her research interest: the curricular design of resident assistant training programs. Koch also has presented regionally and nationally for ACUHO-I, NASPA, and SEAHO on a variety of topics, including RA training and student conduct. Her commitment to innovation, collaboration, and high-quality work in students affairs has been recognized at local, regional, and national levels throughout her career.

CHAPTER 5

JENNIFER M. SCOTT FORRY currently serves as dean of student affairs at Newbury College in Brookline, Massachusetts. In this senior leadership role, she has responsibility for the offices of Counseling and Health Education, Residence Life, Student Involvement, Community Standards, and International Student Services. She also serves as a Title IX deputy and adviser to the Student Government Association. Prior roles include assistant dean of students and director of residence life and community standards.

A graduate of Franklin Pierce University and Suffolk University, Forry is pursuing a doctorate of education in higher education leadership at Regis College in Weston, Massachusetts. She holds several civil rights investigator certifications through the Association of Title IX Administrators (ATIXA) and has been invited to present her Title IX research on the local, national, and international levels, most recently at Trinity College in Dublin, Ireland. Forry is a past president of the Boston Area College Housing Association (BACHA) and Massachusetts College Personnel Association (MCPA) and an active member of NASPA - Student Affairs Administrators in Higher Education. In acknowledgment of her commitment to the profession, NASPA recently invited her to travel to England to collaborate with student affairs professionals to explore best practices in the United Kingdom and the United States.

NICOLE DIBARTOLO is the program coordinator for student conduct for university housing at Florida State University and a part-time student in FSU's Higher Education in Student Affairs doctoral program. She received a bachelor of arts degree from Rutgers University, New Brunswick, and a master's in education from the University of Florida. DiBartolo began her student affairs career as a live-in residence life coordinator for three years before her current role at Florida State University. Her research interests include state and federal laws, and their impact on the university student conduct process.

DERRICK D. DIXON is assistant director for conflict resolution and student conduct for the University of Mississippi in Oxford, where he has worked since 2013. He oversees the student conduct and conflict resolution process for the

Department of Student Housing. In being tasked with updating and developing student conduct practices and implementing conflict resolution programs, Dixon has gained extensive experience in crafting and revising the student conduct process, both campus-wide and within student housing. He has also gained extensive experience using conflict resolution practices, including but not limited to conflict coaching, mediation, restorative justice and practices, and other methods of alternative dispute resolution.

Dixon has extensive experience in training, recruiting, selecting, and advising hearing bodies and officers. His case management experience is robust, hearing cases at all levels, including alcohol, drugs, Title IX, athletics, and student organization misconduct. At the conclusion of the spring 2018 semester, he will complete his doctorate of education in educational leadership at Arkansas State University. He also served as a faculty member in the restorative justice track of the 2018 ASCA Gehring Academy.

CHAPTER 6

MALLORY MARTIN-FERGUSON is the associate director for housing student conduct and conflict resolution for the University of Michigan. In this role she oversees all conduct in residential spaces and works to educate staff in student life on the values of restorative practices and the intersection with diversity and inclusion. Martin-Ferguson attended the University of Colorado where she received her bachelor's degree in international studies and later received her master's degree in educational leadership and policy studies from the University of Washington in 2010. She currently is pursuing her graduate certificate in restorative practices from the International Institute of Restorative Practices. She also is the founder and co-coordinator of the national working group on exploring restorative responses to bias incidents on campus and Midwest Region Chair for The Association of Student Conduct Administrators (ASCA).

DR. DELMY M. LENDOF is director of residential staff and programs at New York University (NYU) and an adjunct assistant professor in the Higher and Postsecondary Education Program at NYU and Teachers College, Columbia University. She has more than 20 years of experience in higher education and serving students at public and private universities. She also is highly involved in regional and national organizations and has presented at a number of conferences. She served as a faculty member for the 2014 James C. Grimm National Housing Training Institute (NHTI) and the 2013 NEACUHO Regional Entry-Level Institute (RELI). At the 2016 NASPA national conference, she presented the first SA Speak session to be done in Spanish on the Latinx/a/o college experience, called *Latinos Aqui*. Lendof earned a doctorate of education degree from

Teachers College, Columbia University; MS in college student development from Long Island University, C.W. Post; and a bachelor of arts in politics, economics, and society from the State University of New York, College at Old Westbury.

DR. DENISE BALFOUR SIMPSON Is the dean of students at Johnson and Wales University in Charlotte, North Carolina, where she oversees athletics, residential life, student involvement and leadership, health services, counseling services, and student conduct. Previously, she served as director for student conduct at the University of Kentucky, and she has additional experiences in residence life, campus recreation, and student involvement. Simpson received her PhD from Old Dominion University in higher education, her MEd in educational leadership from the University of Nevada Las Vegas, and her BA in psychology and communications from DePaul University. Her research in and passion for student affairs are in issues related to student engagement, first-generation students, and the development of new and emerging student affairs professionals.

CHAPTER 7

DR. MARY ANDERSON has been involved in higher education for 20 years. Her experiences include working in admissions, residence life, student activities, student conduct, student support and advocacy, and crisis and threat management. She is an alumna of UNC Greensboro, where she earned her doctorate in educational studies with a concentration in higher education administration. She also holds a master's degree in college student affairs from the University of South Florida and a bachelor's degree in communication arts from the University of West Florida.

Anderson has had the opportunity to work with diverse populations of students in a variety of educational settings, including her work as a resident director for the global study abroad program Semester at Sea. She regularly trains faculty, staff, and students on how to identify students in distress and was hired at UNC Greensboro in 2009 to create a case management process for students who have experienced a mental health crisis. Anderson is active in NASPA and has regularly presented on topics including crisis management, Title IX compliance, and mentorship at NASPA's annual conferences as well as other state, regional, and local conferences.

HEIDI ANDERSON-ISAACSON is finishing her 16th year at St. Catherine University ("St. Kate's") in St. Paul, Minnesota, as the director of residence life. She holds a master's degree in educational leadership from the University of St. Thomas and is working on her doctorate in education, leadership, and learning from the same institution. She cites the assessment, planning, construction, and opening of a 288-bed facility with super-suites and apartments as her most-significant professional accomplishment. While at St. Kate's, she has been involved in many campus-wide initiatives, including the retention and data workgroup; student affairs division assessment lead; and early-alert student team, which addresses student crisis issues. She has taught the course The Reflective Woman, required of all St. Kate's undergraduate students, and has served as a first-year academic advisor. She is an active member of ACUHO-I, having served as chair of the 2018 Senior Housing Institute, on the local arrangements committee for the annual conference, and as a faculty member for the James C. Grimm National Housing Training Institute.

DR. DOUGLAS BELL is the assistant director of residence life at the University of Georgia, where he is also completing his doctoral degree in College Student Affairs Administration. His focus area is in student conduct and he supervises two residential areas. With 11 years of student affairs experience, Bell recently served as senior coordinator for student conduct/assessment. He completed his dissertation, *An Exploratory Study of How Institutions Utilize Systems to Respond to Students Who Are Exhibiting Threatening Behavior*, in 2017. Bell earned his master's degree in college student affairs administration from the University of West Florida and also holds a master's degree in sports administration from the University of Southern Mississippi.

CHAPTER 8

LYNDSAY ANDERSON is the manager of student conduct at Dalhousie University, where she has worked since 2008. She manages residence and campus conduct issues and previously facilitated a restorative justice pilot program for Dalhousie students. Her experience includes eight years as a live-in residence life professional at Dalhousie and St. Francis Xavier University. Anderson holds a bachelor's degree in criminology from the University of Toronto and recently completed her master's degree in women and gender studies at Mount Saint Vincent University, with a research topic of rape culture and sexualization on university campuses. She presents in classrooms and workshops, and at conferences (including TEDxNovaScotia in 2014), on various topics, such as restorative justice, rape culture, sexual consent, and leadership, to share her stories, insights, and research.

NICOLE KOGAN serves as assistant director for student conduct at Kennesaw State University (KSU), where she has worked in the Department of Student Conduct and Academic Integrity since January 2017. Her responsibilities include investigating suspension- and expulsion-level cases, and adjudicating lower-level violation cases. Along with her daily responsibilities, Kogan is the liaison to KSU's Housing and Residence Life staff, who serve as hearing officers. She has established strong partnerships with her colleagues in the Student Affairs division to provide trainings and programs to Kennesaw students, topics of which include interpersonal communication, university policies, rights and responsibilities, involvement, and résumé building, as well as ethical decision making.

Previously, Kogan has served as residential conduct coordinator at the University of West Georgia, residence life coordinator for Conduct and Administration at Florida International University (FIU), and residence life coordinator at FIU and Eastern Washington University. She received her bachelor's degree from Wittenberg University and her master's degree in education from the University of Wisconsin-La Crosse. In 2015, Kagan received the Georgia Housing Officer's Excellence in Housing Award. She is a graduate of ACUHO-I's Stars College (class of 2004).

CHRISTINA LIANG currently serves as an associate judicial administrator in the Cornell University Office of the Judicial Administrator and has been in this role since August 2015. Her primary responsibilities include investigating and adjudicating Campus Code of Conduct violation allegations. She also serves on Cornell University's Bias Assessment and Review Team (BART) and the Alcohol and Other Drug Incident Review Team. Liang completed her bachelor of arts degree in English and psychology and a juris doctorate from the University at Buffalo, SUNY (UB) in New York. Before joining Cornell, she worked in both residential life and student conduct roles at UB. As an active member of ASCA, Liang was awarded the New Professional of the Year award in 2016 and currently serves as treasurer on ASCA's board of directors.

CHAPTER 9

LAUREN TERESA MAURIELLO is assistant director for residential student conduct at the University of Maryland, Baltimore County, where she has worked since 2013, overseeing residential student conduct and residential assessment initiatives. Before that, Mauriello worked in residential life and student conduct at George Mason University and James Madison University, receiving a master's degree in college student personnel administration at the latter. She is completing her doctorate in public policy, specializing in education policy, at the University of Maryland, Baltimore County. Her research interests include restorative practices in higher education as well as in high school and community settings.

In practice at UMBC, Mauriello is a part of a team implementing campus-wide restorative initiatives. She is co-developing a restorative residential curriculum model with residential life colleagues, and teaches a course on conflict resolution in UMBC's First-Year Seminar Program. She also is a licensed trainer through the International Institute of Restorative Practices, and has presented locally, nationally, and internationally on the use of restorative practices in higher education and residential life communities.

MOLLY C.S. PIERSON is an associate director for residential life, responsible for residence education, at Washington University in St. Louis, where she has worked since 2010. She leads a team of 17 fulltime professionals responsible for the residential experience for more than 4,500 students living in residential colleges and on- and off-campus apartment communities. Her areas of oversight include assessment, residential life student conduct, crisis response, living and learning communities, student leadership, restorative justice practice, and student and neighbor relations. Pierson earned her master's degree in college student personnel at Bowling Green State University, where she did a residential life practicum at the University of Michigan, developing their restorative circle program. After graduate school, she worked briefly at Saint Louis University in academic affairs.

Pierson has served as faculty for the restorative justice track at the ASCA Donald D. Gehring Academy and presented on the connection between restorative justice and student learning at several national and international conferences, including the International Institute for Restorative Practices (IIRP), NASPA, ASCA, and ACUHO-I.

CHAPTER 10

CIJI A. HEISER is director for student affairs assessment and effectiveness at Western Michigan University (WMU). She coordinates assessment and strategic planning efforts for the division, manages data integration across programs and services, and leads program review and risk-management processes. Before working at WMU, Heiser spent six years at the University of North Carolina at Chapel Hill working in assessment and strategic planning and at St. Mary's College of Maryland as an area coordinator for international student support.

Heiser received her bachelor's degree in international relations from Bucknell University and her master's in higher education administration and student personnel from Kent State University. She also has a master's of science in educational research methodology from the University of North Carolina at Greensboro and is pursuing a doctorate in the same program, focused on the intersection of culture and methodology.

DR. AMY GAUTHIER is the senior associate director of housing and auxiliary services at the University of Michigan. She oversees residential education, first-year experience, conduct and conflict resolution, and diversity and inclusion. She previously served in roles dedicated to student conduct and housing at the University of North Carolina - Chapel Hill, Connecticut College, University of Rhode Island, Clark University, and Mount Holyoke College. She received her bachelor's degree from University of Puget Sound, her master's degree in education from Oregon State University, and her doctorate in educational leadership from Johnson & Wales University. Gauthier has presented regionally and nationally on topics such as student-faculty interactions, first-year experience, and student conduct.

KATHRYN (KATE) DICATO is the coordinator for housing conduct at the University of North Carolina at Chapel Hill, where she has worked since 2015. She serves as the primary case manager of the housing conduct system, providing functional supervision to 17 hearing officers regarding due process requirements, hearing and sanctioning procedures, and the appeal process. Before working at UNC, DiCato spent more than four years at George Mason University in both residential programs and housing operations. She earned her bachelor's degree in psychology from Boston College and her master's degree in higher education from Florida State University.

KATIE BARTHOLOMEW serves as an assistant director in the Department of Housing and Residential Education at the University of North Carolina at Chapel Hill, overseeing the housing conduct process, compliance, and crisis operations, in addition to supervising community directors and participating on the housing leadership team. Bartholomew has a bachelor's degree in political science from Miami University in Oxford, Ohio, and a master's degree in counseling and college student development from Northeastern University in Boston, Massachusetts. She also serves as a mediator for the North Carolina Office of State Human Resources employee grievance process, which has given her unique insight into how conflict is resolved. Bartholomew enjoys working with students and helping them engage in excellence both in and outside the classroom at UNC-Chapel Hill.